P9-DUA-676

WITHDRAWN

The Strategy of Nonviolent Defense

The Strategy of Nonviolent Defense

A Gandhian Approach

Robert J. Burrowes

State University of New York Press

Published by
State University of New York Press, Albany

For information, address State University of New York Press,
State University Plaza, Albany, NY 12246

Production by Dana Foote
Marketing by Theresa Abad Swierzowski

Library of Congress Cataloging-in-Publication Data

Burrowes, Robert J.
    The strategy of nonviolent defense : a Gandhian approach / Robert
J. Burrowes.
        p.   cm.
    Includes bibliographical references (p.) and index.
    ISBN 0–7914–2587–8 (acid-free). — ISBN 0–7914–2588–6 (pbk. : acid
-free)
        1. Nonviolence. 2. Conflict management. 3. Human behavior.
4. Strategy. 5. Social change. 6. Gandhi, Mahatma, 1869–1948.
7. Clausewitz, Carl von, 1780–1831. 8. Civilian-based defense.
9. International relations.   I. Title.
HM278.R85 1995
303.6'1—dc20   95-2223
                                                                    CIP

10 9 8 7 6 5 4 3 2 1

To All Nonviolent Activists
Past
Present
and
Future

If we are to make progress, we must not repeat history but make new history. We must add to the inheritance left by our ancestors.

It would be wholly wrong for us to lower the standard of [nonviolence] by reason of our own fault or lack of experience. . . . It is necessary for us, therefore, to apply our reason to understand the power of non-violence.

I have always advised and insisted on non-violent defence. But I recognize that it has to be learnt like violent defence. It requires a different training.

A small body of determined spirits fired by an unquenchable faith in their mission can alter the course of history.

If a single *satyagrahi* holds out to the end, victory is absolutely certain.

Mohandas K. Gandhi

Contents

Acknowledgments

In writing this book, I have incurred several debts; it is now my pleasure to acknowledge them. First, I would particularly like to express my appreciation of my partner, Alexandra Perry, for her support and encouragement, and for sharing the consequences of my life as a nonviolent activist. Second, I would like to thank my parents, Beryl and James Burrowes, and an old family friend, Eileen Baysinger, for fundamentally shaping the person I have become. And third, I would like to acknowledge the support of my sister, Catherine Burrowes, who introduced me to the computer age and now happily assists me to remain functional within it.

In relation to the research itself, I wish to thank Don Fletcher, Head of the Department of Government at the University of Queensland, for his support, particularly during the delays caused by my involvement in several nonviolent struggles—including those of the Melbourne Rainforest Action Group and the Gulf Peace Team—and, as a result of my ongoing war tax resistance, the two Federal Court trials that led to my bankruptcy and conviction for contempt.

I owe a particular debt of gratitude to several scholars who helped me to identify and obtain (sometimes obscure) references and/or provided valuable comments on early drafts of the manuscript. My principal debts in this regard are to Ralph Summy (the scholar who has done most to nurture academic interest in the study of nonviolence in Australia); to Thomas Weber (Australia's leading Gandhian scholar), who also gave me unrestricted access to his library; and to Brian Martin, whose careful and thoughtful comments made me more fully appreciate his commitment to nonviolence. In addition, I would like to thank Glenn Paige, Paul Wehr, April Carter, Richard Falk, Norman Freund, and Kevin Cassidy for their comments on the entire manuscript, and Hugh Smith for reading the chapter drafts on strategic theory.

Research sometimes requires access to obscure references or materials that are difficult to obtain. In my case, I was fortunate to have the expert assistance of Bernadine Hardin and Melody Smart of the Royal Melbourne Institute of Technology Central Library, who arranged a long succession of texts through the interlibrary loan service. Their efficiency was critical to the quality of this study, and I deeply appreciate their cheerful help. I was also fortunate to have the expert assistance of Mark Cerin, who helped me to design, and then patiently prepared, four of the diagrams presented in this study.

I must also acknowledge the financial assistance I received in order to undertake this research: a research grant awarded by the Department of Government at the University of Queensland; personal grants from Robert Larkins, Neville Watson, and my parents; and individual contributions to the Peace Fund Team. This fund was thoughtfully organized by Diana Pittock—who deserves special thanks for recognizing my predicament—to supplement my income after I was declared bankrupt. These grants and the Peace Fund Team made the research possible, and I am extremely grateful for them.

This book was produced by a careful, responsive, and efficient group at SUNY Press. For their respective roles in this process, I thank William Eastman, Clay Morgan, Dana Foote, and Wendy Nelson. I also thank typesetter, Kay Bolton, and typesetter and cover designer, Les Bolton.

Finally, I would like to thank the many nonviolent activists with whom I have waged nonviolent struggle over the years. It is difficult to find a greater source of inspiration and ideas, than a jail cell full of empowered activists committed to revolutionary nonviolent struggle. They have also helped to keep me in touch with the reality of the task ahead on those odd occasions when my research made it sound a bit too neat and simple. I hope they judge my effort worthwhile.

RJB
July 1994
Melbourne

Introduction

Can nonviolent defense be an effective strategy against military violence? Despite the ancient and worldwide tradition of nonviolent struggle, many people would regard this question as bizarre. Given the way in which the history of nonviolence has been marginalized, relatively few people have a sense of the rich history of nonviolent struggle or realize that it can be systematically planned and applied. Nevertheless, the historical record illustrates that nonviolent struggle is a powerful form of political action. So powerful, in fact, that, according to this study, a strategy of nonviolent defense[1] is the *most effective*[2] response to an act of military aggression. Much evidence to substantiate this assertion is presented in the pages that follow. We will begin by outlining the structure of the argument and describing the major conceptual frameworks developed to facilitate this research.

The Social Cosmology

An important aspect of this study is the significance it attaches to the notion of "social cosmology." As defined in this inquiry, a society's social cosmology consists of four mutually reinforcing components: the society's specific pattern of matter-energy use, its particular set of social relations, its prevailing philosophy about the nature of society (which includes a conception of human nature), and its strategies for dealing with conflict. These components are described as "mutually reinforcing" because each one helps to shape, as well as reflects, the social cosmology in which it evolves. For example, a society's philosophy (which is usually expressed as a set of spiritual, religious, or ideological beliefs) will justify the pattern of matter-energy use, the set of social relations, and the strategies for dealing with conflict that are characteristic of that society.

While the earliest social cosmologies developed in response to the interaction among three primary elements—the evolutionary forces inherent in humans, the nature of the local matter-energy environment, and the character of the relationships among early societies—many subsequent cosmologies have also been shaped by deep cultural imperatives: those features of earlier cosmologies that, for various reasons, have survived to become dominant. Although the connection between ideology and social relations has long been recognized,[3] this study argues that a society's pattern of matter-energy use and its strategies for dealing with conflict are just as important as both social relations and philosophy in determining the nature of that society. In turn, this cosmology shapes other features of a society, including its conception of security.

Two examples should make this notion of social cosmology clear. It is evident from what we know about nonliterate societies that, in many of them, their pattern of matter-energy use is based on renewable sources.[4] Their social relations are nonhierarchical, highly participatory, and based on communal "ownership." Their philosophy of society is based on a belief in their spiritual and physical connection with the Earth, the premise that all life is sacred, and a conception of human nature that recognizes its variability. And their strategies for dealing with conflict (both within and between societies) are based on egalitarian "laws" and processes that emphasize cooperation and consensus.[5]

In contrast, the dominant social cosmology today (which is Western in origin but which has been systematically introduced into many parts of the world) is quite different. Its pattern of matter-energy use is based on nonrenewable sources. Its social relations are patriarchal, capitalist, imperialist, and racist, to mention its main features. Its philosophy of society is both realist and "scientific"; that is, it characterizes human society as conflictual and regards life as a competitive struggle for existence, it emphasizes a mechanistic understanding of the universe and stresses the importance of material growth, and it believes human nature to be inherently selfish, competitive, and aggressive. And its strategies for dealing with conflict range from the use of state laws that have been enacted by, and for the benefit of, national elites[6] to the use of police and military violence in defense of elite interests. The dominant social cosmology was shaped by patriarchy, Christianity, and, more recently, capitalism.

A secondary task of this study is to substantiate a series of propositions in relation to the notion of social cosmology: to demonstrate, through its use throughout this study, that the notion itself is a valuable analytical and explanatory tool for those seeking to understand the nature of human societies; to substantiate the description of the dominant social cosmology outlined above; to subject the dominant cosmology to critical scrutiny and to demonstrate that this cosmology itself is the cause of the multifaceted "global crisis" that human society is now experiencing; and to demonstrate that in order to change a society, it is necessary to change all four components of its social cosmology. These propositions will be substantiated within the context of the investigation undertaken in chapters 3, 4, 5, 6, 7, and 9.

According to this study, then, in order to understand a particular society, it is necessary to understand the nature of its social cosmology. And for those interested in creating a new local community as part of a new global society, it is necessary to intentionally develop *all four* components of its social cosmology. Moreover, this study will argue, to be functional in the long term, each component of any cosmology must be oriented to the satisfaction of human needs. This means that any strategy for displacing the dominant social cosmology cannot be violent, because violence is inconsistent with the satisfaction of those needs. This study outlines the essential features of each component of any functional social cosmology, but it devotes most attention to just one component: the strategies for dealing with conflict. In particular, it develops a strategic theory and a strategic framework for planning a strategy of nonviolent defense.

The Strategic Theory and the Strategic Framework

In the attempt to demonstrate its principal hypothesis—that the most effective way to resist military violence is to use a strategy of nonviolent defense—this study develops a new and comprehensive strategic theory. It does this by synthesizing selected elements taken from three sources: the strategic theory of Carl von Clausewitz, the conceptions of conflict and nonviolence developed by Mohandas K. Gandhi, and recent research in the fields of human needs and conflict theory. Using this theory, together with insights derived from an analysis of Gandhi's campaigns of nonviolent struggle, the study also identifies twelve components of a strategic framework that can be used to plan a strategy of nonviolent defense. The principal aims of this study are to elaborate this strategic theory and its associated strategic framework and to use them to describe the essential features of a strategy of nonviolent defense.

What Is Nonviolent Defense?

Let us begin by describing the status of research in the field and identifying some of the unresolved issues that this study will attempt to address. This will provide a clear indication of why this study attaches such importance to the notion of social cosmology and the role of strategic theory.

It is apparent that research into nonviolent forms of defense is at an impasse; since the publication of books by Stephen King-Hall[7] and Bradford Lyttle[8] in 1958 and the Civilian Defence Study Conference held at Oxford in September 1964, it is evident that there have been no significant theoretical breakthroughs. Johan Niezing agrees: In his view, the study of nonviolent forms of defense is "stagnating." During the 1980s, he argues, the research produced no new insights or theoretical elaborations.[9] And, according to Christopher Kruegler, the basic concept (of civilian-based defense) as outlined by King-Hall in 1958 and Gene Sharp in 1990[10] is essentially the same.[11]

In part, this impasse can be attributed to the nature of the research. Historically, exponents of nonviolent forms of defense have attempted to formulate their particular approach within the conceptual framework of either classical strategic theory[12] or traditional defense doctrine.[13] However, it is evident that both of these frameworks are prejudicial to the development of nonviolent forms of defense (or even the objective consideration of them) because of the preanalytical assumptions built into prevailing notions of strategy and defense. But the problem is more fundamental than this. As is suggested by the variety of names by which nonviolent forms of defense are known—including *civilian-based defense, social defense, nonmilitary defense,* and *civilian defense*[14]—there are fundamental differences, even among its advocates, regarding the concept itself. This is particularly evident in the debate between exponents of "civilian-based defense" and exponents of "social defense," which is touched on below but explored more fully in chapter 10.

Academic exponents of civilian-based defense, such as Adam Roberts and Gene Sharp, regard civilian-based defense as a functional replacement for military defense and believe it should be separated from other social struggles. In the view of Sharp, its leading advocate, civilian-based defense is defense by civilians using nonviolent means of struggle. It is a strategy intended to deter and defeat military invasions, occupations, and internal coups without the use of military force.[15] Civilian-based defense retains the national and territorial focus of military defense.

Most exponents of social defense prefer a broader definition. Christine Schweitzer, a European activist, argues that social defense is concerned with nonviolent defense against threats to the physical and/or cultural existence of a people and their right to self-determination.[16] Similarly, many African, Asian, and Central/South American activists prefer the broader view and are particularly disinclined to defend the state, which is the instrument of their oppression. Julio Quan, a Central American activist, defines social defense as "the creation of a democratic-based power for economic, social, political, ideological, and ecological security." In his view, civilian-based defense is not relevant for African, Asian, and Central/South American peoples.[17]

It is evident from the above definitions that there are several dimensions to nonviolent forms of defense. Some of these dimensions are made more explicit by the following questions. Is the commitment to nonviolence "principled" or "pragmatic"? Is the violence to be addressed direct or structural in nature? What is to be defended: society or the state? Who is to be responsible for defense: "the people" or the people and "their" government? Against what type of threats is the defense to be carried out: all threats to security or military threats only? How is the defense to be organized: autonomously or hierarchically? How is the defense to be carried out? Subject to a consensus that the defense should not be violent, there is a wide range of views regarding answers to these questions.

However, these are not questions concerning defense strategy as such. They are questions about such things as political philosophy, social relations, security policy, and the conception of conflict that underpins defense strategy. These questions highlight the fact that what should be defended and how it should be defended depend ultimately upon one's conception of the preferred social cosmology. Consequently, for those who are concerned about the violence that results from patriarchal structures and values in society, there is considerable harm in a security policy and defense strategy (in whatever form) that do not functionally undermine patriarchy.

It is therefore important to identify the fact that, of the terms and definitions used in relation to nonviolent forms of defense, each reflects divergent conceptions of society and politics, on the one hand, and strategies for social change, on the other. In each case, but in different ways, a nonviolent form of defense is simply another (important) tool with which to work for the transformation of society. The failure to *systematically* address the more fundamental questions—in relation to society, philosophy, conflict, and security—accounts, in large part, for the lack of progress during the last three decades of research.

This weakness has been touched upon by Antonino Drago. Given the fact that theoretical and historical traditions offer only limited indications of the possibility of a nonviolent form of defense, Drago argues, exponents of such a strategy must provide "a new understanding of society and history" that reflects the total political reality. If they cannot, their notion of nonviolent defense will remain a simple hypothesis without an adequate theoretical base.[18] While any attempt to provide this "new understanding" would be a major undertaking, and one considerably beyond the scope of a single study, this book is one response to the challenge of identifying the historical and theoretical roots that will justify more serious consideration of a nonviolent form of defense. As noted earlier, then, this research is concerned with conceptions of society, philosophy, conflict, and security as well as a particular conception of nonviolent defense.

Given the diversity of terms and meanings attached to nonviolent forms of defense, it should be noted that this study uses the original name—*nonviolent defense*[19]—in order to distinguish the particular form of the defense developed in this study from the other conceptions. The original name is preferred because only this one makes the reference to nonviolence explicit. This is important for two reasons. First, even though the adequacy of the term *nonviolent* will no doubt continue to be debated—particularly given the richness of meaning of equivalent words in Indian languages—it is evident that the unhyphenated word *nonviolent* is now an established part of the English language. Whatever its shortcomings, the word has a clear connotation (if not yet a precise meaning) that is increasingly understood by the general community. Second, use of the word *nonviolent* identifies this form of defense with the history, theory, and practice of nonviolent struggle generally. In this way, nonviolent defense is connected with the roots from which it derives. The precise meaning given to the term *nonviolent defense* for the purposes of this study will be fully explained in chapters 8 and 10.

Methodology

This study combines insights derived from several disciplines in order to suggest the nature of important elements of sustainable social cosmologies, to define a comprehensive security paradigm, and, most importantly, to develop a new interdisciplinary strategic theory. The study then utilizes this theory in order to elaborate the strategy of nonviolent defense.

Using the characterization first identified by Walter Lippmann, this study is empirical, normative, and prescriptive.[20] It is *empirical* in the sense that it seeks to identify and analyze the underlying causes of human behavior in the global strategic environment and to consider the implications of this understanding for questions of security and defense. It is *normative* in the sense that it is deeply concerned with values:[21] The study proposes and develops a radically alternative security policy and defense strategy *that are oriented to the satisfaction of human needs.* And it is *prescriptive* insofar as it provides guidelines for a specific type of action (a strategy of nonviolent defense) in response to military aggression within the existing strategic environment.

The strategic theory developed in this study conforms to the description of a theory offered by Robert Merton. It consists of a set of assumptions from which specific hypotheses are logically derived and that are confirmed by empirical investigation.[22] The validity of this strategic theory stems from its internal cohesion, its explanatory and predictive capacity across cultures and time, and its empirical relevance to contemporary world society. Needless to say, further research and practical experience will be required to test, refute, replace, or improve this theory.

The Structure of the Argument

The strategy of nonviolent defense described in the second half of this study is derived from the strategic theory developed in the first half. Chapters 1 through 7 present the evidence to justify the strategic theory outlined in chapter 8, and, following the definition of a new conception of security in chapter 9, the strategy of nonviolent defense is presented in chapters 10 through 13.

The strategic theory developed in this study is derived from several sources, including the strategic theory of Carl von Clausewitz. But apart from this theory, the study also seeks insights from military strategy. Thus, while chapter 1 describes and evaluates the *strategic theory* of Clausewitz, chapter 2 analyzes several conceptions of military *strategy,* including the "indirect approach" formulated by Basil Liddell Hart. Relevant insights from these and subsequent chapters are incorporated in the new strategic theory presented in chapter 8.

The next three chapters present and criticize important components of the dominant social cosmology. The analyses in these chapters are another important source of ideas for the strategic theory developed in this study. Chapter 3 challenges the traditional but erroneous assumption that national societies are integrated social systems and questions the explanation of conflict that is derived from it. Chapter 4 criticizes the conception of human nature that is characteristic of the dominant social cosmology and examines recent attempts to define human nature in terms of human needs. And chapter 5 criticizes the understanding of conflict that prevails within the dominant social cosmology and outlines an alternative. It also describes the recent conflict resolution process known as "problem solving" and explains why an approach to conflict resolution based on this process alone is inadequate.

Given the importance of power in any conflict, chapter 6 begins with a brief discussion of the nature and meaning of power. The chapter then discusses two theories of power—the consent theory and the structural theory—and identifies their relevance to strategies of nonviolent action. In light of important shortcomings identified in the consent theory, a modified version is presented.

Another vital source of ideas for the strategic theory developed in this study is the life of Mohandas K. Gandhi. Chapter 7 begins by offering a brief explanation of nonviolent action and uses a new conceptual tool—the matrix of nonviolence—to illustrate the four major approaches to it. The chapter then describes and discusses important aspects of Gandhi's social cosmology and illustrates the superiority, as a method for dealing with conflict, of the approach to nonviolent struggle that Gandhi utilized.

Based on the insights derived from the above chapters, chapter 8 outlines the strategic theory and the strategic framework for planning a strategy of nonviolent defense.

Although a defense strategy is shaped by its social cosmology, in more immediate terms it is the product of security policy. Chapter 9 develops a new conception of security and then identifies the major features of a security policy—including a strategy of nonviolent defense—that are designed to achieve it.

The final four chapters explain the strategy of nonviolent defense. Chapter 10 begins by noting the origins of the idea and practice of nonviolent defense and by defining the important differences between two major conceptions of it. It then identifies the main types of military aggression against which a nonviolent strategy must be able to defend. In the following and most important section, the strategic theory described in chapter 8 is used to outline the major features of a strategy of nonviolent defense. The chapter concludes by using this strategic theory to explain five major shortcomings in the strategic orientation of civilian-based defense.

Using the strategic theory and strategic framework outlined in chapter 8, chapter 11 discusses the major planning and organizational components of a strategy of nonviolent defense, chapter 12 explains its operational dimension, and chapter 13 discusses the strategic counteroffensive. In each of these chapters, examples drawn from the history of nonviolent struggle are used to illustrate the argument.

The conclusion discusses one question: How will a strategy of nonviolent defense be introduced?

1

The Strategic Theory of Clausewitz

The strategic theory of Carl von Clausewitz has long been a primary source of ideas for military strategists. But does it offer insights for strategists of nonviolent defense?

This chapter discusses strategic *theory*; strategy is dealt with in chapter 2. The distinction between strategic theory and strategy is important because there is considerable confusion in the literature between the two. The failure to clearly distinguish them and to understand their relationship partly accounts for the shortcomings in existing defense strategies.

A theory is a systematic statement of the principles that explain a set of facts or phenomena. According to Peter Paret, a theory cannot address every variable of its subject, but it should have the capacity to incorporate new findings without its basic hypotheses being proved inadequate or false.[1] In the view of Clausewitz, theory must be comprehensive: It must be able to accommodate all aspects of its subject over all periods of time. The function of theory is to put all factors in systematic order and to trace each action to an adequate, compelling cause. It should explain all relevant phenomena, show how one is related to another, and highlight those that are important. If new principles emerge, theory should identify them.[2] Theory must be realistic and flexible and have the potential for further development.[3] Strategic theory, according to Clausewitz, deals specifically with the components of war and their interrelationships.[4]

Despite the importance of theory, Clausewitz warns, it cannot provide a formula for solving problems nor a set of principles that reveal where "the sole solution is supposed to lie." What it can do, he claims, is provide insight into the relevant phenomena and their relationships. Ultimately, however, theory is only a guide for "the higher realms of action."[5]

Strategic theory is not a well-defined field, but within the context of this study it is considered to have three functions. First, it is a framework for explaining the nature and causes of conflict in the international system and for identifying the causes of conflict in a particular situation. Second, it is a framework for identifying the appropriate strategic aims for dealing with a particular conflict and for guiding the formulation of a strategy to achieve those aims. And third, within the context of this strategy it is a framework for providing tactical guidance. Strategic theories have usually concerned themselves with elements of the second and third functions, although it is historically uncertain how often political or military leaders have used strategic theory to guide the formulation of their strategies. In any case, this chapter will evaluate the suitability of Clausewitzian strategic theory in performing all three functions.

Although other classical strategic thinkers—including Sun Tzu, Niccolò Machiavelli, and Antoine-Henri Jomini—are important, the Prussian theorist Carl von Clausewitz devoted most attention to the question of strategic theory and left the most pronounced legacy in this respect. Like Sun Tzu, Jomini, and other theorists, Clausewitz had much to say on strategy. It is his thoughts on strategic theory, however, that are most important in the context of this study.

Classical strategic theory was first systematically expounded by Clausewitz in his famous book *On War,* published posthumously in 1832. Although the collection of papers, published as a book, represented twelve years of intensive thought, it had not been completed at the time of his death. In a note with the manuscript, Clausewitz wrote: "what I have written so far would . . . only deserve to be called a shapeless mass of ideas . . . liable to endless misinterpretation."[6]

It should be noted at the outset that there is an ongoing debate regarding the value of the Clausewitzian legacy. At one level, this debate includes much discussion regarding the coherence of the argument in *On War.* Although Paret believes that Clausewitz offers "an essentially consistent theory of conflict";[7] Basil Liddell Hart describes his work as too abstract and error-ridden;[8] Raymond Aron maintains it is ambiguous;[9] Azar Gat regards it as unclear and "endemically conflicting";[10] and Michael Howard describes it as "presented with infuriating incoherence."[11] Whatever the case, it is clear that his argument is not straightforward. Some of this stems from the incompleteness of the manuscript itself. In fact, Gat argues, the first book of *On War* reflects the latest stage in Clausewitz's thinking, the middle section reflects the earliest stage, and the last section reflects the intermediate stage; and these sections incorporate "fundamentally contrasting ideas." Gat believes that, given the unfinished state of the manuscript, it is inappropriate to interpret the work as a "coherent whole."[12] Gallie ascribes the complexity of the text not only to its incompleteness but also to Clausewitz's supposed use of a Kantian methodology;[13] Gat points out Clausewitz's supposed use of Hegelian dialectics to resolve the tension between his theoretical conception of absolute war and the reality of historical experience;[14] and Howard simply blames "the tortuous and self-contradictory quality" of much of his writing.[15]

At a more fundamental level, the debate includes a discussion regarding the historical importance and contemporary relevance of Clausewitz's theory itself. While Paret argues that there is "little evidence that soldiers and governments have made use of his theories,"[16] Roger Leonard cites evidence that his work became "a dominating force in the theory and conduct of war" in Europe and elsewhere,[17] and Liddell Hart asserts that the teachings of Clausewitz—taken without understanding and complicated by his errors—have had a great impact on the course of history and "gone far to wreck civilization."[18] In fact, as Howard argues, his influence has been variable: Some central ideas have been largely ignored; some have been distorted yet widely accepted; still others have been adopted into national military doctrines.[19] Whatever its historical importance, Clausewitzian thought is the appropriate place to start an examination of classical strategic theory and to reconsider its relevance to contemporary strategy.

Clausewitz belongs to the mainstream of the realist tradition in international relations. His doctrine is based on the conservative assumptions characteristic of that school of thought. For example, he accepts the statist conception of international politics and considers war to be the business of states and their governments. In addition, he believes war to be a proper instrument for settling conflicts between states and considers law and morality to be of minor significance in the conduct of foreign policy.[20]

The conceptual framework used by Clausewitz is based on his belief in the "dual nature" of war.[21] Thus, while the first few pages of his book discuss the theory of "absolute war" (in terms of which he sometimes described the Napoleonic wars),[22] most of the book is devoted to a description of "limited war." This is highlighted, for example, by his discussion of the resources to be mobilized for war. This can only be determined, Clausewitz argued, following several considerations: an examination of the enemy's political object in relation to one's own; efforts to gauge the strength, character, and abilities of the enemy government and its people in relation to one's own; and an evaluation of the political sympathies of third states.[23] Within this "dual-nature" framework, the notion of absolute war, Clausewitz believed, explained the inner logic of war.[24]

The main elements of *strategic theory* described by Clausewitz are the relationship between politics and war,[25] the principle of polarity and the element of "friction," the principle of the superiority of the defense over the offense, and the concept of the center of gravity. In terms of methodology, Clausewitz often posits the absolute and then describes modifications made necessary by the lessons of historical experience.

There is a strong normative element in Clausewitzian theory. This is reflected in the central tenet—which he emphasizes repeatedly—that the limits of war should be set by policy: "*war is only a branch of political activity; . . . it is in no sense autonomous.*" According to Clausewitz, war does not mean the suspension of political intercourse or change the nature of it: "war is simply a continuation of political intercourse, with the addition of other means." Partly because of its complete subjection to politics, war rarely assumes its absolute form; it remains a halfhearted affair. Though there might be no logical limit to the application of force, there certainly is a political one. Despite the frequent misrepresentation of Clausewitz on this crucial point, in his view "war cannot be divorced from political life" and "policy will determine its character."[26]

According to Clausewitz, policy should represent all interests in the community.[27] The aim of policy is to reconcile all aspects of administration with spiritual values "and whatever else the moral philosopher may care to add."[28] Because strategy cannot be divorced from policy, costs and benefits must be assessed.

The relationship between politics and war is highlighted by the important difference between the political object and the military aim. The *political object*—or "original motive"—of war is "to impose our will on the enemy"[29] in order, as Hugh Smith explains it, to establish a new political relationship between the parties.[30] The reason for wanting to do this varies from one war to the next, but, Clausewitz asserts, the *ultimate objective* is "to bring about peace." The *military aim* of war, however, is always the same: "to disarm the enemy."[31]

At the resort to war, the political object is displaced by the military aim,[32] and it is through this displacement of the object by the aim that each war becomes an indivisible whole in which the different engagements are organized in relation to the single strategic aim. Furthermore, this displacement makes a unified theory of war possible, Boserup and Mack explain, because all wars have the same aim.[33] Also, this displacement of the object by the aim determines the principal characteristic of "absolute" war. War becomes a struggle of polar opposites that tends to escalate to the extreme: "the victory of one side excludes the victory of the other."[34] In the language of game theory, it is zero-sum.

It is evident, however, from a study of military history, "that *immobility* and *inactivity* are the normal *state* of armies in war, and *action is the exception*." The paradox that war is often slow and inconclusive, when in theory it ought to "run its course steadily like a wound-up clock," is explained by several principles at work to which polarity is not applicable: the influence of the political object on the military aim, the retarding influence of fear and indecision, the imperfection of human perception and judgment, the elements of "friction" in war, and, importantly, the superiority of the defense over the attack.[35]

The superiority of the defense derives from the fact that where an attack is not immediately successful, it soon starts to "wear down." In contrast, because the war is being fought on the defender's own territory, it is easier for the defense to maintain, among other things, its communication and supply lines. In addition, mobilization of people and resources is assisted by popular hostility toward the aggressor among the domestic constituency, in previously neutral states, and among allies.[36]

Furthermore, the superiority of the defense derives from the fact that it has the greater say in determining the *nature* and *course* of the war. After the initial offensive strike—which, for effectiveness, would have to be directed against the opponent's "center of gravity"—the defense has the initiative in time. It decides when, where, and how to strike back and in doing so determines how the conflict is conducted; it can choose a strategy to unbalance the opponent and use time to exhaust it.[37] Importantly, then, while this principle does *not* mean that the defense will always prevail in war, it suggests that the superiority of the defense derives largely from the power to choose the *type* of defense.

The final major element of strategic theory explained by Clausewitz is the principle of the center of gravity. The first task in strategic planning, he argues, is to identify the enemy's centers of gravity (sources of power) and, if possible, to trace them back to a single element. By analyzing the dominant characteristics of both belligerents, Clausewitz suggests, it is possible to detect the center of gravity—"the hub of all power and movement, on which everything depends"—which can be weak or strong. Against this point, the center of the enemy's power, all energy should be concentrated and directed. In a very few cases (for example, in circumstances in which multiple opponents act independently of each other) it might not be realistic to reduce several centers of gravity to one. Where this is the case, there is no alternative but to act as if there were two or more wars, with each opponent having its own center of gravity.[38] In some circumstances, the center of gravity may change. For example, the entry of a new ally into the war might shift the center of gravity; this is essentially what happened when the United States entered the two world wars.

Just as it is necessary to identify and attack the opponent's center of gravity, it is also necessary for the defense to concentrate resources in support of its own. How is this center of gravity chosen? Strictly speaking, it is not. What is chosen is a type of defense. As a result, "this imposes a center of gravity *objectively* on both belligerents." If the center of gravity is destroyed, the entire defense will collapse.[39]

How then are the type of defense and the corresponding center of gravity related to the political object of the attacker? In warfare the political object is displaced by the military aim, so the entire activity of the attacker should be directed toward the aim (destroying the center of gravity) and not toward the object. This is so because what is strategically important is *not* the political object but *destruction of the capacity to deny its achievement*. What really matters, then, is that a type of defense should be chosen that allows ready defense of the defender's center of gravity;[40] in this case, strategic withdrawal, counteroffensive, and reconquest are always possible.[41]

While the offense decides what the object of war shall be, the defense "chooses" its center of gravity. It may be such things as their armed forces, the importance of which Clausewitz emphasized, or it may be a capital city, the armed forces of a stronger ally, the community of interest among allies, the personalities of leaders and public opinion,[42] or the economic capacity to sustain the war.[43] Whatever it is, however, the choice of a type of defense determines the center of gravity. This highlights the superiority of the defense over the offense, mentioned earlier: The defense, by "choosing" its center of gravity, also chooses where, what, and how (that is, with what weapons) it should be attacked. "Properly used this is an immense and often decisive advantage."[44]

As noted above there are (at least) two distinct centers of gravity in warfare. One is determined by the defense and should be the point attacked in the first place. If the defense is able to withstand the force of the attack—which will gradually diminish—until its "culminating point" is reached, then a counterattack against the center of gravity of the attacker's defense becomes possible.[45]

The center of gravity must be correctly identified by the opponent in order for there to be a direct attack upon it, and it will determine which weapons can be used and which ones are useless. This is because the means (whether a rifle, a nuclear weapon, an act of sabotage, or a nonviolent action) are useful only insofar as they relate to the center of gravity.[46] For example, in the Vietnam War, the form of warfare was determined by the guerrilla strategy of what was, strategically speaking, the (North Vietnamese) defense. As John Collins has noted, because the United States failed to identify the North Vietnamese center of gravity, it was difficult to define a decisive military aim and to formulate a relevant strategic plan.[47] Moreover, it led to the use of certain weapons, such as strategic bombing, that were, strategically speaking, quite useless.[48] In contrast, during the Gulf War, the center of gravity of the Iraqi defense was clearly its army, a center of gravity with which the United States–led multinational forces were well equipped to deal.

The central point of the argument at this stage can now be identified. It is common in traditional defense thinking—but not deterrence theory—to imagine a range of credible attack scenarios and to design defense countermeasures to meet each one of them; that is, to mold the defense in response to the type of attack. This is a fundamental error arising from a failure to understand the precise strategic meaning of defense—usually by confusing it with some vague political notion like "protection." Defense does not consist of protecting whatever happens to be attacked, although in practice this is what often happens. Any chess player, as Boserup and Mack explain it, knows how ineffective such a piece-by-piece strategy would be. In defense strategy, something is worth defending only to the extent that it serves to defend one's own center of gravity or to attack that of the opponent. Its value can be determined only after a strategy has been formulated, and not before.[49]

Nevertheless, the choice of a defense strategy is not a straightforward one. According to Clausewitz, it is governed by the spirit and limiting conditions of the age (which determine the means available), by the particular characteristics of states, and by the nature of war itself. Moreover, while the political object remains the first consideration, it must still be adapted to the chosen means, "a process which can radically change it." Military strategists are entitled to require that the trend and designs of policy are not inconsistent with the means chosen. Even so, "means can never be considered in isolation from their purpose."[50] This is a view shared by Liddell Hart: While policy should be adapted to the conditions of war, strategy is subservient to policy.[51]

Although he did not make the distinction explicit, it is evident that Clausewitz recognized the existence of two related constraints on the choice of a defense strategy. The first (and more fundamental) is the constraint imposed on strategy by society itself; the second is the constraint imposed on strategy by policy. Howard has noted this distinction as well: War as an instrument of policy, and policy itself, are "the product of certain basic social factors."[52] This is important because it means that even a defense strategy that is vastly superior in the strategic sense must be both politically acceptable and consistent with policy before it can be implemented. The first constraint can be illustrated by reference to the Vietnam War. The use of nuclear weapons by the U.S. forces was virtually inconceivable because their use would have violated "the limits set by political, social and cultural factors."[53] The second constraint can be illustrated by reference to the Gulf War. Although the United States–led coalition had the capability to annihilate the Iraqi army, it did not do so, because U.S. policy did not include the destruction and dismemberment of the Iraqi state.[54] Clearly, there are societal and policy limits on strategy.

The strategic theory elaborated by Clausewitz has been criticized for its failure to address such issues as naval warfare; the role of administrative, institutional, and technological factors; and the significance of economics. But it is evident that many such variables, to which Clausewitz at least alluded, can be fit into his theoretical scheme. It is possible, Paret asserts, "to develop and analyze a concept without illustrating it exhaustively."[55] Nevertheless, it is apparent that Clausewitzian theory is concerned exclusively with military strategy; it is not a theory for dealing with political conflict generally. Nor is it concerned with minimizing the costs of such a strategy. Kindhearted people, Clausewitz asserts, might think that there is some way to disarm or defeat an enemy without too much bloodshed and that this is the true aim of war. "Pleasant as it sounds, it is a fallacy that must be exposed."[56]

Despite Clausewitz's preoccupation with war, many of his admirers credit him with wider political interests. In Gallie's view, however, this is misleading. While Clausewitz regarded war as an extension of policy, his remarks on politics are abstract and meager. Unlike other theorists of war, such as Machiavelli, who were preoccupied with politics, Clausewitz was dissatisfied with certain specifically military doctrines; his main interest was how to wage and win wars. He was not interested in how to use wars in order to achieve certain political ends such as security, liberty, or democracy; nor was he concerned about how war might be contained, limited, or eradicated. Moreover, he was not interested in understanding its causes; he simply accepted that war was inevitable.[57]

This preoccupation reflects his historical period, personal experience, and intellectual environment. Clausewitz saw Europe radically altered by powerful political and military forces and saw his own country lose its independence and status.[58] He endured many terrible experiences during his own life as a soldier; these are reflected in the phrases of "dreadful vividness" that occur throughout his writing.[59] And he was an intellectual product of that period in European history that was noted for its reaction against the ideas of the Enlightenment and that gave rise to the notion that there ought to be something called "a theory of war."[60]

Fundamentally, Howard has warned, Clausewitz was a soldier writing essentially for soldiers, and too much should not be read into his work, "nor should more be expected of him than he intended to give."[61] Nevertheless, while it seems clear that his life during the Napoleonic era tended to distort his conception of strategy and led to his emphasis on its military aspects, there are elements of his strategic theory that suffer less from his preoccupation with the methods of his age. For example, an important element of Clausewitzian strategic theory, which is usually overlooked, is the recognition that in war "many roads lead to success" and that *they do not all involve the opponent's outright defeat.* Possible strategies include the destruction of the enemy forces; the conquest of their territory; a temporary invasion or occupation designed to cause damage; operations that have direct political repercussions (including the disruption of opposing alliances or changes in the political scene) or that increase enemy costs or suffering; and, "the most important method, judging from the frequency of its use," passively resisting the enemy's attacks in order to wear the enemy down. Any one of these strategies might be used to overcome the enemy's will: "the choice depends on circumstances."[62]

Moreover, Clausewitz maintains, the physical and psychological elements interact throughout. Indeed, he argues, in order to overcome an enemy, the effort made must match its power of resistance, which is the product of two inseparable factors: the total means at its disposal and the strength of its will. Even if its armed forces have been destroyed and its country occupied, he asserts, a war cannot be considered to have ended until the enemy's will has been broken.[63]

How adequate, then, is the strategic theory developed by Clausewitz? According to Alexander Atkinson, it is seriously flawed because of its reliance on the implicit assumption that *the social order is stable and inviolable.* Clausewitzian theory, Atkinson explains, assumes that the people of a given society are morally and socially committed (through socialization and behavioral choices) to their particular social order and that this commitment is invulnerable because the people are inaccessible to the opponent. In reality, Atkinson argues, this assumption is false. Moreover, if during war the social order is compromised, then so too is the corresponding strategy. Therefore, Atkinson concludes, Clausewitz's emphasis on the armed forces as the primary instrument of strategy and the center of gravity is quite inappropriate. Atkinson illustrates this point by reference to the Communist Chinese strategy prior to 1949. In this case, the communist guerrilla strategy was only one element of a wider political strategy that was designed to compromise the Kuomintang's will and power to wage war by invading and destroying their social order and replacing it with a new one. This involved, for example, the restructuring of social relations that resulted from the elimination of landlords, the seizure of their land, and its redistribution to landless peasants. The point, Atkinson asserts, is that theories concerning the organization and use of armed force are unthinkable in the absence of social order and yet this social order is quite vulnerable. Therefore, he argues, social order, not the armed forces, is the ultimate source of the will and power to wage war.[64]

In addition, as noted earlier, the strategic theory devised by Clausewitz is anchored in his belief that war's inner logic can be found in the idea of absolute war.[65] This notion, however, is highly problematical. Why should the idea of absolute war explain aspects of war that might otherwise be neglected? In fact, according to Gallie, Clausewitz failed to demonstrate this point, and in many ways his argument is "plainly fallacious."[66] Moreover, while Clausewitz himself discussed the shortcomings of the assumptions underpinning this notion,[67] as Atkinson argues at length, they "infested" his wider theory nevertheless.[68]

Despite the weaknesses identified above, the strengths of Clausewitz's theory lie elsewhere. For example, his recognition that policy should determine strategy is a fundamentally important element of strategic theory that has frequently been ignored or misunderstood by military personnel. However, in elaborating this theme—by making the astute distinction between the political object and the military aim—he oversimplifies the relationship between policy and strategy. Despite several oft-quoted assertions by Clausewitz that emphasize the primacy of policy,[69] in the view of Atkinson, Clausewitz effectively removes political considerations from strategy[70] when he discards the political object—"something not actually part of war itself"—in favor of the aim. This is also evident in his reduction of the aim of war to a narrowly military one—"to disarm the enemy"—and his emphasis on the use of military force—"the *means* of war"[71]—both of which effectively eliminate the political and other elements of strategy. Clausewitz, then, may have believed that politics determines strategy, but he did not consider it to be a *part* of strategy. "What remains peculiar to war is simply the peculiar nature of its means."[72] While one could argue that Clausewitz was correct to concentrate on military factors (given his attempt to write a theory of war), the point is that war itself is essentially political. Despite his statements in this regard, Clausewitz depoliticized war and wrote a theory of military strategy; he did not write a theory of war.

Moreover, it seems clear that his definitions of the political object and the military aim are themselves inadequate. This is essentially because they are based on neither a sound analysis of the *causes* of war nor, perhaps understandably, a sound understanding of the nature of conflict. As a result, his theory is preoccupied with war as a method for dealing with conflict in the international system and does not adequately examine the wider range of strategic methods available. Liddell Hart noted this shortcoming as well. In light of his own research, and reflecting elements that are evident, but not fully developed, in Clausewitzian theory, Liddell Hart offers definitions that are more explicit in their recognition of the realities of conflict. The political object, Liddell Hart argues, is a better state of peace—"even if only from your own point of view." The true aim of war, he asserts, is *not* to seek battle; it is to seek a strategic situation that produces the desired outcome or ensures that a subsequent battle will certainly do so.[73]

The reasoning behind these definitions reflects Liddell Hart's interpretation of the historical record. Consider the political object. According to Liddell Hart, "the conduct of war must be controlled by reason if its object is to be fulfilled." He warns victors against appearing intent to impose a "peace" entirely of their own choosing and stresses the point that, when the military aim is achieved, defeated opponents should not be compelled to submit to onerous conditions. If they are, he suggests, then continuing instability is likely, and perhaps an attempt to reverse the original settlement.[74]

In relation to the military aim, Liddell Hart argues, history demonstrates that military victory is not the same as gaining the object of policy. And yet, given the predominance of military professionals in the formulation of strategy, the historical tendency has been to lose sight of the political object of war and to identify it with the military aim. In consequence, whenever war has broken out, policy has too often become "the slave of strategy." Further, by forgetting the proper relationship between policy and strategy, the military aim has often been distorted and simplified.[75]

In fact, the political object and the strategic aim as defined by Liddell Hart are consistent with the deepest insights of both Sun Tzu[76] and Clausewitz, each of whom regarded the true test of good strategy as its ability to achieve the political object without the use of military force. Nevertheless, although Clausewitz was aware of these considerations, his preoccupation was war itself and he emphasized the effectiveness of military battle.

In his discussion of the principle of polarity and the element of friction, Clausewitz reveals his vast knowledge of, and sensitivity to, the realities of war. In war, he argued, experience counts for more than any number of abstract truths.[77] Thus, while in theory war should escalate to the extreme, he identified at considerable length the many reasons why in practice it does not do so. These included, importantly, his identification of the superiority of the defense over the offense—which does not mean that the best defense strategy will be chosen, that the defense is invincible, or that the defense enjoys a great advantage on the battlefield.[78] Many strategists have argued that the nuclear age has ushered in a period in which offensive weapons are firmly ascendant,[79] but this fact has no bearing on the relevance of this Clausewitzian principle, properly understood. The superiority of the defense is not historically contingent: It has nothing to do with the types of weapons that exist in a particular age.[80] It refers, essentially, to the capacity to choose the *type* of defense, and it remains a valid component of any strategic theory.

Similarly, the notion of the center of gravity remains valid, although there are at least two major conceptions of it. First, there is the original interpretation offered by Clausewitz, which was outlined earlier. This interpretation relies on the *universal acceptance* of the implicit assumption that the social order is stable.[81] And second, there is the more recent interpretation offered by Atkinson. According to this view, the center of gravity is not the armed forces (or any of the other possibilities suggested by Clausewitz). Instead, Atkinson suggests, the strategic center of gravity is the same for all combatants: It is the "finite pool of social resources" that support their strategic efforts. This conception, Atkinson explains, derives from his rejection of the assumption that the social order is stable.[82]

Despite these apparently divergent views, it is possible to offer a third interpretation in which the two conceptions are synthesized. According to this interpretation, the social order itself is considered to be the center of gravity, but under certain conditions the social order can choose a type of defense in order to locate its center of gravity elsewhere. Thus, if the social order appears to be stable, *and if the opponent assumes it to be so* (and, consequently, does not attack it directly), a society may choose a type of defense that shifts its center of gravity to its military forces, for example. But if for any reason (including setbacks in a war that undermine the stability of the social order) the society no longer considers the type of defense it has chosen (such as reliance on its military forces) to be the key to its survival, then the center of gravity automatically reverts to the social order itself (which might then choose another type of defense). Of course, if the society maintains the belief that its center of gravity is in its military forces even as it approaches final defeat, then that is where the center of gravity is located and, in these circumstances, the society will be defeated. To reiterate, then, whereas Atkinson identifies the social order as the center of gravity and Clausewitz believes that the center of gravity is a product of the type of defense chosen, according to the third interpretation the social order itself is the center of gravity but, under conditions in which the social order appears to be stable and the opponent assumes it to be so (and does not attack it directly), the society can *shift* its center of gravity elsewhere by choosing certain types of defense. In this case, a society (as a result of elite manipulation or popular mobilization) might choose a type of defense that keeps the center of gravity within the social order itself. Alternatively, it might choose a type of defense that shifts the center of gravity elsewhere; at any time, however, it might abandon this defense (in which case the center of gravity reverts to the social order). The third interpretation is more consistent with the historical record than either of the other two, or so it seems.

This interpretation has important implications for other elements of Clausewitzian theory. According to Clausewitz, the center of gravity is the point around which any defense should be organized and against which any attack should be directed; moreover, the center of gravity determines which weapons are useful and which ones are useless. Therefore, one important consequence of the above interpretation of the center of gravity (especially given the insight that the social order is not stable and inviolable) is that a defense is most effective if resources are concentrated in support of the domestic social order and that attacks (with the appropriate "weapons") are most effective if they are aimed directly at the opponent's social order (rather than, say, against their military forces). In addition, irrespective of where it is located (and again in contrast to the clear-cut preference of Clausewitz), it is not essential to attack the center of gravity using military means; indeed, this can even be counterproductive. In this regard, as Howard noted, Clausewitz ignored nonmilitary possibilities—such as the possibility of using diplomatic means rather than force to neutralize an enemy's allies, or of using propaganda to undermine public support for a war.[83] Other possibilities will be explored in later chapters.

Finally, as noted above, Clausewitz identified the notions of power and will. Despite the clear indication that he understood the importance of both,[84] there is considerable evidence to suggest that he entertained a rather simplistic understanding of the relationship between them and that he failed to realize the full strategic significance of the role of will. He discussed the strategic implications of the center of gravity (a concept concerned exclusively with power), but he did not devote similar attention to the role of will. Thus, despite his assertions regarding its importance, the notion of will has no clearly defined *strategic significance* within his theoretical framework. Moreover, Clausewitz misunderstood the relationship between power and will: He treated the latter as a function of the former. One description of the thrust of Clausewitzian reasoning goes like this: The object in war is to destroy the enemy's will to resist; its will to resist is a function of its armed forces (that is, its power to resist); therefore, its armed forces must be destroyed.[85] While this characterization discounts the complexity of his analysis, it does indicate the essence of his view. But, as the discussion in the next chapter and in chapter 10 will illustrate, this description of the relationship between power and will is grossly inadequate. Will is not a function of power.

It is now possible to evaluate the strategic theory developed by Clausewitz in terms of the criteria identified at the start of this chapter. First, his theory does not provide a framework for explaining the nature and causes of conflict in the international system and for identifying the causes of conflict in a particular situation. This is a serious weakness, because without this insight a theory cannot help to identify the appropriate strategic aims or offer guidelines for action that address the causes of the conflict itself. Even though Clausewitz argued that theory need not be a manual for action, he still regarded it as a "frame of reference" to guide the action to be carried out.[86] In any case, within the context of this study, guidance for action is a principal function of theory, and the failure of Clausewitzian theory to provide a basis for understanding the causes of conflict is an important shortcoming. Thus, while his theory does provide a framework for guiding the formulation of strategy, it does so within a context oriented to the assessment of relative military power rather than the resolution of conflict or the satisfaction of human needs. And finally, then, although his theory does provide tactical guidance, it does so within this power framework. The shortcomings of an exclusively power-oriented approach to strategy will be discussed in chapters 4 through 7.

Despite the insights it offers, the strategic theory developed by Clausewitz is inadequate. Nevertheless, four elements of his theory—the premise that strategy is an extension of society and policy, the principle of the superiority of the defense over the offense, the insight that the capacity for resistance is the product of power and will, and the concept of the center of gravity—are modified for incorporation into the strategic theory presented in chapter 8.

2

Conceptions of Strategy

Within the discipline of international relations, there are many definitions of strategy. According to Clausewitz, an engagement is a single act, complete in itself, that occurs within the course of a war. Strategy, in turn, is "the use of an engagement for the purpose of the war." Once a war's political object has been determined, the strategist must define the operational aim of the war and draft a strategic plan to achieve it. This plan must include details of the separate campaigns and, within these, the individual engagements of the war.[1]

Despite Clausewitz's belief that strategy should serve and be controlled by policy,[2] and his recognition that limited rather than absolute war is the norm,[3] his emphasis on the use of military violence is evident in many of his statements on strategy. For example, he frequently asserts that the "destruction of the enemy forces" is the most effective means in warfare and that this must always be the primary consideration.[4] It should be noted, however, that Clausewitz offers a precise definition of this oft-repeated expression and qualifies his emphasis of it in important ways. According to Clausewitz, when he refers to the "destruction of the enemy forces," it should be interpreted to mean that the opponent's fighting forces are put in such a condition *that they can no longer carry on the fight.*"[5] How might this condition be induced?

According to Clausewitz, *combat* is the only means in war but, he argues, *it can take many forms*; these range from the physical annihilation of the enemy forces[6] to what Bernard Brodie calls "mere passive resistance."[7] Moreover, although Clausewitz regards destruction of the enemy forces (as defined above) as the most effective form of combat, it is still only *one means* to the end. In fact, he notes that engagements do not always aim at destruction of the opposing forces, because "their objectives can often be attained without any fighting at all." In addition, even when he speaks of destroying the enemy, Clausewitz stresses that this idea is not limited to its physical forces; in his view, the psychological elements must be considered as well.[8]

It is apparent, then, that Clausewitz, like Sun Tzu,[9] believed that the political object could be achieved without using military force. In fact, Azar Gat argues, Clausewitz believed that the perfection of strategy was to achieve conditions that made battle unnecessary.[10] Thus, despite his emphasis on extreme violence, it would be a misinterpretation of his theory to conclude that Clausewitz believed that military force could be countered only with military weapons. Clearly, there are more subtle elements of strategy and other techniques of combat than those related to military battle. In reality, the decisive elements of war have often been the political and psychological ones.

Nevertheless, despite the claim by Peter Paret that Clausewitz's preference for the major decisive battle is "an erroneous assumption" based on an inability to follow the "dialectic" of his argument,[11] Michael Howard has noted that Clausewitz repeatedly emphasized the importance of battle,[12] and Gat argues that Clausewitz held this view throughout his life.[13] Whatever other options there may be, then, and in contrast to Sun Tzu, there is little doubt that Clausewitz regarded annihilation of the enemy forces as the *most effective* means in war. For Clausewitz, again unlike Sun Tzu, it is the engagement itself, rather than the strategy leading up to it, that is ultimately significant. Moreover, he specifically warns that the choice of an alternative form of combat will leave a commander vulnerable should the opponent resort to the "supreme tribunal" of military force.[14] In addition, as Howard noted, even a bloodless victory depended on a willingness to shed blood if necessary.[15] Even if no actual fighting takes place, Clausewitz maintained, "the outcome rests on the assumption that if it came to fighting, the enemy would be destroyed."[16]

According to Basil Liddell Hart, the distinction between policy and strategy is crucial, and considerably more complex than the distinction suggested by Clausewitz. Liddell Hart, in fact, identifies three areas: policy, grand (or higher) strategy, and strategy. While policy governs the object of war, the purpose of grand strategy is to coordinate and direct all the military, economic, moral, and diplomatic resources toward the attainment of the political object of the war; in addition, it looks beyond war to the subsequent peace. Strategy, in turn, is "the art of distributing and applying military means to fulfil the ends of policy."[17]

Liddell Hart rejects Clausewitz's emphasis on battle. Strategy, he maintains, is not absolute in the Clausewitzian sense of seeking to destroy the enemy's military power. Instead, he asserts, when the enemy has military superiority, it might be wise to employ a strategy with the limited aim of draining the enemy's force. For Liddell Hart, the true purpose of strategy is to reduce the possibility of resistance. Ultimately, he argues, the perfect strategy would produce a decision without any serious fighting. However, while Liddell Hart regards strategy as something more than a series of battles, he still considers it to be "only concerned with the problem of winning military victory."[18]

This connection between strategy and military force pervades the conception of strategy held by most recent strategic thinkers. For example, Lawrence Freedman defines strategy as the use of military means to pursue political ends,[19] Hedley Bull describes it as the use of military force in order to achieve given objects of policy,[20] and Howard considers it to be the use or threatened use of force, that is, "organized coercion."[21] However, although this narrow definition might be convenient for distinguishing the concept of strategy used by some students of strategic studies, it is arguably much too narrow. It also highlights a fundamental difficulty associated with definitions of strategy that emphasize a military understanding of it: They encourage the conceptualization of conflict as a military problem rather than a social and political one.

Other analysts have recognized the need for a wider definition. According to Rear Admiral J. C. Wylie, for example, strategy is not limited to war or to military applications. In his view, strategy is a plan of action designed to achieve a particular end; it is an aim together with a system of measures for its accomplishment.[22] More explicitly, in a classic work on the subject, Edward Earle argued that strategy requires increasing consideration of the nonmilitary factors—economic, psychological, moral, political, and technological.[23]

While strategy is often conceived narrowly in terms of military force, these latter conceptions envisage it more widely. Before considering these wider conceptions in more detail, let us consider the work of one prominent author whose work is characteristic of the traditional approach because it is based on the narrow conception of strategy and the effort to identify a set of principles. This case study will help identify the shortcomings of this characteristic approach and will provide a basis for highlighting the advantages of using a wider conception of strategy and a different approach to it.

The Indirect Approach

Basil Liddell Hart has been praised by many, including Raymond Aron, as the greatest military writer of his age.[24] However, it is now clear that the reputation and legacy of Liddell Hart are considerably more clouded than such praise suggests.[25] While Liddell Hart made no attempt to elaborate a strategic theory, he consistently sought to identify the principles that should guide strategic and tactical thinking. This section outlines and evaluates the utility of the "indirect approach" to strategy formulated by Liddell Hart.

In some of his early work in the 1920s, Liddell Hart alluded briefly to the blitzkrieg. The blitzkrieg assumes that the defender has deployed most of its forces near the battlefront and that there is a vulnerable communications network at the rear. When this network is disrupted, it becomes impossible for the defense to keep on fighting. Hence, in the first phase, the attacker endeavors to mass its armored forces at one or more points along the defender's front in order to pierce it; and, in the second phase, to drive deep into the defender's rear in order to sever or overrun key points in its command-and-control network. This deep strategic penetration is the key to success in a blitzkrieg, because the opponent's rear is considered to be its Achilles' heel.[26]

As his interest graduated from strategy to grand strategy and he endeavored to find a way for Britain to defeat a European enemy without having to engage its armies on the continent itself, Liddell Hart started to elaborate the idea of the indirect approach. At the level of grand strategy, this approach was based on the assumption that every nation-state has an Achilles' heel that can cause its collapse in war. This vulnerable point might be some part of its military forces—the belief that underpinned the logic of the blitzkrieg— but it need not be.[27] According to Liddell Hart, then, the aim of grand strategy is to locate and pierce the Achilles' heel of the opponent's power to make war. And the aim of strategy is "to penetrate a joint in the harness of the opposing forces."[28]

The Achilles' heel, in a crude sense, is Liddell Hart's equivalent to what Clausewitz called the "center of gravity." So what is the Achilles' heel of the opponent? Liddell Hart believed that a centralized state is only as strong as its weakest link, and, according to the view he expressed in an early work, the opponent's Achilles' heel is its civilian population and their will to resist. Because the sections of a nation are interdependent, if one section could be demoralized, the collapse of its will to resist would compel *total* surrender.[29] Ultimately, he argued in a later book, the strength of a nation depends "upon its stability of control, morale, and supply."[30] How could the will to resist be destroyed? According to Liddell Hart, the means used could be military, economic, or political.[31] However, while at different times he offered different explanations about how the civilian population could be demoralized—ranging from economic hardship to strategic bombing[32]—he believed that using military weapons was the only appropriate way for doing so during warfare.[33]

Despite his interest in grand strategy, most of Liddell Hart's work focused on strategy, and his description of the indirect approach at this level is one of the most comprehensive expositions of military strategy available. In his view, the principles of war can be condensed into one: "concentration of strength against weakness." More usefully, however, he compiled a set of eight military maxims about strategy that he regarded as fundamental and universal.[34] Like Napoleon, he was interested in practical guides rather than abstract principles. The truth underlying these maxims, Liddell Hart claimed, is that success requires *dislocation* prior to the attack and *exploitation* after it. The attack, in comparison, is a relatively simple act. Physical dislocation results when the disposition of the opponent's forces is upset, when their forces are separated, or when their supplies or routes of retreat are endangered.[35]

However, he asserts, when planning the physical maneuvers of strategy, the psychological element must be kept in mind. Only when both elements are combined is the strategy a truly indirect one. In fact, he argues, the indirect approach can be physical, economic, or psychological in nature, but the last is particularly significant: "in war the chief incalculable is the human will."[36] Nevertheless, although Liddell Hart stresses the importance of psychological factors, whether he is discussing grand strategy or strategy, he considers psychological effects to be the direct result of military activity rather than of anything else.

Despite the significance often attached to this central element of Liddell Hart's legacy, the indirect approach has been systematically criticized by several authors. For example, in a sympathetically critical account of Liddell Hart's work, Brian Bond argues that, in terms of methodology, the historical foundations of the indirect approach are far from secure. In Bond's view, few great battles or wars have been won without some kind of subtlety, surprise, or innovation, and, Bond argues, given that Liddell Hart suggests that the "indirectness" can be strategic, tactical, psychological, or even otherwise, he comes extremely close to offering a circular argument.[37] Similarly, in a book intended to unmask some of Liddell Hart's deceptions and distortions, John Mearsheimer argues that the concept is vague and elastic and its real meaning unclear. He agrees with Bond that, given the way Liddell Hart describes it, every military victory is, by definition, the result of an indirect approach.[38]

Moreover, the assumption on which the indirect approach is based—that every defense has an Achilles' heel—is problematical. Despite the superficial similarity between this notion and what Clausewitz called the "center of gravity," these concepts, and their implications for strategy, are profoundly different. Liddell Hart's concept, as the name implies, assumes that every defense has a weak point. In contrast, Clausewitz does not make this assumption: The center of gravity can be weak or strong. Liddell Hart does not explain why there must be a weak point in every defense nor why attacking this weak point is strategically effective. Striking Achilles in the heel might cause him to stagger briefly or even limp, but there is no guarantee that it will make him collapse!

A broader criticism than those noted above is that some of Liddell Hart's most basic concepts were left undefined, resulting in recurring conceptual confusion throughout his work. For example, despite his frequent references to power and will, there is considerable evidence to suggest that he confused the two concepts, or, at the very least, that he misunderstood the subtlety of the relationship between them.[39] In any case, he does not clearly differentiate between power and will, he does not adequately define them, he does not explain the nature of the relationship between them, nor does he fully and consistently explain their strategic significance. More importantly, and related to this last point, it seems that he did not realize the value of some of his own insights, or perhaps he did not know how to fully integrate them into his conceptual framework. For instance, at the level of grand strategy, he emphasized the importance of the will of the civilian population or, as he later expressed what can be interpreted to be a development of the same notion, that the strength of a nation depends upon its stability of control, morale, and supply. And yet there is no sign of this insight in his "principles of war"; perhaps this is a direct result of his preoccupation with military strategy rather than with war as a whole (grand strategy).

The legacy of Liddell Hart is mixed. There is now considerable evidence to suggest that his idea of the indirect approach might be less significant than originally thought, but his work does contain some useful insights, although Liddell Hart himself failed to fully utilize them. In any case, what is important from the perspective of this study is his typically narrow emphasis on a military conception of strategy[40] and his characteristic approach to it. Before demonstrating the shortcomings of the narrow conception, let us assess the value of this particular approach.

Are There Universal Principles of Strategy?

A characteristic feature of much of the literature on strategy, of which the work of Liddell Hart is a classic example, is the tendency to condense strategy into a set of principles. This method has been popular with a diverse range of theorists and practitioners intent on distilling the essence of strategy into a guide for action. For example, Napoleon identified a series of maxims,[41] Jomini compiled a set of general principles of strategy,[42] Mao Zedong condensed his thoughts regarding guerrilla warfare into a set of principles,[43] Carlos Marighela identified a set of principles to guide the urban guerrilla,[44] Liddell Hart identified eight maxims of his "indirect approach" to strategy,[45] and many national military doctrines include a set of principles of war.[46] Can principles be used to generate a strategy?

While a set of principles may be useful as a frame of reference, they are not, Clausewitz asserted, a precise guide to action.[47] Moreover, André Beaufre argues, the diversity of the various lists of principles highlights the fact that they are really general guidelines for particular situations rather than universal laws.[48] In addition, Brodie notes, each version of the principles is supposed to be constant. However, durability of this sort, he argues, usually means that the principles are too general to be operationally useful. While not denying the utility of generalizations, he contends that trying to identify the principles of war is a modern vice that reflects the contemporary trend to condense and encapsulate knowledge.[49]

Whatever their utility, it is evident that principles cannot be used *to generate* a strategy. Moreover, because many of the principles that appear in the different lists are either too general or not widely applicable, it is clear that existing lists of principles are useful only, if at all, in guiding the conduct of a previously chosen strategy in specific circumstances. For example, if guerrilla warfare is the chosen strategy, Mao's principles might be useful; if strategic bombing is the preferred option, Mao's principles are irrelevant. In addition, these lists usually contain principles, such as the importance of deception or surprise, that contradict the insights provided by recent conflict theory.[50] For these reasons, this characteristic approach to strategy is seriously flawed; it is no substitute for a strategy derived from sound strategic theory.

The Importance of Psychology

A close study reveals that, despite the diversity of their approaches, many strategists—including Clausewitz, Napoleon, Liddell Hart, and Mao[51]—have distilled a common insight: The essence of good strategy is *to overcome the power and will* of the opponent to wage war. Given this shared insight, and the wider conception of strategy held by some strategists, two significant questions suggest themselves. Is a military strategy the *only* way to overcome the power and will of the opponent? And, more fundamentally, are there ways of *altering* (rather than destroying) the opponent's power and will to wage war? Before attempting to answer these questions, a better understanding of the strategic significance of the notion of will[52] is required. This section discusses the relationship between psychology and strategy, and draws attention to the failure of contemporary strategists to adequately utilize psychological insights in their strategic planning.

It is evident that the major strategists and theorists of military history either consciously or intuitively understood the importance of psychological factors in warfare, and that some of the strategists attempted to incorporate such insights into their strategic or tactical planning. However, relatively little of this understanding has been rigorously analyzed and systematically integrated into strategic theories or modern strategies.

Sun Tzu, for example, emphasized the importance of psychological factors. As the first proponent of psychological warfare, according to Samuel Griffith, Sun Tzu regarded the morale of the opponent as the target of highest priority.[53] Clausewitz agrees. In his view, psychological forces "exert a decisive influence" in war. While physical forces may be the "wooden hilt" of the sword, psychological factors are "the finely honed blade." Furthermore, he argues, "will dominates the art of war." Nevertheless, Clausewitz is careful to stress that the importance of psychological factors should not be exaggerated; in his view, no single quality is all-important.[54] Napoleon, too, clearly understood the significance of psychological factors. He expressed the point most vividly in his famous dictum that is usually translated as: the moral is to the physical as three is to one.[55] In addition, Liddell Hart recognized the critical importance of psychological factors in strategy. His research led him to conclude that, in virtually all the decisive battles of history, the victor held a distinct psychological advantage before the battle took place.[56]

Despite the importance attached to psychological factors by earlier theorists and strategists, more recent strategic analysts, with vastly better access to psychological research, are inclined to disregard such elements or to dismiss them as relatively unimportant. Colin Gray, for example, argues that "it is not self-evident that a major commitment by strategists to the study of psychology would yield fresh and useful insights." This, he asserts, is because psychology has "remarkably little" to offer strategic analysts. Paradoxically, Gray also argues that military history is the related discipline of most use to strategists.[57] Given the central importance that classical theorists such as Sun Tzu and Clausewitz, as well as military historians such as Liddell Hart, attach to psychological factors, it is impossible to speculate what use strategists such as Gray would make of their other, less central insights, given his willingness to dismiss their main one.

Of course, in practice the importance of psychological factors to modern strategy is clear-cut. Unfortunately, however, they are used in largely negative roles. This is evident from the importance attached to fear and threats in deterrence strategy.

In short, while the connection between strategy and psychology has been identified by many theorists and strategists, it is evident that their understanding of the connection is still superficial. This is a profoundly important shortcoming, given that one important root of all conflict is psychological and given that no strategic theory can be considered complete, and no strategy can be soundly formulated, without an adequate theory of human behavior to guide it.

As a result of this shortcoming, military theorists and practitioners alike have consistently failed to articulate or implement strategies that *fully* utilize the psychological insights about the nature of conflict already available. What they have done is use their limited knowledge of some psychological factors (such as fear) in attempts to enhance the effectiveness of *military* strategies. It is also evident that most theorists and strategists have yet to appreciate the deeper nature of the connection between psychology and strategy in order to design strategies not reliant on military force. This point is important because the true psychological dimensions of conflict extend well beyond the "battles" themselves: They entail an awareness of the nature and causes of conflict, as well as a sense of the history and preferred future of the relationship between the conflicting parties. The importance of the psychological dimensions of conflict, and the role of will as an element of strategy, will be explored more fully in later chapters.

The Dimensions of Strategy

Despite the various definitions of strategy outlined earlier, it is apparent that strategy is more complex both conceptually and in practice than many of these definitions suggest. This is evident from a consideration of the *dimensions* of strategy.

According to Howard, the major weakness of most historical studies of strategy (including, notably, that of Liddell Hart) is their failure to consider adequately its *four dimensions*. While earlier thinkers had focused attention on the *logistical* dimension—raising, arming, equipping, moving, and maintaining armed forces in the field—Clausewitz drew attention to the principles that govern the military conduct of war: the *operational* dimension of strategy. However, while Clausewitz dogmatically subordinated the logistical dimension to the operational, it is clear that both are important.

The South was defeated in the American Civil War, Howard maintains, as the result of being ground down in a war of attrition. The critical dimension was not the operational one; it was the logistical capacity to transport the largest and best-equipped forces into the operational theater and then to maintain them. This experience, he asserts, has shaped U.S. strategic doctrine ever since,[58] as the Gulf War again highlighted.

The importance of logistics has been discussed in considerable detail by Martin van Creveld. In his view, progressive mechanization has made armed forces increasingly dependent on supplies of fuel, ammunition, and materials. In many cases, he argues, this dependence has made operational strategy "an appendix of logistics."[59] This logistical capacity, however, depends upon a third dimension noted by Clausewitz and Howard: the *social* dimension. This refers to the attitude of the domestic population, whose readiness for sacrifice (including economic sacrifice) ultimately determines the logistical capacity available. Given the importance of public opinion as an element in the conduct of war, there is increasing awareness of the need to comply with or manipulate it. The final dimension, the *technological*, was insignificant during the time of Clausewitz because of technological parity. However, by the last quarter of the nineteenth century, superior military technology was the decisive factor that enabled European powers to dominate the non-European world.[60]

By the beginning of the twentieth century, Howard concludes, war was conducted in these four dimensions: the logistical, the operational, the social, and the technological. In his view, a successful strategy must take account of all four dimensions, although, depending on circumstances, one dimension might dominate. Importantly, however, he argues that the social base must be strong enough to withstand operational setbacks and to support the logistical buildup. The forces raised must then be used to progressively eliminate the operational options available to the opponent in order to eventually destroy its capacity to fight.[61]

Significantly, Howard notes, the inadequacy of their sociopolitical analysis of colonial societies explains the failure of imperial powers to respond effectively to the liberation struggles that characterized the post–World War II era. In these cases, he argues, it was the social dimension of strategy that was the most important, and it was their perception of this that gave the work of Mao and other guerrilla strategists its historical significance.[62] This is because, unlike the vast majority of Western political and military leaders, guerrilla strategists conceive war as political: it is designed to win the allegiance of people. As Robert Taber explains this point, a conventional army fights to control locations; "the guerrilla fights to control people."[63] The awareness of guerrilla strategists in this regard reflects the conception of strategy held by Marxists generally. Conscious of the sociopolitical context in which it evolves and operates, Marxists are among those who conceptualize strategy more widely. This is evident in the contrast between Western and Soviet conceptions of strategy during the Cold War era. While Western strategic thinkers considered Soviet military writing to be excessively politicized, Soviet military theorists specifically criticized Western strategic thinking for being devoid of political content.[64]

Thus, while liberation struggles were essentially conducted in the sociopolitical dimension, Western military thinkers sought solutions in either the operational dimension (by developing techniques such as counterinsurgency warfare) or in the technological dimension (by utilizing superior weapons). When these strategies failed, military leaders invariably complained that the war had been "won" in the military sense but "lost" politically—"as if these dimensions were not totally interdependent."[65] It should be added, given Howard's oversight in this regard, that the social dimension of the independence struggle in India was also critical. Moreover, this struggle was profoundly significant for another reason not considered in Howard's analysis. By using a combination of political, economic, and psychological "weapons" in his nonviolent strategy, Mohandas Gandhi demonstrated that *the operational dimension of strategy is not necessarily a military one.* The historical importance of this development is yet to be adequately studied and fully appreciated and will be illustrated in later chapters.

The vital importance of the sociopolitical dimension of strategy—particularly to strategists who use unconventional forms of "warfare" such as guerrilla war, urban terrorism, or nonviolent struggle—has also been noted by Andrew Mack. In his study of asymmetric conflicts, he observes that the constraints on mobilization "are political, not material" and that the major military powers that have suffered defeat by militarily weaker opponents (as occurred in Indo-China, Indonesia, Algeria, Vietnam, and elsewhere) have *not been defeated militarily.* Success for the militarily weaker party in these conflicts, he argues, depended on the refusal to confront the enemy on its own terms and on the progressive attrition of its political capability to wage war.[66]

Despite the importance of the social dimension, most theoretical works about nuclear war and deterrence emphasize the technological dimension of strategy to the virtual exclusion of the social dimension (and, for that matter, the operational dimension). According to Howard, the technological capabilities of nuclear weapons are considered to be decisive. In this approach, he asserts, the political motivation for the conflict, the social factors involved in its conduct, and the military activity of fighting are all ignored. Drained of political, social, and operational content, deterrence thinking is as barren as pre-Clausewitzian thinking.[67] Moreover, as Julian Lider has pointed out, this focus on the technological dimension, which is particularly characteristic of U.S. strategists, has encouraged a conception of strategy that relies on technical solutions to military problems. No room is left for operational, or other, considerations.[68] Edward Luttwak has noted this technical emphasis as well.[69]

The tendency to conceive war and defense in purely military terms, Boserup and Mack argue, is based on the incorrect assumption that military weapons must be countered in kind. In the case of nuclear weapons, they suggest, the advantages of responding with alternative means are quite obvious. The theater of conflict, in reality, is very wide; and in this theater, politics and culture are powerful weapons.[70] In addition, as Mack has observed, while most strategists would agree that the ultimate aim must be to affect the will of the opponent, in practice, and given available military technology, it is a common military belief that if the opponent's military capability can be destroyed, its will to continue fighting is irrelevant. In fact, of course, as any guerrilla strategist would argue, if the opponent's political will is destroyed, then its military capability is irrelevant.[71] In the words of Mao: "Weapons are an important factor in war, but not the decisive factor; it is people, not things, that are decisive."[72] The importance of this perspective to the guerrilla has been noted by some military strategists intent on countering guerrilla warfare.[73]

It has also been noted by Henry Kissinger. In an analysis of the failure of U.S. strategy in Vietnam, Kissinger observed that the United States fought a military war while the North Vietnamese fought a political and psychological one. U.S. military operations had little bearing on declared political objectives, and even military successes could not be turned to political advantage. In a guerrilla war, he concluded, psychological and political factors are important; "military considerations are not decisive."[74] For quite different reasons, William C. Westmoreland, U.S. army chief of staff during the war on Vietnam, agrees. In his view, it was cracks in the will of U.S. policy makers, rather than military considerations, that led to the U.S. defeat in Vietnam.[75]

The above discussion indicates that strategy is a more complex phenomenon than the narrow definitions cited earlier suggest. It works on at least four dimensions: the sociopolitical, the logistical, the operational, and the technological. In addition, strategy involves the use of many means, not just military force. These means include political, psychological, moral, social, economic, ideological, and diplomatic ones. But the vital insight gleaned from this discussion is that the sociopolitical dimension of strategy is central. Ultimately, Howard argues, the people themselves determine the capacity and will of a government to sustain the technological, logistical, and operational burdens of a particular strategy.[76] And this, as discussed in chapter 1, is precisely the point Alexander Atkinson was making when he identified the center of gravity as the "finite pool of social resources" that support the strategic effort.[77] If the people do not support it, a strategy is highly vulnerable.

In practice, of course, the Vietnam War taught Western strategists this important lesson that Marxist strategists have known all along. As a result, for example, U.S. government policy since Vietnam has been radically different. To minimize the possibility that a consensus against a particular war might have time to build, the executive branch of the U.S. government has favored the use of short-term incursions (such as those in Grenada and Panama) using high-technology weapons, or covert operations (as in Nicaragua) in support of insurgents. Moreover, given the concentration of resources and technical capacity which make it possible—and in an extension of their existing practice of "manufacturing consent" generally[78]—powerful vested interests (including governments) now endeavor to manipulate the sociopolitical dimension of strategy more directly. This was demonstrated, for example, by the explicit manipulation and control, by the U.S. government and military, of media reporting during the Gulf War.[79]

Howard's typology highlights the pivotal nature of the social dimension of strategy, because it is within this dimension that the power and will to wage conflict originate. Moreover, his typology makes it clear that an operational strategy relying on military force is *not* the only way to overcome the power and will of the opponent. In fact, in certain circumstances, as imperial powers in Algeria and Vietnam discovered, a military strategy might even fail.

Given the general failure of strategic theories and military strategies to identify the causes of the conflict they seek to address, it is time to consider the insights offered by other disciplines. And if military strategy is not the only way to overcome the power and will of the opponent, these other disciplines might provide additional insights for answering a related question raised in this chapter: Are there ways of *creatively altering* (rather than destroying) the opponent's power and will to wage war? The next few chapters will consider the evidence available in order to answer this question.

3

Conceptions of Society

It is a contention of this study that a society's social cosmology consists of four mutually reinforcing components: its specific pattern of matter-energy use, its particular set of social relations, its prevailing philosophy about the nature of society (which includes a conception of human nature), and its strategies for dealing with conflict. These components are described as being mutually reinforcing because each one helps to shape, as well as reflects, the social cosmology in which it evolves. For example, the underlying conceptions of human society and human nature have profound implications for the theories of conflict, and the strategies for dealing with it, that a cosmology generates. Thus, within the dominant social cosmology, military violence is often justified on the grounds that national societies are integrated social systems and that conflict is the result of antisocial characteristics inherent in human nature. How accurate are these conceptions of human society and human nature? And do they provide an adequate basis for guiding the development of the strategic theory elaborated in this study? The question of human nature is considered in the next chapter; this chapter considers the nature of modern societies.

An underlying assumption of the dominant social cosmology is that a society is an integrated social system or that it strives to become this. There are two major explanations for this assumption: One emphasizes the importance of shared values, and the other stresses the role of coercion.

Value theory, Ralf Dahrendorf explains, suggests that societies are voluntary associations of people who share certain values and create institutions in order to facilitate cooperation.[1] This conception of society was characteristic of the early European models of the social contract. According to John Locke, for example, because all individuals are free, equal, and independent, none can be subjected to the political power of another without their consent. This consent is expressed when individuals agree to unite into a community "for their comfortable, safe, and peaceable living."[2] And for Jean-Jacques Rousseau, the social contract is a form of association in which the entire community protects the person and property of each member in such a way that each individual, as part of this community, effectively renders obedience to their own will while remaining as free as before.[3] More recently, this consensus view of society was held by the sociologist Emile Durkheim. He argued that human beings need each other because they each perform a function that is needed by society as a whole; this results in what he calls "organic solidarity." The human consciousness that we must realize within ourselves is simply the collective consciousness of our social group. Morality, Durkheim believed, "consists in solidarity with the group." Consequently, the duties of individuals to themselves are duties to society.[4]

In contrast to value theory, Dahrendorf explains, coercion theory suggests that the inequality of power that inevitably accompanies social organization becomes entrenched in the social structure and generates conflict. In these circumstances, it is not shared values but coercion that makes society cohere.[5] This theory is associated with Thomas Hobbes, who believed that society is basically conflictual and that social order is imposed by threat and coercion: "by feare of punishment."[6] There are many critiques of modern society that are consistent with coercion theory. Six of these critiques are explained briefly below, with reference to authors who are representative of each particular perspective.

Karl Marx and Frederick Engels shared the view that society is conflictual. According to the Marxist critique, capitalist society—like its predecessors in recorded history—is characterized by class conflict. However, unlike its predecessors, in which there was a gradation of social rank, capitalism has simplified the nature of this class conflict into a single struggle between those who must sell their labor (the proletariat) and those who own the means of production and who appropriate the surplus value (the bourgeoisie).[7] This relationship is a coercive one that compels the working class to do more work than is necessary in order to sustain itself; it is "reckless of the health or length of life of the labourer." In these circumstances, the "right" to absorb surplus labor is secured not merely through the force of economic relations; it requires the help of the state. Consequently, Marx argues, social order is maintained through the coercive power of the state, which is the instrument of bourgeois capital.[8] Moreover, according to Marx, because the relations of production constitute the foundation of society, on which the political and legal superstructure is built, real change can occur only through a transformation of this economic foundation; it cannot occur through changes to the political or legal institutions that arise from that foundation.[9] This critique has been systematically elaborated and refined in many respects since it was first presented by Marx.

Similarly, the anarchist critique has noted the conflict between civil society and the state and drawn attention to the coercive role of the latter. The state, according to Mikhail Bakunin, is "the most cynical and complete negation of humanity" because it destroys human solidarity. The state unites some people in order to conquer or destroy all others. The "supreme law" of the state, he argues, is self-preservation. This condemns each state to perpetual struggle against its own population and all foreign states. Moreover, in order to succeed in this struggle, the state must augment its power "to the detriment of internal liberty and external justice."[10] In addition, Robert Wolff has highlighted the specific conflict between state authority and individual autonomy. In his view, the defining characteristic of the state is authority—"the right to rule"—and the primary obligation of the individual is autonomy—"the refusal to be ruled." Consequently, Wolff argues, there is no way to resolve the conflict between the autonomy of the individual and the authority of the state.[11]

The feminist critique emphasizes the inherently conflictual and coercive nature of patriarchal society, which denies the most basic needs and rights to women. According to Donna Warnock, patriarchal society grants power and privilege to those who fit the socially defined masculine identity. "Under Patriarchy men are entitled to everything."[12] But, Mary Daly argues, it goes beyond this. "The rulers of patriarchy—males with power—wage an unceasing war against life itself." And because women are essentially biophilic, they are the primary target.[13]

In addition to the above critiques, recent social-critical theories also highlight the conflictual and coercive nature of modern society. For example, amplifying the notions of a "governing elite" and a "nongoverning elite" developed by Vilfredo Pareto,[14] the "elitist critique" emphasizes the role of elites in dominating the military-industrial complex and exercising control over society because of it. C. Wright Mills, for example, argues that the power elite controls the major organizations of modern society: It runs the state machinery, manages the big corporations, and directs the military establishment. According to Mills, because these elites occupy the strategic command posts of the social structure, they are in a position to make decisions of major consequence and to impose them on society.[15]

The "technocratic critique" argues that science, technology, and organization have become a vast, complex, and "quasi-mystical process" that influences or controls all human activity; it is what some critics call a "technocracy."[16] According to Theodore Roszak, the roots of technocracy can be traced to the scientific worldview of the Western tradition. In his view, it is the product not of capitalism but of a mature and accelerating industrialism. In the technocratic state, the business of inventing and marketing "treacherous parodies of freedom, joy, and fulfillment" is an indispensable form of social control.[17] In a technocratic society, Jacques Ellul argues, technique itself prevails over the human being.[18]

Finally, the "cultural critique" argues that culture "is a critical determinant of political, economic, and social systems."[19] This critique is endorsed by Johan Galtung. In his view, culture (itself heavily influenced by religion) shapes the political, economic, and military structures of a society as well as the processes that flow from them.[20] In addition, culture provides the starting point for several critical social analyses. For example, Eldridge Cleaver argues that Western culture (and particularly its manifestation in the United States) generates political, economic, and legal structures based on violence, domination, and competition.[21]

Whether they are concerned with the exploitation of labor, impersonal state control, patriarchal power relations, elite domination, technocratic manipulation, or a cultural predisposition to violence, each of these critiques is compatible with the coercion model of society. They agree that national societies are characterized by high levels of structural conflict and that social systems are far from integrated. However, while each of these critiques can improve our understanding of the nature of any society, none of them is adequate by itself. This point has been made by many authors. In critiques of white feminism,[22] for example, women of color and women from the South have argued that oppression based on gender cannot be separated from other forms of oppression based on nationality, race, ethnicity, religion, sexual orientation, and class. These women have consistently drawn attention to "the simultaneity of multiple oppressions in women's lives."[23] Moreover, as some authors have noted, these multiple oppressions do not function in separate spheres of social life; they "co-define" each other. For example, economic roles within society are not defined, as many Marxists would claim, by class alone; they are co-defined by several influences including class, gender, and race.[24]

According to John Burton, then, the appearance of coherence is misleading, and he rejects both the value theory and the coercion theory. Value theory assumes that the social system is integrated and then endeavors to explain it. And yet, Burton maintains, individuals and groups in society have widely divergent values, and even those values that are described as "shared" frequently impede the satisfaction of universal human needs. Similarly, coercion theory assumes the existence of an integrated social system while arguing that this coherence is maintained through coercion; it offers no evidence that coercion can succeed in promoting system integration.[25]

It is evident that modern industrial societies—which have many different cultural, class, ideological, and interest groups, each of which has its own values and attitudes toward society—are not integrated social systems.[26] According to W. E. Moore: "The conception of an 'integrated' social system, which informs much of the writing in contemporary sociology—often implicitly—is a model useful for many purposes, but is clearly contrary to fact."[27] The apparent and superficial cohesion of societies is due to functional transactions within them.[28]

More importantly, according to sociologist Peter Berger, this apparent cohesion depends on social control—the means used by a society to make its members conform. In Berger's view, a society cannot exist without social control, and the ultimate mechanism of control is violence. In fact, he argues: "Violence is the ultimate foundation of any political order." However, since the constant use of violence would be impractical and ineffective, other means of coercion are more important most of the time: political and legal controls; economic pressure; the mechanisms of persuasion, ridicule, and gossip; the pressures of morality, custom, and manners;

as well as the controls imposed by fellow workers, family, and friends.[29]

In short, the conventional notion that modern societies are integrated does not accord with reality. Moreover, Burton argues, the assumption that societies are integrated and should be preserved as such "may be both a source of many unsolved social and political problems and also a reason why they are not solved."[30] Edward Azar is even more emphatic. In his view, Western political theory has mistaken the centralized state for a socially integrated political system. In fact, he argues, centralized political structures generate conflict because they reduce the opportunity for a sense of community among groups as well as denying these groups the means to satisfy their needs.[31]

The conclusion from this line of argument is that much of the conflict that occurs in national societies is structurally generated. It is the result of a series of mutually reinforcing contradictions inherent in modern society and the state. For that reason, traditional explanations of conflict in the international system—which are based on the notion that national societies are integrated social systems—are inadequate. In such circumstances the important questions are the following: What changes are required in order to eliminate structural conflict from the social system? And under what conditions can there be a harmonious society despite the absence of shared values and the absence of coercion?[32] The answers to these questions require a basic understanding of human nature and the motivations that determine human behavior. These are discussed in the next chapter.

4

Human Nature and Human Needs

It is a contention of this study that a social cosmology includes a particular conception of human nature. This conception helps to shape, as well as reflects, the other components of that cosmology. Consequently, strategies for dealing with conflict in any social cosmology are based, implicitly or explicitly, on fundamental assumptions about human nature.[1] Within the dominant social cosmology, as noted in the previous chapter, military violence is often justified on the grounds that conflict is the result of antisocial characteristics inherent in human nature. To identify the most appropriate conception of human nature for guiding development of the strategic theory elaborated in this study, this chapter does three interrelated things. It begins by explaining and criticizing the conception of human nature that is characteristic of the dominant social cosmology. It then examines recent attempts to define a conception of human nature in terms of human needs. Finally, it presents a summary of the argument that human individuals and their identity groups should replace the state as the focus of political theory and practice.

The Dominant Conception of Human Nature

There is an ongoing debate about human nature in Western literature. Two questions are perennial: Is human nature socially or genetically determined? And, is human nature good or evil? The diversity of answers offered in response to the first question can be illustrated by summarizing the contrasting views of two prominent Western theorists: Karl Marx and Sigmund Freud. This will provide a basis for comparing traditional approaches to this question with the approaches taken by more recent theorists considered later in this chapter. Regarding the second question, this section will explain the conception of human nature characteristic of the dominant social cosmology and identify some important shortcomings of it.

The distinctive feature of Marx's concept of human nature is his belief that human nature is essentially social and that it is determined by social relations that are fundamentally economic in character. The "human essence," according to Marx, is the ensemble of social relations.[2] What makes humans distinctively human, however, is their *production* of their means of subsistence. Consequently, human nature is shaped by the material conditions that determine this mode of production.[3] In fact, Marx argues, the mode of production of material life conditions life in general. "It is not the consciousness of [individuals] that determines their existence, but their social existence that determines their consciousness."[4]

Like Marx, Freud believed that human consciousness is determined by forces acting outside human awareness; unlike Marx, he believed that these causes are individual and mental.[5] According to Freud, there are three types of psychic processes: conscious, preconscious, and unconscious. The latter are psychic processes that cannot become conscious under normal circumstances; moreover, they might lead to behavior that cannot be explained rationally.[6] Freud also distinguished, separately from these psychical processes, three structural systems within the human mind: the *id*, which contains everything that is inherited, including instinctual drives; the *ego*, which mediates between the id and the external world; and the *superego*, that part of the ego left over from childhood that contains the conscience. It is the role of the ego to try to reconcile the demands of the id, the superego, and reality.[7] Freud also attached importance to his theory of instincts. Although he believed that it is possible to distinguish many instincts, he ultimately decided on two classifications: the basic "life" instinct (Eros), which includes self-preservation and erotic instincts; and the basic "death" instinct (Thanatos), which includes aggression, sadism, and self-destruction.[8] In essence then, Freud believed that the individual human personality depends on the influence of hereditary endowment (as contained in the id), the influence of social conditioning (as contained in the superego), and the influence of contemporary personal experience (as contained in the ego). Nevertheless, he emphasized the crucial importance of the experiences of infancy and early childhood.[9]

Although neither Marx nor Freud was able to offer definitive evidence in support of his view regarding the "origins" of human nature, recent research has shed considerable light on this question. This will be considered in a later section. Despite its importance, the debate over whether human nature is socially or genetically determined has been overshadowed by the ongoing debate regarding its character. Is human nature inherently selfish, competitive, and aggressive? Or is it something else?

There are some positive conceptions of human nature in the Western literature; however, descriptions that emphasize its selfish, competitive, or aggressive character are far more common. According to Niccolò Machiavelli, for example, people are ungrateful, greedy, cowardly, and deceitful. They "are wretched creatures who would not keep their word."[10] In the view of Thomas Hobbes, all individuals are engaged in a competitive struggle for power "that ceaseth onely in Death."[11] Among more recent authors, Freud shared this negative view of human nature; in his view, humans are instinctively aggressive.[12]

This negative conception of human nature underpins realism—the political philosophy characteristic of the dominant social cosmology—and is based on the specific notion that conflict is the direct outcome of human aggressiveness. According to Hans Morgenthau, the preeminent exponent of realism, the world is the result of forces inherent in human nature that are essentially malign.[13] Similarly, Kenneth Waltz argues that conflict is the direct result of a small number of behavior traits that reflect defects inherent in humans. The challenge, therefore, is to find ways to repress this evilness. According to Waltz, institutional "force" must be used to control this "rapacious" behavior.[14]

These arguments concerning the origin and essence of human nature are the key features of the "inherency-contingency" debate. This long-running debate is an important element underlying Western discourse about the nature of society and in shaping discussions about human nature and human behavior. According to Harry Eckstein, an event is inherent either if it will always occur or if the potential for it to occur always exists, while an event is contingent if its occurrence depends on the existence of conditions that occur accidentally.[15] "Contingency" thinkers such as Rousseau and Marx have argued that human nature is undesirably molded by the social conditions acting upon it. This view of human nature suggests that satisfying the legitimate demands of people is the way to avoid disruption and conflict. "Inherency" thinkers such as Machiavelli, Hobbes, and Morgenthau have articulated views emphasizing the innate, antisocial characteristics of human nature that are kept in check by socialization, custom, and the law.[16] According to this view, conflict should be contained within a system by enforcing the observance of social and legal norms that have been determined by elites. This logically requires the constraint or punishment of people involved in conflict, both in order to deal with the present situation and to deter future behaviors of this kind. Of course, this approach to conflict also has the effect of distracting attention from the need to further investigate the nature of human behavior and to consider the potential of altering policies and institutions as ways of dealing with conflict.[17]

This last explanation provides an important clue to understanding why the belief that human nature is inherently selfish, competitive, and aggressive is so pervasive within the dominant social cosmology: It is actively promoted by elites because it serves elite interests. It provides a justification for the creation and maintenance of coercive institutions (which are controlled by elites);[18] it deflects attention away from explanations of conflict that identify the responsibility of elite policies or institutions;[19] and it provides an important justification for military spending and military intervention undertaken in "self-defense."[20]

Despite the pervasiveness of this conception of human nature, it is extremely limited. It is patriarchal: It fails to take into account the perspective and experience of women. It is Western: It fails to take into account the perspective and experience of the entire population of non-Western peoples.[21] And it is usually *assumed*: Little or no *evidence* (which is widely accepted even within the limited domain of the Western scientific community) is offered to substantiate the claim that human nature is *innately* selfish, competitive, or aggressive. In fact, for example, there is a substantial body of evidence that systematically refutes the notion that human nature is inherently aggressive.[22]

In summary, the traditional debate about human nature in the literature of the dominant social cosmology has been limited. This is because the notions that human nature is genetically determined and that it is inherently evil serve elite interests. These twin notions have been used to legitimize hierarchical sets of social relations as well as certain approaches to conflict, both of which allow elites to exercise coercive power. While feminist and non-Western perspectives highlighted the incompleteness of the dominant conception of human nature a long time ago, recent research, considered in the next section, has provided new insights for generating a conception of human nature which is better able to explain the diversity of human behavior.

The Importance of Human Needs

If "human nature" actually exists, then any serious attempt to define a universal conception of it—which may then be used to guide the creation of social cosmologies that take real human beings into account—must satisfy several exacting criteria: It must be able to account for changes in the patterns of human behavior that have occurred throughout historical time; it must be able to account for the widely divergent behavioral patterns of people living in different cultures; it must be able to account for the different behavioral patterns of women and men in any culture; and it must be able to explain why individuals within a particular culture behave differently at different times. One recent attempt to define a conception of human nature that satisfies all of these criteria defines human nature in terms of human needs.

Many social scientists have highlighted the importance of identifying the role of human needs in any attempt to understand human behavior.[23] According to Johan Galtung, transdisciplinary efforts have become increasingly focused on the human being, and questions about the meaning of human development and self-realization are now being answered in terms of human needs.[24] In addition, John Burton argues, attention is now directed to these needs as a controlling element in social organization. This development is a logical extension of the work of earlier scholars who were moving toward a general theory of behavior in order to explain a particular phenomenon. What is significant, however, is the shift in emphasis.[25] Paul Sites clearly identifies this shift with his assertion that the influence in society of human needs is much greater than the influence of the social forces that act upon individuals. In his view, society "never completely conquers the individual."[26] What evidence is there to support the contention that human needs exist?

The existence of human needs has been accepted by an increasing number of scholars in a variety of disciplines since 1950.[27] For example, in developing his theory of motivation, Abraham Maslow proposed a hierarchy of human needs.[28] According to Sites, whose work in this field is vitally important, "the most fundamental component in individual and social life is that of control." Individuals seek to control their physical and social environment in order to satisfy their needs. When Sites speaks of needs, he does not mean the secondary needs learned in a specific interaction situation; he is referring to needs that exist "outside" any particular society. For Sites, then, basic needs do exist, and, contrary to the arguments of some behavioral scientists, they are universal rather than specifically cultural. Sites isolates eight needs: the needs for response, security, recognition, stimulation, distributive justice, meaning, rationality, and control. The last four needs emerge, he suggests, because the first four, which emerge from the socialization process, cannot be immediately and consistently satisfied.[29]

For Galtung, there are four classes of human needs: survival needs, well-being needs, identity needs, and freedom needs.[30] In his view, needs differ between individuals and groups and vary over time in accordance with socialization processes. However, although individuals are malleable, they are not infinitely so, and the denial of needs will lead to personal and/or social pathology.[31] According to Galtung, needs are "deeply embedded in the psychosomatic structure of human beings."[32]

According to Dennis Sandole, despite their ambiguous nature, there is evidence that human needs exist. He cites a wide range of examples, from several disciplines, that indicate the existence of various physical and social needs. Sandole shares the view that all basic needs are genetically programmed predispositions, which, he asserts, does not imply "biological reductionism."[33]

Some researchers, of course, reject the contention that human needs are genetically based. Kevin Avruch and Peter Black, for example, argue that to deduce specific human needs from genetics, it is necessary to assume the existence of specific genetic structures connected to the expression of those needs. However, they argue, there is considerable evidence to suggest that such specific genetic control of behavior is highly unlikely: "one wonders what a gene for the expression of 'distributive justice' would look like." According to

Avruch and Black, human culture is responsible for the recurring patterns of human behavior.[34]

Burton and Sandole, however, reject the exclusivity of this argument. They cite the study by Robert Boyd and Peter Richerson that concluded that there is a "dual inheritance" system: one cultural and one genetic.[35] The important conclusion, Burton and Sandole assert, "is that universal patterns of behavior exist." This finding, they argue, is consistent with their view that conflict may involve a clash between culturally determined ways in which needs are expressed rather than a clash between needs as such.[36] Galtung agrees. In his view, human needs are derived from the interaction between physiological and cultural sources.[37] And for Sandole, "it is not a question of nature or nurture but the extent to which each plays a role in the expression of particular kinds of human behavior."[38]

But while there is no significant disagreement about the role of culture in the origin and expression of human needs, what evidence is there to support the claim by Burton, Galtung, Sandole, Sites, and others that needs have a biological basis as well? One argument links needs with emotions. According to Sites, needs directly correspond to human emotions, "thereby giving needs a grounding in the very nature of the human species."[39] Can this claim be substantiated? Since the idea was first articulated by Charles Darwin in 1872,[40] a succession of scholars in various disciplines have argued that emotions entered the evolutionary scheme of things because they enhanced the prospects of survival.[41] This is because emotions are reactions that trigger appropriate behavioral responses to events in the individual's social and physical environment. Though there is still no consensus on the precise definition of "emotions,"[42] their evolutionary role and importance are now widely accepted.

Robert Plutchik summarizes one explanation that identifies the central role of emotions in the human evolutionary process. According to this explanation, the peculiarly human response to the evolution of emotions (such as fear and anger) was the development of enhanced cognitive capacities. This allowed humans to collect, store, and evaluate information about their environment; to develop foresight about future needs; to make predictions about the likely course of events; and to initiate patterns of behavior "in the service of emotions and biological needs." In other words, emotions generate a series of cognitive processes and behavioral responses that are designed to satisfy survival needs.[43]

Widespread acceptance of the adaptive role of emotions in human evolution is coupled with acceptance of the idea that there are a few fundamental or primary emotions and many more derivative or secondary ones.[44] Consequently, many authors have attempted to identify a list of primary emotions. Plutchik, for example, presents a detailed argument to support his identification of eight emotions as the basis, singly or in combination, of all others.[45] More recently, Theodore Kemper has argued that "there are four physiologically grounded primary emotions"—fear, anger, depression, and satisfaction—and that all others are socially constructed derivatives of one or a combination of these. He summarizes seven different approaches to the study of emotions and notes that, regardless of the approach, there is virtual agreement on the existence of these four primary emotions, that is, "ones that are neurologically structured in all human organisms." In addition, he offers convincing evidence on five grounds to support his argument. These include the facts that fear, anger, depression, and satisfaction have evolutionary survival value; they are the first emotions to appear in the development of human infants; they occur in all cultures; and they are the *only* emotions that have been specifically and differentially linked with certain neurochemicals known to activate or modulate the physiological processes associated with emotions.[46]

Whether Kemper is correct or not regarding the *number* of primary emotions, his identification of fear, anger, depression, and satisfaction as primary emotions is consistent with a great deal of research evidence in several disciplines. Consequently, Sites argues, if the evolutionary role of emotions is to enhance the prospects of survival, then humans (as well as other animals) require conditions of life "which will reduce the three negative emotional states of fear, anger and depression and thereby permit the positive emotional state of satisfaction." These conditions of life, he suggests, may be referred to as "needs." Thus, he asserts, corresponding to the emotions of fear, anger, depression, and satisfaction, humans have needs for security, meaning, self-esteem, and latency. These emotions and their corresponding needs, Sites argues, are concerned with survival of "the self" as a whole and not just the physical organism.[47]

As the above discussion illustrates, there is a considerable body of evidence that demonstrates the existence of human needs and that suggests that needs are part of the "very nature" of human beings. According to Roger Coate and Jerel Rosati, human needs do exist "and can provide the basis for empirical theories of politics."[48] And despite the lack of precise knowledge and general agreement about what these needs are, this is not important.[49] Clearly, the lack of consensus regarding the precise definition and use of the concept of power has not prevented political realists from developing a substantial body of theory and practice.[50] Barry Buzan agrees. As he explains it, the failure of theorists to produce a widely accepted definition or measure for power has not prevented constructive discussion.[51]

If these human needs do, in fact, exist, will they be pursued regardless of consequences to society and self? Individuals have no real choice, according to Coate and Rosati. In their view, the drive to satisfy human needs is so strong that individuals will endeavor to satisfy them "even at the cost of personal disorientation and social disruption."[52] Similarly, Burton argues that human individuals *must* pursue their needs, either independently or in association with others, regardless of the consequences.[53] In the beginning, he explains, individuals seek to satisfy their needs by acting within the limits imposed by the norms and laws of their society, their experience, and their knowledge of options. But if these social norms and laws frustrate them, then, subject to the value they attach to their social relationships, they will employ methods that violate these norms and laws. They act this way because there are no other options for satisfying their needs. The threat of punishment, punishment itself, and even isolation from society cannot alter their behavior, because their loss of control over their capacity to satisfy their needs led to their behavior in the first place; consequently, threats or action to aggravate this loss of control will not constrain them. All behavior, then—deviant or otherwise—is that response to the environment that the individual calculates will best satisfy their needs and values.[54]

Sites agrees with this view. He contends that people seek to satisfy their needs and attempt to control their environment in order to achieve this. If this is possible within the framework of socially acceptable behavior, no deviation occurs. If this is not possible, some individuals will attempt to satisfy their needs in socially unacceptable ways and take the risk of paying the social cost for doing so. But in the end, Sites argues, the need wins out, not the society.[55]

In fact, consistently with this view, studies of deviance indicate that individuals are willing to deviate from socially acceptable norms of behavior if they cannot satisfy basic needs within this framework. Individuals, Sites maintains, are not infinitely adaptable to the social environment. They are "self-consciously alive," with certain needs that must be satisfied.[56] Deviant behavior, then, must be properly understood; it is simply "rule breaking." According to Steven Box, it is behavior that is proscribed by elites who have the institutionalized power to create social norms and laws and then to punish those people whose behavior violates those norms and laws.[57] In fact, Burton argues, the term *deviance* cannot properly be applied to the individual, because the individual is needs-oriented and is not able to deviate from the pursuit of needs. The notion of deviance has meaning only when applied to structures, laws, policies, or processes that frustrate the attainment of human needs.[58]

In addition, the *empirical* evidence clearly indicates that individuals will pursue needs irrespective of the cost to society and themselves. As Galtung has noted, history provides a long list of examples to demonstrate that people are willing to sacrifice their lives for the right to speak their own language, for the right to practice their own religion, and for their freedom.[59] This is evident at the micro level as well. According to Victoria Rader: "It is my experience that when individuals are forced to choose their dignity over shelter or food, they will often choose the former even at some risk to their lives."[60]

According to the conception of human nature outlined in this section, emotions evolved because they enhanced the prospects of survival. As a direct result of being driven by these emotions, humans have a corresponding set of needs for conditions of life that will reduce their negative emotional states and thereby permit a positive one. Therefore, the most fundamental evolutionary force experienced by individuals is the drive to attempt to control their environment in order to satisfy their needs. According to this conception, human nature is elastic in the sense that, provided negative emotional states are eliminated by the satisfaction of corresponding needs, the cultural context in which this occurs is irrelevant. Consequently, human nature is neither inherently good nor inherently evil. If a social cosmology provides adequate opportunity to satisfy their needs, individuals will be "good"; if a social cosmology frustrates human needs, individuals may be "evil." This conception of human nature can no doubt be refined; nonetheless, it satisfies the four demanding criteria outlined at the beginning of this section. Given its capacity to explain the exceptional variety of human behaviors, the conception of human nature presented in this section is superior to the dominant one.

Individuals and Their Identity Groups

Given the pervasiveness of the traditional conception of human nature, elite managers within the dominant social cosmology have been able to concentrate their attention on the creation and maintenance of social structures and conflict processes that are designed to contain human "evil." Needless to say, these structures and processes are useful for controlling people for other purposes as well. Although the dominant social cosmology is preoccupied with the institutions and processes characteristic of the coercive state, there is considerable evidence to suggest that human individuals and their identity groups should replace the state as the focus of political theory and practice.

A major characteristic of Western political theory has been its focus on the state as the primary conceptual unit. This has been particularly evident in the disciplines of international relations and strategic studies. Hedley Bull, for example, accepts the notion that states are the primary actors in world politics and "the chief bearers of rights and duties within it."[61]

As a result, Burton claims, conflict persists because mainstream political theory has been preoccupied with preservation of the state and its institutions. This preoccupation derives from the classical assumption that the individual is malleable and can be shaped by the socialization process managed by the state.[62] However, while human individuals are capable of a large degree of adjustment during any socialization process, the traditional view implies that this process has no limits. It presupposes that a person has no inherent or human needs that must be satisfied. But in fact, as the discussion in the previous section illustrated, the evidence suggests that human beings have certain inherent drives that are not within their ability to control and that cannot be suppressed by socialization, threats, or coercion. In other words, people are responsive to opportunities for development and are malleable in this sense, but they cannot be socialized to accept the denial of needs that are necessary for their personal development. In these circumstances, systems and organizations that neglect human needs must generate conflict.[63] Moreover, Burton claims, once basic assumptions are questioned, the empirical evidence suggests that traditional concepts of democracy, law and order, the common good, and the right to rule and to expect obedience, are often at the root of conflict.[64] And deterrence theory, which is the basis of both domestic law enforcement and national defense strategies, is exposed as inadequate because deterrence cannot deter in those circumstances in which human needs are at stake.[65]

For these reasons, Burton suggests a searching reappraisal of the original assumptions and hypotheses of mainstream Western political theory. The aim is to determine which policies and structures generate international conflict. This requires, among other things, a theory of human behavior that is scientific. Consequently, the theoretical foundation of Burton's approach is an assertion that there are certain human needs that are universal. These needs must be satisfied if individual development and socialization are to occur. The failure to satisfy needs is a sufficient explanation of dissidence and deviant behavior as well as of political and social instabilities.[66]

This approach is endorsed by Galtung. The basis of any political analysis, according to Galtung, is the human individual.[67] Galtung highlights the centrality of the individual and the importance of individuals' needs in his discussion of "human-centred development." These needs are human "in the sense that it is in the individual—the body, the mind, the spirit—that they will have to be satisfied." As he explains it, if human needs are not satisfied, then individuals and/or societies will begin to disintegrate. In his view, the nonsatisfaction of human needs explains much of the social disintegration now evident around the world.[68]

In contrast to classical Western political theory, then, many scholars now emphasize the centrality of the individual and the importance of human needs. In fact, according to Sites, it is the existence of needs in humans that makes society possible. Individuals' needs make it necessary for them to attempt to control their environment and, at the same time, to modify their behavior in response to the controls exercised by others.[69]

The organizational-individual debate is thus being resolved by a synthesis: Individuals can adapt to their society and its institutions but only within the limits set by the imperative to satisfy their needs. "In the tension between human needs and institutions, it is change in institutions that is required."[70] It should be stressed, however, that this emphasis on the importance of the individual is not intended to isolate humans from their social context. From a human-needs perspective, networks of individuals and groups are the units of analysis, because these provide the framework in which human needs are pursued and in which values, interests, and power arise.[71]

Edward Azar concurs with this view; he is concerned with the *societal needs* of the individual. According to Azar, the traditional debate over the appropriate unit of analysis in international conflict has been limited by its preoccupation with the individual and the state. "It has ignored the group totally." In his view, the important unit of analysis is the identity group, whether it be racial, religious, cultural, or some other. The nation-state is less important, he argues, because most states in the contemporary international system are unintegrated social units; they are artificial creations of earlier periods of imperial expansion. Despite the elite promotion of nationalism, most contemporary states are totally incapable of inspiring loyalty and a civic culture.[72] This was particularly evident as the Soviet and Yugoslav states began to disintegrate in 1991 in favor of ethnic and cultural identity groups.

To satisfy their needs within these group relationships, individuals must strive for what Christian Bay calls an "authentic community": a group of people who share a sense of solidarity and who have an equal right to influence community decisions. In his view, only this form of community can ensure the satisfaction of human needs.[73] Azar agrees. He believes that decentralized political structures provide the best environment for satisfying the needs of groups. By promoting local participation and self-reliance, they give the groups concerned a sense of control over their own affairs.[74]

Within the dominant social cosmology, the management practices used in supposedly diverse political systems—including those that are labeled "democratic," "communist," or "totalitarian"—reflect elite adherence to a common theoretical and empirical framework. According to this framework, elites are entitled to create social structures and conflict processes in order to manage society in accordance with their ideologically defined notion of the "common good." From the human-needs perspective, whatever the nature of the political system that attempts this form of social control, it must ultimately fail. If the conception of human nature and the arguments concerning the importance of the human individual outlined above are accepted, then it is necessary to develop patterns of matter-energy use, political philosophies, social structures, and strategies for dealing with conflict that are oriented to the satisfaction of individual human needs.

Conclusion

The evidence presented in this chapter demonstrates that the human-needs perspective is a viable alternative to political realism as an approach to international relations. Given its explanatory capacity, several insights derived from this perspective are incorporated into the strategic theory developed in this study. In the meantime, two conclusions derived from arguments presented in this chapter should be highlighted.

The first conclusion is general. If the human-needs perspective—which offers a particular conception of human nature and places the human individual at the center of political theory and practice—is accepted, then it is necessary to develop social cosmologies oriented to the satisfaction of human needs. The second conclusion is more specific. In chapters 1 and 2, the importance of the relationship between psychology (including the notion of "will") and strategy was identified. Is there any relationship between the theory of human behavior outlined in this chapter and what strategists refer to as "will"? While it might be possible to improve on this explanation, it seems reasonable to suggest that will is the disposition or inclination to act in response to the drive to satisfy human needs. This definition of will is incorporated into the strategic theory developed in this study.

5

Conflict Resolution through Problem Solving

Any strategy for dealing with conflict—including a strategy of military violence or a strategy of nonviolent defense—is based, implicitly or explicitly, on a conception of conflict. Given the existence of many different conceptions, which ways of understanding conflict provide the most appropriate guidance for resolving it?

While there is a vast and rapidly expanding literature on conflict, it is clear that research in the subject still suffers from two major shortcomings. First, apart from the efforts of scholars such as Johan Galtung and John Burton, relatively little attention is paid to the development of an adequate and integrated *theory* of conflict. This is a significant shortcoming of modern social science, particularly given the insights now being derived from research in several disciplines. Second, Western literature still pays scant attention to non-Western conceptions of conflict. How, for instance, do Arabs and Polynesians, Buddhists and Hindus, conceptualize conflict? Given the prevalence of conflict in the international system, it is clear that understanding the ways in which different cultures conceptualize conflict is vitally important. Clearly, it would seem, an adequate theory of conflict cannot be culture-specific.

A general theory of conflict is necessary, not just because it helps to explain, predict, and treat some elements of human behavior, but because it provides the basis for understanding particular types of conflict. Despite this, some authors have argued that because different types of conflicts occur in different contexts, a general theory is inapplicable and that a specific theory for each kind of conflict provides greater understanding of the relevant phenomena than a general theory could.[1] These arguments have been systematically refuted by Clinton Fink. In his view, the scientific value of a general theory of conflict is twofold: It provides a more complete explanation of each particular kind of conflict than the one provided by the relevant specific theory, and it provides a more complete explanation of the entire domain of conflict phenomena than any explanation that could be provided by the total set of specific theories. Furthermore, he asserts: "A consistent language for discussing conflict phenomena can only be provided by a unified theoretical framework."[2]

It can be argued, then, that whatever its shortcomings, a general theory of conflict must be the basis of any particular theory of conflict—including that of strategic theory. This is because any valid framework for explaining and dealing with conflict in the international system must be consistent with the more general principles of conflict theory. If it is not, it will lead to erroneous conclusions, policy, and strategy. However, this is not to claim that any new theory, including the one presented in this study, will be the final word on the matter. On the contrary, all that can be claimed is that the attempt represents a step beyond existing theories.

The Dominant Conception of Conflict

In Max Weber's classical formulation, a social relationship is in conflict when one actor carries out their own will against the resistance of another party.[3] For Lewis Coser, conflict is a struggle over values, status, power, and resources "in which the aims of the opponents are to neutralize, injure or eliminate their rivals."[4] As these and many similar definitions illustrate,[5] within the dominant social cosmology conflict is understood to occur when two or more parties compete with each other to secure mutually exclusive outcomes. Moreover, as the definitions of Weber and Coser suggest, there has been a tendency to perceive conflict as destructive.

Despite their apparent variety, the methods used for dealing with conflict in the dominant social cosmology are characterized by several common features. Fundamentally, they share the assumption that a solution exists—and must be found—within the prevailing structural framework. They are designed to deal with symptoms (disputes over short-term interests) rather than causes. They share the notion that conflict outcomes are win-lose by nature or involve some form of compromise. And, for deciding conflict outcomes, they rely heavily on "external" factors such as legal norms (including historical precedents), third parties, relative power, or even goodwill. The traditional methods of dealing with conflict (negotiation, mediation, arbitration, adjudication, and legislation) are all characterized by these features,[6] and, in those circumstances in which negotiable interests rather than human needs are at stake, one of these methods might be able to resolve it. But, as this chapter will explain, when the conflict is structural and/or fundamental needs are at stake, there will be protracted conflict that these methods cannot help to resolve.[7]

Despite the pervasiveness of the dominant conception of conflict, a review of the recent conflict research—and particularly the work of John Burton (international relations), Johan Galtung (peace research), and various scholars in the field of psychology—reveals important, and complementary, insights.

Burton's Theory of Conflict

John Burton distinguishes three types of human motivation: needs, values, and interests. *Needs* are those motivations that are "universal and primordial, and perhaps genetic"; they are required for the development of the human species and will be pursued by all means available.[8] They are essential to the development of the individual as a functioning and cooperative member of society; therefore, they are necessary for the organization and survival of society itself. Needs are fundamental drives that are shared generally by developed organisms.[9] They do not change, unlike values and interests, nor are they scarce.[10] *Values* are those motivations that are culturally specific: They are the customs and beliefs that are peculiar to a particular community. In many circumstances, the needs for identity and security require the defense of values, and in this sense values impinge on needs and can be confused with them. *Interests* are those motivations that change according to circumstances: the social, political, and economic aspirations of individuals and identity groups within a society. They typically relate to such things as social roles and material goods.[11]

As a result of his work, Burton has suggested more precise definitions of the words *dispute* and *conflict* and drawn attention to the distinction between a "settlement" and a "resolution." In addition, he has added a new dimension to conflict management processes by introducing the concept of "provention." According to Burton, a dispute is a situation in which the issues are negotiable, compromise is possible, and consideration of altered institutions and structures is not necessary. It is a normal and constructive feature of social life. In contrast, conflict is deeply rooted in human needs.[12] It involves issues that are not negotiable: human needs that cannot be compromised.[13] It results in behavior that destroys, or has the potential to destroy, people, property, and systems. Burton regards the distinction between disputes and conflicts as vitally important even though the two are sometimes linked, as they are when disputes are symptoms of underlying conflicts.[14]

According to Burton, conflict is *settled*, managed, or suppressed as a result of such mechanisms as negotiation, bargaining, arbitration, mediation, conciliation, or judicial ruling. The outcome—in which some or all of the parties lose—is the result of the application of social or legal norms or the consequence of relative power. Some coercion is usually necessary in order to enforce such a settlement. More fundamentally, conflict is *resolved* when the outcome fully meets the needs of all parties.[15] This frequently requires major policy changes and environmental restructuring.[16] This approach has been labeled "problem solving" and represents a significant shift in thinking about conflict resolution.

However, Burton maintains, there are some areas of conflict—such as those related to drugs, gang violence, terrorism, and the international system—in which there can be no resolution; in these circumstances there must be *provention*. Provention is an approach to conflict in which steps are taken to remove the sources (including the structural causes) of the conflict and to promote conditions in which collaborative and valued relationships control behaviors.[17]

The principal hypothesis of conflict resolution and provention, as Burton conceives them, is that there is a limit to the extent to which any person, acting separately or within a wider ethnic or national community, can be socialized or manipulated. This hypothesis is derived from the assumption that there are human needs that must be satisfied by social institutions if these institutions are to be stable and if societies themselves are to be relatively free of conflict.[18]

In his view therefore, conflict—including that which occurs in the international system—is not over objective differences of interest that involve scarcity, although it is often defined in these terms by the parties themselves. Conflict occurs over needs, including the needs for identity and security, that are not in short supply, although the tactics used in any attempt to satisfy these needs, such as a demand for territory, may involve shortages. Thus traditional approaches to conflict settlement have focused on the allocation of scarce resources, because it is over these that conflicts are thought to be fought; little attention has been devoted to the underlying causes of conflict, which are often not readily apparent to the parties themselves.[19]

Moreover, if conflict is due to drives for identity, security, and other human needs, then it follows that the imposition and enforcement of legal norms is unlikely to succeed. If these insights at variance with the traditional conception of conflict are true, they have profound implications for policy. If conflict is due not to scarcity of resources but to more fundamental human aspirations, "then much of the law-and-order framework on which societies rely for social stability, and much of the deterrent measures that are applied to deviance, are doomed to failure." Furthermore, if competition in the international system is not due to scarcity of resources, and if threats do not deter when needs are at stake, then deterrence strategies will promote conflict to the extent that they frustrate human needs.[20]

In summary, according to Burton, traditional thinking led to the belief that conflict was about interests only, and that for that reason the individual could be socialized and coerced. What both theory and practice reveal, however, is that protracted conflicts are over nonnegotiable human needs. Therefore, it is impossible to socialize individuals into behavior that runs counter to their needs,[21] and conflict resolution depends on the satisfaction of those needs.

Galtung's Theory of Conflict

According to Johan Galtung, there are two basic types of conflict. Direct conflict occurs "over clearly articulated values between conscious, strategy-planning actors"; structural conflict occurs between parties "over interests embedded in social structure—parties that do not even, in a sense, know what is going on."[22]

For Galtung, the "conflict triangle" entails three elements: the attitudinal aspects, the behavioral aspects, and the conflict itself. The attitudinal aspect of conflict can be divided into the cognitive and the emotive. The most important feature of the cognitive aspect is the construction of Self-Other images with significant differences between the two images. The emotive aspect reinforces the cognitive by enhancing Self-love and Other-hatred.[23] The behavioral aspects of conflict build on the attitudinal ones and result in behavioral polarization and a readiness and willingness to undertake destructive action. However, while attitude and behavior reinforce each other, they are only preliminaries to the real conflict analysis. Conflict, according to Galtung, is incompatibility in a goal-seeking system.[24] These goals include needs, values, and interests, although "basic conflicts involve basic human needs."[25]

In Galtung's view, conflict resolution depends on correcting the steep Self-Other attitudinal gradient on both sides, correcting the behavioral polarization patterns and destruction machinery, and removing the goal incompatibilities.[26] This last element of conflict resolution depends on conflict processing. According to Galtung, there are many ways of processing conflict either to resolve or repress it. Conflict processing may lead to resolution through transcendence (a change in the situation or definition of it), compromise, deepening (by adding more issues), broadening (by adding more parties) or withdrawal.[27] Importantly, however, Galtung argues, conflict resolution may require much more than just problem-solving processes. In his view, for instance, structural violence "is not only evil, it is obstinate and must be fought." The strategy he advocates is nonviolent revolution.[28]

Though they often use different definitions and emphasize different elements of conflict theory, Burton and Galtung share the view that the denial of human needs is the central cause of conflict. They also agree that conflict resolution depends on the satisfaction of human needs and that, in some contexts, this will require structural change. Their approaches are different, however, in at least two important respects. Galtung emphasizes the complexity of conflict formations, particularly in relation to attitudinal and behavioral manifestations. And whereas Burton would rely exclusively on problem-solving processes (which will be explained later in this chapter) for dealing with conflict, Galtung recognizes the complementary necessity for nonviolent struggle in many situations.

Conflict Insights Derived from Psychology

Although previously and variously labeled in the literature on psychology as "instincts," "desires," "motives," "drives," and "wants," according to Otto Klineberg, the identification of human needs as part of the attempt to understand human nature has been a continuing preoccupation of social psychology throughout its history. There can be no question as to their significance, he argues, since failure to satisfy human needs "will inevitably lead to unhappiness and frustration at the very least, sometimes to physical or mental pathology, and in extreme cases even to death."[29] For most psychologists, conflicts (or disputes) entail differences of *interests* at various levels; but, importantly, human needs (or "deeper interests") lie at the heart of all serious conflicts.

According to Herbert Kelman, psychological factors contribute to the perpetuation and escalation of conflict, and they cannot be separated from the objective conditions that underlie it. Thus, while conflict must be resolved at the political level using political processes, new possibilities may be created if these psychological barriers can be overcome.[30]

Psychological research into the motives that promote conflict or the kinds of behavior that lead to conflict has emphasized the importance of "nonrational emotions." In the view of Ralph White, the focus of mainstream political scientists on power and security as the major goals behind international behavior has created a gap in their thinking, because emotions intrude on and distort a process that would otherwise be more rational and predictable. He discusses "exaggerated fear," macho pride, anger, hate, and aggression—"an intensely negative image and an impulse to hurt, as an end in itself"—as war-promoting motives.[31]

Moreover, the importance of perception in relation to these motives has been highlighted in much of the psychological research into conflict. In fact, according to Connie Peck, the research suggests that misperception of the other side is virtually automatic in conflict situations.[32] This misperception can occur for several reasons. For example, Robert Jervis makes a distinction between the unconscious motives and the cognitive factors that influence and often distort perception.[33] In turn, White highlights the perceptual side of the emotions of fear and anger in creating distortion. In addition, following Jervis, he discusses some of the unconscious motives (such as a "diabolical enemy-image" and a moral self-image) as well as some of the cognitive factors (including preexisting beliefs) that lead to distortion. He also discusses the elements of "selective inattention" (resistance, repression, rationalization, projection, and compensation), which is the *process* by which uncomfortable or repugnant thoughts are pushed out of a person's consciousness, thus distorting that person's worldview.[34]

Morton Deutsch discusses the tendency for people to perceive their own behavior as "more benevolent and legitimate" than that of others,[35] while White draws attention to the inclination to assume that others perceive our behavior as favorably as we do![36] Dean Pruitt and Jeffrey Rubin suggest that parties in conflict often reduce their level of communication, thereby reducing their ability to understand each other.[37] And Jerome Frank cites evidence showing that lack of communication intensifies dislike.[38]

Irving Janis draws attention to the major problem of "groupthink"—the result of an internal pressure toward uniformity in cohesive groups—which leads to a deterioration in mental efficiency, reality testing, and moral judgment. According to Janis, the eight symptoms of groupthink include an illusion of invulnerability, an unquestioned belief in the group's inherent morality, stereotyped views of the enemy as evil, and suppression of internal dissent. Groupthink has the effect of overriding any motivation to realistically consider alternative courses of action.[39]

Can this high level of misperception normally associated with conflict be corrected? According to White, empathy is the "great corrective" for many forms of misperception. Empathy, unlike sympathy, does not involve warmth or approval, but it does entail realistic understanding of the thoughts and feelings of others.[40] However, as Jervis points out, given the difficulty of accurately perceiving another's perspective, it is necessary to empathize with a variety of outlooks. In addition, Jervis suggests that misperception can be minimized by making beliefs and values more explicit, by exposing implicit assumptions to greater scrutiny, by encouraging the formulation and consideration of alternative images, by subjecting existing approaches to independent assessments of their effectiveness, and by heightened awareness of the ways in which the processes of perception lead to common errors.[41] Clearly, good conflict resolution processes must take these considerations into account.

In addition, Kelman argues, social-psychological analysis indicates that direct interaction between the conflicting parties leads to changes in attitudes and perceptions that facilitate changes at the policy level. In his view, psychological factors interact with political ones, and the two must be integrated in any comprehensive theory of conflict and its resolution.[42] Consequently, Deutsch argues, if one wants to create the conditions for a constructive process of conflict resolution, one should introduce into the conflict the typical elements of a cooperative process. These include good communication, information sharing, mutual confidence and trust, the perception of similarity in values and beliefs, acceptance of each other's legitimacy, and problem-centered processes.[43]

According to Pruitt and Rubin, there are five strategies for dealing with conflict: inaction, withdrawing, contending, yielding, and problem-solving.[44] It is clear that inaction, withdrawal, and yielding are unlikely to lead to conflict resolution; the empirical evidence clearly suggests that contending—a strategy based on models of "hard," "adversarial," "competitive," or "positional" bargaining[45]— does not work either. In addition, the research indicates that although contending might *appear* to be effective, it rarely leads to a stable outcome because it does not address the issues at stake.[46]

Using a different approach, Ury, Brett, and Goldberg argue that interests, rights, and power are three elements of any dispute. Consequently, they distinguish three major ways in which disputes can be resolved: by reconciling the underlying interests of all parties, by determining who is right, and by determining who is more powerful. Problem-solving processes exemplify the interests approach, going to court is an example of the rights approach, and going to war or going on strike are examples of the power approach. According to Ury, Brett, and Goldberg, the interests approach is more rewarding than a rights approach, which in turn is more rewarding than a power approach. They advocate the design of "dispute resolution systems" that provide interests-based procedures for use whenever possible "and low-cost rights procedures (such as advisory arbitration) or low-cost power procedures (such as voting) as backups."[47] However, though psychological research and empirical evidence accumulated since 1970 clearly suggest that the conflict strategy of choice is problem solving, according to Ury, Brett, and Goldberg it is not an adequate strategy in itself. In some cases, they argue, problem solving cannot occur unless rights or power procedures are first employed to bring a recalcitrant party into the process.[48]

According to the conflict perspectives summarized in the last three sections, the denial of human needs is the primary cause of protracted conflict, and problem-solving processes that seek to satisfy these needs are considered vital in resolving it. In addition, given the importance of psychological factors—including the emotional aspects—of any conflict, these must be expressed (and then acknowledged and considered) during the resolution process. However, while many (but not all) theorists implicitly or explicitly reject violence, there is, as yet, no consensus on the role of rights and power in conflict resolution processes. Moreover, for reasons unexplained, many authors do not discuss, or they treat superficially, the issue raised by Galtung as well as Ury, Brett, and Goldberg: How is conflict to be resolved when one or more parties will not participate in the process? In addition, there is no consensus on Galtung's claim that nonviolent struggle, a power procedure, is a vital component of many strategies to resolve conflict. With the preceding observations on recent conflict theory in mind, it is appropriate to consider the empirical origins of conflict in the international system.

The Origins of International Conflict

The claim that violent conflict is an inherent feature of the international system runs strongly through the realist school of international relations theory. For example, Hans Morgenthau argues that each nation is engaged in a struggle for power that is designed to secure its national interests. As a result, conflict is inevitable and much of that conflict will be in the form of war.[49] Similarly, Hedley Bull argues that, given the existence of sovereign states that are politically divided and militarily armed, it is unreasonable to expect peace. He observes: "war is endemic in the system of states."[50] Despite the pervasiveness of this view, the perspectives summarized in the previous three sections provide a different explanation for international conflict.

Burton identifies three reasons for the persistence of protracted conflict in the international system. First, imperial powers have pursued their national interests at the expense of the fundamental needs of people in other states. Second, the underlying causes of conflict have not been understood, nor have the management processes that might have been used in order to resolve it. And third, due to this inadequate understanding of conflict and its resolution processes, imperial elites have relied on violence and adversary negotiations when other processes were more appropriate. These failures, Burton argues, can all be traced to the shortcomings of the domestic institutions of national societies, whether they are capitalist or socialist.[51]

By the 1980s, Burton observes, national societies were characterized by escalating levels of ethnic conflict, street violence, poverty, and unemployment. In these circumstances, many national elites relied on military force to maintain internal control and to resist political change. This was because national elites were intent on defending existing systems and structures—by going to war if necessary—against the pressures for change generated by the external influences that accompanied normal international relations. Thus, for example, while the West was experiencing increasing levels of social violence of various types, demands for change could not be resisted by Western elites if other countries initiated reforms to resolve similar social problems. For this reason, Burton asserts, Western elites gave support to corrupt and repressive regimes that also resisted internal reform, based on the stated fear that the world would "go communist"—a notion that obscured the real fear that capitalism was not able to meet the needs of ordinary people. In essence, he claims, "international problems are a spillover of domestic problems" and these problems are generated by the inability of capitalism and socialism to fulfill the needs of individuals and groups. Accordingly, Burton argues, new emphasis on the failure of domestic systems to satisfy human needs would enrich existing explanations of the causes of conflict in the international system.[52]

In contrast, while Galtung does not deny the importance of domestic problems in generating international conflict, he also stresses the importance of external elements. Therefore, he is particularly concerned with structural features of the international system. The importance of this is readily illustrated by reference to the North-South conflict. According to Galtung, the North-South conflict is a vertical one involving center and periphery nations in which each nation has its own center and periphery.[53] The elites in the center countries (the centers of the centers) are in command of both the ordinary people in the center countries (the peripheries of the centers) and the periphery countries as a whole. However, there is also an alliance between the elites in the center countries and the elites in the periphery countries, and this relationship is a linchpin of imperialism and "the basic configuration underlying the North-South conflict." This alliance between elites provides the bridgehead by which center countries penetrate and exploit periphery countries. The key to exploitation is the vertical division of labor, which means that when products traded are ranked in terms of their degree of processing (the amounts of capital, research, tech-

nology, and management, as opposed to the amounts of raw materials and unskilled labor, that go into the products) and in terms of
the challenges built into the task of creating them, the center gets
much more positive spin-off effects, including value added, than
does the periphery. This economic exploitation—which, in practice,
is reinforced by the cultural, political, and, if necessary, military
power of the center—results in the denial of the basic needs of ordinary people in the periphery. As consciousness of this structural
conflict is generated, it leads to protest behaviors (from demonstrations to direct violence) by the periphery toward the center and
within the periphery itself. The Sandinista struggle against the U.S.
exploitation of Nicaragua was a good example of this.[54]

In short, center-periphery conflicts (and particularly their
structural manifestation) are *not* a spillover of domestic problems in
the periphery countries but are the direct result of policies and structures of exploitation maintained by elites in the center countries.
The origins of international conflict, Galtung argues, may thus be
traced to both domestic and foreign sources.

Despite this difference, these perspectives share three insights
in common: They both contend that international conflict may be
traced to the structural denial of human needs; they both assert
that national elites are committed to the maintenance of the existing structural framework; and they both argue that national elites
will defend this structural framework by using military violence if
necessary. How then can international conflict be resolved?

The Levels at Which Conflict May Be Resolved

Recent Western literature implicitly discusses three different
levels at which conflict resolution may be attempted. At the first
level, conflict resolution might require only policy or process adjustments within an existing system of structures. At the second level,
it might require adjustments to structures within a system—for
example, changes to an adversarial legal structure. And at the third
level, it might require changes to a system itself—changes to the
more fundamental structures, such as patriarchy and the economy.
Each of these levels is important in the conflict resolution process.

At first glance, there might seem to be little difference between
traditional Western approaches to conflict and recent descriptions
of how to resolve conflict through policy and process adjustments

alone. In fact, even at this level, the differences are profound. The recent conflict literature emphasizes a significantly different focus (on human needs), identifies a particular type of outcome (one that satisfies all parties), and describes a procedure (the problem-solving process) substantially different from those associated with traditional methods. This process will be described in the next section.

Nevertheless, it is the recent literature's identification of the importance of structural change that distinguishes it most clearly from traditional approaches. Among conflict theorists, Johan Galtung has played a preeminent role in identifying the structural nature of protracted conflict. In his view, structural conflict is conflict that is built into social structures. It appears as unequal power and unequal life chances. According to Galtung, structural conflict demands structural change.[55] The importance of structural change to conflict resolution has also been emphasized by Edward Azar. In his view, war and poverty are the main causes of human suffering, but they are only symptoms of underlying structural conditions. Groups that seek to satisfy their needs through conflict are actually seeking changes in the structures of their society. It is now clear, he argues, that structural change is an essential part of the process of conflict resolution.[56] The need for structural change, it should be noted, includes the need for changes in process: that is, changes in the way decisions are made. Structural change and improved conflict processes, rather than deterrence and punishment, are what is needed, because through these behavior can be reoriented toward problem solving.[57]

The third level at which conflict resolution may need to occur is at the level of the system itself. Several authors have identified the fact that entire systems of structures, nationally and globally, will need to be changed, if human needs are to be universally met. Galtung, for example, has argued that the whole global economy must be restructured in order to resolve the North-South conflict.[58] And many feminists have argued that the global system of patriarchy must be destroyed if the needs of women are to be met. System level change will be considered in more detail later in this chapter and in chapter 6.

Problem Solving as an Approach to Conflict

This section describes the conflict resolution process known as problem solving. The description relies heavily on the work of Burton because he is the most representative and prolific author on the problem-solving process. Moreover, the quantity of his work makes it easier to identify the weaknesses of this approach—and, importantly, the reasons for them—which will be discussed in the next section.

In Burton's view, a problem arises because the prevailing conflict theory is unable to explain or resolve it; therefore, an important feature of problem solving is its ongoing examination of the theory itself. Can the problem under consideration be solved within the framework of the existing theory and its assumptions, or is it necessary to review this theory together with any resolution process derived from it? According to this approach, while the preliminary analysis of a problem may include a series of steps, the most important one is to examine the conflict theory and the process themselves. Otherwise, the problem might be tackled in a context that excludes the possibility of solution.[59]

Burton maintains that since the early 1980s the theory and practice of conflict resolution have been in a period of transition from one main approach to another.[60] There is an ongoing shift from traditional approaches to one that relies on "interactive analytical problem solving processes."[61] This problem-solving process has four distinctive features: its ongoing nature (in which each "solution" contains its own set of problems to be solved), its recognition of the need to reconceptualize problems in terms of an adequate theory of human behavior, its consideration of the total environment over which there can be little or no control, and its focus on dealing with problems at their source.[62] Problem solving, then, is the facilitated analysis of the underlying sources of a conflict by the parties themselves. It is a process in which both policies and institutional frameworks are adjusted so that the needs of all parties are met.[63] This approach implies a set of assumptions: that conflicts can be resolved to the satisfaction of all parties, that processes exist for achieving this, that there is a distinctive difference between management and resolution, and that this process expands the range of possible outcomes.[64]

In most conflicts, and particularly those at the international level, there is a set of disputes involving many parties and various issues. Consequently, a conflict must be broken down into its various parts so that it can be defined and analyzed. This implies an exploration for, and an analysis of, the causes underlying the declared issues. It is useful, therefore, to distinguish between tactics and goals;

for example, a territorial claim might be a tactic designed to achieve the goals of identity and security. To be effective, the resolution process must also include high levels of direct communication between the parties,[65] because problem solving implies a concern for the relationship and not just the conflict itself.[66]

For this reason, the process must begin with the opportunity for all parties to express their emotions and to have them acknowledged as legitimate.[67] This is important because emotions are a central element of any conflict formation, and the experience of conflict facilitators indicates that emotions must be dealt with before systematic progress can be expected on the issues at stake. Therefore, in any problem-solving process, all parties should be given the opportunity to honestly express their feelings and to have these feelings acknowledged by the other parties. "Freed from the burden of unexpressed emotions, people [are] more likely to work on the problem."[68] According to A. J. R. Groom, this initial stage of the process might also involve the recitation of a litany of past grievances, which it is important for the facilitators to acknowledge: The negative elements of the past must be mourned. Nevertheless, the past must not be allowed to capture the future. For this reason, the process is future-oriented and draws attention to the mutuality of problems: "the remedy to our difficulties lies in us helping them to overcome their problems."[69]

The conflict resolution framework provided by needs theory involves a workshop approach in which the components of the conflict are revealed by analysis. A facilitation panel, which is expert in human behavior and conflict theory, seeks to help the parties to be analytical, that is, to concentrate on an analysis of existing relationships rather than legal norms or past events; to identify the perceptions of reality of all participants (particularly those from different cultural backgrounds); to filter out false assumptions, ideological orientations, and personal prejudices; to reveal underlying motivations; to differentiate cultural values and negotiable interests from nonnegotiable human needs; to define their separate goals clearly; to distinguish tactics from goals; to correct misperceptions; to provide an opportunity to assess the cost of ignoring, suppressing, or failing to promote needs; to provide an opportunity to explore options and to discover outcomes that meet the needs of all; to assist parties to deduce what alterations in policies and structures are required to enable the fulfillment of needs; and to assist the parties to monitor events and communications perceptively. The facilitation panel should also suggest, in advance, a combination of creative need satisfiers that will attract parties to the process in the first place.[70] This framework can also be used, if necessary, to decide the nature of system alterations.

This workshop approach is endorsed by other conflict theorists, some of whom have made complementary suggestions. For example, Galtung maintains that a facilitated conflict resolution framework should involve the following elements: All parties should be participants in the process (and a vacant space should be left for those who have not yet chosen to participate); there should be no prior conditions; all issues should be open for discussion; issues should be grouped in "baskets" in order to reduce them to a manageable number; trading between "baskets" should be acceptable; and the dialogue should occur among the parties themselves.[71]

The problem-solving approach considers cultural differences to be part of the problem to be solved;[72] nevertheless, it is important to retain a sensitive appreciation of cultural factors when elaborating versions of the process. For example, as Raphael Patai points out, in the Arab world, mediation at the tribal and village level is the traditional method of resolving conflicts. More recently, it has been adapted for resolving political and military conflicts within and between Arab states. The purpose of the mediation process is to find an honorable way out of the conflict without "loss of face" by any party. The mediator is someone who commands respect and is clearly impartial but who has the necessary prestige to create the desire, on the part of the conflicting parties, to conform with the mediator's wishes. Mediators often try to increase their personal influence over the parties by invoking the presumed desires of other individuals whom the disputants are bound to respect. Modifying a demand (in relation to an opponent) "for the sake of" a relative, for example, is a manifestation of generosity (a value important in Arab culture) and rebounds to the honor (another important value) of the kin group. Importantly, then, within traditional Arab culture, mediation by a third-party (who commutes between the parties in order to avoid direct contact between them) is the only acceptable method of resolving conflict, because, unlike direct negotiations between the parties themselves, mediation is seen to provide a solution without loss of face.[73] Thus, though awareness of cultural factors in the development of a problem-solving process is important, it must not be forgotten that cultural traditions for dealing with conflict are frequently dysfunctional.[74]

According to arguments presented earlier in this chapter, protracted conflict can be resolved only when policies, processes, structures, and systems are oriented to the satisfaction of human needs. The problem-solving process described above is one (conflict resolution) process designed for this purpose. This process can be used to design policies, structures, and/or systems that, in their turn, are oriented to the satisfaction of human needs.

Needs or Power?

The satisfaction of human needs might be central to conflict resolution, but power remains the principal determinant of conflict outcomes. Given this reality, why, despite its desirability, is an approach to conflict resolution that relies exclusively on problem-solving processes not adequate? For the reasons indicated in the last section, Burton's work will be examined in order to identify the weaknesses in the analysis and prescription associated with this approach.

Burton acknowledges that conflict over political, economic, and environmental problems is increasing. In fact, he identifies the increased use of lethal weapons, the possible disintegration of societies into separate enclaves, and further military interventions as outcomes of this conflict.[75] In such circumstances, and given the intractable nature of many problems that will make continuing societal disruption inevitable, how can need-denying structures and systems be removed or transformed? On this fundamentally important question, most conflict theorists are conspicuous by their silence, and others offer solutions that are clearly inadequate. Burton is in the latter category.

Burton's earlier work strongly suggested the importance of structural and systemic changes;[76] his more recent research is characterized by its emphasis on changes in system *operation*. "The system structure is not the problem, it is system operation that determines whether human needs are met."[77] This significant shift is the result of the increasing importance he attaches to *process* in any conflict resolution strategy (which *may* lead to structural or systemic change), but it also reflects another important element of his approach: its orientation to elites.

Burton explicitly rejects "revolution" as a mechanism for transforming system structures. In his view, changes in system operation should occur as a result of "ripening" as well as ongoing assessments of "political realities" and costs. Therefore, he concludes, before problem solving is applicable in the wider political domain, there must be a consensus shift from power-oriented to problem-solving processes, a shift that requires both experience and education. Rhetorically he asks, do we have time?[78]

Time is obviously critical, but this question is certainly not the vital one. From the evidence presented throughout this study, it is clear that the fundamental needs of most people, as well as those of nonhuman species, can never be satisfied within the framework of the dominant social cosmology. In these circumstances, the protracted social conflict we are now experiencing is of critical concern to those who are the immediate and ongoing victims of it and to many others besides. The important question, therefore, is surely this: Is a strategy that hopes for a consensus shift from power to problem solving, as a result of experience and education, adequate? The evidence suggests that it is not.

To begin with, exclusive reliance on a strategy of experience and education ignores the many factors that encourage resistance to new ideas. These include subtle psychological factors and the conservative role played by intellectuals. In relation to psychological factors, resistance to new information occurs at both the conscious and the unconscious level. Thus, some of the reluctance to respond to experience and education can be traced to unconscious factors such as "irrational consistency" (the tendency to act on the basis of one dominant value in the first context and a different value in the second) and the tendency for people to fit new information into preexisting beliefs in order to maintain consistency in their belief structure.[79] Another factor of this nature is "role defense." One important way in which individuals attempt to satisfy their needs for security, meaning, and self-esteem is to acquire and occupy an appropriate role. As a result, individuals are strongly inclined to defend their role and, in fact, usually confuse defense of their role (the means) with defense of their needs (the end).

In relation to the role of intellectuals, Noam Chomsky points out, it is their responsibility "to speak the truth and to expose lies." However, by working for the state—the source of their power, prestige, and economic reward—most intellectuals adopt an approach characterized by obedience, self-deception, and an uncritical attitude. They are responsible for articulating and justifying the narrowly defined elite perspective and distracting attention from taboo subjects. They create the ideological cover for "the doctrines of the faith"—elite power, profit, and privilege. In addition, Chomsky argues, few are willing to challenge "the right to lie in the service of the state."[80] Apart from these factors, reliance on this strategy ignores a number of other "political realities" as well. This is because the strategy involves the acceptance of several unexamined assumptions and naively relies on the willingness of elites to initiate reforms.

First, the strategy entails acceptance of the ongoing suffering caused by existing structural and systemic problems as well as a series of risks that threaten potential disaster for the planetary ecosphere and the future of humankind. In view of this suffering (including the death through hunger-related diseases of forty thousand children in Africa, Asia, and Central/South America each day) and these accelerating risks (including depletion of the ozone layer, emission of greenhouse gases, and destruction of the world's rainforests), there is no valid justification for waiting (perhaps in vain) for the development of a new consensus and then hoping that elites will act upon it. Justice and ecological common sense demand that more vigorous strategies (with shorter timeframes) be devised.

Second, the strategy assumes that once there has been a consensus shift from power to problem solving, elites will respond by facilitating the necessary changes[81] rather than simply reinforcing their existing strategy of repression and coercion combined with minor reform. This assumption is highly problematic. On the one hand, there is little evidence to suggest that elites will facilitate fundamental change (or even tolerate the process by which a new consensus might emerge), particularly in circumstances in which such change will require the voluntary surrender of their own privileged roles. On the other hand, elite use of repression and coercion to resist change in a wide variety of circumstances has been extensively documented and is a prominent feature of political life in all societies.

Third, the strategy ignores the self-sustaining nature of structures and systems of power; it assumes that they can be readily dismantled once the decision is made to do this. The problem of structural power will be considered in chapter 6.

And fourth, the strategy is based on unexamined assumptions about the nature of "revolution" and apparent ignorance of the potential (and complementary nature) of nonviolent struggle. This will be considered in chapter 7.

Given the complexity and protracted nature of much social and political conflict, Ury, Brett, and Goldberg explicitly reject an approach that relies exclusively on the use of problem-solving processes. In their view, problem-solving processes cannot occur in some cases unless rights or power-based procedures are first employed to bring reluctant parties into the process. The challenge is to design a process that promotes the satisfaction of human needs while simultaneously providing low-cost ways of determining rights or exercising power in those conflicts that cannot be resolved by focusing on needs alone.[82]

It is evident that recognition of the importance of human needs and the adoption of problem-solving processes do not constitute a complete strategy for dealing with unsolved social and political problems; nor is this strategy an adequate substitute for the use of power. However, though this strategy is clearly inadequate, the insight that the satisfaction of human needs is central to the resolution of conflict remains critically important to the success of any alternative or complementary strategy. Moreover, because the needs approach is analytical rather than ideological, it also provides a moral basis for political action intended to resolve conflict. For this reason, it points to a consideration of the value of nonviolent struggle—and particularly its Gandhian conception—as a possible part of any strategy designed to resolve deep-rooted or protracted conflict.

6

The Nature of Power

According to Max Weber, power is the ability of one actor within a social relationship to carry out their will despite resistance.[1] Although social science disciplines within the dominant social cosmology offer an exceptional number of explanations of this type,[2] a close examination suggests that this definition of power is much too narrow. According to Joanna Macy, for example, this definition conceives power exclusively in terms of "power over."[3] In fact, as feminists in general have noted, this definition reflects a bias that is characteristic of Western social science: Power is described in a way that reflects elite preoccupation with political, economic, and social control.

In stark contrast to the "traditional" theorists, others have focused attention on the importance of power sharing as part of the solution to political, economic, social, and environmental problems. As a result, they have suggested more elaborate descriptions of power that go beyond the prevailing view that power is a mechanism of domination and control.

Inspired by his study of Gandhi and others, Johan Galtung, for example, argues that power is a reciprocal relation; it is not a property possessed by someone or something. He identifies three ways in which power can work. Normative power, based on persuasion, requires an element of submissiveness. Remunerative power, based on bargaining, requires some kind of dependency. And punitive power, based on force, requires an element of fear. As power is a relation, Galtung argues that there are two kinds of countervailing power available to the receiver. In the balance approach, the receiver uses their own resources of persuasion, bargaining, and force to resist the power exercised against them. In the autonomy approach, the receiver refuses to receive the power exercised against them by developing "power over oneself": self-respect (to eliminate submissiveness), self-reliance (to eliminate dependency), and fearlessness (to eliminate fear). Galtung also identifies three sources of power: innate (or being) power, such as charisma, intellect, or muscle; resource (or having) power, such as that which comes from owning assets or weapons; and structural power, which is the result of occupying an exploitative position. Importantly, Galtung notes, these sources of power are convertible.[4]

In addition to those male scholars whose descriptions of power challenge the dominant conception of it, the contemporary feminist literature contains many descriptions of power that are fundamentally different from the Western patriarchal view.[5] According to the ecofeminist Starhawk, for example, there are three types of power, and each of these is rooted in a different worldview and mode of consciousness. Power-over means domination and control; it shapes every institution in our society. Power-over views the world as an object composed of separate parts that have no intrinsic life or value; value must be earned or granted. It motivates through fear and offers "the hope of relief in return for compliance." Power-from-within refers to the mysteries that awaken our deepest abilities and potential; it relies on our willingness to act. Power-from-within stems from a consciousness that is in touch with the immanent value of all things. Power-with is the influence we wield among equals—the ability to act as a channel to focus the will of the group. Power-with embodies a consciousness that views the world as a pattern of relationships to be shaped and molded. Unlike power-over, which is backed by violence, power-from-within and power-with are grounded in another source: spirit. This is important, Starhawk asserts, because Western culture particularly has absorbed the delusion that power-over can be countered only by power-over; that spirit, mystery, bonding, community, and love are weak rather than powerful forces of resistance.[6]

Within the dominant social cosmology, power is widely understood to mean the capacity to dominate and control. However, as the above discussion suggests, power is a complex and multifaceted phenomenon that can manifest itself in a variety of ways. These will be explored more fully in the remainder of this chapter.

The Consent Theory of Power

The consent theory of power has been chosen for discussion for three reasons: It has a long history within the discipline of political theory, starting with the sixteenth-century philosopher Étienne de La Boétie.[7] It is endorsed by many theorists (some of whom are cited below), including theorists of nonviolent struggle such as Gene Sharp. And it has been accepted by a diverse range of political practitioners, including Mohandas Gandhi and Mao Zedong, who have effectively applied its basic insight.

The roots of political power, Sharp maintains, reach below the structure of the state into society itself.[8] It is the people, according to David Hume, who are "the source of all power."[9] Power, then, Sharp and others contend, is not intrinsic to political elites; the power of elites is based on external sources. These sources include authority (the acceptance by people of the elite's right to command), human resources (the elite's supporters, with their knowledge and skills), intangible factors (such as psychological considerations and ideological conditioning), material resources, and the type and extent of sanctions at the elite's disposal.[10]

These sources of power, in turn, depend on the obedience and cooperation of the people. The relationship between command and obedience is an interactive one, and elite control can be exercised only with the active or passive compliance of subject peoples and particularly the compliance of key specialist groups. This does not always occur. Even when political power is backed by sanctions, there is always some degree of interaction between elites and those they try to dominate. The use of political power is not, therefore, a one-way process; it is a series of interactions that take place within a political and social setting subject to a variety of influences.[11]

Obedience in such circumstances is therefore necessary, but not inevitable. Why then, La Boétie and many other theorists have asked, do some individuals obey others? In the view of Thomas Hobbes, subjects obey elites primarily because of fear.[12] But fear alone, as Hobbes acknowledged, is not the only reason for obedience. The other reasons, as Aristotle noted, include habit.[13] According to Robert MacIver, individuals obey because they are socialized and indoctrinated in the ways of their society.[14] Moreover, obedience becomes so familiar, that most people "never make any inquiry about its origin or cause."[15] It is so deeply ingrained, as the experimental evidence has demonstrated,[16] that "it sneaks up on us even when we intend the opposite."[17] In addition to fear of sanctions and habit, there are other reasons for obedience—respect for authority, moral obligation, self-interest, psychological identification with elites, the existence of zones of indifference, ignorance, and disempowerment.[18] Moreover, La Boétie argues, consent is engineered: Elites use various devices—such as ideology, selective distribution of material benefits, and distractions like sport and entertainment—to induce obedience.[19]

But there is another reason for obedience that is vitally important and that draws attention to the structural theory discussed in the next section. Most people comply, La Boétie argues, because elites create hierarchies of privilege that attract key supporters, including intellectuals, from the wider population.[20] As a result, Michael Mann observes, most people lack the organization to resist. They are "organizationally outflanked"; that is, they are locked within organizations that are controlled by others.[21]

According to the consent theory of power, then, elite power depends upon the degree of obedience and cooperation offered by those subject to domination. This obedience and cooperation are not inevitable. Despite incentives and the threat of sanctions, cooperation is essentially voluntary. "Even in the case of sanctions, there is a role for an act of will, for choice." Elite control, then, is based upon consent. According to Sharp, based on this theory of power, three conditions must be satisfied in order for nonviolent action to be effective. First, consent must be withdrawn; that is, there must be a clear refusal to cooperate. Second, there must be a collective commitment to action. And third, there must be a coherent strategy.[22] In the absence of these conditions, success is unlikely. This is because, as Gaetano Mosca pointed out, the ruling elite is usually unified and able to act in concert, whereas the majority is unorganized. According to Mosca, an organized minority will inevitably dominate the unorganized majority.[23] Consequently, corporate resistance that is strategically organized is essential.

Both Mao and Gandhi shared these insights into the nature of power. Despite his oft-quoted assertion that "political power grows out of the barrel of a gun,"[24] Mao held a more sophisticated view of political power than this statement suggests. In his view, power (whether economic, military, or otherwise) "is necessarily wielded by people"; for that reason, he claimed, the coercive power of elites is limited.[25] Similarly, Gandhi argued, a superficial study of history has led to the conclusion that all power percolates from parliaments to the people. The truth, he claimed, is otherwise: Power resides in the people themselves.[26] In politics, he asserted, "government of the people is possible only so long as they consent either consciously or unconsciously to be governed."[27] In fact, he argued, a government requires the cooperation of the people; if that cooperation is withdrawn, government will come to a standstill.[28]

In summary, as figure 1 illustrates, the consent theory of power identifies people as the ultimate source of all power and highlights the notion that elites are dependent on the cooperation of the people they dominate. Whatever its insights, however, the consent theory of power is the subject of three major criticisms.

First, several authors argue, it is incomplete. This is because, as Lewis Lipsitz and Herbert Kritzer explain it, there are situations in which elites *do not* depend on the cooperation of the people they dominate.[29] Alex Schmid and Steven Huxley agree. As Schmid explains it, not all power is delegated by the subject people themselves as the consent theory suggests. Power can be exercised over a subject people using a combination of means: the assistance of nonsubject peoples, agents who are loyal to the elite, and nonhuman resources (such as weapons). People, he argues, are *not* the only source of power, and in those conflicts in which an elite is not dependent on them (for example, in circumstances in which an invader is not dependent on the citizens and resources of an occupied territory), "their fate can be sealed without their cooperation."[30] This point has been illustrated by the Palestinian Intifada against the Israeli occupation. According to Andrew Rigby, the strategic thinking behind the Intifada was influenced by the consent theory of power. However, Rigby notes, the Intifada has been less effective than expected because "Israel wants to rule over the *land* of Palestine, it does not want the *people*." Unlike the explanation offered by Rigby,[31] the critique offered above suggests that at least one reason for the limited effectiveness of the Intifada is the direct result of applying the (incomplete) consent theory of power. In brief, because the cooperation of the Palestinians is only one of the factors that make the occupation possible, their noncooperation cannot be decisive. Though elites are always dependent, they are not necessarily dependent on the cooperation of the people they actually oppress or exploit.

In an attempt to address this concern, Galtung has suggested that for power (in the form of nonviolent action) to be effectively exercised in such cases, it is necessary to *create* a dependency relationship between the elite and the people they dominate. This might be done through what he calls "the great chain of nonviolence." In cases where no dependency relationship exists, where there is too much social distance between the elite and the oppressed group or where the elite has dehumanized the group they dominate, a third-party might choose, or be induced, to intervene on the side of the oppressed; this might weaken the elite's resolve *if the elite identifies (even partially) with the third-party.* For example, middle-class whites played this role in the civil rights struggle in the United States.[32]

But even this may not be adequate or possible. Given the imperial world order that now exists—in which national elites mutually reinforce each other—some elites (such as the military junta in Burma) are principally dependent on other state and corporate elites rather than their own people or any third-party of the type Galtung has in mind. Thus, as the diagram in figure 2 implies, it may be necessary to develop a strategy in which solidarity groups, with which the aggressor elite does *not* identify, conduct campaigns to undermine cooperation with it.

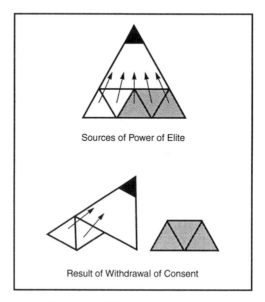

Sources of Power of Elite

Result of Withdrawal of Consent

Figure 1. Consent Theory of Power

The second major criticism of the consent theory of power is that it fails to adequately consider the cultural dimension. According to Ralph Summy, a variety of cultural factors will influence the degree of psychological and intellectual freedom that people are able to exercise when they choose to offer or withdraw their consent. He cites several important factors, including traditions of independence and attitudes towards authority, approaches to conflict management and values in relation to violence, religious beliefs about "chosenness," and, importantly, the ways in which people process knowledge and experience. Nevertheless, while he believes that more explicit consideration of cultural factors would improve consent theory, he does not believe that this shortcoming invalidates its key point that power is diffused throughout society and does not emanate from above.[33] A more elaborate version of this type of criticism is offered by Kate McGuinness. The consent theory of power, she argues, is based on at least two unstated assumptions. It assumes that all individuals are fully constituted members of civil society and that these members share the same political culture.

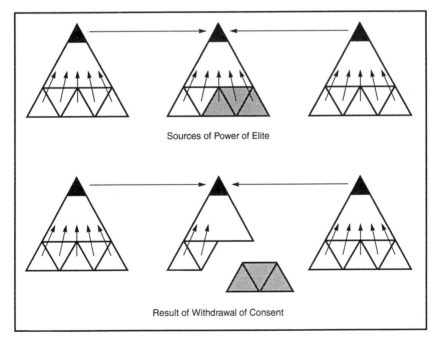

Sources of Power of Elite

Result of Withdrawal of Consent

Figure 2. Modified Consent Theory of Power

However, McGuinness asserts, both of these assumptions are problematic. On the one hand, she agrees with Carole Pateman[34] that women are not fully constituted members of civil society. "Hence, consent is not their privilege." On the other hand, she argues, men and women do not share the same political culture, "because their positions within the dominant patriarchal culture are very different." These differences lead to divergent views regarding the nature of, and the solutions to, problems of social organization. In the absence of a common view of how society is organized, the notion of consent is neither very meaningful nor very useful. McGuinness concludes that the consent theory of power has limited value in explaining the relationship between men and women within the power structure known as patriarchy.[35] This criticism points to the third one as well.

The third major criticism of the consent theory of power is that it pays inadequate attention to social structures. La Boétie identified the importance of social structures,[36] but most subsequent theorists have either ignored them completely or failed to identify their significance. In particular, Brian Martin suggests, Sharp's focus on consent is both individualistic and voluntaristic. It describes little of the complexity associated with the array of contending forces in a conflict.[37] Moreover, Koen Koch argues, Sharp ignores the dependence of individuals on social structures and the coercive nature of those structures.[38] In essence, then, many recent exponents of the consent theory fail to consider the nature and role of the structures that underpin a conflict or to consider how these structures, and the actors within them, interact. What insights into the nature of power can be derived from structural analysis? This question will be considered in the next section.

In essence, the consent theory of power identifies people as the ultimate source of all power and highlights the notion that elites are dependent on the cooperation of the people they dominate. According to this theory, strategically organized resistance is necessary if opposition to elite domination is to be effective. However, there are at least three major criticisms of the consent theory, and in combination they provide compelling evidence that, as it is usually conceived, this theory provides an incomplete and inadequate explanation of power. Consequently, strategies based on this theory may ultimately fail.

The three criticisms of consent theory suggest the need for at least two modifications. First, if an elite does not necessarily depend on the cooperation of the people it dominates, then if its power is to be systematically undermined, it is necessary to organize corporate resistance by those constituencies on which the elite does depend. This might require the implementation of a strategy that goes beyond that implied by Galtung's "great chain of nonviolence" hypothesis. Second, any insights that may be derived from this modified consent theory should be complemented by insights derived from the structural theory.

The Structural Theory of Power

From the perspective of structural analysis, social structures and systems are regarded as by-products of certain types of social interactions that have become so regular and entrenched that they have acquired a life of their own.[39] Structural analysis is important for at least two reasons. First, it highlights the fact that while individual choice exists in theory, in practice tradition, social process, and social structures limit the capacity for individual decision making. This is because while there might be no overt conflict and no obvious parties, it is structures and systems, rather than individual choices, that determine social outcomes. Knowledge of these structures and systems is necessary if strategies to resolve conflict are to be effective. And second, in situations of overt conflict in which one party is willing to resist satisfying the needs of their opponents, identifying the structural and systemic sources of that party's power is a crucial step in the formulation of an effective strategy for dealing with their resistance.

Consequently, structural analysis is concerned with the structures and systems themselves. The best known structural analyses are the feminist critique of patriarchy, the Marxist critique of capitalism, and the anarchist critique of the state. The following discussion will outline the structural critique of patriarchy in order to illustrate the nature of the insights that structural analysis can provide.

According to feminist analysis, patriarchy is both a political institution and a system of power. It is a relationship of domination in which "males rule females." According to Kate Millett, patriarchy is the most pervasive ideology in human culture and its most fundamental system of power. While its particular form has varied throughout history and across cultures, it permeates all other political, economic, and social relations, including caste, class, and religion.[40]

Traditional patriarchy, Millett argues, has used an extensive variety of mechanisms to oppress and exploit women (and contemporary versions of patriarchy show little evidence of breaking down these mechanisms). It has used socialization to condition women and men to accept two different cultures: This socialization requires women to cultivate a submissive and ignorant temperament, to accept an inferior social status, and to perform a gender role that is limited to domestic service and child care. Patriarchy has undermined women's solidarity and created antagonisms within and across class lines. It has denied women the power of knowledge by imposing on them what Millett calls "systematic ignorance," including an educational syllabus characterized by its distinction between "masculine" and "feminine" subject matter. It has made women economically dependent and denied them economic justice and ownership of property. And it has intimidated women by the manner in which it has shaped legal systems and by its use of physical (including sexual) violence.[41]

Moreover, patriarchy has used a variety of psychological and ideological techniques in order to justify and reinforce its oppression and exploitation of women. According to Millett, "patriarchy is a governing ideology without peer." In her view, it is unlikely that any other system has ever exercised such complete domination over its subjects. It has used "biology" to argue women's "natural" inferiority. It has concocted a whole series of beliefs about women that invade the consciousness, and condition the thinking, of both women and men. It has created ideas, images, and symbols of women for the benefit of men. As a result, the ideology of patriarchy is internalized, and women are denied the most fundamental needs of identity, dignity, and self-respect. Ultimately, Millett argues, perhaps patriarchy's most important psychological weapon is its universality and longevity. In her view, patriarchy has a tenacious hold because of "its successful habit of passing itself off as nature." When a system of power is dominant, she asserts, it does not need to proclaim itself.[42]

Perhaps most importantly of all, however, patriarchy has systematically destroyed a wide range of spiritual traditions that valued women, including the "Old Religion" of Witchcraft—the spiritual foundation of prepatriarchal Western culture. According to Starhawk, legends suggest that Witchcraft is more than thirty-five thousand years old. Unlike patriarchal religions (such as Judaism and Christianity) that worship a male God outside of nature, Witchcraft is a religion of ecology: The Earth is sacred, and nature provides the inspiration for the teachings. Symbols and rituals are used to trigger altered states of awareness in order to reveal insights that can be discovered intuitively but never explained. In Witchcraft, the Goddess is the primary symbol: She *is* the world, and she is present in each one of us. The basic ethic of Witchcraft is love for all life; it sees that all being is related and therefore mutually responsible. "An act that harms anyone harms us all." Unlike patriarchal gods, which pronounce an external truth, in Witchcraft "each of us must reveal our own truth."[43]

Patriarchy, then, is pervasive. Moreover, it permeates other structures of power, including capitalism and socialism, the state, churches, and the military. The gender division of labor, state legislation, Church dogma, and military practice have all been used to exploit, oppress, or discriminate against women and are structural manifestations of patriarchy. But just as patriarchy has acquired a life of its own, so too have other structures. For that reason, while there is a tendency for structures of power to be mutually reinforcing (and this tendency is vital to their ongoing domination), any particular system outcome is co-defined by the interaction among structures. For example, some states have intervened in order to limit some forms of sexism.

According to the structuralists, a structure such as patriarchy or capitalism is a system of power in itself. And these structures are sustained by at least three factors: the support of national elites, the acceptance of elite hegemony by most of society, and the support of other structures, including the coercive power of the state.[44] The principal conclusion of any structural analysis is that *the structures themselves must be challenged.*

A related consideration that is important to an understanding of structural power is the role played by such factors as language, knowledge, ideology, religion, and technology in the defense of elite power.

Language, for example, is not neutral. People are constrained in their actions by the way in which language is constructed and by the manner in which images are conveyed. For instance, sexually exclusive language and media advertising that consistently portrays women in particular roles both express and reinforce a patriarchal set of social relations. Similarly, particular uses of language and various forms of media (such as violent cartoons and video games) legitimize and encourage the use of violence for dealing with conflict.

Another important factor is the role of knowledge and experience and the ways in which these are gained. According to Martin, knowledge is not something found in books or experts. It is a social relationship that reflects the exercise of power. For example, governments finance the development of certain kinds of knowledge (such as those related to military strategy and weapons); educational institutions define and validate certain things (such as patriarchal and Eurocentric interpretations of history) as knowledge; and the media selects and presents knowledge in particular ways.[45]

Similarly, ideology is used to defend elite power. Marx and Engels noted: "The ideas of the ruling class are . . . the ruling ideas."[46] All structures of power depend on systems of ideas to legitimize them. Realist ideology, for example, legitimizes the dominant social cosmology and its distribution of power, provides the intellectual resources to maintain it, discredits ideas that challenge it, and limits the need to apply coercive power to defend it. Despite the crucial role played by ideology: "The connection between ideas and political power usually remains hidden."[47] More specifically, ideology is used to shift attention away from unmet needs within society; this is why liberal ideology directs attention to the unmet needs for identity and participation in socialist societies, while Marxist ideology is critical of the unmet needs for security and distributive justice in capitalist societies. Liberal ideology is also used to obscure the political foundation of economic relationships so that political responsibility for economic inequality and deprivation can be avoided. Moreover, ideology is used to alter individuals' awareness of their needs and to influence the nature of their political involvement; this fact helps to explain historical cases in which unmet needs did not lead to social disruption.[48]

Likewise, patriarchal religion is used to legitimize elite power. It is used both to rationalize exploitative social relations and to stifle the development of the critical consciousness necessary in order to resist those relations. For instance, though some Christians (including those committed to liberation theology in Central/South America) preach a theology intended to mobilize people to resist injustice, most of the Catholic and Protestant church hierarchies— and particularly the fundamentalist Christian groups—preach a conservative theology. They use Christian doctrine (for instance, the meek shall "inherit the earth")[49] to encourage passive obedience to dictatorial rule and to obstruct the struggle for revolutionary change. They concentrate people's attention on the individual effort to achieve "salvation" for a life in heaven rather than the collective struggle to achieve justice for their life on Earth.

In addition, David Dickson argues, technology plays an explicitly political role in society that is related to the distribution of power and the exercise of social control. In his view, technology promotes the material interests of elites while at the same time propagating the legitimating ideologies used by those elites.[50] As Martin elaborates, certain technologies are more easily used for some purposes and by some groups than others. Nuclear weapons might be useful to national elites, for example, but they are of no use to environmentalists or even the police.[51]

Clearly the practical possibilities for resisting a particular power structure depend on such factors as the knowledge and experience of individuals and the infrastructure of the society in which they live. An intellectually independent, technologically decentralized, and economically self-reliant community, for instance, is better able to resist than one that is politically and technologically centralized and economically dependent.[52]

Concerns about structural power, however, are not confined to what occurs in national societies and the global system. Structural analysis is also concerned with the manifestations of structural power that occur at the levels of individual behavior and group process. These will be explained in chapter 11.

Finally, it is worth repeating that the structural analyses referred to above highlight the existence of *a series of interacting and mutually reinforcing contradictions.* As Galtung has argued, there is no single, preeminent contradiction (such as capitalism) that is the key to the elimination of them all. Similarly, there is no single class of exploited actors that is the "vanguard" of structural change; suggesting otherwise is an unfortunate way of excluding a variety of exploited groups from the frontline of the struggle against violence in all its forms.[53]

In summary, it is evident that structures such as patriarchy, capitalism, and the state usually reinforce each other; it is not so evident that noncooperation by individuals—even organized noncooperation by large numbers of people—will be an adequate strategy for removing these solidly entrenched structures of violence, exploitation, and oppression. Therefore, a comprehensive strategy for dealing with conflict must take these structures into account. It must also create new structures that are able to resist the capacity of existing institutions to co-opt, corrupt, or destroy them and that are designed to satisfy human needs.

Conclusion

The modified consent theory that was presented in this chapter suggests that the way to undermine the power of an elite is to organize corporate resistance *by those constituencies on which it actually depends*; in this sense, the modified consent theory implies that a conscious choice about how power is applied is a central question of strategy. On the other hand, structural analysis provides a richer and more sophisticated explanation of structural power and highlights the importance of strategies that challenge its manifestations at the personal, group process, and political levels.

It seems evident that any form of political action will be enhanced if it includes thoughtful consideration of both the modified consent and the structural theories of power. One of the reasons why Gandhi's contribution to politics and history is so important and lasting is that he combined insights derived from both of these theories in his formulation of political strategies of nonviolence. The next chapter introduces the theory of nonviolence and discusses Gandhi's conception of it in detail.

7

The Gandhian Conception of Nonviolence

The strategic theory developed in this study is derived from several sources, including the Gandhian conception of nonviolence. The doctrine of nonviolence—in one form or another—runs through a rich variety of cultural, spiritual, religious, and philosophical traditions.[1] In addition, the practice of nonviolent action is thousands of years old and has been documented in all cultural contexts in which it has been investigated.[2] Recently, the terms *nonviolence* and *nonviolent action* have become umbrella terms for describing a range of methods for dealing with conflict;[3] at the very least, they share the principle that physical violence against human beings should not be used.

According to Gene Sharp, nonviolent action is a *technique* by which people can address conflict, including threats to their security, without using violence. It is not an attempt to ignore or to avoid conflict. It is *one* of the possible responses to the problem of how to use power effectively. As a technique, therefore, "nonviolent action is not passive. It is *not* inaction. It is *action* that is nonviolent."[4] In Sharp's view, there are three categories of nonviolent action: acts of protest and persuasion, noncooperation, and nonviolent intervention.[5]

Nonviolent protest and persuasion is a class of methods that are "mainly symbolic acts of peaceful opposition or of attempted persuasion, extending beyond verbal expressions." These methods include demonstrations, vigils, pickets, the use of posters, street theater, painting, and protest meetings.[6]

Noncooperation—the most common form of nonviolent action—involves the deliberate withdrawal of cooperation with the person, activity, institution, or regime with which the activists are engaged in conflict. These methods include the provision of sanctuary (social); strikes, boycotts, and war tax resistance (economic); and boycotts of legislative bodies and elections (political). Political noncooperation also includes acts of *civil disobedience*—the deliberate, open, and peaceful violation of particular laws, regulations, or instructions that are believed to be morally objectionable or unreasonable.[7]

Nonviolent intervention is a class of methods involving the disruption or destruction of established behavioral patterns, policies, relationships, or institutions that are considered unacceptable; or the creation of preferred alternatives. The *disruptive* class of methods includes nonviolent blockades and occupations, fasting, seeking imprisonment, and overloading facilities (such as courts and prisons). The *creative* class of methods involves establishing alternative political, economic, and social institutions, such as nonhierarchical cooperatives, markets for organically grown food, ethical investment groups, alternative schools, and energy exchange cooperatives, as well as parallel media, communications, and transport networks or even parallel "governments."[8] The creative class of methods is what the Gandhian literature refers to as the "constructive program."

Four Major Approaches to Nonviolence

There are many types of nonviolence. Sharp has identified nine: nonresistance, active reconciliation, moral resistance, selective nonviolence, passive resistance, peaceful resistance, nonviolent direct action, satyagraha (Gandhian nonviolence), and nonviolent revolution.[9] While such typologies[10] illustrate the diversity of types of nonviolence "as they seem to exist,"[11] for the purposes of this study it is more useful to classify the major approaches to nonviolence by using a set of previously identified criteria. This allows each approach to be assessed in terms of the conflict theory outlined earlier in this study. Consequently, this section identifies two dimensions of nonviolence and describes important characteristics of each. The labels used to identify these dimensions might not be ideal, but they are useful for describing and distinguishing the four different approaches to nonviolence discussed below.

Gandhi distinguished between those committed to nonviolence as a creed and those who used it as a policy.[12] More recent authors have recast this type of distinction in a variety of ways. Most frequently, a distinction is made between those whose commitment to nonviolence is "principled" and those whose commitment is "pragmatic."[13] This distinction is also employed throughout the remainder of this study. Specifically, the *pragmatic-principled* dimension is used to indicate the nature of the commitment to nonviolence and the approach to conflict that activists utilize, including the importance attached to the relationship between means and end and the attitude toward the opponent. Separately from this distinction, another dimension may be identified. The *reformist-revolutionary* dimension is used to indicate the type of analysis, the ultimate aim, and the operational timeframe that activists utilize.

Practitioners of *pragmatic* nonviolence believe it to be the most effective method available in the circumstances. They view conflict as a relationship between antagonists with incompatible interests: Their goal is to defeat the opponent and, if this entails any suffering (short of physical injury), to inflict that suffering on the opponent.[14] Practitioners of *principled* nonviolence choose it for ethical reasons and believe in the unity of means and end. They view the opponent as a partner in the struggle to satisfy the needs of all; if anyone suffers, it is the practitioner of nonviolence. More fundamentally, this practitioner may view nonviolence as a way of life.

Practitioners of *reformist* nonviolence are guided by an analysis that identifies particular elite policies as the cause of social problems. They use short- to medium-term campaigns to change these policies within the existing social framework; their aim is reform. Practitioners of *revolutionary* nonviolence are guided by a structural analysis of political and economic relationships and believe there is a need for fundamental structural change; particular campaigns (which may have a short- to medium-term timeframe) are thus conducted within the context of a long-term revolutionary strategy.

The criteria underpinning these two dimensions of nonviolence are itemized in table 1. By reference to their standing in relation to these criteria, it is possible to identify the orientation of individual activists and particular campaigns, and to locate them in one of four categories of nonviolence. For instance, most antinuclear and environmental campaigns (such as the campaign to prevent the damming of the Franklin River in Australia) fall into the pragmatic-reform category. Most campaigns with a Christian per-

Table 1. Nonviolence Criteria

THE PRAGMATIC-PRINCIPLED DIMENSION		
CRITERION	PRAGMATIC NONVIOLENCE	PRINCIPLED NONVIOLENCE
Nature of commitment	Most effective	Ethically best
Means and end	Separate	Indivisible
Approach to conflict	Incompatible interests	Shared problem
Approach to opponent	Inflict suffering	Accept suffering
Nonviolence as a way of life?	No	Probably

THE REFORMIST-REVOLUTIONARY DIMENSION		
CRITERION	REFORMIST NONVIOLENCE	REVOLUTIONARY NONVIOLENCE
Analysis of conflict	Policy problem	Structural problem
Aim	Policy change	Structural change
Constructive program?	No	Yes
Operational timeframe	Short/medium-term	Long-term

spective (such as the Montgomery bus boycott led by Martin Luther King, Jr.) are examples of the principled-reform category. The Palestinian Intifada is probably the best recent example of the pragmatic-revolutionary category. And many of Gandhi's campaigns (including the Salt Satyagraha) were clearly in the principled-revolutionary category.

It should be stressed that these categories are intended to be broadly descriptive rather than definitive. This is because individuals or campaigns might adopt a particular approach but utilize some characteristics normally associated with another approach. For example, many activists in the Intifada used features typical of the principled approach; nevertheless, insofar as it can be classified as nonviolent, the Intifada as a whole is more accurately categorized as pragmatic.

The commitment of individual activists and the nature of particular campaigns can also be illustrated graphically—according to the strength of their standing in relation to each of the criteria identified in table 1—on a matrix. They may be located in any quadrant on the matrix, near to or far from a particular axis, and at various distances from the origin, as illustrated in figure 3.

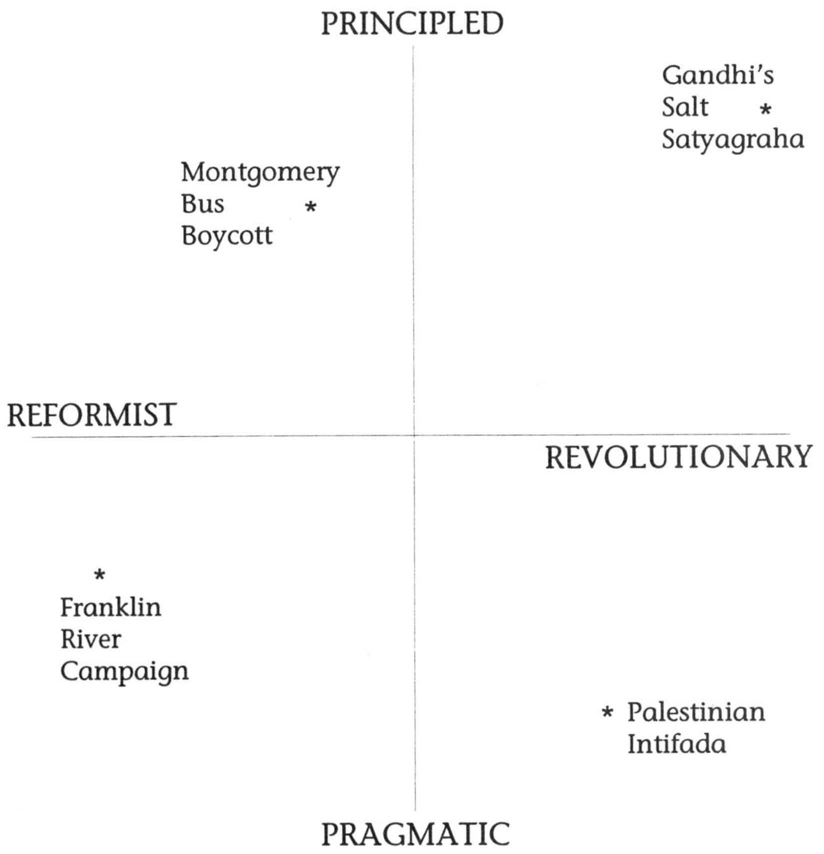

PRINCIPLED

Montgomery
Bus   *
Boycott

Gandhi's
Salt   *
Satyagraha

REFORMIST

REVOLUTIONARY

*
Franklin
River
Campaign

* Palestinian
Intifada

PRAGMATIC

Figure 3. Matrix of Nonviolence

Now that the four major approaches to nonviolence have been identified, the discussion that follows will concentrate on the principled-revolutionary (or Gandhian) conception of nonviolence—which goes considerably beyond nonviolent action as a "technique." A later section will specifically identify the shortcomings of the reformist and pragmatic approaches.

The Gandhian Conceptions of Society and the Individual

Gandhi's approach to politics entailed three essential elements: personal nonviolence as a way of life, constructive work to create the new society, and nonviolent resistance to direct and structural violence. All of these are firmly grounded in a concern with human needs and the realization that the satisfaction of needs is central to conflict resolution. The remainder of this chapter is primarily concerned with describing and analyzing Gandhi's conceptions of society, the individual, conflict, and nonviolence.

There are three reasons for this concentration on Gandhi. His views on these subjects are the most comprehensively developed of those offered within the nonviolence tradition. As the discussion will illustrate, his approach to conflict is consistent with, but an extension of, the recent conflict theory discussed in chapter 5. And Gandhi's views constitute a complete social cosmology: They offer guidance on the difficult tasks associated with creating new patterns of matter-energy use, new sets of social relations, new philosophies of society, and new strategies for dealing with conflict that are inherently nonviolent and mutually reinforcing. This section describes Gandhi's conceptions of society and the individual.

An awareness of the importance of human needs is not new (for example, it runs strongly through Christian and Hindu traditions), but, as discussed in chapters 4 and 5, it has never been a focus of concern (in either the theoretical or practical sense) within the dominant social cosmology. Moreover, while needs have been of considerable interest to some radical theorists, including Karl Marx,[15] few radical thinkers and even fewer radical activists have made the important connections between human needs and the nature of society, on the one hand, and between human needs and the process of conflict resolution, on the other. The most notable exception to this is Gandhi, who used a needs-based conception of society and conflict as the foundation of his strategically oriented nonviolent campaigns.

Gandhi's conception of society is based on a rejection of both capitalism[16] and socialism.[17] In relation to capitalism, he rejected the competitive market and private property,[18] with their emphasis on individual competitiveness and material progress and their consequent greed and exploitation of the weak.[19] He also rejected the major institutions of capitalism, including its parliamentary system of democracy (which denied sovereignty to the people),[20] its judicial system (which exacerbated conflict and perpetuated elite power),[21] and its educational system (which divorced education from life and work).[22] In relation to socialism, he rejected its conception of conflict in terms of class war,[23] its claim that state ownership and centralization are conducive to the common welfare,[24] its emphasis on material progress, and its reliance on violent means.[25]

The Gandhian vision of future society is based on a decentralized network of self-reliant and self-governing communities using property held in trust, with a weak central apparatus to perform residual functions. His vision stresses the importance of individuals being able to satisfy their personal needs through their own efforts—including "bread labor"—in cooperation with others and in harmony with nature.[26] For Gandhi, this horizontal framework is necessary in order to liberate the exploiter and exploited alike from the shackles of exploitative structures. This is vitally important because, in his view, "exploitation is the essence of violence."[27] Self-reliance and interdependence must be built into the structure in order to enhance the capacity for self-regeneration and self-defense and to eliminate the potential for structural violence inherent in any dependency relationship.[28]

This social vision was clearly evident in Gandhi's "constructive program," which was intended to restructure the social and economic life of all Indians; it was a vital part of his strategy for the liberation of India. The constructive program was designed to satisfy the needs of each individual member of society and was centrally concerned with the needs for self-esteem, security, and justice. The program entailed many elements, some of which are outlined below in order to illustrate this point.

A crucial feature of the constructive program was the campaign for communal unity. This was intended to encourage reciprocal recognition of the identity of Hindus, Muslims, Christians, Jews, and those of other religions. According to Gandhi, all people should have the same regard for other faiths as they have for their own.[29] The campaign to liberate women was intended to secure self-esteem, security, and justice for those most systematically oppressed by India's patriarchal society. "Woman has been suppressed under custom and law for which man was responsible. . . . In a plan of life based on non-violence, woman has as much right to shape her own destiny as man."[30] The campaign for the removal of untouchability was meant to restore self-esteem, dignity, and justice to the Harijans (Gandhi's term for those without caste) in Hindu society. Similarly, the constructive program was concerned with recognizing the needs of indigenous peoples and lepers throughout India. "Our country is so vast . . . one realizes how difficult it is to make good our claim to be one nation, unless every unit has a living consciousness of being one with every other."[31] The khadi (handspun/handwoven cloth) and village industries programs were intended to make the villages largely self-reliant and Indians proud of their identity after centuries of oppression and exploitation under British imperial rule. Khadi, Gandhi argued, "is the symbol of unity of Indian humanity, of its economic freedom and equality."[32] The struggle for economic equality was aimed at securing distributive justice for all. It meant "leveling down" the rich, who owned the bulk of the nation's wealth, while raising the living standards of "the semi-starved" peasant millions.[33]

Thus, Gandhi stressed the centrality of the individual and the importance of creating a society that satisfied human needs. "The individual is the one supreme consideration";[34] individuals are superior to the system they propound.[35] In fact: "If the individual ceases to count, what is left of society? . . . No society can possibly be built on a denial of individual freedom."[36]

But how is this nonviolent society to come into being? For Gandhi, the aim is not to destroy the old society now with the hope of building the new one later.[37] In his view, it requires a complete *and ongoing* restructuring of the existing social order using nonviolent means. And while it might not be possible to achieve it, "we must bear it in mind and work unceasingly to near it." The foundation of this nonviolent society, according to Gandhi, can only be the nonviolent individual: No one need wait for anyone else before adopting the nonviolent way of life. Hesitating to act because the whole vision might not be achieved, or because others do not yet share it, is an attitude that only hinders progress.[38] The point, he argued, is that by doing the right thing and by acting in accordance with one's ability, there comes a time when the individual has an "irresistible" power to make others act.[39] Moreover, this power is enhanced by the individual's ability to exercise self-control, which in turn might entail suffering and sacrifice.[40] For Gandhi, then, the nonviolent transformation of society depended on the nonviolent transformation of the individual. "As with the individual so with the universe."[41] Thus, although Gandhi emphasized the centrality of the individual, he also stressed the importance of personal responsibility. We must learn, he argued, "to strike the mean between individual freedom and social restraint."[42] Gandhi's reasoning in this regard stemmed directly from his analysis.

According to Marx, the crisis of civilization was created by the production relations of capitalism; for Gandhi, it was created by the process of industrialization itself. This process both stimulated and was fueled by the unrestrained growth of individual wants. The remedy, according to Gandhi, lay in individuals transforming themselves and, through this transformation, founding a just social order. He argued that social transformation, no matter how profound, would be neither adequate nor lasting if individuals themselves were not transformed.[43] A part of this strategy was "the deliberate and voluntary reduction of wants."[44] Gandhi did not begrudge people a reasonable degree of physical well-being, but he made a clear distinction between needs and wants. "Earth provides enough to satisfy every [person's] need but not for every [person's] greed."[45]

Gandhi saw clearly that humans had created the predicament in which they found themselves. He also believed that the egotistic conception of the human individual adhered to by the liberals and by Marx was not only outmoded but also disastrous for the individual, for society, and for nature. To Gandhi, therefore, freedom was the result of developing the self in harmony with, not antagonism to, society and nature.[46] "Willing submission to social restraint for the sake of the well-being of the whole society enriches both the individual and the society of which one is a member."[47] Nevertheless, in Gandhi's philosophy, "the individual stands first" because the individual has a soul while society does not.[48]

The importance attached to individual responsibility is also evident in Gandhi's conception of nonviolence as a way of life. Gandhi had a very positive view of human nature. He believed that humans could respond to "the call of the spirit" and rise above selfishness and violence.[49] Moreover, this was necessary in their quest for self-realization. Self-realization, as the Gandhian scholar Arne Naess explains it, "involves realizing oneself as an autonomous, fully responsible person."[50] This quest is an individual one that relies on nonviolence, self-reliance, and the search for truth. "To find Truth completely is to realize oneself and one's destiny."[51] But what should guide this search? According to Gandhi, *it can only be the individual conscience*: The "inner voice" must always be "the final arbiter when there is a conflict of duty."[52] And in his view, "the voice of God, of Conscience, of Truth or the Inner Voice or 'the still small Voice' mean one and the same thing."[53]

This point is centrally important, because the usual descriptions of Gandhian nonviolence stress its morality, humility, and sacrifice while neglecting the fundamental norm "that *you* should follow *your* inner voice *whatever the consequences*"[54] and "even at the risk of being misunderstood."[55]

In practice, of course, there is no other way; the quest for self-realization is inherently personal. But for the nonviolent individual the path is easier, as the following explanation illustrates. In Gandhi's view, violence is anything that impedes individual self-realization. This violence can be direct or structural in nature. Under normal circumstances, whether one is the perpetrator or the victim of violence, self-realization is impeded. But for the perpetrator, the violence is self-inflicted.[56] In the case of the nonviolent individual, however, the situation is different. According to Gandhi, while self-realization is the "highest" need, it depends on the satisfaction of other needs. For this reason, he attached immense importance to personal identity and dignity; loss of self-respect had to be avoided. Without self-respect and inner security, he argued, one cannot reach the road leading to self-realization or start on the road to nonviolence.[57] However, once an individual has assimilated the nonviolent spirit, they should not feel humiliated or provoked by the insulting words or violent behavior of others, because their self-respect nullifies its effect.[58] For the nonviolent individual, self-realization cannot be impeded by the behavior of others.

In practice, according to Gandhi, self-realization is achieved through service to humanity.[59] But because the capacity for service is limited by our knowledge of the world, we must start with service to those "nearest and best known" to us.[60] In fact, this reflected Gandhi's concept of political obligation. Real rights, he argued, are a result of the performance of duty.[61]

Though Gandhi placed individuals at the center of society and stressed the importance of satisfying their needs, he attached equal importance to individual responsibility. This responsibility was threefold, entailing responsibility in the quest for self-realization, as a member of society, and as an agent of nonviolent social change.

The Gandhian Conceptions of Conflict and Nonviolence

Gandhi's conception of conflict, and the approach to nonviolence he developed in order to resolve it, is consistent with the conflict theory outlined in chapter 5. It also goes beyond this theory.

Conflict, according to Gandhi, is both positive and desirable. It is an important means to greater human unity. Johan Galtung explains this point: "far from separating two parties, a conflict should unite them, precisely because they have their incompatibility in common."[62] More fundamentally, Gandhi believed that conflict should remind antagonists of the deeper, perhaps transcendental, unity of life, because in his view humans are related by a bond that is deeper and more profound than the bonds of social relationship.[63]

Gandhi also saw conflict as built into social structures and not into people. Hence, he made a clear distinction between the actor and the deed: "Hate the sin and not the sinner."[64] According to Gandhi, British imperialism and the Indian caste system were both examples of structures that were perpetuated, in large part, as a result of people performing particular roles within them. The evil, however, was in the structure, not in the people who performed their duties. The essence of Gandhi's approach was to identify approaches to conflict that preserved the people while systematically demolishing the evil structure. Nevertheless, he firmly believed that structural purification alone is not enough; self-purification is also essential.[65]

Given this positive and structurally oriented conception of conflict, Gandhi was not seeking a conflict-free society, nor did he believe that it was soon to be realized. On the contrary, because he saw conflict as a perennial condition, his discussions about future society are particularly concerned with how to manage conflict and how to create new social arrangements free of structural violence. This emphasis is in stark contrast to Marxist doctrine, which provides no guidelines for dealing with new types of conflict (including those related to class) as they emerge in socialist or even communist societies.[66]

So how is conflict to be resolved? In essence, the Gandhian approach to conflict recognizes the importance of resolving all three corners of what Galtung calls the "conflict triangle": the attitude, the behavior, and the goal incompatibility itself.

The Gandhian method of conflict resolution is called "satyagraha," which means "a relentless search for truth and a determination to reach truth";[67] it is somewhat simplistically but more widely known in English as "nonviolent action." While the perpetrator of violence assumes knowledge of the truth and makes a life-or-death judgment on that basis,[68] satyagraha, according to Gandhi, excludes the use of violence precisely because *no one is capable of knowing the absolute truth.*[69] Satyagraha was Gandhi's attempt to evolve a theory of politics and conflict resolution that could accommodate his moral system. It has been characterized by Naess as "the ethics of group struggle."[70]

Satyagraha, as Gandhi conceived it, is a way of struggling that is *goal-revealing*.[71] It is a dialectical process that is both creative and constructive, and it is centrally concerned with human needs: Through nonviolent action "the truth as judged by the fulfillment of human needs will emerge in the form of a mutually satisfactory and agreed-upon solution."[72] For the satyagrahi (practitioner of satyagraha), this wider truth cannot be achieved through violence ("which violates human needs and destroys life"), because violence itself is a form of injustice. In any case, violence cannot *resolve* conflict, because it does not address the issues at stake.[73]

To resolve conflict, Gandhi employed a combination of three basic approaches. First, he used what Galtung calls "decoupling." Noncooperation involved breaking relations at the level of social structure while reinforcing the deeper structure of human unity through greater interaction at the personal level.[74] In other words, while satyagraha implies cooperation with the opponent *as a person* in the context of the human unity structure—the deep structure to which everyone belongs—it implies noncooperation with the opponent's *role* in the context of the social structure.[75] Second, he was willing to compromise when basic principles had not been challenged.[76] This reflected his desire to cooperate with opponents whenever possible throughout the struggle in order to build relationships and to create the basis for a sound postconflict life.[77] Third, he sought synthesis or transcendence. He would never yield on what he believed to be the truth, or make concessions with the intention of "buying over" the opponent, but he was always ready to be persuaded that the opponent's position was nearer the truth. The aim, according to Gandhian theorist Joan Bondurant, was to create new choices and to restructure the opposing elements of a conflict in order to achieve a synthesis that was satisfactory to all parties and superior to any one of the original positions. Nonviolent resistance continued "until persuasion has carried the conflict into mutually agreeable adjustment."[78] And this adjustment, in the formula used by Galtung, entailed three elements: correction in the steep Self-Other attitudinal gradient, reversal of the behavioral polarization pattern, and removal of the goal incompatibility—if necessary, by creating new social structures.

The essential point about conflict resolution in the Gandhian sense is that resolving the conflict is only one aspect of the desired outcome. For Gandhi, success also implies the creation of a superior social structure, higher degrees of fearlessness and self-reliance on the part of both satyagrahis and their opponents, and *a greater degree of human unity at the level of social relationships.*[79]

This point is centrally important. As illustrated in chapter 5, within the dominant social cosmology conflict is usually perceived as a zero-sum contest with both parties having the desire to dominate. This perception, Thomas Weber argues, is often the result of fear or insecurity: the suspicion that if one yields or shows trust, the opponent will take advantage. The aim of Gandhian satyagraha is neither to harm the opponent nor to impose on them a solution against their will. The aim is to help both parties to achieve a more secure, creative, and truthful relationship.[80] According to Richard Gregg, several elements in satyagraha tend to reduce the feeling of insecurity. These include an attitude of respect and goodwill toward the opponent, the adherence to truth, the maintenance of discipline, the belief in human unity, "and a steady series of deeds in accord with that belief."[81]

Satyagraha, then, involves consistent effort in the search for truth while converting the opponent into a friend as part of the process: It is not used against someone; it is done *with* someone.[82] "It is based on the idea that the moral appeal to the heart and conscience is . . . more effective than an appeal based on threat of bodily pain or violence."[83] For Gandhi then: "Satyagraha *is not a set of techniques.*" This is because the actions cannot be detached from the norms of nonviolence that govern attitudes and behavior. Therefore, an action or campaign that avoids the use of physical violence but that ignores the attitudinal and behavioral norms characteristic of satyagraha cannot be classified as Gandhian nonviolence. Moreover, the lack of success of such actions or campaigns is often directly attributable to a failure to apply these fundamental norms.[84]

It is evident from this discussion that three principles underpin the Gandhian approach to conflict: the unity of means and end, a recognition of the unity of all life, and a willingness on the part of the satyagrahi to undergo suffering. We will discuss each in turn.

Gandhi's ultimate aim was to bring about a just and peaceful society. To do this, he believed in the unity of means and end. For Gandhi, truth is the end, nonviolence the means.[85] "The means may be likened to a seed, the end to a tree; and there is just the same inviolable connection between the means and the end as there is between the seed and the tree."[86] Moreover, he observed: "They say 'Means are after all means'. I would say 'means are after all everything'. As the means so the end. . . . There is no wall of separation between means and end."[87] And: "if one takes care of the means, the end will take care of itself."[88]

This vital connection between means and end has been noted by Aldous Huxley as well. In his view, a good end is the direct result of appropriate means. "The end cannot justify the means, for the simple and obvious reason that the means employed determine the nature of the ends produced."[89] Hannah Arendt has made a similar observation. Because the end of human action cannot be predicted, Arendt argues, the means used to achieve a political end have more bearing on the future world than the goal itself.[90]

According to Leroy Pelton, the link between means and end is vital. If the goals are peace, justice, and freedom tempered by social responsibility, then we must behave peacefully, justly, and as free and responsible individuals.[91] Huxley suggests that the golden rule to be kept in mind when means are chosen is to ask whether the result will be merely the attainment of some immediate goal, or to transform the society to which they are applied "into a just, peaceable, morally and intellectually progressive community of non-attached and responsible men and women."[92]

In addition to recognizing the unity of means and end, the Gandhian approach to conflict presupposes the unity of all life. Nonviolent resistance, according to Gregg "is based upon the idea of unity."[93] This idea runs strongly through the major cultural and spiritual influences on Gandhi's life—India, Hinduism, and Jain-ism—which provides some explanation for the *central importance* of this concept in Gandhian thinking. The core of Indian thought, Hajime Nakamura maintains, "is the idea of the unity of all things."[94] It is also characteristic of Hinduism, which is inclined "to emphasise Universal Being, to which all individuals and particulars are subordinated."[95] And it is a central tenet of Jainism, which urges humans to realize "that all souls are like oneself."[96]

Thus, as an Indian, a Hindu, and a person deeply respectful of other religions, Gandhi had a profound sense of the unity of all life. For him, the practice of nonviolence was not confined to his relationship with other human beings; it included the noninjury of all living things.[97] According to Gandhi: "*Ahimsa* [nonviolence] means not to hurt any living creature by thought, word or deed."[98] The individual, humanity, and other life forms are one: "I believe in the essential unity of [humanity] and for that matter of all that lives."[99] "The life of a lamb is no less precious than that of a human being. I should be unwilling to take the life of a lamb for the sake of the human body."[100] Nevertheless, Gandhi was not bound by a dogmatic interpretation of this principle; there are circumstances in which killing is justified.[101]

A third principle underpinning Gandhi's approach to conflict is that of self-suffering, and there are many reasons for it: It is central to Gandhi's conception of nonviolence that the satyagrahi is willing to suffer the violence of others without inflicting violence and suffering in return; this will result in the least total loss of life and the greatest degree of moral enrichment for humanity as a whole.[102] This is the price paid for conducting resistance that is specifically nonviolent.[103] The willingness to suffer for the sake of others is also the ultimate test of love in action, as well as a method of dramatizing the injustice to be remedied. It is a demonstration, too, of sincerity and of the commitment to satisfying the needs of the opponent. It will strengthen appeals to the opponent's conscience and may evoke their sense of justice; it may also elicit the support of third parties. It is a means of strengthening self-control and discipline for the struggle against injustice generally: "it frees one from the manipulative attempts of others."[104] And, finally, it is the means for ensuring that others do not suffer because of the satyagrahi's mistakes.[105]

Nevertheless, certain historical incidents[106] and recent experimental evidence[107] suggest that awareness of others' suffering can induce dislike for victims *because they suffer.* According to the experimental evidence, perpetrators might respond in this way because their responsibility for inflicting the suffering might lead them to devalue the opponent. Observers might have this response because suffering violates their need to believe in a just world: they are motivated to convince themselves that the victims deserved their fate.[108]

If suffering is to be functional, then, it must be designed to elicit respect rather than rejection or condemnation. Factors that will help to elicit respect include prior knowledge of the issues and the activists who are suffering. In addition, the activists can evoke respect by their sincerity, openness, commitment to an ideal, outward displays of fearlessness and dignity even in the face of threats, good humor, maintenance of nonviolent discipline, and displays of goodwill toward opponents.[109] Such qualities, Eleanora Patterson asserts, can be demonstrated only if the suffering is undertaken voluntarily by someone who has a high level of self-worth.[110] In this case, the suffering is likely to be both liberating and empowering.[111]

Because suffering is a means of conversion only when it occurs in the appropriate context, Gandhi specifically warns against brutalizing the opponent by compelling them to inflict punishment. In his view, given the principle of spiritual unity, this would "drag down" the satyagrahi as well. He counsels "exemplary self-restraint" in the face of provocation and repression, "even at the risk of being charged with cowardice."[112]

In Gandhi's view, conflict is the result of the structural denial of human needs. If these needs are to be satisfied, new structures are necessary. This requires a method of struggle that satisfies three conditions: It must destroy need-denying structures, create need-satisfying structures, and respect the needs of the conflicting parties during the struggle itself. Satyagraha was Gandhi's attempt to devise a method of struggle that satisfied all three conditions.

The Reformist and Pragmatic Approaches to Nonviolent Action

While Gandhi's conception of conflict and the principles he devised for its resolution are consistent with the recent conflict theory outlined in chapter 5, the approach to nonviolence adopted by many other activists and theorists is not. Using the conception of conflict and the desirable features of a problem-solving process described in chapter 5, coupled with the insights provided by Gandhi's approach to conflict and nonviolence outlined above, we can now identify the major shortcomings of an approach to conflict based on the reformist or pragmatic use of nonviolent action.

The reformist approach to nonviolent action is characterized by two main features: its analysis of social conflicts as problems that are independent of the political framework and its intention to remedy these problems through internal reform. Although this approach is appropriate in certain contexts, given the fact (identified by Gandhi and the conflict theory discussed in chapter 5) that most serious social conflict is structural in origin, this approach is often inadequate, as the discussions in chapters 5 and 6 highlighted. There is no need to discuss it further here.

The main feature of a pragmatic commitment to nonviolent action is the belief that it is the most effective method of struggle. In itself, there is nothing of concern about this belief; indeed, it was shared by Gandhi. While Gandhi was deeply concerned with the spiritual, religious, and ethical aspects of nonviolence, in his view, it is still "the most practical politics."[113] In fact, he asserted, "if any action of mine claimed to be spiritual is proved to be unpractical it must be pronounced to be a failure. I do believe the most spiritual act is the most practical in the true sense of the term."[114] "Satyagraha is, as a matter of fact and in the long run, the most expeditious course."[115] According to Gandhi, then, there is no conflict between ethical and practical politics.[116]

However, other common features of the pragmatic approach to nonviolent action are a belief in the divisibility of means and end, a conception of conflict in terms of incompatible interests, and a negative conception of the opponent. These run directly counter to Gandhi's conception of nonviolence and the approach to conflict suggested by the conflict research outlined in chapter 5.

Many pragmatic activists choose nonviolent action because it is the most effective *means*; they are less concerned with questions regarding the relationship between means and end. This is evident from the willingness of many pragmatic activists to consider, and sometimes use, tactics involving deception, secrecy, or sabotage.

It is clear from the above discussion that deception, secrecy,[117] and sabotage cannot be used without violating such fundamental Gandhian norms as adherence to truth, respect for the opponent, and belief in the sacredness and unity of all life; it is equally clear that such tactics are at variance with basic elements of the conflict theory discussed in chapter 5: Such means preclude the possibility of satisfying human needs, including the needs for self-esteem, participation, and security. They do nothing to correct the steep Self-Other attitudinal gradient, to reverse the behavioral polarization pattern, or to remove the goal incompatibility. And they make it impossible to improve understanding, correct misperceptions, and cultivate empathy with the opponent. In fact, they create additional barriers by intensifying the opponent's fear (an emotional state it is imperative to eliminate) and mistrust.

Moreover, pragmatic activists regard conflict as a contest over incompatible interests; their goal is to defeat the opponent. This is clearly at variance with the Gandhian approach and the approach developed by those recent conflict theorists discussed in chapter 5.

If conflict resolution depends on satisfying the needs of all parties, then an approach to conflict that seeks defeat for one party is inconsistent with a resolution of it. Specifically, this approach fails to recognize the importance of satisfying the opponent's needs for participation, justice, and control—needs that cannot be met if the opponent is not meaningfully involved in determining the outcome.

In addition, this intention to defeat the opponent is usually accompanied by a negative conception of them; this, in turn, may lead to their dehumanization. This is highly counterproductive. According to Gandhi, dehumanization is not just a prologue to violence, "dehumanisation *is* violence."[118] In any case, whether or not it is aggravated by a process of dehumanization, a negative image of the opponent (a steep Self-Other attitudinal gradient) is an impediment to conflict resolution. It is inconsistent with an approach to conflict that acknowledges the opponent's needs for self-esteem, recognition, and rationality, among others.

In his careful study of the nature and meanings of nonviolent action, Douglas Bond concluded that the nature of nonviolence is less elusive than the frequent misuse and abuse of the concept might suggest. "There does seem to be an essence or core of nonviolence rooted in the idea of sanctity of life *and* manifest in a sense of unity or community between antagonists achieved at a cost of self-suffering or sacrifice."[119] This core is missing when the commitment to nonviolence is pragmatic, because the aim of pragmatic activists is to defeat the opponent; there is no desire to seek unity with them (if necessary, through personal suffering).

In order to appreciate the "magic" of nonviolent action, Theodor Ebert maintains, it is necessary to understand that it works at various levels and in different ways. In essence, it is the result of a dynamic interplay between human psychology and political power. Thus, while the capacity of nonviolent action to function effectively at the level of power relationships is very important, and directly contradicts the popular notion that only violence can be effective at that level, it is the *intention* and *capacity* of Gandhian nonviolence to radically transform human relationships that makes it unique as a method of political action.[120]

The debate over the principled and pragmatic conceptions of nonviolent action is sometimes projected as a contest between two central elements: an approach based on a moral appeal to the opponent's conscience (amplified through personal suffering) and an approach based on undermining their sources of power. In fact, there is *no* tension between these conceptions *in this particular sense* in the Gandhian scheme of nonviolence; they are both fundamental elements of it. The first element describes the approach to the opponent *as a person*. The second element describes the approach to the opponent's *role* in the structures of oppression. By combining these two elements, the struggle is meaningfully transformed from a struggle between individuals to a struggle between people, on the one hand, and structures, on the other. "My non-co-operation is with methods and systems, never with [people]."[121] The intention is to strip the opponent of the dehumanizing effects inherent in their structural role so that they must confront the most obvious manifestation of their own humanity—their conscience. Pragmatic activists fail to utilize the benefits of the psychological elements of nonviolence.

In fact, unlike the pragmatic approach to nonviolent action, recent psychological studies indicate that Gandhi's conception of nonviolence is likely, from the opponent's perspective, to generate the minimum degree of psychological resistance and to increase the rationality of seeking creative outcomes. For example, by stating openly and completely the nature of the grievance, by focusing attention on the issue and respecting the opponent, by being truthful, consistent, trusting, and ready for dialogue, the activist should reduce the frustration, fear, and hostility (and the amount of overt hostility that can be justified to third parties) that occurs when opponents feel that they are the victims of arbitrary situations or when they feel that they are under threat.[122] Moreover, Pelton argues, by utilizing the capacity for reflective rather than reflexive action, the Gandhian approach makes it possible to love the opponent—in the sense of having understanding, empathy, and goodwill (important elements in conflict resolution)—and to channel cognitively controlled anger into creative nonviolent action.[123]

From the conflict perspectives developed by Gandhi and those recent conflict theorists discussed in chapter 5, there are major weaknesses associated with both the reformist and the pragmatic approaches to nonviolent action.

The Importance of Power and Will

Clearly Gandhi used a conception of conflict and an approach to its resolution that are consistent with the conflict theory outlined in chapter 5. He went beyond this theory by offering a way of using power ethically in circumstances in which approaches to conflict based on needs or rights are inadequate. This section discusses Gandhi's conceptions of power and will and the importance he attached to each of these as elements of any struggle. The next section considers the question of power in more detail.

According to Pelton, Gandhi's conception of power is humane and constructive. It is respectful of human needs both now and in the future. It is power that can reconcile opponents and resolve conflict, power "that can transform and not destroy."[124] Gandhi was keenly aware of the difference between power-over and power-with, and his own conceptions of society and conflict are firmly rooted in the latter. "Power is of two kinds. One is obtained by the fear of punishment and the other by acts of love. Power based on love is a thousand times more effective and permanent than the one derived from fear of punishment."[125] Gandhi also believed that, independent of these manifestations, there is another dimension of power: "power from within,"[126] or power-over-oneself. "Government over self is the truest swaraj [self-rule]."[127]

As Raghavan Iyer has noted, Gandhi explicitly rejected the notion that society is governed by laws "which are beyond the ability of any individual to alter."[128] Unlike conservative thought, which locates rationality outside the individual and which assigns individuals a very limited role, Gandhi had a profound belief in the moral autonomy and status of the individual and in the capacity of *individual will* to bring about fundamental social and political change.[129] "Strength does not come from physical capacity. It comes from an indomitable will."[130]

What does the notion of will mean to Gandhi? It is an expression of the needs for identity, self-reliance, and self-realization and of the moral commitment to self-chosen values. And it is essential to nonviolence. Nonviolent resistance is "the resistance of one will against another."[131] It means "the putting of one's whole soul against the will of the tyrant."[132]

To Gandhi, the frailty of human nature is a direct result of the weakness of the will.[133] But this weakness has social roots. In his critique of industrial civilization, Gandhi observed that while it promised to increase physical comfort, it undermined the will by draining moral and physical courage.[134] Admitting that people usually live according to habit, he believed that it is better for individuals to live by the exercise of their will. Strength of will is gained through action and suffering that are the products of thought and conscience.[135] But there is more to it than this.

Gandhi's struggle against injustice was a fight against power. However, unlike those who seek to concentrate coercive, political, economic, or moral resources in an effort to acquire *power-over* the opponent, Gandhi's approach was quite different. According to Gandhi, illegitimate power can work only in certain circumstances. Normative power (appeals to values or ideas) works because people are "empty," remunerative power (incentives and rewards) works because people are dependent, and punitive power (the threat or use of force) works because people are afraid. The way to minimize or eliminate the effectiveness of this power, Gandhi believes, is to build *power-over-oneself* through the development of personal identity, self-reliance, and fearlessness. Building identity is the result of identifying with what Galtung calls "the trans-personal Self," that is, identifying with all humans rather than just some; cultivating self-reliance involves reducing one's wants to a minimum and developing a self-sufficient capacity to satisfy those wants; and fearlessness results from developing these two qualities and from the performance of duty.[136] Power-over-oneself is also strengthened by taking personal vows—a deliberate commitment to a moral principle[137]—and the experience of suffering. The key to countervailing power, then, according to Gandhi, is power-over-oneself.

So what is the relationship between power and will? Most fundamentally, according to Gandhi, individuals need this power-over-oneself in order to give full expression to their will.

It was noted in chapters 1 and 2 that some military thinkers from Clausewitz to the present have identified the importance of power and will as elements of strategic theory. It is quite clear that Gandhi identified their importance as well. In addition, Gandhi was clearly aware of the different manifestations of power, including its structural manifestations as described in chapter 6. However, as this section has discussed, Gandhi made another, unique, contribution: He identified certain elements of both power and will and illustrated the important relationship between one manifestation of power—power-over-oneself—and the notion of will. This is vitally important given the preeminent role Gandhi ascribed to the individual in strategies for creating a nonviolent society. It is also important in developing a strategy of nonviolent defense.

Nonviolent Action and Coercion

It was apparent from the discussion at the end of chapter 5 that a strategic approach to conflict based on a willingness to satisfy human needs is not adequate unless it includes a method of exercising power that is both ethical and effective. Is it possible to use coercive power ethically?

Coercion, asserts Christian Bay, refers to actual physical violence or the use of sanctions that are strong enough to force individuals to abandon their preferred course of action.[138] For Pelton, coercive power is the influence derived from the ability to use punishment or the threat of punishment.[139]

According to Clarence Case, coercion is usually regarded as a process involving the application of physical force. In his view, this interpretation is not correct. For Case, coercion entails the application of force that is either physical *or* moral.[140] Bondurant agrees with this interpretation. In her view, coercion involves the application of physical or moral force; it is intended to compel action against a person's will.[141]

Is nonviolent action coercive? It can be. According to Bondurant, nonviolent action does contain an element of coercion. In her view, noncooperation in the form of boycotts and strikes is a tool that involves an element of compulsion that might induce a change on the part of the opponent that is contrary to their will.[142] In contrast, while she agrees that nonviolent action is coercive, Barbara Deming argues that it constitutes force only in the sense that the activist insists on acting out their own will. It does not involve coercion of the will of the opponent.[143]

More emphatically, William Borman asserts that, contrary to both Gandhi's interpretation and the canons of strict nonviolence, satyagraha is an essentially coercive force. The object of satyagraha, he continues, *is* coercion. "The principal motive is to have one's way."[144] Reinhold Niebuhr agrees. In his view, as long as nonviolent action places restraints on the desires and actions of others, it is a form of coercion.[145]

Adopting a different approach, Gene Sharp offers a clarifying typology. He distinguishes four mechanisms of change by which nonviolent action might work: conversion, accommodation, nonviolent coercion, and disintegration.[146] In his view, the demands of a nonviolent group can be achieved by conversion of the opponent, through accommodation by the opponent, through the disintegration of the opponent, or, in some cases, *against the will* of the opponent. That is, they might be *nonviolently coerced*.[147]

Nonviolent coercion is an important tool for many pragmatic exponents of nonviolent action. However, in principle it was never

acceptable to Gandhi; nor is it acceptable to many principled exponents of nonviolence. This is because coercion is inconsistent with
the moral development of the conflicting parties, it fails to express
the respect in which the opponent is held, and it does nothing to establish the justice of the objectives sought.[148] In fact, according to Gandhi
there is no such thing as compulsion in the scheme of nonviolence.
"Reliance has to be placed upon ability to reach the intellect and the
heart—the latter rather than the former."[149] Indeed, "no one has a
right to coerce others to act according to [their] own view of truth."[150]

Despite this, several authors claim that Gandhi used coercion.
Case, for example, argues that Gandhi's 1919 campaign against
the Rowlatt Bills (which were intended to subject "any suspected
person" to arrest without warrant and secret trial without appeal)
was explicitly *nonviolent* but implicitly *coercive* because the aim was
to compel the imperial government to withdraw the legislation
against its will.[151] In addition, though some of Gandhi's fasts were
obviously instruments of self-purification, others, some authors
argue, were clearly coercive. For instance, Gandhi's fast for communal peace in January 1948, according to Weber, "had no selfish
motive but did have a coercive element." The leaders of the religious communities gave assurances of peace because they did not
want to risk blame for Gandhi's death.[152] In fact, Borman argues,
Gandhi's use of the fast provides an appropriate focus for examin-
ing the coercive character of his principles, because fasting was
intended to produce certain specific results. In his view, the coercive
character of fasting is "undeniable." This derives from several factors. For example, given Gandhi's personal moral status, the moral
pressure that attached to his fasting was clearly coercive and "subversive of moral autonomy."[153]

Gandhi, however, consistently refused to acknowledge any
element of coercion in satyagraha. "The satyagrahi's object is to
convert, not to coerce."[154] In fact, Gandhi asserted that the person
who uses coercion is guilty of deliberate violence. "Coercion is inhu-
man."[155]

Gandhi believed that motive and intent are determinative in
deciding whether an action is coercive. "In any examination of
moral conduct, the intention is the chief ingredient." Coercion, in
his view, means the use of harmful force *against* another person.
"Surely, force of self-suffering cannot be put in the same category."[156]
However, in Borman's view, disclaiming the coercive intent does *not*
remove the coercive effects and repercussions. Further, he argues, the

justification of self-suffering is inadequate: the force that communicates itself, "whether produced by directing suffering against oneself or others, is an externally impinging factor."[157]

Krishnalal Shridharani has considerable sympathy with Gandhi but believes that it is misleading to call satyagraha a pure and simple process of conversion. In his view, satyagraha does contain an element of what some people might call "coercion." However, because the word *coercion* implies revenge and punishment, it is not an appropriate term for describing satyagraha—a process that is concerned with self-purification and self-suffering rather than punishment. For this reason, Shridharani suggests that satyagraha entails an element of compulsion rather than coercion.[158]

Gopinath Dhawan disputes even this claim. In his view, satyagraha as practiced by Gandhi exerted "moral pressure" intended to evoke the best in the opponent. The satyagrahi undermines the moral defenses of the opponent, and the pressure of the resistance, while compelling, is persuasive.[159]

In any case, Shridharani's distinction between the inclination to self-purification and self-suffering, on the one hand, and revenge and punishment, on the other, is important, despite Borman's objection. It highlights one vital difference between satyagraha and other approaches to conflict (including the pragmatic approach to nonviolent action). But whether an action entails coercion, compulsion, or even moral pressure, there is another important distinction that must be made.

An inherent feature of group struggle, Naess contends, is "a conflict of wills." During a successful satyagraha campaign, the wills of *both* parties are changed so that both wills end in harmony. This occurs even though each party would have rejected the final solution had they known about it beforehand. Despite this, Naess argues, "Coercion is not conceptually implied." Suppose a person wills one thing initially and another at a later time. Clearly, something has changed their will. However, from this influence upon their will, one cannot infer that they were coerced. A number of things, such as a change of opinion, may have influenced their will. Moreover, if the person was led to acquire new information or to receive certain impressions of suffering that altered their "reasoned judgment," one would not claim they were coerced.[160]

If a change of will follows the scrutiny of norms in the context of new information while one is "in a state of full mental and bodily powers," this is an act of personal freedom under optimal conditions. Naess highlights this point with the following example: Suppose that one person carries another *against their will* into the streets where there is a riot and, as a result of what they see, the carried person changes some of their attitudes and opinions. Was the change coerced? According to Naess, while the person was coerced into seeing something that caused the change, the change itself was *not* coerced. The distinction is important, Naess argues, because satyagraha is incompatible with changes of attitudes or opinions that are coerced.[161]

But what if, after being coerced to witness something, the opponent does *not* change their attitude or opinion? Such a change clearly cannot "be predicted without fail."[162] In these circumstances, it would seem, either the satyagrahi has made a mistake (and while their use of nonviolence has prevented injury to the opponent, it has not necessarily prevented loss) or, if the injustice remains unresolved, nonviolent resistance (perhaps in another form) must continue until the opponent *does* change their attitude or opinion.

Even if changes of attitude or opinion are uncoerced, then, opponents might still be coerced to witness particular events or to hear certain arguments. However, Naess warns, "coercion within a campaign decreases the degree of its consistency." And Gandhi maintained that by training and outlook, the satyagrahi should be able to detect and eliminate coercion, although Gandhi himself did not always succeed.[163] For example, during the struggle against the Ahmedabad mill owners in 1918, he fasted in order to encourage the striking mill hands to persevere until a settlement was reached.

My fast was not free from a grave defect. . . . With the mill-owners, I could only plead; to fast against them would amount to coercion. Yet in spite of my knowledge that my fast was bound to put pressure upon them, as in fact it did, I felt I could not help it. The duty to undertake it seemed to me to be clear.[164]

As a result, this satyagraha was of less than perfect purity. But Naess maintains that this does not invalidate the contention that satyagraha can be carried out *without* coercive pressures.[165] Nor, as Pelton would emphasize, does it invalidate the desirability of doing so. As the psychological evidence (such as that derived from cognitive dissonance theory) indicates, given the resentment and resistance that coercive power generates, if behavior is to be coerced in an attempt to change attitudes, then it is important to apply the *minimal pressure necessary* in order to obtain the behavioral change.[166]

Clearly then, there are widely divergent views regarding the relationship between satyagraha and coercion. For some, like Borman, there is no justification for differentiating between the pressure created by satyagraha and that meant by the word *coercion*.[167] Others, like Anders Boserup and Andrew Mack, accept Gandhi's interpretation and distinguish satyagraha from nonviolent coercion. In their view, satyagraha is not a means for coercing the opponent into particular forms of behavior; it is a way of helping them to understand the true nature of the conflict and of making them consider the moral issues anew.[168] Still others, like Naess (and in contradiction to his argument outlined above!), contend that if someone is ultimately persuaded about something, the influences leading up to the change are not, and should not be, classed as coercive.[169]

For pragmatic exponents of nonviolent action, the issue is largely irrelevant. According to James Farmer, when change by other nonviolent methods is considered unlikely, neglect of the mechanism of nonviolent coercion only creates opportunities for advocates of violence. "Where we cannot influence the heart of the evil-doer, we can force an end to the evil practice."[170]

It is evident from the above analysis that nonviolent action *might* entail the use of moral (or even economic) coercion; this, however, is incompatible with the spirit of satyagraha. Nevertheless, according to Weber, moral coercion "is always preferable to physical coercion." It is more indicative of sincerity, it is more likely to lead to conversion, and it can galvanize public support.[171]

Despite this, from the Gandhian perspective there is a clear injunction against using nonviolent power to coerce a change in the opponent. In circumstances in which activists are not yet capable of devising strategies employing exclusively noncoercive means, however, tactics involving nonviolent coercion will inevitably be considered. If the intention of this coercion is to compel the opponent's participation in a dialectical process that will satisfy the needs of all, then at least the action is within the domain of what Naess calls "more or less unavoidable weaknesses in practice"[172] and involves no direct coercion of their will.

Moreover, if, as Gandhi claims, intention is the chief ingredient in any examination of moral conduct, then nonviolent coercion may indeed be used under strict conditions. First, the compulsion must take place in circumstances in which the satyagrahi is committed to realizing the truth of the situation and in which the satyagrahi holds a deep respect for the shared humanity of the opponent (the Gandhi conditions). Second, the satyagrahi must have a clear willingness to experience self-suffering and no intention to punish the opponent or to extract revenge (the Shridharani condition). Third, the only compulsion must relate to compelling the opponent's *participation* in a problem-solving process (designed to satisfy the needs of all parties) and must not entail direct coercion of their will (the Naess condition). In these circumstances, the truth, including the opponent's true will, should be realized.

Conclusion

Gandhian satyagraha is not perfect nonviolence. "Satyagraha has been designed as an effective substitute for violence. This use is in its infancy and, therefore, not yet perfected."[173] Moreover, perfect nonviolence is not possible in a world in which life itself entails violence. "Perfect non-violence is impossible so long as we exist physically, for we would want some space at least to occupy. Perfect nonviolence whilst you are inhabiting the body is only a theory like Euclid's point or straight line, but we have to endeavour every moment of our lives."[174] And we must endeavor, Gandhi insisted, because nonviolence itself is an "eternal principle" and the shortcomings of those who practice it, or even the difficulty of doing so in this imperfect world, cannot be blamed on the principle itself.[175]

Clearly, life is not a choice between violence and no violence. It is a choice between violence and less violence; the latter sometimes expressed through the medium of nonviolence. In a political context, nonviolent struggle is about the use of power. In its Gandhian conception, nonviolence is about the use of power in a way that is both highly effective (in the sense that it can resolve conflict) *and* highly ethical (in the sense that it does not subvert the moral autonomy of the opponent). Nonviolent struggle, including those occasions requiring the use of coercion, is the most effective and ethical way of exercising political power in an imperfect world.

8

The Strategic Theory and Framework of Nonviolent Defense

In this study, a strategy of nonviolent defense is one conducted in accordance with the strategic theory and the strategic framework outlined in this chapter. The *strategic theory* has three functions: (1) to explain the nature and causes of conflict in the international system and to identify the causes of conflict in a particular situation; (2) to identify the appropriate strategic aims for dealing with a particular conflict and to guide the formulation of a strategy to achieve those aims; and (3) to provide tactical guidance within the context of this strategy. In turn, the *strategic framework* has a single function: to provide specific guidance for those planning a strategy of nonviolent defense by identifying twelve components of any strategy.

The Strategic Theory of Nonviolent Defense

The *human-needs theory* incorporated below is based on research undertaken by Paul Sites and others. The *conflict theory* is based on research linking conflict with the denial of human needs. This research has been undertaken by peace researchers such as Johan Galtung, by conflict theorists such as John Burton, and by various psychologists. The conflict theory also draws significantly on the conceptions of conflict and nonviolence developed by Mohandas K. Gandhi. The *strategic theory* outlined below is derived from three primary sources: the human-needs and conflict theories just mentioned, the strategic theory of Carl von Clausewitz, and the strategic insights of Gandhi. The evidence justifying each of the assumptions and hypotheses within these theories was presented in chapters 1 through 7.

Human-needs theory is based on four interrelated assumptions and a central hypothesis, which were discussed in chapters 4 and 5. The first assumption is that emotions evolved because they enhanced the prospects of survival. There are relatively few primary emotions—fear, anger, depression, and satisfaction (happiness)— and these appear very early in human infants of all cultures. As a direct result of being driven by these emotions, humans have a corresponding set of needs for conditions of life that reduce the negative emotional states of fear, anger, and depression and thereby permit the positive emotional state of satisfaction. The second assumption is that these human needs are innate and universal. It is not yet possible, nor necessary, to precisely define or reach general agreement on what these needs are, although most researchers agree that they include the needs for security, meaning, self-esteem, and latency. (This list might also include the needs for identity, response, recognition, stimulation, freedom, distributive justice, participation, rationality, and control, although some authors argue that these are *necessary conditions* for the satisfaction of needs, rather than needs in themselves. For the purposes of this theory, they will be treated as needs in themselves.) The third assumption is that these needs *must* be satisfied (regardless of consequences to society and self) and that individuals will identify with other individuals in pursuit of these needs. In other words, the most fundamental evolutionary force experienced by individuals is the drive to attempt to control their environment in order to satisfy their needs. The fourth assumption is that the inherent drive to satisfy these needs—irrespective of socialization, threats, or coercion—is the ultimate determinant of human behavior. The only constraint is the value attached to relationships (although *awareness* of needs can be altered by such factors as role defense, propaganda, religion, and ideology).

The central hypothesis of human-needs theory is that the frustration or denial of human needs (derived from genetically encoded emotions) leads to conflictual behaviors; if needs generally are not satisfied, then deep-rooted problems and protracted conflicts arise. Such conflict may entail policy, process, structural, and/or systemic elements. In any case, it is concerned with issues that are not negotiable: issues that relate to innate needs that cannot be compromised.

For the purposes of this theory, then, a dispute involves incompatibility in a goal-seeking system in which the goals at stake—interests and values—are negotiable. And conflict involves incompatibility in a goal-seeking system in which the goals at stake—fundamental human needs—are not negotiable.

The *conflict theory* outlined here accepts the assumptions and hypothesis of human-needs theory. In turn, it postulates two principal hypotheses that are derived from arguments presented in chapters 5 and 7. First, the satisfaction of human needs will resolve conflict. According to this hypothesis, all disputes and some conflicts can be resolved to the satisfaction of all parties within the framework of prevailing structures and systems. However, given the inadequacy of many methods for dealing with conflict within the dominant social cosmology, these conflicts require processes that are interactive, analytical, and problem-solving in approach. In these cases, conflict resolution might require only changes in policies and/or processes as well as efforts to promote conditions in which collaborative and valued relationships control behaviors. However, some conflicts cannot be resolved within the framework of prevailing structures and/or systems. Their resolution requires an approach in which steps are taken to remove the structural and systemic causes of the conflict. This can also occur as a result of participation in a facilitated problem-solving process.

The second hypothesis of the conflict theory outlined here is derived from the Gandhian conception of nonviolence discussed in chapter 7. In those circumstances in which one or more parties will not participate in a problem-solving process, nonviolent action (with a Gandhian orientation) is the most effective means of compelling their participation in a way that is also consistent with the intention of satisfying the needs of all parties. Nonviolent action, used for this purpose, must satisfy three conditions: The action must take place in circumstances in which the activist(s) hold a deep respect for the shared humanity of the opponent; the activist(s) must have a clear willingness to experience self-suffering and no intention to punish the opponent; and any coercion must be limited to compelling the opponent's participation in a problem-solving process.

This hypothesis is based on three assumptions that also were discussed in chapter 7. First, it assumes that the means used to deal with conflict shape the end produced. For example, the use of violence (which negates the needs for self-esteem and security among others) cannot satisfy human needs; consequently, it cannot resolve conflict. Means and end are one. For that reason, correcting negative attitudes held toward the opponent and eliminating behavioral patterns that tend to isolate the opponent are important elements of the means. This assumption reflects the related Gandhian notions that conflict provides an excellent opportunity for conflicting parties to develop their relationship and that conflict resolution requires a high level of positive interaction between them. This interaction, in turn, will help to improve understanding, develop empathy, correct misperceptions, and minimize the impact of "nonrational" emotions. Second, this hypothesis assumes the unity of all life. If human needs are to be satisfied, the needs of all living beings must also be satisfied. Otherwise, deep-rooted problems and conflicts (including degradation of the ecosphere and loss of biodiversity) cannot be resolved. Third, this hypothesis assumes that the willingness to undergo self-suffering is, independently of its other functional attributes, the most credible demonstration of the commitment to satisfying the needs of the opponent.

The *strategic theory* outlined here accepts all of the assumptions and hypotheses of both human-needs theory and conflict theory identified above. In addition, it makes five further assumptions justified by the arguments presented in chapters 4, 5, and 6: (1) that the cause of international conflict is the result of policies, processes, structures, and/or systems that deny the satisfaction of human needs in a national context; (2) that these policies, processes, structures, and systems are actively supported by national elites; (3) that, in some circumstances, national elites will use military violence to defend these policies, processes, structures, and systems; (4) that the most relevant units of analysis in protracted international conflict are ethnic, cultural, religious, class, and other identity groups, rather than nation-states; and (5) that progress toward peace, security, and stability in the world system is dependent on steps that create decentralized structures that serve the psychological, economic, and relational needs of all individuals and groups within society.

Three hypotheses are derived from these assumptions, the conflict theory outlined above, and the arguments presented in chapters 5, 6 and 7. The fundamental hypothesis is that nonviolent action (with a Gandhian orientation) and problem-solving processes are the only methods for dealing with deep-rooted conflict (including military violence) that can reliably satisfy unmet human needs. This is because the strategic means used will shape the end gained. The second hypothesis is that any strategy for dealing creatively with conflict in the international system must, *as its central feature*, undermine the structural and systemic causes of that conflict—including manifestations of patriarchy, statism, capitalism, socialism, imperialism, and colonialism. The third hypothesis is that because of the human needs for self-esteem, participation, and control, among others, any strategy for resolving conflict must actively involve all individuals and identity groups directly concerned.

In circumstances in which conflict erupts in the form of military aggression (in this theory, *military aggression* is a general term that refers to all forms of military intervention and military repression), the strategic theory outlined here incorporates four elements of Clausewitzian theory (although each of them is given a new interpretation) that were identified and discussed in chapter 1: the premise that strategy is an extension of society and policy (and the derivative notion that the strategic aim should displace the political object), the principle of the superiority of the defense over the offense, the insight that the capacity for resistance is the product of power and will, and the concept of the center of gravity. This theory also incorporates several insights derived from Gandhi.

According to Clausewitz, strategy is an extension of society and policy. However, this theory assumes that a society's social cosmology includes its pattern of matter-energy use, its social relations, its philosophy of society, and its strategies for dealing with conflict and that each of these components *helps to shape*, as well as reflects, the social cosmology in which it evolves. It also assumes that to be functional in the long term, each component of a social cosmology must be oriented to the satisfaction of human needs. Consequently, even in response to an act of military aggression, policy should identify a strategy that will reliably satisfy those needs.

The superiority of the defense over the attack derives largely from the power to choose the *type* of defense that is conducted; it does not mean that the best defense strategy will be chosen, that the defense is invincible, or that the defense enjoys a great advantage "in the field." According to Clausewitz, it is the choice of the type of defense that *determines* the center of gravity. In contrast, the conception of the center of gravity developed for this theory (which, as described below, is the same for all parties) is independent of the type of defense chosen. Thus, it is a hypothesis of this theory that the superiority of the defense derives from the power to choose the type of defense (irrespective of the nature of the act of aggression) that will most effectively defend the center of gravity. A wise choice in this regard can be a decisive strategic advantage in itself.

In the narrowly strategic sense, power is the capacity *to conduct* or *to resist* aggression, and will is the inclination to do so (in response to the drive to satisfy human needs). In some cases, one of these factors can be decisive. For example, if the will to conduct an act of aggression is altered (by satisfying needs), then the power to conduct it is irrelevant. Conversely, if the power to conduct an act of aggression is removed, then the will to conduct it is immaterial (which is not to say that the unmet needs driving this will should be ignored). Significantly, then, and in contrast to military strategists generally, this strategic theory rejects the belief that power alone is determinative. It is a hypothesis of this theory that will and power are both important and that, depending on the circumstances, it might be sufficient to alter one of these factors or it might be necessary to alter both.

Though conflict (including war) is characterized by strategic polarity (incompatibility of strategic aims), it is an assumption of this theory that there is always an underlying (but invariably unrealized) political symmetry in the shared desire to satisfy human needs. Thus, in conditions of strategic polarity in which the opponent elite uses military aggression, while their strategic aim must be resisted, their political purpose (as an expression of human needs) must ultimately be addressed.

Consequently, the *political purpose* ("what you want") of resisting military aggression is to create the policy, process, structural, and systemic conditions that will satisfy human needs. This, in fact, is what "peace and security" means, whether for one party or for all. In practice, the political purpose might be expressed in the form of a political program or as a list of demands.

In turn, the *two strategic aims* ("how you get what you want") are as follows. The strategic aim of the defense is to consolidate the power and will of the defending population to resist the aggression. The strategic aim of the counteroffensive is to *alter* the will of the opponent elite to conduct the aggression—in favor of their participation in a problem-solving process that will create the conditions necessary to satisfy human needs—and to *undermine* their power to do so. In practice, the strategic aims might be achieved via a series of intermediate strategic goals.

According to one hypothesis, then, the opponent elite may be induced to participate in a problem-solving process by successfully identifying their unmet needs (for example, their needs for self-esteem, security, justice, and participation) and by offering a bracket of specific satisfiers that will meet those needs. (Of course, their perception of these needs can be distorted by such factors as role defense, propaganda, religion, and ideology, and this must be taken into consideration when planning the defense.) This might *alter their will* to conduct the aggression.

According to another hypothesis, the opponent elite might be nonviolently coerced to participate by conducting a series of strategically focused campaigns of nonviolent action that are *directed at their center of gravity*. This will *undermine their power* to conduct the aggression.

For each party in conflict, there is a specific center of gravity—a center of power on which the entire defense effort depends. In contrast to Clausewitz's position on this point, this theory accepts the argument of Alexander Atkinson that was presented in chapter 1 and that is consistent with the insights of guerrilla theorists, and authors such as Michael Howard and Andrew Mack, that were discussed in chapter 2. According to this hypothesis, the strategic center of gravity is the same for all parties: It is the finite pool of social resources that support their strategy.[1] This conception of the center of gravity is consistent with the modified consent theory of power that was outlined in chapter 6; that is, it identifies the support of people within the society of the opponent elite and, in some circumstances, the support of people within the society of the opponent elite's allies (rather than the cooperation of the victims of aggression themselves) as the vital sources of power that must be undermined.[2]

In those circumstances in which the will of the defense or the opponent elite cannot be altered directly, the center of gravity becomes critical for each party. Moreover, it defines which weapons are useful and which ones are useless. Therefore, if their strategy is to have a chance of being successful, the opponent elite must correctly identify the center of gravity of the defense (that is, the social groups that support the defense strategy) and then "attack" it with the appropriate "weapons." For the same reason, the defense must mobilize to defend it. This means that the defense must aim to mobilize key social groups to participate in the strategy of nonviolent defense.

Similarly, in those circumstances in which the will of the opponent elite cannot be altered directly, the strategic counteroffensive by the defense should be directed at their center of gravity and it should employ the most relevant and effective "weapons." That is, the defense should precisely identify the key social groups (within and outside the society in question) whose support is necessary for the opponent elite to conduct the aggression. Then, the strategic counteroffensive should specifically endeavor to alter the will of these groups (usually, but not always, including their armed forces) to support it. Given the complexity of most conflict formations, this might require the organization of specific campaigns as part of a protracted defense struggle.

In addition, good strategy requires wise use of the relevant weapons. If the opponent elite fails to recognize that the support of key social groups for the strategy of nonviolent defense is the ultimate target of their aggression, then their use of inappropriate weapons may consolidate the defense rather than help to destroy it. Similarly, from the perspective of the nonviolent defense, each campaign of the counteroffensive should employ a strategically selected combination of nonviolent tactics, as well as other means (including various forms of dialogue), that are designed to undermine support for the opponent elite's aggression.

The Strategic Framework of Nonviolent Defense

Using the strategic theory outlined above, together with insights derived from an analysis of Gandhi's campaigns of nonviolent struggle, it is possible to identify twelve components of a strategic framework that can be used to plan a strategy of nonviolent defense:

1. The political and strategic assessment
2. The political purpose (which may be derived from the strategic theory outlined above) and the list of specific political demands of the defense
3. The twin strategic aims (which may be derived from the strategic theory outlined above) and the set of intermediate stra-

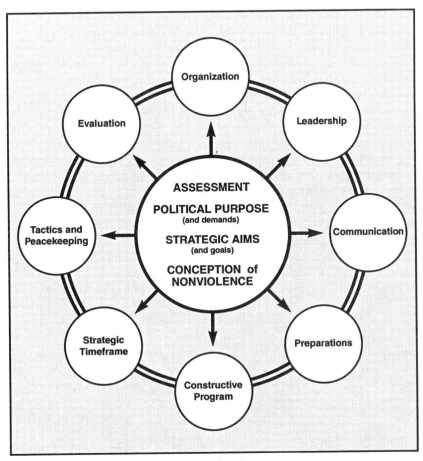

Figure 4. Nonviolent Strategy Wheel

tegic goals that will guide the individual campaigns of both the defense and the strategic counteroffensive

4. The conception of nonviolence that the defense will utilize
5. The organizational framework, including the decision-making structure and process
6. The leadership structure and the process that will be used to ensure the maintenance of effective strategic coordination
7. The nature of the communications systems and the style of communication that will be used internally, with the opponent, and with third parties

8. The advance preparations
9. The key elements of the constructive program
10. The strategic timeframe, stages, and campaigns of the defense
11. The strategic considerations in relation to the selection, organization, and application of nonviolent tactics, as well as peacekeeping
12. The procedures for ongoing evaluation of the strategy

The strategic framework can be presented in the form of a nonviolent strategy wheel[3] as in figure 4. This diagram highlights the importance of the political and strategic guidance provided by the first four items listed in the strategic framework.

Conclusion

The strategic theory and the strategic framework outlined in this chapter can be used to plan a strategy of nonviolent defense. This strategy can be adapted for resisting military intervention or repression in all its forms. The theory and components of a strategy of nonviolent defense will be discussed and illustrated in chapters 10 through 13. Chapter 9 will consider the nature of a security policy that is oriented to the satisfaction of human needs.

9

The Search for Security

Unlike the concepts of conflict and power, the concept of security has not generated an extensive and multidisciplinary literature of its own. This fact, coupled with the realist orientation within the dominant social cosmology, has led to a conception of security, and an approach to it, that is extremely narrow. Within the discipline of international relations, for instance, security has long been defined in terms of the policy and strategic interests of national elites. For example, in one frequently cited definition, Walter Lippmann argues that a nation has security insofar as it does not have to sacrifice its legitimate interests in order to avoid war and is able, if necessary, to defend those interests by resort to war.[1] The international relations literature is replete with definitions and discussions of security in terms such as these.

Despite claims of a shift to a more inclusive conception, the recent literature on security within this discipline has retained its state-centric and military orientations as well as its focus on the interests and value norms of national elites.[2] This is the case in respect to most of the recent literature on "alternative" defense as well, including that which describes territorial defense[3] and nonoffensive defense.[4] Despite its widespread use, this notion of security is now under serious challenge from authors outside the international relations community because it actually ignores the security needs of ordinary people. Most obviously, it ignores the needs of women, indigenous peoples, Africans, Asians, and Central/South Americans. It also ignores the needs of nonhuman species and the environment. For these constituencies, the failure to identify their security needs leads to two further problems: It makes it possible to ignore the structural causes of their insecurity, and it diverts attention from the need to develop responses that address these structural causes.

Despite recent developments in the notion of security, there is still room for improvement. The next four sections offer brief discussions intended to identify the sources of insecurity and the perspective of security of four important constituencies that are usually ignored.[5] Although these perspectives are only outlined—and space prevents the full consideration of all arguments pro and con—they will provide the basis for defining a conception of security that is highly inclusive.

Feminist Perspectives on Security

According to human-needs theory, security for individual women requires the satisfaction of their needs, including their needs for self-esteem, participation, stimulation, distributive justice, and control. More fundamentally, it requires a set of social structures that facilitate the satisfaction of those needs. In such circumstances, the obvious question is this: Can the needs of women be meaningfully satisfied within the structures of patriarchal society? This section describes the perspective of security offered by a selection of authors who are widely considered to represent central elements of feminist thought.[6]

While not the first woman to identify or resist patriarchal society, Mary Wollstonecraft was the first feminist author to systematically expose "the tyranny of man." Rejecting the "nonsense" of Rousseau and other prominent male thinkers of her time, Wollstonecraft argued that "the grand end" of a woman's efforts should be the development of her own faculties—not the cultivation of qualities designed to please men. This, she noted, was exceptionally difficult, given the subjugation of women since "the remotest antiquity."[7]

Since Wollstonecraft, many feminist authors have identified patriarchy as the principal source of women's oppression. According to Simone de Beauvoir, patriarchal society compels women to occupy a subordinate position to men. It denies women dignity and autonomy.[8] In the view of Marilyn French, patriarchal culture controls women and attempts to control everything they produce.[9] For

Rosalind Miles, the social and mental systems of patriarchy deny women their most fundamental human needs: their freedom, autonomy, and control, including the "basic right of control over their own bodies."[10] In these circumstances, Barbara Zanotti concludes, life for women is found "only outside the patriarchy."[11]

There is now an extensive body of literature demonstrating that patriarchy impedes the satisfaction of human needs, and particularly the needs of women. This is because, according to Kate Millett, patriarchy is both a political institution and a system of power for perpetuating male domination.[12] In these circumstances, it is virtually impossible for women to fully satisfy their needs. For example, patriarchal cultural practices (such as marriage) have been used to deny women their need for a complete and independent identity, patriarchal governments have been used to deny women their need to participate in the decisions that affect their lives, patriarchal economic relations have been used to deny women their need for distributive justice, and patriarchal laws have been used to deny women their need for control, including their need—separately from their right—for control over their own bodies. Moreover, given the ways in which patriarchy sanctions the use of violence against women,[13] patriarchal social relations have been used to deny women their need for personal security.

It is a central tenet of feminist analysis that mainstream institutions reinforce patriarchal values and practices. Religion, for example, plays a key role. Christianity, Judaism, and Islam all reinforce the patriarchal domination of women and nature. For that reason, many feminists would argue, we need a return to the nature-based spirituality of our ancestral past. We must reconceive the sacred as immanent (something "within us") rather than transcendental (something "outside us"). In fact, this conception of the sacred is central to the feminist spirituality movement that practices the ancient religion of Witchcraft. The three core principles of Witchcraft, Starhawk asserts, are immanence, interconnection, and community. Immanence means that we are each a manifestation of the Goddess; it calls on each one of us to live our spirituality here in this world and to live with integrity and responsibility. Interconnection is the realization that all being is related; we are parts of one living organism. And this type of spirituality is lived in community, a community that includes not just our personal friends but everything in our bioregion and, ultimately, the whole Earth.[14]

Recognizing the impact of patriarchy on women's lives, much feminist literature has drawn attention to a conception of security that is meaningful for women. This conception of security requires, among other things, the creation of a nonpatriarchal society and measures improvements in women's security in terms of the steps taken to achieve this. According to Millett, social change is meaningless if it has no effect upon patriarchy.[15] And in Starhawk's view, true social change can occur only "when the [patriarchal] myths and symbols of our culture are themselves changed."[16]

Indigenous Peoples' Perspectives on Security

Despite the lack of a clear-cut consensus regarding an appropriate designation, the expression *indigenous peoples* is the name most widely accepted by the peoples themselves. And despite the lack of an agreed definition, indigenous peoples are widely regarded as those who are descendants of the original inhabitants of a territory that was conquered (and is now occupied by an alien and dominant culture) or they are nomadic and seminomadic peoples. They have the characteristics of a national minority, no centralized political institutions, and, most importantly, a different worldview. This worldview includes a custodial and nonmaterialist attitude to the land and natural resources.[17] This section discusses the worldview and perspectives on security characteristic of indigenous peoples.

A study of their traditional knowledge of the natural world reveals that indigenous peoples have a profound understanding of the shared origins of all life, the integrity of ecological systems, and the ancient bonds of kinship between human beings and nonhuman species.[18] In the words of the Lakota shaman Black Elk, "we are related to everything that exists."[19] This knowledge highlights the fundamental relationship between life and land and illuminates the cyclic processes of nature. It also provides warning of the damaging, long-term consequences of human greed, arrogance, and neglect.[20] According to the Brundtland Commission, indigenous peoples have accumulated a vast amount of knowledge and experience that links humanity with its ancient origins and that enables them to sustainably manage complex ecological systems. In fact, their very survival has depended on their ecological sensitivity.[21] For example, the !Kung people of southern Africa have accumulated such an extraordinarily detailed understanding of their natural surroundings that, despite their desert environment and a high proportion of dependent members, the adults hunt or gather plenty of food by each devoting just fifteen hours to the task each week; this leaves considerable time for leisure and spiritual activities. And the Kayapo of Amazonia use a variety of ingenious strategies to more effectively utilize the food and materials available in the rainforest. For instance, to facilitate their highly mobile lifestyle, the Kayapo plant hardy varieties of food and medicinal plants along their extensive network of trails.[22]

It is probably their relationship to the land that most clearly distinguishes indigenous peoples from nonindigenous societies. For that reason, the struggle of indigenous peoples has always focused on the land. It is the source of their (spiritual and cultural) identity and their economic survival.[23] According to the Sioux Mary Crow Dog: "The fight for our land is at the core of our existence. . . . Once the land is gone, then we are gone too."[24] Moreover, for indigenous peoples, land has a sacred quality.

> The Earth is the foundation of Indigenous Peoples. It is the seat of spirituality, the fountain from which our cultures and languages flourish. The Earth is our historian, the keeper of events and the bones of our [ancestors]. Earth provides us food, medicine, shelter and clothing. It is the source of our independence. . . . We do not dominate Her: we must harmonize with Her.[25]

The struggle for security by indigenous peoples is a struggle to satisfy their needs for identity, justice, participation, and control (among others) in circumstances characterized by their domination by powerful external forces. Brief descriptions of the struggle by two indigenous peoples will give some indication of the variety of circumstances in which this domination may occur.

In Australia, Aboriginal people were systematically murdered or displaced following the continent's invasion and occupation by the British. Like indigenous peoples everywhere, Marcia Langton stresses the spiritual significance and economic importance of the land and the maritime environments for Aboriginal people in Australia. In her view, the immediate security risk to Australia's indigenous people stems from the Australian government's continuing refusal to ensure that all Aboriginal communities have secure land tenure and proper access to the resources necessary to satisfy their physical needs. In addition, some northern Aboriginal communities are aware of the potential threat to their security should the Australian government decide to pressure Aboriginal land councils into agreeing to the establishment of military facilities on land already controlled by Aboriginal people. To resist could jeopardize future land rights claims. To accede would put pressure on Aboriginal people to support militarism against their will, and, Langton argues, given the Australian government's cooperation with the United States and the demonstrated willingness of both governments to intervene militarily, this could compromise Aboriginal solidarity with other indigenous peoples in the Asia-Pacific region.[26] Security for the Aboriginal people of Australia involves recognition of their sovereignty and their distinctive spiritual and cultural identities as well as their right to self-determination and economic self-reliance.

In the Malaysian state of Sarawak, the Dayak natives have long practiced a form of shifting cultivation—an economic activity full of deep social and spiritual significance—which is ecologically sustainable in tropical forest conditions. They have also developed a sophisticated social system centered on the longhouse and guided by customary law, which reflects their deep respect for the land and its resources. However, these traditional cultures are now rapidly disintegrating under the combined pressures of the "development" being imposed on them by the Malaysian state and the insatiable demands of multinational corporations (especially from Japan) for the commercially valuable timber in the rainforests of their ancestral lands. In addition, the rainforest ecology is being systematically destroyed.[27] Security for the natives of Sarawak involves recognition of their right to live on their traditional lands without interference by the Malaysian state and imperial interests.

As these examples illustrate, for indigenous peoples the connection between their relationship with the local environment and their security is profound. The point, according to the Brundtland Commission, is that security for indigenous peoples begins with the recognition of their need for land and the other resources that sustain their traditional way of life. For that reason, security includes recognition of their traditional rights, measures to protect indigenous institutions that regulate resource use in harmony with nature, and processes to ensure meaningful participation by indigenous peoples in the decisions that affect their lives.[28] For indigenous peoples, land is the principal means of satisfying their needs for identity, justice, participation, and control.

The South's Perspective on Security

Until the 1960s the conventional development strategy that is being followed by the "developing" nations was not widely questioned in the West. This strategy assumes that by accelerating the rate of economic growth, higher levels of national wealth will be generated and that enough of this will "trickle down" to raise the living standards of all. This approach to "development" is still widely endorsed by elites such as those represented by the Brundtland Commission.[29] The *experience* since World War II, of course, is that this strategy—and the "modernization" or economic rationalist theory that underpins it—is fundamentally flawed: Though growth in terms of economic output has undoubtedly occurred, this strategy has facilitated the exploitation of vast numbers of people (as well as nonhuman species and the environment) and led to unprecedented levels of indebtedness on the part of developing nations.[30] It has also led to the death, through systematic starvation, of millions of African, Asian, and Central/South American people.[31] This section will briefly identify the principal causes of underdevelopment and then use this information as a basis for offering a perspective on security that is meaningful for those people in the South for whom "development" has so far meant dispossession and starvation.

Critiques of "underdevelopment" date back to the nineteenth century, but most of the now huge literature on this subject has been written since 1960. This literature includes the major critique, offered in various forms, by the dependency (later called "neo-Marxist") theorists.[32] Insofar as its exponents have offered an alternative model of development, this critique offers some valuable insights, but its exponents share the capitalist commitment to at least one major cause of underdevelopment and ecological imbalance: *indiscriminate* economic growth. Recognition of this fact led some authors to formulate "development" theories that incorporated an ecological perspective as well. These include the theories formulated by advocates of the steady-state economy[33] and the more recent bioregional economy.[34]

While the diverse development literature offers some complicated and technical explanations of underdevelopment, there is
still no consensus regarding its causes among the various schools of
thought. Nevertheless, without oversimplifying an extremely complex problem, it is possible to offer a clear and plausible explanation of underdevelopment derived from this literature. According to
Johan Galtung, as explained at greater length in chapter 5, the
structural nature of imperial relations between the North and the
South facilitates the former's exploitation of the latter.[35] The key to
this exploitation, he argues, is the vertical division of labor. This
means that when products traded are ranked in terms of their
degree of processing (the amounts of capital, research, technology,
and management, as opposed to the amounts of raw materials and
unskilled labor, that go into the products) and in terms of the challenges built into the task of creating them, the countries of the
North get much more positive spin-off effects, including value
added, than do the countries of the South.[36]

    Another way to illustrate the causes of underdevelopment
(bypassing much of the sophistication, and complexity, inherent in
the explanation touched on above) is to focus attention on the way
market forces work: That is, what happens when access to commod-
ities is decided by who can pay the most? And what happens when
investment decisions are based on profitability rather than the satisfaction of human needs? According to Ted Trainer, markets have
an overwhelming tendency *"to make the wrong development and distribution decisions."* This occurs for two main reasons. First, because
the market allows rich countries to outbid poor countries, it has
ensured that when goods become scarce only the rich can buy
them.[37] In the words of Barbara Ward: "Markets as masters of society enrich the rich and pauperize the poor."[38] Moreover, as Mahbub ul Haq has illustrated, unlike developed societies, in which
there are usually pressures and mechanisms for the redistribution
of income and wealth (for example, through public ownership, tax-
ation, and welfare payments), in the international economy and in
many "developing" countries there are no such factors at work. In
these circumstances, the market ensures that poor countries and
poor people cannot buy what they need.[39] And second, market
forces have skewed "development" in the wrong direction. Instead
of developing clean water supplies, locally required foodstuffs,
appropriate technologies, rural health clinics, local education programs, and cheap housing, market forces have geared most of the

world's productive capacity to the demands of Western consumers rather than the needs of local people. Driven by the desire to maximize their profits, for example, multinational corporations have taken over vast tracts of land in Africa, Asia, and Central/South America in order to produce cash crops (such as coffee) for export. The core problem, Trainer argues, is not lack of development; it is inappropriate development. There is a direct contradiction between what is most profitable and what is most needed. In addition, he notes, because the market itself is not entirely "free," powerful actors such as governments and corporations are often able to manipulate or override market conditions and to directly influence the type and direction of development.[40] In other words, markets allow powerful actors to exercise disproportionate influence. For instance, as Susan George has documented, because the United States has cornered the world food market, it now uses food as a weapon of political and economic control.[41]

Whatever the preferred explanation for the underdevelopment of the South, it is a direct result of the structural exploitation (which occurs in many forms) inherent in the mechanisms of capitalism. However, it would be naive to think that capitalism operates independently of political processes; clearly it does not. Therefore, it is important to identify the fact that these structures of exploitation thrive as a direct result of the political decision by certain national elites to support capitalism and to actively and systematically destroy alternative economic systems. This support stems directly from elite awareness that the structures of capitalism serve their own interests best. This is evident in the work of the Trilateral Commission—one of the more prominent efforts to facilitate elite cooperation for the purposes of world management. According to Holly Sklar, the commission's purpose "is to engineer an enduring partnership among the ruling classes of North America, Western Europe, and Japan . . . in order to safeguard the interests of Western capitalism."[42] As Edward Herman more bluntly explains this point, there is "a huge tacit conspiracy" between Western governments and multinational corporations, on the one hand, and local business and military cliques in the developing nations, on the other, "to assume complete control of these countries and 'develop' them on a joint venture basis." Nevertheless, it is not necessary to resort to conspiracy theories in order to explain this exploitation: It flows directly from the structures, values, and relationships that are characteristic of the dominant social cosmology.[43]

In essence, the conventional development strategy subverts the struggle for security in two related ways: It accepts the structural exploitation generated by capitalism, and it requires imperial elites in the industrial countries to defend these structures of exploitation by using terror and violence to crush dissent in the developing nations. This can be achieved by supplying client regimes with repression technologies,[44] through covert operations (including coups) organized by such bodies as the Central Intelligence Agency (CIA), or, when necessary, through direct military intervention by the imperial nation itself (usually to defend or install a client regime).[45] A principal purpose of such intervention, as noted above, is to ensure that alternative, noncapitalist approaches to development fail. As Noam Chomsky has observed, the smaller and weaker countries (like Grenada and Nicaragua) are the most dangerous in this regard. If an impoverished nation can begin to utilize its own limited resources to undertake development geared to the needs of its people, then more important developing countries might follow suit, thus denying corporations in the major capitalist economies unimpeded access to the world's resources.[46]

The above discussion suggests that security for people of the South requires the restoration of political processes that allow decisions about the production and distribution of resources to be made by the people themselves (rather than local or foreign elites) in accordance with their needs for participation, distributive justice, and control. According to Amechi Okolo, this will require the political and economic restructuring of developing societies in ways that respect indigenous identities and traditions.[47] It will also require the redistribution of productive capacity, and especially land,[48] in order to enhance their capacity to achieve self-reliance. And it will require a strategy that will enable developing societies to defend their security against local and imperial elites that are militarily powerful.

The Deep Ecological Perspective on Security

Since Rachel Carson first succeeded in drawing widespread public attention to the increasingly devastating impact that humans are having on the planetary environment[49] and the Club of Rome published its reports on the limits to growth,[50] there has been a steady increase in the level of public concern with issues of "ecological security." This concern has developed at two levels, first identified by Arne Naess. At the superficial level, the "shallow ecology" movement has retained a human-centered concern that pollution and resource depletion should not adversely affect the quality of human life.[51] More profoundly, the "deep ecology" movement has rejected a concern for the environment based on human interests only; it has adopted a holistic view that venerates all forms of life for their own sake.[52] In order to provide a nonhuman-centered outlook on security, which might offer insights that enhance the conception of security being developed in this chapter, let us consider the deep ecology perspective.

Modern biological research, David Suzuki notes, is based on the knowledge that organisms have a shared evolutionary history. Despite that shared history, uncontrolled human activity (such as rainforest destruction) has multiplied the rate of species extinctions. In addition, and quite deliberately, vast numbers of animals and insects are exploited in painful research designed to benefit human individuals while millions of farm animals are killed annually for human consumption. These troubling facts raise the important question of where humans fit into the natural world.[53] For those with a deep ecological perspective, the answer is simple. In the words of Aldo Leopold, the human species is a "plain member" of the biotic community.[54] And for animal rights activists such as Peter Singer, all species deserve *equal consideration*.[55] From the perspective of deep ecology,[56] then, humans are physically, biologically, and spiritually *part of* the Earth; they are neither separate from it nor superior to it.

This holistic perspective is vitally important, given the range of human-induced ecological crises that are destroying global security. The destruction of old-growth forests, the emission of carbon dioxide and chlorofluorocarbons, the depletion of the ozone layer, the release of radioactive and toxic wastes, soil degradation, and the exploitation of the oceans constitute an ongoing assault on ecological systems that has already driven countless life-forms to extinction.

In her discussion of ecological security, Patricia Mische draws attention to the dangers of the homocentric view of security, including the elite practice of conceiving it in terms of state sovereignty. In her view, this impedes the realization of global security, because *"the sovereignty of the Earth is indivisible."* The Earth, she observes, is an ecological whole consisting of interactive ecosystems and bioregions.[57] This view is endorsed by James Lovelock, who has gone one step further in suggesting the Gaia hypothesis. According to Lovelock, the Gaia hypothesis contends that all life on Earth, from whales to viruses, "could be regarded as constituting a single living entity" that is capable of manipulating the Earth's physical environment to suit its needs. Gaia is thus defined as a complex entity involving the Earth's biosphere, atmosphere, oceans, and soil that seeks an optimal physical and chemical environment for maintaining life. The Gaia hypothesis has not yet been proven, but Lovelock claims that it has already led to some valuable insights.[58]

The deep ecological worldview is comprehensive: It includes the whole Earth and all its species, and is intergenerational. In addition, it includes biological, psychological, philosophical, cultural, political, economic, and spiritual dimensions. To achieve security in the ecological sense, Mische argues, we must live with "consciousness and intentionality," given our responsibility for the future.[59] This requires, among other things, a development strategy that rejects indiscriminate economic growth, particularly in the industrialized North. Given the ecological limits to growth, which are now well documented, further growth would exacerbate the enormous and increasing damage that is already being done to the Earth's ecosystems by the high levels of production and consumption characteristic of industrial economies. But given the level of underdevelopment in the South, is an ecologically sustainable development strategy possible?

The empirical evidence accumulated since 1960 suggests that it is not possible to solve the problems associated with underdevelopment and environmental exploitation within the framework of the dominant social cosmology. This is because the pattern of matter-energy use characteristic of the dominant cosmology is unsustainable; and it is important to understand why. According to the first law of thermodynamics, energy cannot be created or destroyed; it can only be transformed. According to the second law, the amount of *available* energy (that which can be used) is always decreasing. Given that the basis of all life on Earth is energy—ultimately derived from the Sun—the shape, form, and movement of everything that exists is only "an embodiment of the various concentrations and transformations of energy."[60] On Earth, there are only two sources of available energy—the terrestrial stock and the solar flow—both of which are limited. The terrestrial stock is of two types: those resources (such as topsoil) that are renewable on a human time scale and those resources (such as fossil fuels) that are renewable only over geological time. For human purposes, resources in the latter category must be treated as nonrenewable.[61] In essence, then, the pattern of matter-energy use that helped to shape (and forms part of) the dominant social cosmology is unsustainable, because it relies on nonrenewable sources ("geological capital") such as fossil fuels. Moreover, despite claims to the contrary, the consequences of this reliance cannot be ameliorated by technology or any other factor.[62]

But it is not just the pattern of matter-energy use within the dominant social cosmology that impedes any shift to ecologically sustainable development. As argued throughout this study, the components of a social cosmology are mutually reinforcing. Thus, for example, the philosophy that prevails within the dominant social cosmology—a philosophy characterized by a "scientific" outlook that emphasizes a mechanistic understanding of the universe, a view of life as a competitive struggle for existence, and a belief in unlimited material growth—sanctions the ruthless exploitation of nature. And while this philosophy has several sources, many authors have drawn attention to the importance of religion, and particularly Christianity, in shaping its essentially Western worldview and its arrogant attitude toward nature. According to Lynn White, for instance, Christianity is homocentric. Its biblical texts and its historical practice have sanctioned human domination and exploitation of nature.[63] Similarly, within the dominant social cosmology, the prevailing social structures function in ways that exploit people and nature. For example, given its drive to maximize profits at the expense of human needs, its drive to overproduce and waste at the expense of the planetary ecology, and its drive toward global economic integration (which will make the fate of every household dependent upon the few gigantic players at the center), capitalism is a singularly inappropriate form of economic system.[64]

In any case, according to an increasing number of activists and theorists, any shift to a cosmology that is oriented to the satisfaction of human and planetary needs requires higher degrees of economic self-reliance and ecological sustainability at the household, community, and bioregional levels. This will require a change to different types of economies and a shift to significantly lower levels of economic activity, which of course will require most people in the industrialized countries to adopt a simpler material lifestyle while providing new opportunities to explore the possibilities of spiritual and cultural fulfillment.[65] Under what circumstances might human communities prosper without destroying the ecological integrity of the planet itself?

According to Kirkpatrick Sale, a bioregion is a part of the Earth's surface that is defined by distinctive natural features. These features include the flora, fauna, water, climate, soils, and landforms as well as the human settlements and cultures based on them. From an ecological perspective, human society, and particularly its economics and politics, should be based on the bioregion. A bioregional economy would seek to maintain rather than exploit the natural world. It would use and recycle the natural resources within the bioregion for energy, food, shelter, clothing, art, and manufacture in order to maintain balance and self-sufficiency.[66] For example, there would be more, but much smaller, cities. These "ecocities" would be characterized by communally owned property and community-controlled production; the existence of small urban forests, meadows, ponds, and orchards; the use of appropriate and decentralized energy and transport technologies; highly self-sufficient food production based on sustainable agricultural practices such as permaculture; and an emphasis on leisure and cultural activity.[67] Similarly, bioregional politics would reflect the scale, decentralization, and diversity of nature and the particular needs of local human communities.

It is worth stressing that the bioregional approach to economics and politics implicitly recognizes two historical realities: It acknowledges the success of traditional village life in satisfying human needs in ways that were ecologically sustainable; and it acknowledges the fact that, historically, not only have identity groups satisfied the needs of their individual members within the context of a distinctive cultural tradition, but each of these traditions has been shaped by its long, intimate, and knowledgeable association with a particular bioregion and its history.[68] This is useful experience on which to build contemporary approaches to human community that are ecologically (and economically) secure.

The deep ecological perspective on security is based on the twin principles that all things are connected through cyclical processes and that nature is active and alive.[69] For nonhuman species, security will require recognition of these principles by their human counterparts. As Theodore Roszak puts it, "The needs of the planet and the needs of the person have become one."[70] In practical terms, ecological security will require strict adherence to Leopold's famous "golden rule" of ecology: "A thing is right when it tends to preserve the integrity, stability, and beauty of the biotic community. It is wrong when it tends otherwise."[71]

Cooperative Security

In contrast to the conception of security that prevails within the dominant social cosmology, the discussion above illustrates that feminists, indigenous peoples, theorists about the South, and deep ecologists share elements of a conception of security that better serves the interests of both ordinary people and nonhuman species. In fact, given the single constituency these perspectives collectively represent (all living beings), there is little doubt that ordinary people should reject the elite perspective on security in favor of a radically new conception of it. This section defines a new conception of security and identifies (without elaboration) the key elements of a security policy that will help to achieve it.

The conception of security adopted for the remainder of this study is consistent with the human-needs theory discussed in chapter 4 and the four perspectives on security discussed above. Security, then, is a condition of certainty regarding the ongoing viability of the ecological, political, economic, social, and psychological circumstances necessary for all individuals and identity groups, as well as the Earth and all its species, to satisfy their needs, to live in harmony, and to survive indefinitely.[72] The term *cooperative security* is used to describe this particular conception of security. Decisions about security are decisions about policy. It is within the context of security policy that defense strategy is decided.

Given this conception of security, what should security policy entail? Consistent with the argument developed throughout this study, the security policy outlined below is intended to identify key steps that need to be taken to establish new patterns of matter-energy use, new sets of social relations, new philosophies of society, and new strategies for dealing with conflict that are normatively oriented to the satisfaction of human and planetary needs.

Given the structural factors and elite interests that impede the realization of security, this policy must provide guidance for enhancing security in ways that take these impediments into account. Consequently, the security policy outlined below is designed to systematically undermine structures of exploitation and the vested interests of national elites. It is intended to inform and guide the efforts of ordinary people in the struggle for security in their daily lives. This policy (and the strategies that derive from it) will meet powerful and ongoing opposition from national elites; nevertheless, it is important (as the earlier discussions of conflict theory and Gandhian nonviolence concluded) to conduct the struggle for security using means that are consistent with the satisfaction of needs, including the need for participation. Therefore, efforts by individuals and communities to implement this security policy at the local level are the only basis for implementing it on a wider scale.

This security policy is also distinctive for two further reasons. First, it is designed to facilitate transformation of the state-centric international security system; undoubtedly this will be a long process characterized, as is already evident, by the slow demise of state power and the steady rise of alternative structures that are more responsive to human needs. And second, it rejects deterrence as a component of security policy. Instead, it is designed to promote security through a variety of cooperative activities and processes at several levels. In contrast to the case with deterrence, the reliance on the human capacity for cooperation as the basis of security policy is theoretically and empirically sound. Since the human faculty for cooperation was first systematically documented,[73] extensive research evidence in the biological and social sciences has proven that "cooperation is central to human existence." Moreover, the evidence indicates that cooperation is partly innate and partly the result of socialization and that it can be strengthened in several ways. Notably, it is enhanced by the performance of interdependent activities designed to achieve shared goals.[74] Nevertheless, for those occasions when cooperative approaches to security are obstructed by elites, this security policy includes a strategy for using nonviolent struggle (or, in the case of military aggression, nonviolent defense) in order to resist the intervention of those elites.

Security, then, can be enhanced in a variety of ways, and security policy should identify processes for doing this. In essence, according to Galtung, security requires communities to increase their "degree of invulnerability," or capacity for resistance (rather than their destructive capacity), at four distinct levels: the levels of the "nature system," the "human system," the "social system," and the "world system."[75]

At the level of the nature system, security can be enhanced by increasing the resilience of ecosystems. As the deep ecological perspective on security suggested, this requires respect for the biodiversity and symbiosis inherent in pristine ecosystems and recognition of the fact that economic self-reliance ultimately depends on the sustainable use of renewable resources.

At the level of the human system, the perspectives on security outlined earlier all emphasize the importance of individuals within their political, social, economic, and ecological contexts. In this sense, security can be enhanced by increasing the degree of "power-over-oneself" of individual members of the community. This requires an approach that facilitates development of each person's body, mind, and spirit in ways that enhance their identity, fearlessness, and self-reliance.[76] Real strength, Narayan Desai argues, comes from within. It is faith, patience, perseverance, and self-reliance. Personal power is vitally important, he believes, because the "enemy" is not one or several individuals, but the system itself, "which is anti-people and anti-nature."[77]

At the level of the social system, security requires the development of a just and equitable set of social relations, as well as political and economic structures (including those related to decision making and conflict resolution) that tend to reinforce these. Security can also be enhanced by increasing the degree of decentralization within a society so that there is no "central nervous system" (such as a capital city) that is vulnerable to attack.[78] Therefore, as the security perspectives outlined earlier suggest, a program to increase system self-reliance would emphasize decentralized development and would encourage smaller-scale local communities[79] to work toward self-reliance in the political, social, economic, and cultural spheres *within their own bioregions*; that is, to rebuild cultural identities that are directly related to ecosystems. It would also encourage the development of self-reliant defense strategies.

Finally, at the level of the world system, security can be enhanced by developing more networks of mutually supportive communities. This is important given the extensive variety of elite-sponsored programs to drive cleavages between non-elite constituencies, such as those between Western workers and people of the South. An important task, then, is to keep developing worldwide networks that foster mutual respect and high levels of interaction and cooperation at the personal and community levels. These networks require facilitation mechanisms and, in some cases, nonstate regional and global agencies (that are representative of, and accountable to, ethnic, cultural, religious, and other identity groups rather than nation-states)[80] in order to coordinate the shared responsibilities that arise from functional interdependence.[81] However, unlike those alternative conceptions of international security that emphasize the role of centralized institutions, this approach is more concerned with creating decentralized processes (and facilitation mechanisms) that encourage active participation by ordinary people.

The approach to security described in this section requires political will and long-term vision. It requires political will because the task ahead is difficult. And it requires vision: not because the vital changes are necessarily distant, but because thinking beyond the life span of the current generation should expand dramatically the range of possible alternative futures. Few would argue that the states-system will last indefinitely, so thinking that is focused beyond this paradigm may provide insights on its supersession in the shorter term.

The remaining four chapters of this study will explain how to use nonviolent defense in response to one particular kind of threat to security: acts of military aggression.

10

The Strategic Theory of Nonviolent Defense

Although the improvised use of nonviolent resistance as a defense strategy (particularly by indigenous peoples against imperial invasions) has been previously documented,[1] the idea that a nonviolent form of defense against military aggression could be *consciously planned and prepared* can be traced to an article written by Bertrand Russell in 1915.[2] According to Gene Sharp and Christopher Kruegler, four broad influences have contributed to the contemporary concept of "nonviolent defense," and particularly that version known as "civilian-based defense." These are the early antecedents arising from pacifism and radical antimilitarism; the insights of major theorists such as Étienne de La Boétie (in relation to the consent theory of power) and Basil Liddell Hart (in relation to military strategy); historical examples of improvised nonviolent defense— such as those in Germany in 1923 and Czechoslovakia in 1968; and the development of nuclear weapons, which inspired some people to search for radical defense alternatives.[3] In addition, Sharp identifies a fifth major influence: the projection by various practitioners of nonviolent action, and particularly Mohandas K. Gandhi,[4] that defense against foreign invasion could be waged effectively by nonviolent struggle.[5] This last factor is probably most significant from the viewpoint of activists concerned with the social defense version of "nonviolent defense." In any case, the publication of books by Stephen King-Hall[6] and Bradford Lyttle[7] in 1958 marked the start of more systematic consideration of the concept by activists and scholars alike.

Two Conceptions of "Nonviolent Defense"

There are two major conceptions of "nonviolent defense": They can be referred to as "civilian-based defense" and "social defense."[8] *Civilian-based defense*, according to Kruegler, is an alternative defense system in which nonviolent resistance by civilians, coupled with economic and diplomatic sanctions, would replace or supplement military weapons "as a means of deterring and defending against unwanted internal and external military aggression."[9] *Social defense*, according to Brian Martin, is "nonviolent community resistance to aggression as an alternative to military defence." It relies on the use of protest, persuasion, noncooperation, and intervention to resist military aggression or political repression.[10] These definitions suggest a certain similarity, but in fact these conceptions are fundamentally different. The major differences are outlined below.

First, exponents of civilian-based defense would use nonviolent sanctions because of their practical value; they make no claims regarding the "moral superiority of nonviolent behavior."[11] In contrast, while not all exponents of social defense are practitioners of principled nonviolence, concerns regarding the morality of the means would usually weigh at least as heavily with them as pragmatic concerns for the outcome. For exponents of social defense, then, a commitment to nonviolence is equal to, if not more important than, the "rational superiority" of social defense.[12]

Second, proponents of civilian-based defense use a narrow, actor-oriented definition of violence. They understand violence to be "overt physical damage, or the threat of such damage, to actual persons." Thus, civilian-based defense might include some sanctions, such as sabotage, that are usually associated with military strategies.[13] In contrast, most advocates of social defense would favor a definition of violence that specifically emphasized its structural elements; and, for different reasons, many would reject the use of sabotage.

Third, advocates of civilian-based defense are concerned with defense of the nation-state, its government and territory. According to its leading exponent, Gene Sharp, it is a form of national defense that is designed to deter and defeat foreign military invasions and occupations, as well as domestic coups ("that is, seizures of the physical and political control of the state machinery").[14] In contrast, while advocates of social defense are less specific about their defense preoccupation, their focus is clearly non-statist and anti-elitist. Social defense is variously described as concerned with defense "at the community level,"[15] defense of "the social fabric,"[16] defense of "the values of a society, such as freedom, equality . . . the integrity of the individual, and an atmosphere in which all of these values may be nurtured and developed,"[17] and, even more broadly, "the creation of a democratic-based power for economic, social, political, ideological, and ecological security."[18]

Fourth, and related to the point above, advocates of civilian-based defense seek its adoption (in whole or in part) by national governments, and it involves a nonviolent strategy working under the direction of a government.[19] Like military defense, it would rely on centralized decision making and hierarchical organization for its implementation.[20] In contrast, exponents of social defense seek its acceptance by the community at large; social defense "refers to nonviolent defence based on grassroots initiatives."[21] It would rely on cooperation and communication among community-based groups for its implementation.[22]

Finally, proponents of civilian-based defense regard it as a functional equivalent for military defense that is capable of practical operation "under existing political and international conditions";[23] it has no direct relationship to other social struggles. In contrast, advocates of social defense usually consider the problem of defense to be a part of the wider struggle for fundamental structural changes in society. Consequently, there is a vital link between social defense and revolutionary social movements. This includes "movements which pose a challenge or alternative to military and state power."[24]

There is a significant literature dealing with civilian-based defense, considerably less dealing with social defense. This reflects the preference for civilian-based defense among scholars in the field. A perusal of the literature suggests that there are several reasons for this preference. First, most academics in the field wish to promote the credibility of civilian-based defense in the eyes of political and military elites in the hope that it will eventually be adopted by governments; their approach is "essentially reformist."[25] In the view of these scholars, in order for civilian-based defense to be seriously considered as a national defense option, further research, analysis, and policy studies are needed.[26] Research, they believe, will solve outstanding problems associated with civilian-based defense, and this research must ultimately be sponsored by govern-ments because only governments have the resources to conduct the scale of research that is required.[27] Second, certain military strate-gists had a personal influence on the early theorists. Adam Roberts and Sharp, for example, were both influenced by Liddell Hart.[28] This reinforced the elite orientation of these scholars as well as their inclination to separate civilian-based defense from principled non-violence.[29] Third, and related to the second point, the preference for civilian-based defense is a function of the narrow intellectual and theoretical foundation on which it is based. Apart from pragmatic nonviolence, civilian-based defense has been heavily influenced by a particular military conception of strategy (the indirect approach described by Liddell Hart);[30] it has not been significantly influenced by other disciplines such as conflict theory and psychology. This has reinforced the narrow conceptual framework in which many schol-ars of civilian-based defense are already working.

In contrast to the preference of these scholars for civilian-based defense, this study rejects it entirely. A major purpose of the remainder of this study is to elaborate a new and more strategically rigorous conception of nonviolent defense. Before doing this, sev-eral major criticisms of civilian-based defense will be considered.

Arguments against Civilian-Based Defense

There are three main sets of arguments against civilian-based defense. These are summarized here in order to clarify why this study rejects it as a strategic defense option.

First, as noted above, a distinctive feature of civilian-based defense is the pragmatic nature of its commitment to nonviolent action. As discussed at greater length in chapter 7, several features characteristic of the pragmatic approach are inconsistent with the resolution of conflict. For example, civilian-based defense utilizes an approach to conflict based on the traditional win-lose concep-tion of it. This is evident from the emphasis placed on the intention to "defeat" the aggressor.[31] This approach ignores the insights derived from the recent conflict research discussed in chapter 5 and summarized in chapter 8. Briefly, it fails to recognize the impor-tance of satisfying the opponent's needs for self-esteem, participa-tion, justice, and control through meaningful involvement in decid-ing the outcome.

In addition, the pragmatic approach of civilian-based defense entails a negative conception of the opponent. This is evident from the emphasis placed on its deterrent capacity.[32] Apart from the fact that deterrence does not deter (except in circumstances which are trivial),[33] deterrence is based on the notion that "no matter what we do, the enemy will never become good." This notion is clearly at odds with the attitude of principled resisters who believe in "the worth and dignity" of their opponent.[34] According to the strategic theory developed in this study, conflict resolution requires the correction of negative attitudes held toward the opponent, the elimination of behavioral patterns that tend to isolate the opponent, and the satisfaction of the needs of all parties (including the opponent's needs for self-esteem, recognition, and rationality). On this basis, the negative conception of the opponent characteristic of civilian-based defense is a direct impediment to the resolution of the conflict.

However, rejecting civilian-based defense on this basis does not mean a complete rejection of the pragmatic use of nonviolent action. Many, if not most, historical examples of improvised nonviolent "defense"—especially those against military coups—have neither had an ethical base nor been characterized by "monolithic ideological unity." For example, the nonviolent resistance to the French Generals' Revolt in Algeria in 1961 "was not the consequence of any ethical beliefs or political theories about 'non-violence.'"[35] Moreover, it is true that nonviolent action generally is most frequently used "on behalf of narrowly conceived interests" rather than because people "desire to eradicate the root causes of conflict" or engage in "transformationalist politics."[36] However, there is a difference between what has occurred in particular historical contexts and what constitutes sound strategic planning for future conflicts. Given the depth of the global crisis and the profound nature of the transformation required to resolve it, it is highly desirable to educate defense activists—both to expand their appreciation of the links between their particular conflict and the global crisis, and to improve the quality of the nonviolent action they use to address local conflicts.

Strategic planning should be based on sound strategic theory and should nominate methods that are consistent with that theory. Insofar as the pragmatic use of nonviolent action is inconsistent with recent conflict theory, it is an inappropriate component of any defense strategy. However, in the strictly limited sense that some (or even most) people might choose nonviolent action because they believe it to be effective, rather than because they have an ethical commitment to it, their participation is valuable provided that it occurs within the framework of an overall strategy based on the strategic theory outlined in chapter 8. In part, this strategy will reflect the elements characteristic of a principled (rather than pragmatic) approach to the use of nonviolent action as it was described in chapter 7.

Second, for critics of civilian-based defense concerned with the wider struggle for fundamental structural changes in society, there are two related concerns: They are skeptical about the prospects of political elites implementing a civilian-based defense strategy except "insofar as such a project can be integrated within the limits of the existing societal relations." Equally importantly, many are concerned that if it *were* implemented within the context of existing political institutions, it would neutralize the revolutionary dynamics of the strategy.[37] In fact, for that reason, Theodor Ebert has specifically drawn attention to the dangers associated with the selective interest in civilian-based defense being shown by those Western European governments that see it exclusively as a possible complement to the military defense apparatus.[38]

The idea that civilian-based defense is "a functional equivalent" for military defense that can be integrated within the context of existing social relationships has attracted considerable criticism. According to this view, Gustaaf Geeraerts notes, civilian-based defense is "a socio-technical innovation," the advantages of which can be weighed against those of a traditional military defense. This approach "only takes into account the manifest functions of the military apparatus"—that is, the deterrence and defense functions. It neglects the latent functions fulfilled by both the military apparatus and the military-industrial complex. These include the role of the military apparatus as an instrument of "internal repression and imperialist control" and the role of military structures and ideologies as socializing agents leading to "authoritarian patterns of behaviour."[39]

Recognizing the many roles of the military is vitally important because it highlights why the proposal to use a civilian-based defense strategy in defense of the nation-state is both politically unsophisticated and highly problematical. The social and economic privileges now enjoyed by Western nations are the direct result of earlier periods of imperial violence and colonial exploitation that have now been structurally institutionalized through the international division of labor. These privileges, which primarily accrue to elites in the West, must be defended militarily against foreign competition, the developing nations, and exploited classes within the Western nations themselves.[40] Thus, national elites are not likely to seriously consider a defense strategy that undermines their capacity to defend their vested interests and that could not be used to defend those interests even if they chose it.

Russell noted this latter point in his visionary article on nonviolent defense written in 1915,[41] Gandhi was certainly well aware of it,[42] and Sharp himself made the observation in one of his earlier works on the subject.[43] Other authors,[44] including Dave Dellinger, have made the point as well. Dellinger observed that it would be impossible to defend the United States nonviolently because an inherent feature of the nonviolent method is a very important strength: "nonviolence cannot be used successfully to protect special privileges that have been won by violence." For example, a civilian-based defense strategy could not be used to maintain the dominant position of the United States in Central/South America. Nonviolent defense, Dellinger argues, requires not only a willingness to risk one's life, but a willingness to renounce "all claims to special privileges and power at the expense of other people."[45]

In summary, the idea that civilian-based defense could be "a functional equivalent" for military defense ignores the reality, discussed in earlier chapters of this study, that national societies are dominated by a series of mutually reinforcing structures, including the state, that serve elite interests. Within this framework, the military plays a vital role, which is *not* confined to national defense. The military helps to maintain the state and is the mechanism by which the state can, if necessary, impose the "common will" on its citizens, whether that "common will" is determined by a parliamentary elite or a military dictatorship.[46] Therefore, Martin argues, elite-sponsored civilian-based defense would have little impact on dominant institutions. The state and the military system "would not be challenged in any fundamental way."[47] In fact, Egbert Jahn asserts, this approach ignores "the emancipatory social and moral potential of abolishing the military approach as a whole and with it the traditional state as we know it."[48]

Despite this, it has been argued that, because more people question military defense than capitalist social relations, state-organized civilian-based defense might be a means of social reform.

However, Jahn asserts, it is undesirable for theorists of nonviolent struggle in any context to nourish illusions that genuine peace and structural change can occur "within the framework of the existing capitalist and socialist system of nation-states."[49]

Finally, there is a third set of reasons for rejecting civilian-based defense; in a sense, these encompass and expand on those given above. Fundamentally, as indicated in the introduction, the different notions of "nonviolent defense" reflect the different preferred social cosmologies of their proponents. Like military defense, the notion of civilian-based defense is implicitly based on five assumptions: that existing patterns of matter-energy use are acceptable, that national societies are integrated social systems, that realism (including its negative conception of human nature) offers an adequate explanation of human society, that conflict is largely actor-oriented, and that security is narrowly conceived in terms of nation-state interests. However, as the discussions in earlier chapters revealed, there is considerable theoretical and empirical evidence to suggest that existing patterns of matter-energy use are inequitable and unsustainable, that national societies are not integrated social systems, that realism offers a grossly inadequate explanation of human society and behavior, that much of the deep-rooted conflict characteristic of modern society is structural in nature (and derives, in fact, from such structures as the nation-state and the institutions of government), and that security is a complex and multifaceted concept deeply rooted in human emotions and needs. Thus, from the perspective of the analysis offered in this study, civilian-based defense is a deficient strategy for dealing with military violence because of the inadequate conceptions of society, philosophy, conflict, and security on which it is based.

As the analysis in earlier chapters indicated, dealing effectively with the many manifestations of conflict in the international system will require fundamental structural and philosophical changes. While such changes may be a long-term goal of advocates of civilian-based defense, they are certainly not the primary and ongoing focus of their attention nor a goal of the strategy itself.[50] In fact, according to Sharp, civilian-based defense should not be coupled with any "grand conception of social change."[51] Moreover, from the perspective of Sharp's personal social cosmology, efforts to link it in this way only lead to "conceptual confusion" and complicate the efforts of those who are attempting to extricate civilian-based defense from the "grip of doctrine and ideology" that interferes with its sympathetic consideration by political and military elites.[52] However, as this study has sought to demonstrate, this type of approach—which seeks limited system reform, seeks to separate the elements of this reform, and relies for its success on the persuasion of elites—seriously misunderstands the nature and causes of conflict in the international system and what is required in order to resolve it. In contrast, this study has argued that it is necessary to create entirely new social cosmologies, that the components of any newly evolving cosmology (its pattern of matter-energy use, its social relations, its philosophy of society, and its strategies for dealing with conflict) must be developed concurrently, and that ordinary people have an *innate need* to participate in this process. Therefore, given the ongoing resistance to these changes that must be expected from national elites, a strategy of nonviolent defense, as it is conceived in this study, is designed to assist activists and ordinary people in their struggle to create social cosmologies that satisfy human needs. In this sense, nonviolent defense is both one component of any new social cosmology of this type *as well as* a strategy for helping to achieve it.

In summary, the concept of civilian-based defense is based on elite-oriented conceptions of society, philosophy, conflict and security; is indifferent to structural violence; aims at elite-oriented reform; and fails to concern itself with satisfying fundamental human needs. It remains caught in the framework of the dominant social cosmology. In the worst case, Jahn warns, advocates of civilian-based defense will so adapt themselves to elite interests that they will simply integrate civilian-based defense "into the existing defense and deterrence establishments."[53]

For the sake of completeness, and for reasons outlined in earlier chapters as well as those given above, it should be noted that this study also considers the combination of civilian-based defense with military defense to be inadequate.[54]

Because it has been ignored by most scholars in the field, social defense lacks a clearly developed strategic orientation. Nevertheless, the strategy of nonviolent defense advocated in this study is much closer in conception to social defense than to civilian-based defense. In its approach to conflict, security, and defense, however, nonviolent defense (as it is conceived in this study) goes considerably beyond the stated concerns of the existing social defense literature; in this sense, nonviolent defense is quite distinct from social defense. For purposes of clarity, then, any future references to civilian-based defense and social defense will be consistent with the explanations of these concepts given above. And the term *nonviolent defense* will be used to refer to a defense strategy conducted in accordance with the strategic theory and the strategic framework outlined in chapter 8.

Military Aggression and Nonviolent Defense

The selection of a defense strategy is a political decision that can be guided by ethical criteria as much as any other. But whatever the criteria guiding its selection, the defense strategy must be based on sound strategic theory if it is to be a functional mechanism for dealing with conflict. The strategy of nonviolent defense elaborated in the remainder of this study is based on the strategic theory outlined in chapter 8 and is consistent with the cooperative security policy described in chapter 9. This strategy is based on the insight that it is not possible to use military violence to resolve social, political, and economic conflict; of course, it might be used to destroy certain symptoms of it, including, as Krishnalal Shridharani put it, "the very existence of opposing claims."[55] The strategy, then, is based on the fundamental assumption that exponents of nonviolent defense wish to *resolve the conflict* underlying an act of military aggression. For this reason, and unlike military strategies generally, nonviolent defense shifts the struggle "decisively to the political arena."[56] This section identifies the main types of military aggression against which a nonviolent strategy must be able to defend.

War is almost always described as a conflict between nation-states. This description is misleading. As illustrated throughout this study, war is the result of military aggression organized by state elites in defense of their imperial interests and structures of exploitation. There are no ways in which ordinary people benefit from war: It brings no benefits to national societies *as a whole*, nor can it satisfy the needs of ordinary individuals.[57] Of course, these facts are contrary to the impression carefully projected by national elites and reinforced by various socializing agents, including educational institutions, dominant ideologies, and the mainstream media. Moreover, Western elites generate fear and foster nationalist feeling in order to maintain a perception that ordinary people in non-Western countries are in competition with (or are the "enemies" of) ordinary people in Western societies. In this way, the possibilities of cooperation between members of different peripheries can be controlled and minimized. This is done for several reasons, including the desire to maintain the inequitable international division of labor; it also means that, when necessary, members of the peripheries can be readily manipulated or coerced into fighting wars against each other in pursuit of elite interests.

Given this conflict configuration, there are several types of military aggression against which a nonviolent defense strategy must be able to defend.[58] Of particular importance in this regard are two major categories: the military repression used by some national elites against their own people, and the military interventions that imperial elites organize against the people of other states. Several examples will illustrate the variety of forms such repression and intervention can take.

Consider the following cases of military repression. In South Africa the constitutional entrenchment of apartheid was accompanied by escalating levels of paramilitary violence in an attempt to repress the struggle to establish a nonracist South African government and society. Even as the constitutional elements of apartheid were finally being dismantled during the leadup to the first all-race election in 1994, there was ongoing violence—including killings, torture, and other "extrajudicial" practices—in the black townships, carried out by the state security apparatus and its agents. Following a well-worn pattern of the postcolonial era, Burma has been governed by a long-running military dictatorship characterized by its willingness to use gratuitous military violence against the Burmese people (particularly its ethnic minorities) and to ignore the results of the 1990 election, which should have seen power transferred to a civilian government.[59] And the Chinese communist dictatorship has demonstrated its willingness to use military violence against the Chinese people in order to defend its own autocratic vision of how Chinese society should develop.[60]

In addition to military repression, there are a variety of ways and circumstances in which military intervention can occur. Five brief examples will illustrate this diversity. In 1950 the Chinese government sent troops to invade and annex Tibet. Since the invasion, the Chinese army has systematically destroyed Tibetan culture and particularly its religious heritage. In the early years, particular efforts were made to persecute, humiliate, and discredit the Buddhist clergy—the most cohesive group in Tibetan society. More than three thousand monasteries and nunneries were ransacked of their treasures and then destroyed. Crops have been looted (causing widespread famine), mineral ores have been mined, and the environment has been devastated through such practices as deforestation and toxic waste dumping. At least one million Tibetans (a sixth of the population) have been barbarically exterminated.[61] During the Six Day War in 1967, Israeli military forces seized and occupied the West Bank (of the River Jordan) and Gaza. From this date until the signing of the "Gaza-Jericho First" agreement in 1993, when the official violence subsided, Palestinians in the Occupied Territories were subjected to beatings, torture, deportations, shootings, land seizures, house demolitions, school closures, and many other forms of abuse at the hands of the Israeli forces.[62] In 1975 the Indonesian government sent troops to invade and occupy the former Portuguese colony of East Timor. Since the invasion, the Indonesian army has carried out a policy of genocide against the East Timorese people. This has ranged from cultural suppression and forcible relocation to direct military repression: arbitrary arrests, torture, "disappearances," and massacres.[63] Throughout the 1980s, during its long-running military operation to destabilize the Sandinista government in Nicaragua, the government of the United States mined Nicaraguan harbors and financed the Contras to spread terror and to attack nonmilitary (as well as military) targets.[64] And in 1989, the U.S. government dispatched troops to attack Panama in order to defend a range of elite interests related to the Panama Canal and U.S. military bases.[65]

The strategic theory and the strategic framework developed in this study can be used to guide the formulation of a strategy of nonviolent defense for use against any type of military aggression. It provides a framework to guide the efforts of ordinary people (rather than political and military elites) who wish to defend themselves effectively *and*, given existing knowledge, in the way which is most likely to lead to a satisfactory resolution of the underlying conflict.

Nonviolent defense, as it is presented here, is a strategy designed for use within the wider context of the nonviolent struggle against violence in all its forms. It is intended for use in response to military aggression, including that directed by militarized elites against their own people, that aimed by coup-makers at grassroots resistance movements, and that undertaken by imperial elites against foreign populations. Thus, in the first place, and unlike civilian-based defense, the strategy can be directed against the militarized state itself. This is important. As Julio Quan implies, in countries like Guatemala, Honduras, and El Salvador the only relevant nonviolent defense is one that is organized by ordinary people to defend themselves against the militarized state that represses them.[66]

A nonviolent defense strategy can also be used to defend against internal coups or attacks by imperial elites. However, unlike civilian-based defense, this approach is not concerned with defense of the nation-state itself. The focus of this study is how ordinary people can respond nonviolently to military attacks in defense of whatever bioregion, social structures, or way of life they choose to defend. This approach does not preclude the possibility of a people using nonviolent defense in order to defend an existing state, but if they choose to use it for this purpose, it will reflect a conscious choice and not be an inevitable concomitant of the strategy they have adopted.

In this context, whatever social entity is to be defended, it must be defended in its entirety, *the good with the bad*; otherwise the defense risks being halfhearted and unnecessarily divided. Contrary to first impressions, this approach does not pose a dilemma to those concerned with aspects of the existing social order. This is because nonviolent defense has the potential to accelerate existing processes of social evolution. At the very least, as April Carter claims, resistance "is a political activity which may modify whatever political and social system emerges from the struggle."[67] More positively, Ebert argues that resistance that is nonviolent will help to purify and strengthen a defective social order.[68] The validity of these claims was illustrated, to different degrees, by the defeat of the 1991 Soviet coup. In the year prior to the coup attempt, it was evident that there was a high level of popular discontent with the Soviet government. Despite this, it was clearly preferred to the alternative offered by the coup leaders. In any case, the successful nonviolent defense of the existing government provided impetus to the reform process, including the disintegration of the Soviet state. Thus, nonviolent defense is concerned with defense of "the people" even if they happen to live in a particular nation-state and choose, at times, to defend that state.

However, given the many problems inherent in the nature of the state itself, and the importance of creating new nonhierarchical social structures if human needs are to be met, this study specifically suggests the use of alternative organizational models for planning and implementing a nonviolent defense. Some suggestions in this regard will be outlined in chapter 11. The importance of creating and using alternative structures and processes cannot be over-emphasized. If new types of structures are not being created to replace the old, then even a successful nonviolent struggle or defense will, at least in the short term, merely precipitate the emergence of new versions of the old structures rather than new and more appropriate structures. This is what occurred after the nonviolent removal of the Shah of Iran in 1979, Marcos of the Philippines in 1986, and a succession of military-backed communist dictatorships in Europe during 1989; it also occurred following the defeat of the Soviet coup in 1991.[69] In each case, while the elite managers of the postrevolutionary state structure were different, and the structures themselves underwent some changes, the latter remained largely inaccessible to ordinary people and quite inappropriate for implementing the profound changes that are necessary if human needs are to be met. If the gains won as a result of a successful nonviolent defense are to be consolidated, then, among other things, new nonhierarchical structures are necessary. Thus, the preparation and implementation of a nonviolent defense should include an ongoing shift to structures of this nature.

There is insufficient space in any single study to identify and discuss all elements of a nonviolent defense strategy or to consider all possible contingencies in each conceivable defense context. The remainder of this study will discuss the major theoretical and practical issues that should be considered and, where appropriate, illustrate how these issues have been tackled in the past. Hopefully, future studies will elaborate the details of nonviolent defense strategies that might be used in particular contexts.

The Strategic Theory of Nonviolent Defense

Throughout this study it has been argued that a society's cosmology includes its pattern of matter-energy use, its social relations, its philosophy of society, and its strategies for dealing with conflict and that these components help to shape, as well as reflect, the cosmology itself. It has also been argued that to be functional in the long term, each component of a cosmology must be oriented to the satisfaction of human needs. Because a defense strategy is one of the components that shape the social cosmology, policy should identify a strategy that will satisfy those needs. Nonviolent defense, as it is conceived in this study, is such a strategy. This section uses the strategic theory described in chapter 8 to outline the major features of a strategy of nonviolent defense. It is based on the five assumptions and three hypotheses outlined on pages 128–129.

An important observation that emerged from the discussions in chapters 1 and 2 is that while most military strategists would agree that the ultimate aim is to destroy the opponent's will to fight, in fact most of them believe that if the opponent's military capability can be destroyed, then either their will to fight is also destroyed or else it is no longer relevant. In contrast, the guerrilla strategist would argue that if the opponent's will is destroyed, then it is their military capability that is irrelevant. These widely held but contradictory beliefs illustrate the conceptual confusion that underpins most strategic thinking and complicates efforts, despite Clausewitz's imperative, to define an appropriate strategic aim.[70] There are two primary elements of this confusion, both of which can be traced to Clausewitz himself. First, there is confusion regarding the precise meaning, in the strategic sense, of three vital concepts: power, will, and the center of gravity. And second, there is confusion regarding the nature of the relationships among them. The remainder of this section will explain how important elements of the strategic theory developed in this study apply to a strategy of nonviolent defense and, in so doing, will answer two questions: What, in the strategic sense, do the notions of power, will, and center of gravity mean? And what are the relationships among them?

Within the literature on strategic studies, as the discussions in chapters 1 and 2 illustrated, there is a tendency to equate power with military capability. However, as the discussion in chapter 6 highlighted, power is a complex phenomenon that can manifest itself in a variety of ways. Moreover, in practice it has many sources. The power of elites, for example, stems from their influence within structures of power as well as from the human and material resources (including the military forces) made available to them. *In the narrowly strategic sense*, power is the capacity to conduct, or to resist, aggression. However, as the discussions in chapters 1 and 2 demonstrated, *effective resistance does not depend on military capability*. Furthermore, unlike those military strategists who incorrectly believe that the military power of the opponent must be destroyed, practitioners of nonviolent defense utilize the insight that *the opponent's power can be undermined at its source*. So what about the notion of will?

Like the military strategists considered earlier in this study, several advocates of civilian-based defense have identified the role of will. According to Jessie Hughan, one of the early theorists, the real battle is between enemy violence and "the will of a . . . civilian population."[71] Similarly, King-Hall noted that "the will to win is the first essential" and that the individual "must never give in mentally."[72] And in a list of factors that determine the effectiveness of civilian-based defense, Sharp includes "the population's will to defend against the attack."[73] The role of will has been noted by other theorists of civilian-based defense as well.[74]

Despite the references to the notion of will in the strategic studies and civilian-based defense literature, there is little discussion regarding its precise meaning and no serious attempt to identify its strategic significance. It is simply understood to refer to the disposition or inclination to fight (or struggle) and is presumed to reflect such factors as one's confidence in oneself as well as in one's comrades, leaders, country, and cause. For Gandhi, as noted in chapter 7, will is more complex. It is an expression of the needs for identity, self-reliance, and self-realization and of the moral commitment to self-chosen values. In any case, as the discussion in chapter 4 concluded, it seems reasonable to define will in terms of the theory of human behavior outlined in that chapter; that is, will is the disposition or inclination to act in response to the drive to satisfy human needs—including the needs for self-esteem, security, freedom, and justice. Given that needs will be pursued regardless of cost, the will to conduct aggression should reflect the degree to which needs are not satisfied and the will to resist it should reflect the degree to which needs are threatened. Of course, the perception of this will can be distorted by such factors as role defense, propaganda, religion, and ideology, and this must be taken into consideration when planning a strategy of nonviolent defense.

Because there is a dynamic interplay between political power and human psychology inherent in any defense strategy, although the notions of power and will are conceptually distinct, they are strategically related. As previously noted, in the narrowly strategic sense, power is the capacity to conduct or to resist aggression, and will is the inclination to do so. In some cases, as the discussion in chapter 2 illustrated, one of these factors can be decisive. However, unlike a military strategy in which the intention is to *destroy* the opponent's power and will, in a strategy of nonviolent defense the intention is to *alter* the opponent's will to fight[75] and to *undermine* their power to do so. This strategy is based on the insight that, properly understood, the political and psychological considerations in war are decisive; military factors are incidental.

According to the strategic theory developed in this study, the political purpose and the strategic aims of a nonviolent defense strategy are those defined on pages 130–131. But if campaigns of nonviolent action are necessary as part of the strategic counteroffensive, where should they be directed?

Within the literature on civilian-based defense there is a minor "debate" regarding the relevance of the concept of the center of gravity. Those who use a Clausewitzian framework, such as Boserup and Mack, consider it relevant and use it explicitly. Most authors, including those whose conceptual framework owes more to Liddell Hart than to Clausewitz, do not refer to it at all. In any case, there is no consensus regarding its identity. According to Boserup and Mack, the center of gravity in a civilian-based defense is the *unity* of the resistance.[76] In contrast, Roberts argues, unity is obviously an advantage, but "it is not an absolute necessity."[77] Gene Keyes agrees. In his view, the center of gravity, for both the aggressor and the defender, is *morale*. Should unity be impaired, he argues, "let the parties bearing the burden of defense carry on with morale unshaken, and national integrity will remain intact." If the morale of one party collapses, however, "all is over" for them.[78]

It is evident that unity and morale are important factors; however, neither of these is the center of gravity of a nonviolent (or any other) defense. In fact, this brief discussion illustrates the point made earlier: There is considerable confusion regarding the precise meaning of this vital concept.[79] Nevertheless, in Clausewitzian terms the meaning is unequivocally clear: The center of gravity is the center of *power*.[80] Even though the meaning is clear, there are strong grounds, as the discussion in chapter 1 illustrated, for varying the interpretation of the center of gravity preferred by Clausewitz.

According to the strategic theory described in chapter 8, there is a specific center of gravity—a center of power on which the entire strategy depends—for each party in a conflict. This center of gravity is the same for all parties: It is the finite pool of social resources that support their strategy. In other words, the power of the defense to resist aggression depends on its capacity to mobilize key social groups to participate in the defense strategy. And the power of the opponent elite to conduct the aggression depends on the level of support their strategy commands. This includes the support that is offered from within the elite's own society (especially by key social groups, or "*loci* of power")[81] as well as that which is offered by third-party elites (who, in turn, depend on support from within their societies). Therefore, a strategy to undermine the *power* of the opponent elite should be directed at their center of gravity; that is, it should aim to alter the *will* of those key social groups in both the opponent and third-party societies that support the aggression. This will require an understanding of the ways in which these key social groups reinforce, or conflict with, one another; the ways in which such factors as role defense, propaganda, religion, and ideology shape their perception of their needs; as well as the ways in which solidarity groups within these societies can help to alter the support of these groups for the aggression.

In those circumstances in which the will of the defense or the opponent elite cannot be altered directly, the center of gravity becomes critical for each party. Moreover, it defines which weapons are useful and which ones are useless. This means, for example, that the utility of a rifle is not measured by its ability to shoot but by its capacity to destroy the center of gravity. If it cannot be used to help do this, Boserup and Mack explain, "it is just a piece of iron."[82] If the opponent elite fails to recognize that the support of key social groups for the strategy of nonviolent defense is the ultimate target of their aggression, then their use of inappropriate weapons may consolidate the defense rather than help to destroy it; this is one reason why the use of violence can be highly dysfunctional. Similarly, from the perspective of the nonviolent defense, each campaign of the counteroffensive should employ a strategically selected combination of nonviolent tactics, as well as other means (including various forms of dialogue), that are designed to undermine support for the opponent elite's aggression.

To illustrate the explanation above, consider a situation in which a military dictatorship violently represses its civilian population. The dictatorship might successfully dominate national life in the short or even medium term; yet the dictatorship is subject to removal *unless it has also achieved what should be its strategic aim*: to destroy the *power* of the defense to resist the repression *as well as* its *will* to do so. Until it has done that, the potential to resist, and to ultimately remove, the dictatorship remains; this is why it is necessary to maintain high levels of repression on a continuous basis. Using the strategic theory outlined in chapter 8, from the defense viewpoint the political purpose of the resistance is to create the policy, process, structural, and systemic conditions that will satisfy human needs—including the removal of the repression and the dictatorship itself. This is done by achieving the twin strategic aims: first, to consolidate the power and will of the defending population to resist the repression; second, to *alter* the will of the dictator to conduct the repression and to *undermine* their power to do so. On the one hand, the dictator might be induced to participate in a problem-solving process by offering them a bracket of specific satisfiers that will meet their needs; this might *alter their will* to maintain the repression. On the other hand, the dictator might be nonviolently coerced to participate by *undermining their power* to conduct it. This may be achieved by subjecting them to a series of strategically focused campaigns of nonviolent action that are directed at their center of gravity—in this case, the key social groups supporting the dictator's strategy, whether these groups are from within the dictator's own society or from within the societies of the dictator's elite allies. In some circumstances, as in the case of Burma, the support of elite allies is very important.

To illustrate the explanation above using a different type of example, consider a situation in which an imperial elite uses military force to invade and occupy another territory. While the imperial elite might successfully occupy the invaded territory, overthrow its government, and even install a client regime, the occupation is subject to reversal *unless it has also achieved what should be its strategic aim*: to destroy the *power* of the defense to resist the occupation *as well as* its *will* to do so. Until it has done that, the potential to resist, and to ultimately reverse, the occupation remains; this is why it is necessary to keep occupation troops in the invaded territory. From the defense viewpoint, the political purpose of the resistance is to create the policy, process, structural, and systemic conditions that will satisfy human needs—including the removal of the occupation forces. This is done by achieving the twin strategic aims: first, to consolidate the power and will of the defending population to resist the aggression; second, to *alter* the will of the invader to maintain the occupation and to *undermine* their power to do so. On the one hand, the invader might be induced to participate in a problem-solving process by offering them a bracket of specific satisfiers that will meet their needs; this might *alter their will* to maintain the occupation. On the other hand, the invader might be nonviolently coerced to participate by *undermining their power* to conduct it.

This may be achieved by subjecting them to a series of strategically focused campaigns of nonviolent action that are directed at their center of gravity—in this case, the key social groups supporting the imperial elite's strategy, whether these groups are from within the imperial elite's own society or from within the societies of the imperial elite's allies. In some circumstances, as in the case of the Israeli occupation of Palestine, the support of an occupying government's elite allies is very important.

According to the strategic theory developed in this study, military aggression is one aspect of the political and strategic activity of national elites that is intended to satisfy their own unmet needs. A strategy of nonviolent defense is designed to resist this aggression without destroying the capacity of individual members of these elites (and their agents) to satisfy their needs in legitimate and more effective ways.

Shortcomings in the Strategic Orientation of Civilian-Based Defense

There are five major shortcomings in the strategic thinking that characterizes civilian-based defense. As discussed in this section, each of these shortcomings can be addressed by the strategy of nonviolent defense as it is conceived in this study. The alternatives are explained more fully in subsequent chapters.

In the literature on civilian-based defense, there is no strategic theory; this makes it impossible to offer specific strategic guidance.[83] As a result, suggestions about strategy are very general,[84] and there is no clear-cut basis for gauging the appropriateness of a particular decision or action. This has assisted the spread of some erroneous notions—such as the belief that an important aim of civilian-based defense is to increase the cost of occupation[85]—and contributed to the failure to fully appreciate, for example, the importance of strategic considerations in the selection of nonviolent tactics. First, then, as it is conceived in this study, a strategy of nonviolent defense should be specifically designed in accordance with the strategic theory and strategic framework outlined in chapter 8.

In the main English language works on civilian-based defense, there is no attempt to define the notion of will or to identify its strategic significance.[86] Where it is mentioned, it is either listed as one of several considerations,[87] coupled inexplicably with the notion of power,[88] or simply identified as important without further explanation.[89] Given its strategic importance, this is a serious shortcoming. As discussed in chapter 2, if the will to conduct aggression is altered, then the power to conduct it is irrelevant. Second, then, the strategy of nonviolent defense developed in this study uses a precise definition of the notion of will and recognizes its particular strategic significance.

In the literature on civilian-based defense, there is a diversity of opinion regarding the strategy that should be adopted. For example, in the context of an invasion, authors have offered at least four different strategic approaches: resistance by nonviolent defenders at the invaded frontier (sometimes called the "living wall"),[90] a strategy of total noncooperation (sometimes called a "nonviolent blitzkrieg"),[91] a strategy based on the continuing use of the existing political and economic system (sometimes called "work-on without collaboration"),[92] and a strategy of selective resistance.[93] These different approaches reflect the divergent opinions regarding what should be defended (for example, a territorial frontier, a government, or an ideology). In fact, Gene Sharp lists six questions that are supposed to help identify the appropriate points for resistance in each particular case.[94] This, of course, is one legacy of using the "scenario approach,"[95] an approach that is strategically flawed, as the discussion in chapter 1 illustrated. In contrast to this approach, according to the strategic theory developed in this study (and irrespective of the nature of the act of aggression) defense of the center of gravity and reinforcement of the will to resist are what are strategically important. Third, then, any strategy should be designed to defend the center of gravity and the will to resist; it should not be tailored to a particular act of military aggression or the location at which it occurred.

In much of the literature on civilian-based defense, there is a popular misconception that the opponent has a weak point (or points) against which resources should be concentrated. This misconception can be traced to the influence of Liddell Hart,[96] to a misunderstanding of guerrilla theory,[97] or to both of these sources.[98] In relation to the first influence, as indicated in chapter 2, Liddell Hart does not explain why there must be a weak point in every defense nor why attacking this weak point is strategically effective. And in the case of the second influence, while guerrilla theory emphasizes the *tactical* importance of attacking the opponent's weak points in the *military* sense, this imperative should not be confused with the *strategic* aim of destroying the internal cohesion of the opponent in the *political* sense. This task, in the view of Mao Zedong, will require "protracted" struggle precisely because "the enemy is strong."[99] Clausewitz believed that, in contrast to the notion that the opponent has a weak point, their center of gravity may be weak or strong. For example, in the case of the Chinese occupation of Tibet or the U.S. invasion of Panama, the center of gravity of the invading forces was very strong. Similarly, in the case of the Burmese junta's repression of the Burmese people, the center of gravity of the junta is strong. Fourth, then, according to the strategic theory developed in this study, the only strategically effective plan is to identify the opponent elite's center of gravity and then, irrespective of the difficulty and time involved in doing so, to conduct the strategic counteroffensive with the aim of undermining it. Of course, the fact that the opponent elite might not have a weak point in the strategic sense does not mean that it does not have weak points in the moral sense. Thus, the strategy may identify a carefully framed set of political demands (which, among other things, might expose the moral weak points of the opponent elite) in order to mobilize support for a particular campaign.

In some of the literature on civilian-based defense, considerable emphasis is placed on the importance of denying the opponent's specific objectives, whether they be political, economic, territorial, or otherwise.[100] This leads Johan Galtung, for example, to argue that if an occupier orders that there should be no public meetings, then public meetings should be held.[101] It also leads Sharp to argue, for instance, that if the opponent's objective is political control, the resistance "would thus be primarily political: strikes and boycotts on economic issues would not be appropriate." Moreover it leads Sharp to argue that if the opponent's objective is to seize an isolated location, then its defense would be "difficult" because, according to the widely held conception of civilian-based defense, the defense of this location would depend primarily on the resistance that could be offered at the site.[102] This emphasis on denying the opponent's objectives is a major shortcoming and is the direct result of failing to maintain the important distinction between the opponent's political purpose and their strategic aims.[103] This distinction can be illustrated again by brief reference to the Tibetan resistance to Chinese occupation. In this extreme case, while the Chinese government has achieved its political purpose (including the objectives of governing Tibetan territory and mining its resources), it has not been able to achieve its strategic aim: to destroy the power and will of the Tibetan resistance. As a result, the Chinese government must maintain a massive occupation force in Tibet and still faces the possibility that the Tibetan resistance will ultimately succeed. Finally, then, as the discussions in earlier chapters demonstrated and the Tibetan example illustrates, it is not strategically important to deny the opponent elite their political or other objectives.[104] Instead, it is important both to reinforce the will of the defense to resist the aggression and to consolidate its power to do so, and to alter the will of the opponent elite to conduct the aggression and to undermine its power to do so. This will require, among other things, the implementation of a series of strategically focused campaigns of nonviolent action.[105]

For the reasons discussed in this section, the strategic orientation of civilian-based defense is seriously flawed.

The final three chapters will describe the strategy of nonviolent defense.

11

Planning and Organizing Nonviolent Defense

In the final three chapters of this study, the term *strategy* refers to a planned series of actions (including campaigns) that are designed to achieve strategic aims in accordance with the strategic theory outlined in chapter 8. This chapter discusses the major planning and organizational components of a strategy of nonviolent defense. Examples drawn from the history of nonviolent struggle are used to illustrate the argument. The operational dimension of strategy is considered in the final two chapters.

Strategic Planning

According to Clausewitz, strategy is an extension of policy. Therefore, the strategic aim of conflict must be in accordance with the political purpose. In planning a strategy, the first task is to define the strategic aim. Once this aim is defined, the strategist should plan a strategy for achieving it. The strategy should identify the individual campaigns as well as the sequence of actions within each campaign. Strategic control should be maintained throughout.[1]

In the past, many nonviolent struggles (including several cases of improvised "nonviolent defense") have lacked the strategic orientation necessary for success. For example, and in spite of their many tactical successes, the lack of a sound strategic orientation was a major shortcoming of the Defiance Campaign against the Pass Laws organized by the African National Congress in South

Africa in 1952, it was a major factor in the eventual failure of the Czechoslovakian defense against the Warsaw Pact invasion in 1968, and it was one of the many shortcomings of the Chinese pro-democracy movement in 1989.[2]

Nonviolent defense, like any defense, requires a sound strategic orientation. This, in turn, requires a thoughtfully designed strategic plan. According to the strategic theory developed in this study, this plan should be generated by using the strategic framework (or "strategy wheel") outlined on pages 132–134. This strategic framework can be adapted to plan the individual campaigns of the defense strategy as well.

Before we proceed, an important point must be clarified. The strategic theory developed in this study represents a determined effort to "encapsulate knowledge" derived from certain historical experience, but in fact theory and practice exist in a dynamic relationship. For that reason, there will be contexts in which there is tension between what this theory suggests and what empirical circumstances will allow.[3] In these cases, it may not be possible to implement every facet of the strategic theory in the manner described here. It is important, therefore, that activists who choose to implement a strategy of nonviolent defense, as it is conceived in this study, use this theory to guide their efforts in a manner sensitive to local conditions. And it is even more important that activists use their experience to improve this theory or, better still, to develop superior ones. The discussion that follows will elaborate the strategy of nonviolent defense derived directly from the strategic theory outlined in chapter 8; in some cases, it will also indicate modifications that may be necessary in light of difficult local circumstances.

The Political and Strategic Assessment

Though many of the components of a strategy of nonviolent defense can be implemented prior to an act of military aggression, precise strategic planning in response to a particular act must be based on an accurate political and strategic assessment. In essence, this requires four things: (1) knowledge of the vital details about the act of aggression; (2) a structural analysis and understanding of the causes behind it, including an awareness of the deep cultural imperatives that exist in the collective unconscious of the aggressor society and that might drive elites within that society to perform certain political acts; (3) an assessment of the prevailing political circumstances, both locally and globally, in relation to the particular act (for example, how powerful is the opponent elite in relation to the defending population and its solidarity allies? What is the attitude of third-party elites?); and (4) a series of judgments about what will be possible at different times throughout the stages of the defense strategy in light of the first three factors. These elements are considered in context in the following discussion.

The Conception of Nonviolence

Given the existence of various conceptions of nonviolence, the strategic plan should identify the particular conception that the defense strategy will utilize and, to maximize the benefits of adopting this strategy, make this commitment to nonviolence explicit and widely known. The plan should also define the code of discipline that will guide defender behavior.

As the discussion in chapter 7 illustrated, there are several conceptions of nonviolence. However, from the perspective of recent conflict research, some of these have serious shortcomings. In circumstances in which nonviolent strategists drift into the use of an inferior conception of nonviolence, or in which they do not exercise the necessary strategic coordination, tactics that undermine the nonviolent dynamic may be implemented. The cost of utilizing a flawed conception of nonviolence and of failing to maintain the necessary strategic coordination has been starkly illustrated by the shortcomings of the Palestinian Intifada. During the period from 1987 to 1993, the Palestinian resistance to Israeli occupation was frequently characterized as "nonviolent." However, the conception of nonviolence that underpinned the Intifada during this period was essentially pragmatic (as this term was defined in chapter 7). This was illustrated by the language used in the Intifada leaflets, which was devoid of the spirit of nonviolence,[4] and by the calls for "stone-throwing or the use of petrol bottles."[5] In fact, according to Andrew Rigby, the Intifada was more accurately described as "unarmed," given the "wilder acts" carried out by undisciplined gangs and the frequent use of stones and firebombs.[6] While Rigby identifies the use of these weapons as "counterproductive" from the perspective of removing the Israelis, elsewhere he blames "the limitations of nonviolent resistance" in the particular context of the

Palestinian struggle.[7] However, from the perspective of the strategic theory developed in this study, the reliance on a flawed conception of nonviolence,[8] aggravated by the lack of strategic coordination and activist discipline—or, as Rigby himself puts it, an approach that "has not been *nonviolent* enough"[9]—was, in itself, a major shortcoming in the Intifada strategy during this period. Nafez Assaily is one Palestinian who, given the failure of forty-three years of armed struggle by the Palestinians and the many recent examples of effective and disciplined nonviolent resistance in the Occupied Territories,[10] has argued the case for developing a comprehensive strategy based on the Gandhian conception of nonviolence.[11] It is important, then, to make a *deliberate strategic choice* regarding the conception of nonviolence that will underpin any strategy. If the intention is to utilize the strategic theory developed in this study, it is vitally important to recognize that this theory is based on the *Gandhian conception* of nonviolence. And it is essential to recognize the strategic importance of developing the level of discipline required to carry this strategy out.

To maximize the benefits that accrue from the adoption of a strategy of nonviolent defense, the commitment to it should be explicit and widely known. It is apparent from the historical record that, no matter how weak and insignificant a group may be, if it relies on a military defense then it is easier for an internal or imperial elite to justify the use of violence against that group. In contrast, the use of violence against a people who have declared their commitment to nonviolence is clearly seen to violate major norms of international behavior, as the widespread outrage over the Beijing massacre in 1989, the Dili massacre in 1991, and the Bangkok massacre in 1992 illustrated. Of course, aggressive elites will try various methods to discredit a nonviolent defense; for example, they might use propaganda to spread the false belief that the defense is actually violent, and they might use provocateurs to incite or to carry out violence. But once the nonviolent defense has acquired credibility through explicit commitment and consistently nonviolent behavior, as the movement led by Gandhi did, it would be very difficult "to make the charge of violence stick."[12] It is clear that for smaller national groups generally, such as the Tibetans, the East Timorese, or the people of Grenada, no military defense is adequate against the unprovoked military aggression of imperial elites. However, by publicly declaring their commitment to a nonviolent defense and by actively developing a strategy to implement it, they would (at least marginally) reduce the risk of military intervention (given the existence of the norms mentioned above) and, if occupied, would improve their chances of ultimately removing the invader. The strategic plan should identify the specific ways in which the commitment to nonviolence will be conveyed to all parties.

While it is important to make an explicit commitment to nonviolence and to make this commitment widely known, these are not enough. It is also necessary to develop the level of discipline required to carry out the defense strategy. The principal reason for this is that nonviolence, in the Gandhian sense, is "disciplined and rule-based." Too often, Michael Nagler argues, people try a kind of nonviolence that is unsystematic: They may have the best of intentions, but their nonviolence is of the "make-it-up-as-you-go-along" variety. This is grossly inadequate. As Nagler points out, nonviolence has precise rules for success, and they must be learned and applied.[13] Psychologist Jerome Frank agrees. In his view, nonviolent action "probably cannot succeed as a set of tactical maneuvers unsupported by ideals, and it will probably also fail if based on ideology without discipline." Nonviolent defense requires as much group discipline as a military one does.[14]

However, as Horsburgh has noted, the maintenance of nonviolent discipline is doubtful if the commitment to nonviolence is purely pragmatic—that is, if the commitment is based on a belief in the effectiveness of nonviolence as a technique. This is particularly the case in those circumstances in which nonviolent defenders are expected to maintain their discipline under extreme provocation or in which they must engage in a protracted defense struggle.[15] While not all defenders need to share a principled commitment to nonviolence, in Frank's view it is questionable whether nonviolent tactics can succeed in the total absence of such commitment, because the temptation to abandon these tactics "as soon as they appear not to be working" is very strong.[16]

For Gandhi, discipline was crucial. In his view, success depended entirely upon "disciplined and concerted" action,[17] and his use of highly disciplined nonviolent tactics was central to his success as a strategist. In fact, Gandhi considered discipline so important that he regarded it as one of his most serious mistakes ("a Himalayan blunder") that he had taught civil disobedience to those who had never learnt the art of discipline. In his view, "rigid discipline" is necessary for nonviolent struggle,[18] and a nonviolent lifestyle, together with nonviolence education, is intended to cultivate that discipline. Discipline, in the Gandhian sense, means the personal selection of certain principles and the determination to live by them. In his view, this is "the only way" in which political life can be built up.[19] It includes the willingness to perform humble tasks and to acquire the knowledge and skills necessary to act with greater effectiveness.[20] Discipline is necessary for power-over-oneself, and this is necessary in order to achieve individual self-realization and to develop the community self-reliance characteristic of a nonviolent society. Discipline must be developed conscientiously and may be reinforced by vows: the commitment to do "at any cost something that one ought to do."[21] As a component of nonviolent defense, therefore, discipline means "self-discipline and inner discipline."[22]

In practical terms, there are many reasons for maintaining discipline in the often stressful circumstances encountered during nonviolent action. Given the individual needs for self-esteem, security, participation, rationality, and control, discipline is vitally important from the perspective of individual activists and their group. It will help people to control and to overcome their personal fear; it will enhance self-respect and self-reliance; it will help build trust among individuals and groups within the resistance (by increasing the degree of activist predictability) so that each activist can be confident of others' commitment to act in accordance with the agreed-upon plan; it will help groups involved in the action to act decisively and with unity; it will help activists readily identify and deal decisively with the disruptions of provocateurs; and it will help activists withstand repression. In addition, the psychological and historical evidence illustrates that the maintenance of nonviolent discipline has tangible political benefits. It is more likely to convey the gravity of the issue at stake, to encourage increasing participation in the defense struggle, to win the respect of the opponent and third parties, to inspire support among the wider audience, and to generate a lasting political impact.[23] This was illustrated on 21 May 1930 by the exceptional discipline displayed by the Indian activists at the Dharasana salt works. Despite receiving severe physical beatings, which resulted in the serious injury of more than three hundred activists and the death of another two, the activists maintained their nonviolent discipline throughout. Their supreme courage in the face of such brutality had a major impact on world opinion and functionally undermined support for British imperialism in India.[24] There can be no guarantee about the outcome when high levels of discipline are maintained, but the historical evidence is conclusive in at least two respects: if discipline is maintained, violence is less likely and the outcome is more likely to reflect nonviolent goals; and if discipline is not maintained or actions by provocateurs to undermine it are successful, these results are likely to be reversed.

To make the commitment to nonviolent discipline explicit, activists should be asked to pledge themselves to a widely publicized "Code of Nonviolent Discipline" that identifies important behavioral agreements. Ideally, this code should be developed by the individuals who will be asked to commit themselves to it. The following covenant is adapted from two primary sources: the one prepared by Gandhi for the 1930 independence campaign[25] and the one that is used widely in Brazil.[26] It provides a strong sense of the necessary elements, although in practice such covenants are usually less comprehensive. Many movements dedicated to nonviolent resistance have developed similar covenants.[27]

1. I will speak the truth.
2. I will endeavor to overcome my fear of punishment and death.
3. I will work conscientiously to purify my personal life.
4. I will treat each person with honesty, openness, caring, and respect.
5. I will harbor no anger or hate. I will suffer the anger and assaults of my opponents.
6. I will protect opponents from insults or attack, even at the risk of my own life.
7. I will act in accordance with the decisions and planned program of the organizing group and will respond promptly to requests from the action focalizers.[28] In the event of a serious disagreement, I will withdraw from the action. I will not initiate or participate in any spontaneous action.
8. I will accept responsibility for my actions; I will not use secrecy.[29]
9. If my arrest is sought, I will accept it voluntarily; if I am taken prisoner, I will behave in an exemplary manner.
10. I will protect the property of my opponents and property held in trust.

11. I will not run or use any threatening motions.
12. I will not carry any weapons.
13. I will not bring or use any drugs or alcohol.
14. I will encourage others to maintain their commitment to this covenant.

It should be clear from this covenant that nonviolent activists require great courage and that the price of that courage might be death. All defense strategies, whether violent or nonviolent, involve a cost. But, unlike the soldiers who are willing to kill for what they believe, the nonviolent activist is willing to die. This, more than anything else, distinguishes the nonviolent activist from the soldier. Of course, nonviolent action will not always result in death, and as the discussion in one section of the next chapter will demonstrate, it will usually minimize the suffering and deaths in any struggle. Nevertheless, a strategy of nonviolent defense is based on the insight that, ultimately, the best way to demonstrate sincerity and commitment to a cause is through personal sacrifice. And this requires great discipline.

According to the strategic theory developed in this study, an effective strategy of nonviolent defense requires a commitment to the Gandhian conception of nonviolence. Moreover, this strategy can be made more effective by making the commitment explicit and widely known and by developing the discipline necessary to carry it out. In fact, throughout Africa, Asia, and Central/South America, where military aggression is often directed against unarmed peasants and workers, this commitment and discipline are already widely evident.[30]

Organization

Thorough organization is crucial to the success of nonviolent struggle in any context. Gandhi, for example, emphasized this. The most important thing, he argued in relation to the 1920–22 nonco-operation campaign, "is to evolve order, discipline, co-operation among the people, co-ordination among the workers. Effective non-co-operation depends upon complete organization."[31] However, the importance of good organization has not always been recognized. For example, the organizational shortcomings of two major nonviolence campaigns sponsored by the African National Congress during the 1950s were a principal reason for their failure.[32] Nonviolent defense, like nonviolent struggle generally, must be well organized. But how? Some authors have argued that a civilian-based defense should be organized around the equivalent of a standing army.[33] However, this approach is inconsistent with the strategic theory that guides the conception of nonviolent defense developed in this study. For that reason, different organizational structures and processes are necessary. What forms might these structures and processes take? And are there particular advantages associated with them? This section addresses these questions.

Decentralization is important, Anurag Ratna argues, as a means of creating "proper political consciousness." It is needed in order to make people realize their responsibilities and to facilitate their involvement in making and implementing decisions.[34] Chadwick Alger agrees. Emphasizing the importance of participation in the defense planning process as one element of a democratic polity, Alger argues that nonviolent defense could be organized by regional communities, which in turn might choose to coordinate their preparations and "manoeuvres."[35] How might this be achieved? And what principles should guide the formation of any new structures?

The fundamental principle, according to John Burnheim, is that each person or group should have the opportunity to influence decisions on any issue in direct proportion to their "legitimate material interest" in the outcome.[36] Moreover, these new structures should satisfy the needs of each individual, including their needs for self-esteem, participation, and control. The empirical evidence and the research suggest that this organizational model should be based on small groups of people (such as affinity groups and collectives) as well as community organizations (including trade unions and religious assemblies). These should be firmly rooted in local communities that are part of wider identity groups. In turn, these groups and communities should be part of local, regional, and international networks.

Identity groups are racial, religious, ethnic, cultural, or class groups that display high levels of social cohesion because of shared values, attitudes, and beliefs. As was argued in chapter 4, they are more relevant than nation-states as units of analysis in international relations because they command greater loyalty than do artificially integrated states. Within these identity groups, local communities would be important elements of the nonviolent defense. Theodor Ebert suggests that citizens' councils—perhaps modeled on the workers' *soviets* formed during the Russian revolutions of 1905 and 1917—could be organized.[37] But there are many possibilities. These include collectives (like those self-managing organizations developed by anarchists during the Spanish Revolution),[38] communes, "church base communities" (like those in Central/South America),[39] and various forms of tribal organization. The relevant model would be determined by local circumstances.

In turn, community organizations would be important. According to Gene Sharp, a major part of any nonviolent defense would be conducted through the independent organizations and institutions of society.[40] Community groups such as trade unions, worker cooperatives, professional associations, cultural organizations, and religious bodies would all provide forums for planning and organizing components of the defense and could be major vehicles of the resistance itself.[41] The importance of community groups to nonviolent defense was illustrated by the Norwegian resistance to Nazi occupation in World War II.[42] For example, despite the incredible hardships they suffered, more than six hundred teachers who were imprisoned for eight months in a concentration camp north of the Arctic Circle resisted the Nazi demand that they join the new teachers' organization.[43]

Within these local communities and organizations, smaller groups of people, such as affinity groups and collectives, would be necessary; most of the detailed planning, preparation, and organization of the nonviolent defense would occur at this level. These smaller groups are also important because they would provide the basis for every person being able to resist "in an organized manner as a member of a group."[44]

The *affinity group* is an organizational unit that usually consists of between five and thirteen people.[45] It is designed to satisfy a range of individual human needs—including the needs for response, recognition, stimulation, meaning, and participation—and usually does so in an atmosphere of shared philosophical commitment and group trust. Affinity groups are important because "banding together with people one trusts is a precondition of political action."[46] The affinity group is one example of what Jane Mansbridge calls a "unitary democracy": It is characterized by relationships built on common interests, face-to-face contact, mutual respect, and consensus decision making—"the natural conditions that prevail among friends." The unitary ideal, Mansbridge argues, is the oldest form of human social and political organization because it is "natural" and "organic."[47] The importance of the affinity group derives partly from the intimacy of the relationships it allows; people feel needed, included, and accepted. This, in turn, encourages a congruence of interests among its members. In this context, *interests* are defined as enlightened preferences among policy choices; these include matters of personal taste, altruistic motives, and ideals. *Common interests*, then, can arise for three reasons: They can occur through a coincidence of personal tastes; altruism, or empathy, might lead an individual to consider another's well-being as their own; and ideals might lead an individual to adopt the well-being of the entire group.[48] Insofar as affinity groups cultivate empathy and idealism in these particular senses, affinity groups are also important tools for building wider networks of solidarity. In essence, an affinity group is created by its members in order to perform a range of political task and personal support functions. For this reason, the affinity group accepts responsibility for deciding its membership—it is not open to everyone—and it usually functions in accordance with a set of agreements. A typical set of agreements, which members may be asked to sign, would include a statement of commitment to the nonviolent principles of the group; a statement of commitment to participate in the nonviolent actions of the group; a set of behavioral guidelines (including agreements to respect and support each other, to use inclusive language, and to deal with conflict within the group); a set of group process guidelines (including agreements about sharing leadership roles and using some form of consensus decision making); and agreements about how the group will balance the intellectual, emotional, and spiritual aspects of its time together.

In contrast, the *collective*[49] is usually chosen as an organizational model for use within a structure designed to perform a particular range of service functions. Because the purpose of a collective in this sense is different from that of an affinity group, its membership is usually chosen according to different criteria and it is more likely to exhibit internal tension as a result of power differentiation, ideological diversity, and the tension between personal and collective identities. In fact, diversity and differences are often perceived as threatening to the larger goal of collective identity. Collectives are important, however, because they provide the opportunity to deal meaningfully with diversity and differences "in order to build solidarity and foster alliances."[50]

Irrespective of their degree of homogeneity, however, the real importance of small groups—whether affinity groups, collectives, "grassroots circles,"[51] witches covens,[52] "radical caucuses,"[53] or other culturally and spiritually appropriate models—derives from the opportunities they provide for individuals to interact meaningfully with the wider world: to satisfy their needs, to challenge the structural violence inherent in certain personal behaviors and group processes, and to participate meaningfully in the decisions that affect their lives.

In relation to structural violence, small groups provide the opportunity to work on important manifestations of the structural conflict described earlier in this study. As noted in chapter 6, the concern with structural conflict is not confined to the major political and economic structures of national societies. It is equally concerned with the structural violence inherent in certain types of individual behavior and group process. Thus, at the *personal* level, small groups provide the opportunity to challenge the structural violence inherent in social relationships stigmatized by the juxtaposition of privilege and oppression. For example, sexually exclusive language and behavior reflects the patriarchal structures and values characteristic of national societies, but it is important to recognize that eliminating this form of structural violence requires meaningful changes at the level of individual values, attitudes, and behavior. Consequently, within the context of small groups, individuals have the opportunity to explore the meaning and importance of various types of privilege and oppression, and to adopt an alternative value set that should manifest itself, among other things, in the use of nonexclusive language and behavior. According to Roxanna Carillo, no one is to blame for the country, class, or race they were born into, but we all must take responsibility and work conscientiously "to change the aspects of our lives . . . that are oppressive to others."[54]

Similarly, at the level of *group process*, small groups provide the opportunity to challenge the structural violence inherent in those forms of group dynamics that are hierarchical, that are dominated by men, and in which decisions are made by majority vote. Although these processes also reflect dominant social structures and values, eliminating this form of structural oppression can be achieved only through substantial alteration of small-group processes. Moreover, given the historical experience of social change groups,[55] it seems clear that unless nonhierarchical forms of organization are combined with antihierarchical measures designed to counter specific forms of oppression, much informal power will remain in the hands of privileged groups, such as middle-class men. Consequently, this analysis encourages the adoption of empowering group processes: no hierarchy; decisions by consensus; systematic efforts to neutralize gender, racial, national, class, and other power imbalances within the group; and a genuine commitment to skill sharing.[56]

Clearly, structural violence cannot be eliminated simply by adopting new norms regulating individual conduct and group process, yet these are vitally important components of the overall strategy. The importance of grassroots groups also derives from the opportunities for participation they provide. The evidence seems to support the hypothesis that political participation of various kinds, including leadership activities, are more equally distributed in small groups.[57] In addition, by rejecting an organizational model that is hierarchical and relies on centralized decision making, the networks of small groups should be able to minimize, if not avoid altogether, the worst effects of what Guida West and Rhoda Blumberg have labeled "the iron law of patriarchy": the tendency for the division of roles in gender-integrated social movements to result in male domination.[58] Given the needs-based conception of human nature upon which this study is founded, this consideration is centrally important.

In summary, there are several advantages associated with organizing nonviolent defense, particularly given its role in nonviolent struggle generally, in accordance with this model: It provides higher-quality opportunities for all individuals to satisfy their needs. It provides the opportunity for people to acknowledge diversity and to learn to utilize individual differences in order to build collective strength. It provides a manageable framework in which people can challenge the structural violence inherent in certain personal behaviors and group processes as part of the overall struggle against structural violence. It allows people to meaningfully participate in the decisions and activities that affect their lives. And finally, it minimizes the vulnerability to defeat inherent in a defense system reliant on a centralized leadership, which can be destroyed. How then are various small groups and local communities to coordinate their activities and responses in the context of a nonviolent defense?

Leadership

There is a clear division of opinion in the literature on civilian-based defense regarding the preferred nature of the leadership. The major issues concern the degree of centralization and openness that should characterize the leadership arrangements. How should the nonviolent leadership be organized and what are its essential functions?

The hierarchical model of organization relies on one or a few individuals to perform all leadership tasks and then authoritatively disseminate their decisions to lower levels; in this model, "unity of command" is the mechanism for exercising *strategic control*. This is reflected in the arguments used by some authors to advocate the adoption of traditional models of leadership in a civilian-based defense. The major advantages of a centralized leadership, it is claimed, are that it can design and disseminate a unified strategy of resistance and can accumulate the necessary expertise and intelligence for doing so. The advantages of an underground leadership, it is claimed, include the fact that it can serve instrumentally in guiding the resistance and that it is not vulnerable to direct repression by the attacker.[59] The nonviolent resistance to the Nazis in Norway during World War II was run by a centralized and underground leadership.[60] And as the nonviolent resistance to the Russification of Finland during the period 1898–1905 gained momentum, the centralized leadership "was obliged to go underground."[61]

Despite the above arguments, it is clear that a decentralized and open leadership structure is superior to a centralized and clandestine one. There are several reasons for this, related to individual needs for participation and control, the strategic advantages of this type of leadership, and the requirements of the wider strategy for social change, of which a nonviolent defense is only a part. The advantages of an open and decentralized leadership will be considered below; the separate question of whether secret tactics should be employed will be considered in the next chapter.

The first reason for developing an open leadership is that people need to participate in the decisions that affect their lives. As the discussion in chapter 7 illustrated, the use of secrecy is inconsistent with the principles that underpin both Gandhian nonviolence and the recent conflict theory discussed in chapter 5. Secrecy creates informed elites; it disempowers and excludes those not privy to the planning process. It is crucial, therefore, that the leadership be open and accessible so that it can involve and empower everyone. It is also worth noting that, given the increasing availability of highly sensitive surveillance technologies, as well as old-fashioned infiltration,[62] it is naive to assume that opponent elites can be effectively prevented from monitoring secret planning, should they choose to do so. Consequently, a secret leadership will exclude the defenders but not their opponents!

The second reason for developing an open leadership structure is that it has important strategic advantages. The willingness of leadership figures to act openly and fearlessly in the face of repression is vitally important in giving others the confidence to act.[63] The liberating and inspirational impact of an open leadership has been noted by Jawaharlal Nehru: "we had a sense of freedom and a pride in that freedom. The old feeling of oppression and frustration was completely gone. . . . We said what we felt. . . . What did we care for the consequences? Prison? We looked forward to it; that would help our cause still further."[64]

The third reason for developing an open leadership is that it is one of the requirements of the wider struggle for profound structural change. According to Gandhi: "No underhand or underground movement can ever become a mass movement or stir millions to mass action."[65] Insofar as a nonviolent defense is only one part of this wider struggle, it should use a leadership model consistent with the needs of the wider movement.

Historically, as noted above, some nonviolent movements have relied on an underground leadership in order to avoid direct repression of the leaders. However, the desire for secrecy may also reflect other considerations. For example, in the case of the Palestinian Intifada during the period from 1987 to 1993, it is usually claimed that there was a deliberate policy to protect activists at risk.[66] However, given that the Israelis captured three successive leadership groups within two months in 1988,[67] and that this did not seriously impede the Intifada, there are obviously other reasons why the Unified National Command of the Uprising (UNC) remained clandestine. These include the fact that the UNC consisted exclusively of men, many of whom regarded underground organization as a corollary of resistance, given their personal experience of the secret networks used by Palestinian activists in Israeli prisons; the need for secrecy to plan violent tactics (given the equivocal nature of the commitment to nonviolence); the ideological commitment to, and history of, this form of organization among the member bodies of the UNC during the earlier period of armed struggle; and the complexity of the Intifada leadership's relationship with that of the Palestine Liberation Organization (PLO).[68] Nevertheless, as noted above, there are strong theoretical and empirical grounds for adopting an open and accessible leadership. The weight of historical evidence, Ebert argues, supports the contention that openness is an integral element of nonviolent resistance. In his view, the dangers of secrecy must be understood by all those involved in planning a nonviolent defense.[69] The case against an underground leadership is related to the case against one that is centralized. Why should the leadership of a nonviolent defense be decentralized?

The first reason reflects the importance, noted by Arne Naess, of involving people in the decisions that vitally affect their own lives. In his view, people must learn to make decisions individually and in small groups without reliance on leaders. The decentralization of decision-making power is vitally important because it nurtures personal responsibility, local initiative, and the ability of people "to resist encroachments on their freedom."[70] In fact, what the strategic theory developed in this study indicates is that people *need* to be involved in these decisions; and, it seems clear, they have a right to be involved as well. Thus, the important question is this: In the context of a nonviolent defense, how can leadership be organized to be consistent with people's needs for participation in, and control of, the process?

The second reason for developing a decentralized leadership is that its strategic advantages (and the advantages of the high level of organizational preparation that goes with it) have been demonstrated historically. The outcome of a resistance campaign has often depended on whether rank-and-file activists have been sufficiently well organized and disciplined to continue the struggle after leaders have been arrested or rendered ineffective.[71] This was illustrated by the difference between the noncooperation movement in India during 1920–22 and the civil disobedience campaign in 1930–31, notwithstanding the distinctive role of Gandhi. Despite the noncooperation movement's apparent power, by 1922 it was disintegrating. According to Nehru: "All organisation and discipline was disappearing; almost all our good [leaders] were in prison, and the masses had so far received little training to carry on by themselves."[72] By 1930, however, the organization and network of the

Indian National Congress were vastly stronger. As Gopal noted: "The policy of arresting only the leaders was obviously ineffective in countering a movement which drew its strength from local organizations."[73] It is evident, according to Gene Keyes, that a "plenitude of quietly competent self-starters is preferable to one heroic leader" or leadership group;[74] it also involves fewer strategic risks. For example, once a centralized leadership has compromised (as the Czechoslovakian government did following the Soviet invasion in 1968),[75] submitted, or been removed (as happened to successive leaders of the African National Congress during the 1950s),[76] the nonviolent defense might be seriously undermined, and perhaps fatally weakened. On the other hand, a network of strong, independent organizations can compensate for weak or irresolute central leadership. After the long colonial war against the Algerian nationalists, for instance, in 1961 the French government indicated its willingness to negotiate with the nationalist leadership. However, a section of the French army resented this change of policy, and in the Generals' Revolt conducted shortly afterward they captured the city of Algiers. This inspired fears of a coup in Paris or an invasion of France from Algeria. The French government was so unprepared for this revolt that their initial response was most notable for its lack of resolution. According to Adam Roberts, however, even when the French government was inactive and threatened, "individuals and independent bodies proved ready and able to act in a decentralized form of defence." A wide variety of nonviolent actions—including a one-hour general strike by ten million workers—was organized by nongovernmental organizations, including the trade unions.[77]

The third reason for developing a decentralized leadership reflects the requirements of the wider strategy for revolutionary social change. According to the strategic theory developed in this study, the creation of decentralized structures (including leadership structures) is necessary in order to serve the psychological, economic, and relational needs of all individuals and groups within society. For at least three important reasons, then, the leadership of a nonviolent defense, like its organization generally, should be decentralized.

The strategic advantages of a leadership that is both open and decentralized have been demonstrated frequently. In one form, they were evident during the Indian independence struggle. More recently, in another form, they were demonstrated by "the Mothers of the Plaza" in Argentina. These women used open meetings to dis cuss strategy and to organize their most well known tactic—the weekly demonstrations in the Plaza de Mayo of Buenos Aires. The demonstrations, which began in 1977, were designed to draw attention to their "disappeared" relatives. Despite the kidnap and murder of a dozen women—including Azucena De Vicenti, the woman who started the movement—and the violent harassment and arrest of hundreds more, other women continued to effectively organize their various activities. Although compelled by the sustained violence of the military junta to abandon their weekly protests for a few months in 1979, gatherings of over a hundred women met secretly in the churches to organize their eventual return to the plaza. Despite renewed and massive repression when they did return, the women refused to go underground again. As a result, "Their visible courage was contagious."[78]

Nevertheless, given the experience of many social movements whose commitment to the conduct of open meetings has ultimately proved dysfunctional, there is one further point that must be stressed. Open leadership, as it is defined in this study, *does not mean that everyone can attend meetings*. It means that members of the leadership group are clearly identified and readily accessible. In practice, therefore, participation in this type of leadership should be measured by the capacity of the leadership structure and process to involve people through such mechanisms as representation and rotation. It should not be measured by the number of people who attend any given meeting and "clog" the efficiency of its decision-making process.

Notwithstanding the evidence presented above regarding the desirability of developing an open and decentralized leadership, it was noted earlier in this chapter that precise strategic planning in a particular situation should be based on an accurate political and strategic assessment of the prevailing circumstances and a series of judgments about what will be possible at different times throughout the stages of a defense strategy in light of these circumstances. For this reason, the nature of the leadership structure in a particular situation might diverge sharply from that discussed in the preceding paragraphs. In circumstances characterized by brutal repression, for example, it might be strategically unwise to attempt to organize an open leadership. In summary, while the prevailing political circumstances will have a decisive influence on the nature of the leadership structure adopted, activists would be wise to remember that secrecy and centralization should be employed only when they are considered to be functional imperatives, that is, when organization of the defense is impossible without them. Even then, Polish Solidarity activist Wiktor Kulerski argues, under the conditions of a modern police state, "a long-term, nationwide secret organization is not possible."[79] Given the compelling reasons for adopting a decentralized and open leadership whenever circumstances allow it, what form might this leadership take?

In the past, decentralized groups (of many different types) have experimented with various forms of coordination. Many of these forms, depending on the cultural context, remain relevant today. In the specific context of nonviolent defense, however, it is clear that the problem of coordination can be separated into two distinct phases. First, how should the planning and preparation phase be coordinated? And second, how should its integrated implementation be coordinated, given the short notice characteristic of most military attacks? While there is a clear need for further action and research on this point, there seem to be three major options available for consideration at this stage: groups may coordinate one or both phases by using a federated council, a network facilitator, or a demarchy.

A *federation* consists of several organizations, each of which retains control over its own affairs. It is designed to encourage participation at the grassroots level while allowing consultation and some decision making by a central body of elected delegates. If the federation is large, it may have several tiers.[80] Given the problems frequently associated with a federal system (such as delegates "hardening" into permanent representatives subject to factional influence and vote trading), variations on its basic character should be considered. For example, a federation might divide responsibility for its functions among several councils, and delegates from member organizations might be strictly rotated or chosen by lot after a predetermined period. This should equalize participation and share responsibility more completely.

A *network* consists of a multiplicity of small groups, each of which makes decisions for itself. It is designed to emphasize collective participation, local autonomy, and decentralization.[81] For a network to function efficiently, it requires a facilitator—a group that has no policy positions of its own but is responsible for facilitating communication, coordination, and resource gathering within the network. Importantly, the network facilitator should provide a communications framework to expedite the flow of information; this framework should be capable of distributing urgent information efficiently when necessary. It may also support coalitions of groups that choose to work on one issue.[82]

Demarchy is a system in which representative groups of people make sets of decisions within strictly limited domains on behalf of a larger population. It is decentralization by function. The only eligibility requirements for membership in any group are a particular interest in the issue—in this case, the various aspects of nonviolent defense—and a commitment to acquiring adequate knowledge and skill for the tasks of planning and implementing it. Under the principles of demarchy, representative groups would be chosen once a statistical characterization of the demographic features and the various interests to be represented from the larger population had been established; for example, if there were 50 percent women in the sample population, there would be 50 percent women in each of the representative groups. The representatives would be randomly selected from the various categories of representative volunteers. These volunteers would serve a fixed term before being replaced in a staggered rotation of the membership, which ensures continuity within the groups but prevents the entrenchment of particular cliques. The work of all groups would be subject to public scrutiny. In essence, small groups of volunteers—who are highly motivated, well informed on the issues, statistically representative of the wider population's range of interests, rotated periodically, and chosen by lot—would design the various aspects of the best possible nonviolent defense strategy and then supervise its implementation.[83]

A variation on demarchy that has already be tried in the United States is what Ned Crosby calls a "policy jury." A policy jury is a method of citizen participation in which randomly selected people are paid to attend a series of meetings, usually for about five days, in order to learn about the major viewpoints on a specific issue and to make recommendations about what should be done. The juries are chosen so that they represent the larger population in terms of sex, age, education, race, and political attitudes. In large geographical areas, several juries may be used, and there is usually a second-level jury, made up of delegates from the original juries, to resolve disagreements and make final recommendations.[84]

If a federation is used, each organization within it could work on one or more components of the defense strategy—for example, strategic planning, communications, the constructive program, a specific campaign—while separate councils of delegates, each responsible for one component, works to achieve consensus on that component within the federation as a whole. If a facilitated network is used, each group within it could work on one or more components while the network facilitator communicates the progress of each group to the others. If a demarchic approach is used, several groups would need to be formed, each with the responsibility for planning and coordinating one component of the strategy. Of course, a combination of these (and other) approaches could be used. Federations and networks of various types exist already and, in some cases, have played a part in past attempts to resist military aggression nonviolently, but more advanced models, together with practice in the use of demarchy, will enhance the capacity of grassroots groups to coordinate the planning and rapid implementation of a nonviolent defense.

Some of the strengths and weaknesses of decentralized forms of coordination were illustrated by the leadership of the Palestinian Intifada, which was loosely federal in form. Despite being clandestine, the UNC managed to remain in close touch with people throughout the Occupied Territories. This was possible because of the decentralized nature of the decision making, the roots of which were firmly embedded in neighborhood committees, and the practice of rotating the individual delegates who represented each of the five main nationalist organizations at meetings of the UNC. As a result of this rotation, which was also practiced at other levels, the degree of political specialization remained low and the emergence of a political elite with interests that diverged from those of Palestinians generally was obstructed. Within this decentralized structure, the role of the UNC was confined to the establishment of political guidelines and the coordination of activities in direct response to the initiatives of local committees throughout the Occupied Territories.[85] The responsiveness and resilience characteristic of this type of leadership structure are among its greatest strengths, but are they enough?

Good nonviolent leadership requires people who have an understanding of, and deep commitment to, nonviolence. In addition, good leadership requires that each of several functions be performed; these functions can be learned and shared. First, it requires people who keep the strategic aims in focus, develop strategies, and take a long-term view. Second, it requires people who monitor the level of energy for the resistance, generate ideas and enthusiasm when necessary, and draw people into the struggle. Third, it requires people who draw attention to how people are feeling and who draw conflicts out into the open. Fourth, it requires people who keep the struggle grounded in reality and who define its limits. And fifth, it requires people who keep everyone connected by facilitating communication and interaction.[86] When all of these tasks are being performed well, it may be claimed that the leadership is exercising effective *strategic coordination*.

Regrettably, however, the strategic coordination required for effective nonviolent struggle is often lacking. Moreover, this shortcoming can be aggravated by the use of a decentralized leadership structure. This defect was evident during the Palestinian Intifada and was a critical failure of the Chinese pro-democracy movement in 1989. In the case of the Intifada, partly because of the decentralized nature of Palestinian decision making (coupled with the equivocal commitment to nonviolence), the UNC was not able to fulfill all of the necessary leadership functions identified above. For example, despite being considered a sensitive and responsive leadership, the UNC was not able to help ordinary Palestinians to keep the Intifada's aims clearly in focus, to maintain the energy and discipline necessary for a long-term nonviolent struggle, and to ground the struggle in a realistic assessment of its costs. This was evident, for instance, in the use of certain violent tactics and the slaying of collaborators, both of which seriously undermine a strategy of nonviolent resistance.[87] In the case of the Chinese pro-democracy movement, it is clear that the fluid and divided leadership was never capable of performing the leadership functions identified above and, therefore, of exercising the necessary strategic coordination. For example, despite a strong move in late May to initiate a departure from Tiananmen Square in favor of other tactics, the pro-democracy leadership lacked the cohesion and strategic perspective necessary to help their fellow students and workers to make wise strategic choices and to use an appropriate strategic timeframe. Thus, the occupation of the square continued after 28 May 1989 because at a vote taken on that date the students who lived outside Beijing outvoted the students who lived within Beijing. This decision reflected such factors as the cost of traveling to and from Beijing rather than the strategic imperatives of a long-term nonviolent struggle and the campaigns within it.[88]

While a decentralized leadership that is genuinely responsive to its grassroots constituency must reflect the divisions and wishes of that community, *it must also monitor its own capacity to perform each of the leadership functions identified above and, in the early stages, to facilitate widespread debate about the strategy itself.* By asking local groups to identify and consider the merits of different strategies, *as well as their requirements for success,* the leadership will facilitate the development of a cohesive and comprehensive strategy as well as the commitment necessary to carry it out. The leadership structure may vary in form, but it must still perform the vital function of strategic coordination.

As nonhierarchical forms of social organization gain acceptance, there will be more opportunities to explore a wide range of possibilities for coordinated decision making. In the meantime, organizational flexibility and experimentation should be encouraged. In addition, existing efforts to increase the levels of communication and cooperation (including solidarity work) among groups and networks in the peripheries is vitally important and should be sustained. One useful addition to this work would be to put more effort into specifically linking existing networks of women, indigenous peoples, workers' organizations, and activist groups to the nonviolence networks that exist locally and transnationally.

The historical experience contains clear lessons on how to prevent the defeat of a nonviolent defense through the elimination of any "leaders." Such a defense requires an unequivocal commitment to nonviolence, clearly defined strategic aims, and a widely understood strategic plan. It requires thorough preparation and an efficient communications system. Finally, it requires a decentralized organizational structure (with the capacity to develop locally relevant campaigns and tactics) and a decentralized leadership. This last point involves developing leadership capacity in as many people as possible and sharing leadership functions widely. According to Gandhi, each satyagrahi should become their own "general and leader."[89] This is important given the possibility, noted by Michael Walzer, that a ruthless opponent might dispatch squads of soldiers to detain, torture, exile, or kill civilian leaders.[90]

Despite the many gaps that remain in the historical experience, and the limited research on how to organize a decentralized nonviolent defense, there are important reasons why we should work to create alternative leadership structures rather than revert to more traditional models.

Internal Communication

One important feature of a well organized nonviolent defense strategy is a viable communications network. According to Alex Schmid, the social unit that is being defended must be able to communicate within its own ranks, with third parties, and with the social basis of the aggressor.[91] This requires a system that facilitates both internal and international communication. The discussion in this section will concentrate on the role of internal communication; the role of communication with the opponent and third parties will be considered more fully in the next chapter.

Internal communication channels are necessary in order to provide an ongoing account of the military aggression, to report international reactions to it, to provide analyses of political events, to explain nonviolent defense strategy, to communicate tactical ideas, to help maintain morale and discipline, and to legitimize the defense strategy.

Given the degree of elite control of mainstream media channels (newspapers, radio stations, and television networks) in most national societies, these cannot be relied upon either before or during a nonviolent defense. This is certainly the case in societies engaged in resistance to high levels of internal military repression. The stifling effect of elite control of the media was illustrated in the 1952 Defiance Campaign in South Africa. In this case, control of much of the mainstream media by racist interests not only prevented these channels from being used for the purposes identified above, it also ensured that most news of the campaign did not reach the white population. The stifling effect of this control was intensified by the fact that alternative news-sheets had only a very limited circulation, even among blacks.[92] The reporting of the 1961 "stay-at-home" strike was even worse, with many accounts in the mainstream media deliberately falsified.[93] Similarly, in cases in which nonviolent defense is being used to resist an invasion or coup, control of mainstream media channels may be lost during the initial stages of the attack.

In some circumstances, telephone, facsimile, and telex systems, as well as computer networks, may be very useful. During the pro-democracy struggle in China in 1989, for example, fax machines and computer networks were a vital means of communication between Chinese activists and the outside world. However, in many circumstances these channels will also be subject to elite control and might be shut down. For this reason it is important to develop alternative communication networks that are not centrally controlled. These must be widely accessible and should allow both internal communication and contact with peoples' networks in other countries. These channels might include pirate radio transmitters, short-wave radios,[94] duplicated posters, and even personal communications such as face-to-face conversations and letters. During the Norwegian resistance to the Nazi occupation in World War II and the Czechoslovakian resistance to the Warsaw Pact invasion in 1968, personal communications were vitally important.[95] In addition, personal communications have been a major source of information about the Tibetan resistance to Chinese occupation.

The historical record contains many examples in which the opponent's control of major media channels did not halt the communication of resistance information. During the French Generals' Revolt in 1961, the rebel generals controlled all of the newspapers and main radio transmitters in Algeria. However, they were not able to control the broadcast points outside Algeria or the less formal means of communication. In this case, transistor radios became especially important.[96] Similarly, during the nonviolent revolution in Iran in 1978–79, the Shah retained control of the state media, but cassette tapes containing revolutionary messages were smuggled into the country and distributed through the bazaars.[97] In the case of Fiji, despite military control of the mass media following the coups in 1987, activists continued to rely on short-wave radio for inter-island communication.[98] And during the Soviet coup in August 1991, despite the fact that all media outlets were banned, employees of eleven newspapers in Moscow published a "general newspaper," which they printed on photocopying machines. Large quantities of this newspaper were pasted to the walls and cars of the railway system, at bus stops, and in other gathering places. This helped to spread accurate information about the coup, encourage discussion of it, and psychologically transform the mood of the city. The quantity of papers was so great that any attempt to tear them down would have been pointless.[99]

Communication is a vital component of nonviolent defense.[100] Given the likelihood that centrally controlled media channels might be unavailable during a crisis, alternative communication networks—which allow both internal and international communication—should be developed and maintained.

Advance Preparations

Nonviolent defense, like military defense, will work more effectively if it has been thoroughly prepared in advance. Preparation involves several major aspects, including those discussed in other sections of this chapter. In addition, it should include the following: research designed to more fully understand the power structures within the societies of opponent elites; educational programs to teach people the history and theory of nonviolent action; opportunities for people to acquire confidence in nonviolent defense through their participation in local nonviolent struggles; advance contact with solidarity groups and grassroots networks in other countries; and an ongoing shift to more self-reliant social structures. This section briefly explains each of these aspects in turn.

For the strategic counteroffensive to be fully effective, it is necessary to understand the power structures within the societies of opponent elites. This will require research and may require the assistance of solidarity groups in the societies in question. For example, to undermine the Chinese government's occupation of Tibet, it is necessary to identify those social forces within China as well as those social forces in the United States and other third-party societies that support the occupation. Leaving aside the vital question of China in this example, why does the United States government support the occupation? One reason is suggested by the U.S. approach of encouraging the Chinese authorities to portray the Tibetan struggle as one of ethnic tension. This approach shifts the focus away from questions about Tibet's sovereignty and right to self-determination;[101] an approach that is consistent with that of a government that has long been intent on denying the sovereignty and right to self-determination of indigenous peoples generally, whether they be in Africa, Asia, or Central/South America or within the United States itself.[102] Within the United States, who supports the Chinese occupation of Tibet, and why? How can their support for the occupation be undermined? Who is likely to act in solidarity? These and related questions must be answered before an effective strategy of nonviolent defense can be developed. The strategic counteroffensive will be discussed more fully in chapter 13.

Preparation should also include campaigns to raise the level of awareness of nonviolent defense as well as ongoing educational programs to teach the theory and principles of nonviolent action and defense to a wider variety of social change and community groups. This will include role-plays[103] and may include more elaborate simulations[104] or maneuvers.[105] A nonviolent defense strategy will work most effectively in those circumstances in which a high proportion of the population understand what it entails and know the part they must play in order to implement it. In the words of Julio Quan: "The power of nonviolence has to be learned by the majority of the people."[106] Ideally, this means that a wide variety of educational forums (including workshops in schools and workplaces) should be used to help teach it. In addition, and particularly in those circumstances characterized by ruthless repression, preparation may need to include activities that allow people to deal with their fear.

However, while nonviolence education is important, it is evident that a nonviolent defense strategy will work most effectively if people have learned how to use nonviolent action and have experienced its effectiveness for themselves. For that reason, the *most valuable* component of the preparation for nonviolent defense is active participation in local campaigns of nonviolent struggle. Narayan Desai has noted: "Action is the best method of mass education."[107] This participation will provide the best opportunity to develop the knowledge and skills necessary to organize a nonviolent defense.

Sound preparation for nonviolent defense also requires advance contact and regular communication with solidarity groups and grassroots networks in other countries. This will widen the possibility of effective solidarity action in the societies of the opponent elite and their elite allies. There are many factors that complicate the way in which the people in grassroots constituencies interact; these include cultural and language differences. Much more importantly, they include the ways in which elites use fear, nationalism, racism, ideological distortion, censorship, and propaganda to maximize the degree of social distance among grassroots constituencies. Consequently, there are significant practical problems associated with any strategy to undermine the support of foreign constituencies for the aggression of their elites. For this reason, direct links with grassroots networks are necessary. This will make it possible, for example, to circumvent the elite practice of suppressing vital information (as was the case regarding the genocide in East Timor) and the complicity of the elite-controlled media in this practice.[108] Similarly, direct links with grassroots networks will make it possible to provide accurate information about the nature of any aggression and the nonviolent resistance to it—particularly given the elite preference for the use of military force and their willingness to justify it, if necessary, by using propaganda to deliberately exaggerate the potential for violence of even nonviolent opponents.

Preparation should also include an ongoing shift to self-reliance in the political, cultural, and economic spheres so that the defending population is better able to resist aggression and to minimize the effectiveness and rewards of military control. At the level of economic infrastructure, for example, it is necessary for the defending community to be able to maintain its essential services despite military disruption; these services include the water supply, the food production and distribution system, health services, the energy supply, and transport and communication systems. In addition, depending on the community, it might require the maintenance of a certain type and level of industrial production. It is evident that highly centralized societies (and particularly industrial cities) are more vulnerable to military interference in these respects than are decentralized communities.[109]

The Constructive Program

The conception of nonviolent defense developed in this study draws heavily on the conception held by Gandhi.[110] As outlined in chapter 7, nonviolence for Gandhi was more than just a technique of struggle or a strategy for resisting military aggression; it was intimately related to the wider struggle for social justice, economic self-reliance, and ecological harmony as well as the quest for self-realization. For Gandhi, nonviolent defense required the reconstruction of the personal, social, economic, and political life of each individual. "We shall get nothing by asking; we shall have to take what we want, and we need the requisite strength for the effort." He identified nineteen elements of this personal "strength" that was the prerequisite for effective nonviolent defense.[111] In essence, this program meant two things, both of which are also essential for the creation of a nonviolent social cosmology. For the individual, it meant increased power-from-within through the development of personal identity, self-reliance, and fearlessness. For the community, it meant the creation of a new set of political, social, and economic relations. So what should the constructive program[112] include?

For Gandhi, the development of personal identity is the result of identifying with what Johan Galtung calls "the trans-personal Self," that is, identifying with *all* humans rather than just some. In Gandhi's view, self-identification requires identification with both the oppressor and the oppressed in the struggle against the antihuman structure.[113] Václav Havel agrees. As he explains it, individuals must grasp their sense of "higher responsibility" to cultivate "a new experience of being" in their relationship with other people, the human community, and the universe as a whole. This is the basis for the "moral reconstitution of society."[114] For Gandhi and Havel, identification with "the trans-personal Self" is a concrete expression of the belief in the unity of all life, which has political, moral, and spiritual dimensions. It is a prerequisite for conflict resolution because the opponent's need for identity must be satisfied. It is a prerequisite for societal reconstruction given the moral void characteristic of the modern state. And it is a prerequisite for self-realization. Moreover, a person who has a strong sense of personal identity is well equipped to resist the normative power (that is, the cultural imperialism) of others.

This identification with all others requires that all persons reduce their wants to a minimum and develop a self-reliant capacity to satisfy those wants. "If each retained possession only of what [they] needed, no one would be in want, and all would live in contentment."[115] It is the desire for more than is needed that leads to dependence on the labor of others; this exploitation is avoided by those who are modest and self-reliant. Moreover, a person who is self-reliant is free of the bargaining power of others.

The higher the level of identification with all others, the greater the degree of fearlessness.[116] For Gandhi, fearlessness means freedom from all external fear, including the fear of dispossession, ridicule, disease, bodily injury, or death. These fears, he believed, derived from attachment to the body and the passions that arise from it. "Fear has no place in our hearts, when we have shaken off attachment for wealth, for family and for the body." This is because nothing in this world "is ours." According to Gandhi, people should enjoy things from the perspective of trustees, not proprietors. Progress toward the goal of fearlessness requires "determined and constant endeavour." In his view, the brave are those who are armed with fearlessness; those who use weapons "are possessed by fear."[117] A person who is fearless is unbowed by the punitive power of others.

According to the strategic theory developed in this study, progress toward peace, security, and stability in the world system is dependent on steps that create decentralized structures that serve the psychological, economic, and relational needs of all individuals and groups within society. At the community level, then, the constructive program is that part of the strategy designed to facilitate the development of new social structures that foster political participation, cultural diversity, economic self-reliance, and ecological resilience. As noted in chapter 10, if new types of structures are not being created to replace the old, then even a successful nonviolent defense will merely deliver control of the old and inadequate state structure to a new elite.[118] According to Havel, because ordinary people have been denied any direct influence on, or involvement in, the existing structures, "those who have decided to live within the truth" must create their own. The structures characteristic of this "second culture" must satisfy "the authentic needs of real people"; they must be small, community-oriented, and self-managing.[119] The important features of these new structures have been identified in earlier chapters and above.[120]

A comprehensive strategy of nonviolent defense requires a community of empowered individuals; in turn, it should help to create one. The constructive program, outlined in principle above, is central to that strategy.

Evaluation

The strategic plan should identify a process by which the strategy can be periodically evaluated. Importantly, these evaluations should include an assessment of the degree to which each strategic goal has been achieved. Ongoing evaluation is important because good strategy requires flexibility, a willingness to shift the focus of resistance and constructive work when necessary. Failure to seriously evaluate their strategy in light of changing circumstances was an important reason for the strategic inflexibility, and failures, of the Chinese pro-democracy movement in 1989. On the other hand, the capacity to debate and evaluate its strategy and tactics was a major strength of Solidarity's campaigns in Poland during the 1980s.[121]

12

The Strategy and Tactics of Nonviolent Defense

There is now a significant literature on civilian-based defense and social defense; an inadequate proportion of this literature, though, is devoted to the *operational* dimension of strategy. This shortcoming reflects several problems that plague thinking in the field: the lack of a shared conception of "nonviolent" defense (discussed in chapter 10), the lack of sufficient case studies that are considered to fit the "standard" model from which common principles can be deduced, the cultural and contextual diversity characteristic of the case studies that do exist, and the lack of a coherent strategic theory. This chapter discusses the operational dimension of a strategy of nonviolent defense based on the strategic theory and strategic framework outlined in chapter 8. While it concentrates on the defensive component of the strategy, it includes much discussion that is also relevant for the strategic counteroffensive: the topic of the final chapter.

The Political Purpose and the Strategic Aims

It has been argued throughout this study that strategy both reflects and shapes a society's cosmology. Therefore, while strategy is determined by policy, in any struggle the political and strategic components interact throughout. To make the relationship between politics and strategy more explicit, this study has significantly revised the original distinction drawn by Clausewitz. We now turn to a discussion of the meaning of, and the relationship between, the political purpose and the strategic aims in a strategy of nonviolent defense. These are illustrated in figure 5.[1]

According to the strategic theory developed in this study, the political purpose of a strategy of nonviolent defense is to create the policy, process, structural, and systemic conditions that will satisfy human needs. In practice, this purpose may be publicized in the form of a political program or as a list of demands. This program or list is vitally important and should be compiled with five criteria in mind: (1) According to Gandhi, the demands must be concrete, easily understood, and "within the power of the opponent to yield";[2] (2) they should accurately reflect the needs of the people engaged in the defense effort in order to mobilize widespread support for the struggle; (3) they should include an explicit commitment to the needs of the opponent; (4) they may expose moral weak points in the position of the opponent elite; and (5) they should constitute the substance of the political purpose. Some political programs in the past have satisfied several, if not all, of these criteria. For example, in the 1930–31 independence campaign, Gandhi chose eleven specific demands,[3] which, as Gopal noted, "were shrewdly chosen to win the sympathy of every social group" in India;[4] moreover, they highlighted the injustice of British imperialism and constituted the substance of independence. Similarly, the Congress of the People held in South Africa during 1955 adopted the Freedom Charter, which identified the broad aspirations of many South Africans, highlighted the moral weaknesses of the apartheid regime, and described the general elements of a democratic South African state.[5] However, the charter failed to clearly identify specific and concrete demands that reflected the day-to-day needs of ordinary Africans. This fact, coupled with the failure by the African National Congress (ANC) to do likewise, was a major reason for the inability of the ANC (despite its involvement in six major campaigns throughout the 1950s) to mobilize the increasing level of participation and support necessary to achieve the wider political demands described in the Freedom Charter.[6] As Narayan Desai has noted, people are more quickly and thoroughly mobilized when the issues are immediate and concrete.[7] And finally, in Palestine, fourteen demands announced in January 1988 became the political program of the Intifada. These demands were followed by the Declaration of Independence in November 1988 and the release of a program calling for a resolution of the conflict. Importantly, this program acknowledged Israel's right to exist within secure borders and, although this

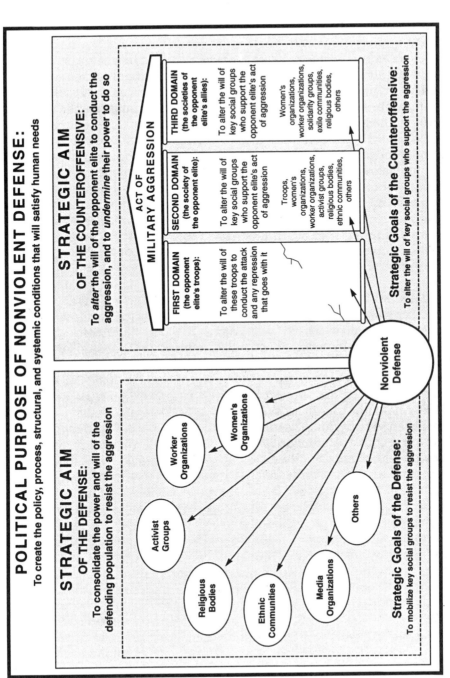

Figure 5. The Political Purpose and the Strategic Aims

provision was not fully adopted, renounced the use of violence in the Occupied Territories.[8]

Though identification of the political purpose ("what you want") is important, it does not provide strategic guidance; that is the function of the two strategic aims ("how you get what you want"). These are as follows. The strategic aim of the defense is to consolidate the power and will of the defending population to resist the aggression—that is, to maintain the nonviolent defense organization and to mobilize key social groups to participate in the strategy of nonviolent defense. And the strategic aim of the counteroffensive is to alter the will of the opponent elite to conduct the aggression—in favor of their participation in a problem-solving process—and to undermine their power to do so. The opponent elite might be induced to participate in a problem-solving process by offering a bracket of specific satisfiers that will meet their needs. This might alter their will to conduct the aggression. Or the opponent elite might be nonviolently coerced to participate by undermining the support of those key social groups (within and outside the country in question) whose support is necessary for the opponent elite to conduct the aggression. This will undermine their power to conduct it. In situations in which the opponent elite is powerful and a protracted struggle is likely, it is wise strategy to identify a series of intermediate strategic *goals*. This will make it possible to concentrate effort on particular goals within a sensible timeframe; it will also allow defense strategists to measure progress toward achievement of the strategic aims. A strategic goal should be specific: It should identify the group(s) it will affect and specify whether its achievement will increase the sources of power available to the defense or reduce those available to the opponent elite.[9]

The importance of clearly identified strategic aims and an appropriate set of intermediate strategic goals has been illustrated by the shortcomings of the Palestinian Intifada. According to the consent theory of power, which influenced the strategic thinking behind the Intifada,[10] withdrawal of cooperation by the Palestinians should have undermined the Israeli occupation strategy. However, it did not do so to the degree to which this theory would suggest because the Israelis are not sufficiently dependent on the Palestinians. As Andrew Rigby notes, the Israeli elite wants to rule the *land* of Palestine; "it does not want the *people*." While Rigby blames "the limitations of nonviolent resistance" as it applies in this particular case,[11] in fact the Intifada demonstrates the shortcomings of both the consent theory of power, which were discussed in chapter 6, and the strategy of the Intifada itself. According to the strategic theory developed in this study, it is the support of people within Israeli society and the support of people within the United States—rather than the cooperation of the Palestinians themselves—that are the vital sources of power that must be undermined.[12] Therefore, while one strategic aim of the Intifada should have been to consolidate Palestinian support for the Intifada itself, the other strategic aim should have been to alter the will of the Israeli government to maintain the occupation and to undermine its power to do so. The will of the Israeli government might have been altered by offering to satisfy certain Israeli needs, including the needs for identity and security.[13] The power of the Israeli government would have been undermined by mobilizing key social groups within Israel and the United States to publicly withdraw their support for the occupation. This, in turn, would have required a series of intermediate strategic goals. For example, an important strategic goal would have been to alter the will of the occupation troops to carry out their duties. The importance of this goal was recognized by Yesh Gvul ("There is a limit!"), the organization of Israeli soldiers who refuse to serve in the Occupied Territories. The potential impact of a campaign to achieve this strategic goal is illustrated by the fact that refusal of this type influenced the Israeli government to withdraw from Lebanon.[14] Of course, efforts to achieve this goal would have required a new and exceptional nonviolent discipline on the part of many Palestinians, a profoundly different attitude toward individual Israeli soldiers, new patterns of behavior toward these people (including a systematic program to eliminate stone throwing and the use of more lethal weapons against them), as well as considerable time. In summary: It is inaccurate to blame "the limitations of nonviolent resistance" when, in addition to the defects identified in the previous chapter, the shortcomings of the Intifada can be attributed to the incompleteness of the consent theory of power on which it was based, the major weaknesses in the Intifada strategy itself, and the crucial fact, highlighted by Rigby,[15] that the Intifada was *not* a nonviolent uprising: It was a predominantly *unarmed* one! For the Intifada to have been fully effective as a nonviolent defense strategy, its major strategic weaknesses, including those identified above, would have had to be corrected. This would include identifying the strategic aims and setting appropriate strategic goals.

To achieve the strategic aims, it may be necessary to organize a series of campaigns. These campaigns should highlight key political demands and concentrate on important strategic goals. In this way, it will be possible to move steadily and systematically toward the strategic aims, no matter how difficult it might be to achieve those aims. The following example highlights the way in which political and strategic factors interact at all levels throughout a defense struggle; it also illustrates the relationship between the political purpose and political demands, on the one hand, and the strategic aims and strategic goals, on the other.

As Gandhi conceived it, the political purpose of the Indian independence struggle was to create the conditions that would satisfy the needs of all Indians; this purpose was described by the word *independence*. In turn, the two strategic aims were, first, to consolidate the support of Indians for the independence struggle, and second, to alter the will of the British government to maintain its occupation—in favor of its participation in a conference to discuss the details of Indian independence—and to undermine its power to do so. To achieve the strategic aims, Gandhi organized a series of campaigns, one of which was the 1930–31 Salt Satyagraha. At the beginning of this campaign, Gandhi identified eleven political demands (which, as noted above, constituted the substance of independence), including removal of the salt tax. However, in parallel with these political demands, which were designed to reflect the needs of a wide cross-section of the Indian population, he envisaged a set of limited strategic goals. The first set of goals was intended to increase the sources of power available to the defense by mobilizing specifically identified sectors of Indian society for the independence struggle;[16] its achievement could be measured by the increased level of participation—particularly among women and villagers—that the campaign generated. The second set of strategic goals was intended to undermine the sources of power available to the British government by mobilizing public opposition within Britain and elsewhere to the imperial exploitation of India, exemplified in this campaign by the salt tax.[17] Its achievement could be measured by the decreased level of support among certain social groups, including the English working class and Americans generally, and by concessions in relation to the political demands, including the salt tax. In the Salt Satyagraha, both sets of strategic goals were achieved, and therefore progress was made toward the strategic aims; however, because the strategic aims of the independence struggle as a whole had not yet been fully realized, the political demands (as an expression of the political purpose) were only incompletely met.

As part of any strategy to achieve its strategic aims, the defense must be able to establish and maintain its legitimacy, build and maintain a high degree of social unity, and demonstrate its political resolve.

In many historical cases of nonviolent resistance, Adam Roberts argues, the political idea that inspired the resistance was "the idea of legitimacy."[18] According to Alex Schmid, a viable nonviolent defense strategy requires legitimacy in two distinct senses. First, the people of the defending society must enjoy some "legitimate status" in the eyes of their opponents or the wider community so that their concerns are taken seriously. In Western society, for example, indigenous peoples have usually lacked this status. And second, the society being defended must have a political system that is widely regarded as legitimate by its own population.[19] For instance, despite its well-known shortcomings, the Soviet government enjoyed "legitimate status" in the eyes of the civilian population, which the 1991 coup leaders clearly lacked.[20] Consequently, while the political systems represented by such groups as the National League for Democracy (NLD) in Burma, the Assembly of Tibetan People's Deputies, and the Palestine Liberation Organization (PLO) enjoy widespread legitimacy among their own people, an important part of their respective defense struggles is to enhance their legitimacy as social groups in the eyes of their opponents and the world community.

It is also important, as Schmid notes, for the defending society to achieve and maintain "a high degree of social cohesion" in order to minimize opportunities for the opponent elite to exploit political cleavages.[21] For example, as April Carter has noted, ethnic, religious, or class divisions (particularly those that coincide with political or ideological conflicts) can weaken the defense.[22] This was illustrated by the British success in exploiting Hindu-Muslim rivalry during the Indian independence struggle. More recently, it was illustrated by the apartheid regime's success in exploiting divisions between the black communities in South Africa and by the Israeli government's success in exploiting the strains between secular nationalists and Islamic activists during the Palestinian Intifada.[23] Nevertheless, unity in this sense is a goal to be achieved, not a precondition for nonviolent defense. In another sense, however, unity may be expressed in the form of a unified strategy, and the lack of this is a major risk. For example, the wide disparity of viewpoints among leaders of the African National Congress during the 1950s made a unified strategy "impossible."[24] More importantly, the failure of the Pan-African Congress to coordinate its campaign against the Pass Laws in 1960 with the more elaborate plans of the ANC was one of the main reasons for the defeat of the nonviolent movement in South Africa during that year, as well as the subsequent shift in emphasis, after twelve years, away from nonviolent struggle.[25] Unity among its organizers is a prerequisite for the effective implementation of a strategy of nonviolent defense.

It is also necessary for the defending society to demonstrate its political resolve. In some contexts, as the spontaneous nonviolent resistance by the Danes and Norwegians to Nazi occupation in World War II demonstrated, factors such as nationalism can supply the necessary fortitude for nonviolent defense.[26] However, in the context of this study, political resolve is a reflection of the ongoing efforts to develop the self-esteem, self-reliance, and fearlessness of the defending population. Such resolve can be demonstrated through either constructive work or campaigns of nonviolent resistance.

Throughout the defense struggle, the political purpose and the strategic aims should be kept clearly in mind, although the strategy should retain a capacity to maneuver in response to initiatives of the opponent elite. There is more than one way to achieve the strategic aims, but every intermediate goal should bear directly upon one of them.

The Strategic Timeframe

The notion of strategic goals suggests two related considerations: the need to adopt a *realistic* strategic timeframe, and the need to decide the number, nature, and duration of the *stages* and *campaigns* of a strategy of nonviolent defense. These are considerations to which Gandhi attached great importance.[27]

The adoption of a realistic strategic timeframe and a thoughtfully designed sequence of stages and campaigns will allow the defense to make steady progress toward the strategic aims. It will also reduce the risks associated with an unrealistic timetable (including the possibility that people will become prematurely disenchanted with the strategy and advocate the abandonment of nonviolent defense) and the danger of sudden and excessive doses of repression.

This approach is important in all cases but especially those in which the early removal of a dictator or an occupier is unlikely. On the basis of a limited understanding of the historical record, it is easy to assume that a short timeframe is adequate. For example, the nonviolent revolution in Iran during 1978–79 and the nonviolent revolutions in Eastern Europe during 1989 are often described as taking only several months, the nonviolent removal of Marcos in the Philippines in 1986 has been attributed to just four days of "people power," and the Soviet coup of 1991 is widely considered to be the result of just three days of intensive resistance. But in each of these cases there had been long periods of struggle of one sort or another, and the climax was built on this earlier preparation. For instance, the nonviolent revolution in the Philippines was the culmination of ten years of struggle.[28] Of course, from the perspective of the strategic theory developed in this study, these strategies were also incomplete; this explains the failure of the postrevolutionary societies to transform, in a positive way, the lives of ordinary people. Consequently, while a strategy (or some part of it) might succeed sooner than expected, it is wise to plan a long timeframe. In planning a strategy to remove the Chinese from Tibet or the Indonesians from East Timor, for instance, a long timeframe is essential. The colonists of North America intuitively recognized the importance of phased campaigns of nonviolent resistance;[29] the Chinese pro-democracy activists of 1989 did not.[30] While the approach described in this study stresses the wisdom of preparing for a protracted defense struggle, this should not be interpreted to mean that all strategies of nonviolent defense necessarily involve long timeframes. It simply emphasizes, as in the case of the nonviolent resistance to the Soviet coup, that a quick outcome in relation to a particular act of aggression is more likely if the conditions necessary for success already exist or have been created during previous stages of the struggle.

There are several points to consider in planning the stages of a nonviolent defense, but, like the advance preparations, both the initial response to an act of military aggression and all subsequent stages should be designed to systematically consolidate the will and power of the defense. What points should be considered when planning these stages?

First, the appropriate timeframe for the strategy, as well as the number, nature, and duration of its stages, should be decided following a realistic assessment of the existing will and power of the defense compared with those of the opponent elite; the appropriate timeframe is unrelated to the nature of the act of aggression. When the opponent elite is committed and much more powerful than the defense, several stages of lengthy duration—involving both constructive work and campaigns of nonviolent resistance—will be necessary. For example, due to the will and power of the British government compared with that of the Indian nationalists, the Indian independence struggle lasted for more than three decades and consisted of several stages during which a number of nonviolent campaigns were conducted and an elaborate constructive program was undertaken. When the opponent elite lacks both will and power compared to the defense, when both sides are approximately equal or when the levels are at least significant in each case and the situation is extremely fluid, then (apart from the period of advance preparation) one or two stages of extremely short duration *might* be adequate to defeat an act of aggression. For example, the will and power of the Soviet people and of the 1991 coup leaders were significant, and the situation was highly fluid. In these circumstances, the Soviet people were able to implement a single campaign of nonviolent resistance—involving massive noncooperation and nonviolent intervention—to consolidate their power and to undermine that of their opponents in just three days. The danger of failing to make a realistic assessment of the will and power of the defense compared with those of the opponent elite, in order to determine the appropriate strategic timeframe, was clearly illustrated during the early months of the Palestinian Intifada. In this case, the failure led the Palestinians to work under an untenable timeframe and to ignore the need for the resistance to proceed in a series of thoughtfully designed stages and campaigns. Given the heavy cost of the economic tactics employed in the first few weeks of the Intifada, the Palestinians were quickly exposed to unproductive strain.

Second, because a strategy of nonviolent defense is based on the participation of ordinary people, both the nonviolent campaigns and the constructive program should be designed to encourage new people to become actively involved during each stage of the defense. The strategy should aim to enlist "the passive sympathy, if not the active co-operation" of all individuals and groups.[31] This requires an astute assessment of the level of "psychological preparedness": the capacity of people to risk something during each new stage of the defense.[32] For example, the first stage of any protracted defense struggle should include simple things, including nonviolent tactics, that everyone can do—bearing in mind the possibility that some sections of the defending population might need to deal with considerable personal fear. Planning should therefore include the preparation of a code of nonviolent discipline (including guidelines regarding the appropriate attitude and behavior toward individual opponents)[33] as well as the preparation of a set of simple actions (such as wearing a symbol of resistance or solidarity, or engaging in minor acts of noncooperation) that can be implemented in immediate response to an act of military aggression. These activities will build confidence, strengthen solidarity, and "prod the population into involvement."[34] If a symbol is to be used, the type chosen is very important. As the discussion in a later section will illustrate, the choice of inappropriate symbols can be very dangerous. A symbol should be meaningful, easily recognizable, and readily duplicated. For example, symbols, such as the Tibetan flag, that emphasize shared religious and cultural heritage have been a crucial and unifying element in the long Tibetan struggle against Chinese military occupation.[35]

Moreover, as this example suggests, there is another factor that should be considered if the strategy is to encourage people to become actively involved during each stage of the defense. This factor concerns the role to be played by cultural and spiritual activities. During the long Soviet occupation of Latvia, for example, both resistance and constructive activities often had a cultural or spiritual nature. Latvians resisted participation in Soviet cultural activities such as learning the Russian language or singing Soviet songs, and they worked hard to maintain and develop Latvian cultural and spiritual traditions, including art, literature, music, and religious celebrations.[36] The "Culture Front" was an important part of the Norwegian resistance to Nazi occupation in World War II as well. In fact, by mid–1942, a representative group of musicians, painters, and writers had issued a set of guidelines identifying "acceptable behavior for loyal Norwegian artists."[37] A strategy that identifies appropriate cultural and spiritual activities as part of each stage of the defense offers the general population easy opportunities for involvement and should help to draw people into the struggle. At a more mundane level, each stage of the defense should provide ample opportunity for involvement in other ways—for instance, by contributing labor or other resources.

Third, in planning the stages of a nonviolent defense, careful thought should be given to the number, nature, duration, and stages of the individual campaigns. Gandhi paid close attention to these factors.[38] Each campaign should be planned to achieve a previously identified strategic goal. Its nature should be determined by the goal itself; for example, a campaign intended to mobilize a specific group of potential defenders will be quite different in nature from a campaign conducted in the society of the opponent elite with the goal of undermining the support of a key trade union for that elite. The duration and stages of any campaign should be determined by a realistic assessment of the time necessary to achieve the strategic goal.

Fourth, in relation to the strategic counteroffensive, the stages should be designed so that support for the opponent elite's aggression is systematically undermined and so that the climax of the strategy is neither reached prematurely (as occurred during the 1989 Chinese pro-democracy struggle) nor unnecessarily drawn out. This means that each stage should consist of a combination of activities (including specific nonviolent campaigns) that are thoughtfully designed to undermine the support of key social groups within the constituency of the opponent elite and within the constituencies of their elite allies in accordance with a precisely identified strategic sequence. If this has not been done during the period of preparation, the first stage of the strategic counteroffensive should include direct communication with solidarity groups and grassroots networks in order to encourage their active participation in the resistance and to request their help in identifying those social groups within their countries whose support for the aggression it would be strategically useful to undermine. For example, if trade unionists are responsible for handling weapons that are being supplied to the opponent elite, then one part of the strategy might include dialogue with the trade unionists and, if necessary and possible, a local solidarity campaign to have this labor withdrawn. This will be considered more fully in the next chapter.

In summary, all stages and campaigns of a strategy of nonviolent defense should be designed to enhance the will and power of the defense to resist aggression and to diminish those of the opponent elite to conduct it. In this way, achievement of the strategic aims should be the culmination of a carefully planned series of stages during which the defense retains the initiative.

Communication

A section in the previous chapter discussed the importance of communication systems to nonviolent defense and illustrated this with particular reference to internal communication; this section will concentrate on the role of communication with the opponent and third parties. Communication with *the opponent* can occur at three levels: with the opponent elite directly, with the opponent elite's troops and functionaries, and with the people in the opponent elite's domestic constituency.

To establish the basis for future cooperation with the opponent *elite*, it is important that the selected representatives of the defense create or accept opportunities for dialogue. This is strategically important because it will provide the opportunity to listen to the opponent elite and to clarify what they declare they want; this may lead to an early opportunity to identify and satisfy their needs and thus alter their will to conduct the aggression. At the very least, it will provide the opportunity to start cultivating personal relationships and to explain the commitment to nonviolent discipline and the determination to resist. Even if it produces no immediate results, this approach will assist when the problem-solving process to resolve the conflict is ultimately commenced. Telling the truth throughout this dialogue is vital to the process of building trust, particularly given the inevitability of misperception. It should be stressed at this point that nonviolence never means noncommunication. For example, despite the ongoing atrocities committed by the Chinese army in Tibet, the Dalai Lama has consistently demonstrated his willingness to engage in dialogue with the Chinese leadership.[39]

As the defense struggle makes progress toward the strategic aims, further opportunities to discuss the substantive issues will arise. As they do, the selected representatives of the defense should make clear their willingness to participate. In the past, nonviolent leaders have been criticized "for their willingness to negotiate and to make concessions."[40] Gandhi, for example, was strongly criticized for negotiating the Gandhi-Irwin Pact of March 1931 to conclude the Salt Satyagraha.[41] However, as Gandhi argued, there comes a time when satyagrahis must negotiate with their opponent.[42] Moreover, he believed, any agreement should reflect precisely those gains made during the struggle and nothing beyond that.[43] In any case, unlike his critics, Gandhi believed that any negotiations were only partly concerned with the conflict outcome; more importantly, they were concerned with building superior human relationships.[44] Ultimately, of course, negotiations are an essential corollary of nonviolent defense, "making it possible for an opponent to withdraw from policies and positions which the resistance has shown to be impossible or unprofitable."[45] Unlike traditional forms of negotiation, however, the process advocated in this study is a problem-solving one designed to meet the needs of all parties.

Nonviolent defense can also provide the opportunity for various types of contact with the opponent elite's *troops and functionaries*; this might be negative or positive. On the negative side, it might entail ostracism of individual soldiers or forms of social boycott. For example, in Czechoslovakia in 1968, citizens argued with the Soviet soldiers, refused them food, and denied them normal social relationships. This had a demoralizing impact on the occupation troops.[46] Where contact is used more positively, it might be limited to friendly fraternization, it might include political propaganda about the aims of the nonviolent resistance, or it might involve "deliberate and carefully calculated attempts" to make the troops realize the degree of suffering their actions are causing.[47] When their personal safety is not at risk, soldiers are likely to have an attitude of curiosity.[48] In the nonviolent resistance to the Soviet coup in 1991, mingling with the soldiers entering Moscow was vitally important. Spontaneous meetings took place around military vehicles and tanks, and soldiers were given food and cigarettes. Importantly, no one "displayed a personal hatred for the soldiers," and the attitude of goodwill, as well as the provision of otherwise unavailable information, undermined "the 'fighting spirit' of the conscripts." This action made it necessary for the coup leaders to constantly replace the military units patrolling the city. In addition, barricades were built from trolleybuses, delivery trucks, and rubbish skips. Though these did not present a serious obstacle to armored vehicles, they were capable of stopping soldiers for a few minutes. "These minutes could be used to agitate among the soldiers." Activists who spoke the languages of non-Russian nationalities were selected out "in order to appeal to soldiers in their native tongue." One crucial result of these discussions was that six tanks ordered to seize the Russian White House defected to the people's side.[49]

It is clear, as Schmid's study concluded,[50] that in those circumstances in which it is feasible, personal contact with the opponent elite's troops should be encouraged; in fact, as the next chapter will explain, it can be a vital aspect of the strategic counteroffensive. However, given the diversity of historical experience, there is no consensus in the literature regarding the form this contact should take and in what atmosphere it should occur. Despite this, the answer is clear. The recent conflict theories outlined in chapter 5 indicate that a negative approach to the opponent (including the use of verbal insults) is likely to induce role defensiveness and a threatening approach is likely to generate fear. In either case, these approaches are likely to consolidate a soldier's commitment to their military role. Therefore, according to the strategic theory developed in this study, personal contact with individual opponents should be positive and should involve reflective listening, including the acknowledgment of feelings, as well as educative elements. Given the inherent needs for recognition and self-respect, interactions that affirm the dignity and worth of the individual are most likely to induce soldiers to consider alternative information, to question their orders, and, ultimately, to challenge the legitimacy of their military role. This approach will help to reduce the steep Self-Other attitudinal gradient and may induce behavioral changes as well; both are important elements in the conflict resolution process.

To counter the subversive impact that can result from the defenders' contact with soldiers, the opponent elite might rotate troops frequently or use troops who speak a different language. More seriously, the opponent elite might scare the troops with deliberately inaccurate warnings of probable defender violence or simply provoke violence by using provocateurs. Rotation and language differences can be met by rostering teams of defenders who speak the appropriate languages to undertake the dialogue on a continuing basis and by printing leaflets in the languages of the opponent elite's troops. Troop fears can be allayed by seeking contact with them long before they reach their final (and most feared) destination. The risk of deliberate provocations resulting in violence can be minimized by encouraging defenders to adhere to nonviolent discipline and by using specially trained peacekeeping teams to identify and isolate inappropriate behavior. The problem of provocateurs will be considered more fully in a later section.

Communication with the people in the opponent elite's *domestic constituency* should concentrate on the nonviolent and determined nature of the resistance and the illegitimacy of the aggression. The concurrence of interests between the respective peripheries should be emphasized. Ideally, as the next chapter will elaborate, it should include discussions about how the aggression can be undermined by campaigns of nonviolent action undertaken by solidarity activists within the society of the opponent elite.

Communication with *third parties* is another vital aspect of the defense. This communication should also emphasize the nonviolent nature of the defense and include discussions about how the aggression can be undermined by nonviolent action undertaken by solidarity activists in third-party societies. Solidarity action of this type will be discussed in the next chapter.

Communication with the opponent and third parties is a vital element in any nonviolent defense. Effective communication may alter the opponent elite's will to conduct the aggression, it may undermine the commitment of their troops and functionaries, it may undermine the support of their domestic constituency, and it may undermine the support of their allied elites.

Strategic Considerations in the Selection of Nonviolent Tactics

As noted previously, the strategic plan should identify an appropriate set of strategic goals. To achieve each strategic goal, it will be necessary to engage in dialogue and it might be necessary to conduct a well-focused nonviolent action campaign. Any campaign should be carefully planned using a modified version of the strategic framework outlined in chapter 8. Importantly, it should identify the combination and sequence of nonviolent tactics and indicate how, where, and when to apply them. To be strategically effective, the tactics chosen must be directed at the strategic goal and applied in accordance with the conceptions of conflict and Gandhian nonviolence that underpin the strategic theory developed in this study. This section discusses some of the strategic considerations that should guide the selection, organization, and application of nonviolent tactics used in any campaign.

Within any strategic plan, according to Clausewitz, there are two possible types of operational pattern: the sequential and the cumulative. The sequential approach entails planning a series of carefully selected tactics, with each action building on the one that preceded it. The cumulative approach is one in which the entire pattern consists of a collection of tactics that are not sequentially interdependent. In practice, Clausewitz argues, the sequential approach is superior, but these operational patterns are not mutually exclusive and are often interdependent in strategic impact.[51] In contrast, Mao Zedong contends, in the case of guerrilla warfare the cumulative effects are decisive.[52] In a strategy of nonviolent defense, each campaign should identify a carefully selected sequence of nonviolent tactics, although in most situations tactics that have a cumulative impact will still be useful. For example, in circumstances or locations in which it is difficult to plan strategically sequential tactics, but in which action may be necessary in order to maintain morale, build unity, or intensify resolve, even tactics that are likely to have only a marginal cumulative impact are important. The plan should identify a combination of tactics and design them to have impact in one or more ways: politically, psychologically, morally, socially, economically, or physically. These tactics should be feasible, creative, culturally appropriate,[53] and designed either to consolidate the power and will of the defense or to undermine those of the opponent elite.

In planning any campaign strategy, defense activists should consider the three major categories of tactics—protest and persuasion, noncooperation, and nonviolent intervention—and the vast array of tactics in each category.[54] Given this variety, careful thought needs to be given to selecting the tactics that are most likely to help achieve the strategic goal of the campaign. For example, if the campaign plan includes the decision to resist the occupation of an important media installation in order to counter its propaganda function, defense activists might choose (among other tactical options) to picket the entrance and use moral suasion on the occupiers (a form of protest), to refuse to service and supply it (a form of noncooperation), or to blockade it (a form of nonviolent intervention).[55] Clearly, there are significant but different strategic implications associated with each tactic. These need to be carefully considered in light of the strategic aims and the stages of the strategy.

Certain classes of tactics involve a cost, and in many cases this cost falls disproportionately on a particular sector of the defending population. While self-suffering is an important element in any nonviolent defense, it is still necessary to make a realistic assessment of the capacity of those affected to bear the cost. This is vitally important because tactics that exact an inappropriately heavy cost may jeopardize the strategy itself. This was graphically illustrated during the early months of the Palestinian Intifada, which resembled a "nonviolent blitzkrieg." In this case, the economic tactics employed—particularly the frequent general strikes, the mass resignations, and the tax resistance—seriously interfered with the capacity of the Palestinians to sustain the resistance. Eventually these tactics had to be revised.[56] The defense planners should identify a sequence of tactics that is based on a realistic assessment of their cost and is consistent with the capacity of the resistance to sustain these costs.

In addition, certain classes of tactics have particular requirements for effectiveness. Effective noncooperation, for instance, usually requires the involvement of larger numbers of people and longer periods of time.[57] During the 1930 independence campaign, Gandhi rejected the notion of concentrating solely on the boycott of foreign cloth, because it would have required the cooperation of 300 million Indians. Instead, he focused attention on civil disobedience of the salt laws because, he believed, it required the active participation of only ten thousand defiant people.[58] The defense planners should identify tactics that will be effective in the circumstances.

While more powerful nonviolent tactics have the potential of working quickly, there are greater risks to the activists and wider strategic implications and dangers. These tactics require more careful preparation, higher levels of nonviolence education and discipline, higher quality organization and leadership, and, usually, supplementary use of more moderate tactics.[59] In Gandhi's view: "The quickest remedies are always fraught with the greatest danger and require the utmost skill in handling them."[60] Gandhi often used the public response to a specific tactic as a gauge to determine the wisdom of using more extreme measures.[61] For example, on one occasion he used the public response to a *hartal* (voluntary closure of businesses) to gauge the readiness for civil disobedience.[62] The defense planners should identify an appropriate combination of both moderate and powerful tactics.

Careful consideration should also be given to the factor of dispersion or concentration.[63] Tactics involving *dispersion* (such as a strike or boycott) provide the opportunity for more people to participate in the action and are more likely to overextend the opponent; they also minimize the opportunities for repression. This last factor was recognized by the Solidarity leaders in Poland. During earlier periods of social unrest in Poland, police had often provoked and used violence against workers involved in street marches. Consequently, the tactic most frequently employed by Solidarity during the early 1980s was the sit-in strike, which minimized the opportunities for such violence.[64] Tactics involving *concentration* (such as a street demonstration) provide the opportunity to share commitment and build solidarity and, when the opponent elite's power has been functionally undermined, to deliver a decisive "blow." Moreover, such tactics may be deliberately used—as Gandhi did at the Dharasana salt works[65]—to expose the opponent elite's willingness to use violence.[66] However, in circumstances in which the correct tactic involves concentrating people in one place even though the opponent elite is likely to attempt decisive repressive action, more elaborate preparation should be undertaken. This will be discussed in a separate section below.

A vitally important strategic consideration is how to seize and retain the initiative. In Gandhi's view, good leaders always choose the time and place of "battle." They always retain the initiative in these respects and never allow it to pass into the hands of the opponent.[67] But retaining the strategic initiative is not a straightforward task. During the 1952 Defiance Campaign in South Africa, for example, the apartheid regime used provocateurs to provoke riots; as a result, the initiative was lost to the government.[68] Retaining the initiative requires ongoing assessment of the defense strategy and the careful selection of tactics.[69] Four considerations are vital.

First, the strategic plan should include only tactics that are designed to achieve the strategic aims; the defense should not respond automatically, as suggested by some authors,[70] by offering resistance to specific objectives of the opponent. For example, in response to a bout of repression (including a ban on public political activity) directed at opponents of the Uruguayan dictatorship in 1983, activists organized a street demonstration. This demonstration was brutally repressed. Concerned that another street demonstration would achieve only limited participation while playing into the military's strategy of terrorizing the population, the organizing group—Servicio Paz y Justicia (SERPAJ)—regained the initiative by organizing a tactic more likely to reinforce the will and power of the resistance. The tactic involved a fifteen-day fast (undertaken by two priests and a pastor) followed by "an hour of national reflection," at the end of which time people were asked to turn off their houselights in silent protest. At the appointed time, the entire city went dark.[71] To retain the initiative, the strategic aims must be kept clearly in focus and the temptation to respond automatically to each new provocation of the opponent elite must be resisted.

Second, retaining the initiative requires strategic coordination (which was explained in the previous chapter). This includes the capacity to maintain nonviolent discipline and to share costs for the duration of the struggle. In addition to the considerations mentioned earlier, this might require use of the "relay effect": When excessive pressure is being applied against one section of the resistance responsible for a particular function, another group or groups may assume responsibility for that function. In this way, important activities can continue without undue interruption, because they are being performed by the group best able to do so at the particular time. For example, during the Czechoslovakian resistance to the Warsaw Pact invasion in 1968, a succession of media channels was used to convey resistance information. When newspapers were censored, newsreels, theaters, and humorous magazines were used. As these fell under the threat of censorship, leaflets and chain letters were used in order to relieve the pressure on other channels. By exercising the discipline and self-control necessary to use the relay effect, the resistance was able to improve its durability and to avoid having important functions isolated and destroyed.[72] To retain the initiative, strategic coordination is vital.

Third, retaining the initiative requires strategic flexibility. This can be easily lost and can happen for a variety of reasons, including attachment to a symbol. In nonviolent defense, a symbol is important insofar as it represents important values and norms. It provides a unifying reference point, reminding defenders what is being defended and why.[73] But it is important to remember that it is not the symbol itself that is being defended. A symbol, by definition, represents something else.[74] Consequently, activists should not become transfixed by a particular symbol, no matter how important it may seem. If they do, the defense will lose its strategic flexibility. For example, there is compelling evidence to suggest that Tiananmen Square—including the statue known as the "Goddess of Democracy"—had become a strategically immobilizing symbol for the Chinese pro-democracy movement in 1989. Despite the strategic advantages of shifting the focus of the struggle elsewhere, the square itself had acquired a magnetizing influence over the activists; this was starkly illustrated by the oath, taken by several thousand students a few hours before the massacre, to "defend Tiananmen Square with my young life." The square, rather than what it represented, had become the focus of the struggle. More importantly, the movement had failed to maintain the important distinction between its political purpose (democracy) and its symbols (including Tiananmen Square), on the one hand, and its strategic aims, on the other. In the strategic sense, the square, like any symbol, was important only insofar as it could be used to mobilize particular social groups (students, workers, and intellectuals) to support the pro-democracy struggle in a strategically focused manner; control of the square itself was strategically irrelevant.[75] Similarly, during the Soviet coup in 1991, the Russian White House was strategically important only insofar as it was a suitable symbol for mobilizing individuals and groups to resist the coup; control of the building itself was strategically irrelevant *except* insofar as a mistaken belief in the importance of this control may have led to loss of the building having an adverse affect on the will and power of the defenders to resist.[76] In summary, it is important that defenders do not become transfixed by a symbol,[77] and, as noted earlier, it is possible to choose a type of symbol that minimizes this risk. Belief in the importance of a particular symbol (as distinct from what it represents) can lead to three undesirable strategic outcomes: It can lead activists to defend a strategically irrelevant point; it can make it difficult to shift the focus of the resistance, if a shift is negatively interpreted to be a retreat; and it can lead activists to believe that they have suffered a defeat if a symbol is "lost." Each of these outcomes, and particularly the last, can undermine both the will and the power to resist, at least in the short term, as the 1989 setback to the Chinese pro-democracy struggle graphically highlighted. If the initiative is to be retained, strategic flexibility is essential.

Fourth, retaining the strategic initiative requires ongoing assessment of the political situation in order to gauge the suitability of particular tactics. For example, in circumstances characterized by severe repression or in which the atmosphere is temporarily inflamed, a tactic involving direct confrontation with the opponent elite will increase the risk that they will resort to the use of extreme violence—which will brutalize their soldiers—and might endanger the immediate continuity of the defense. In these circumstances, a different tactic, perhaps one involving a high degree of dispersal, should be chosen. To retain the initiative, the defense must keep the strategic aims clearly in focus, it must exercise strategic coordination and flexibility, and it must continually assess the political situation.

It should be clear from the discussion above that the choice of tactics is not an arbitrary one: *It should reflect a careful assessment of which tactics are most likely to help achieve the strategic aims.* Once tactics have been selected, there are several factors that need to be considered during the detailed planning of each tactic. How is the tactic to be organized (particularly if there is a possibility of ruthless repression)? How many activists should be involved, and what level of nonviolence education or experience should they have? Where and when should the action take place? And who will be responsible for peacekeeping?

To achieve the desired strategic outcome, it is vitally important that each nonviolent tactic be thoroughly organized, from planning to debriefing. Given his political and strategic orientation, Gandhi was disinclined to leave anything to chance. For example, in preparation for the Salt March, there was a remarkable degree of organization; this included identifying the route (according to several criteria) and the formation of two advance parties that were to prepare alternate villages for the arrival of the marchers themselves.[78] To organize a tactic thoroughly, an action-planning group may be formed. When planning a tactic, the organizers should be aware of the sensibilities of their opponents and third parties so that the action works to humanize the defenders in the eyes of these parties.[79] For some actions, such as a large rally, the planning group may appoint people to fill several important roles, including that of action focalizer. It is the task of the action focalizers to create the atmosphere for a particular action. This includes identifying the goal of the action, indicating its nonviolent nature (and asking people to respect this discipline or to withdraw from the action), and creating the appropriate mood (for example, one of celebration or mourning). It may also include drawing attention to the distribution of an "action leaflet" (which explains the main details of the action and identifies the important behavioral guidelines) as well as outlining any safety precautions or contingency plan (particularly if a violent response from the opponent is possible). This information will assist people to understand the nature of the action and to resist the initiatives of individuals or groups with a competing agenda. It is also the responsibility of the focalizers to facilitate the action through the stages agreed upon during the planning process. To perform their role, the focalizers require the support of people in other roles: public speakers, media spokespeople, liaison personnel, and those organizing any equipment. In addition, they require the support of marshals and peacekeepers. In summary, though there is room for elements of creativity during any action (and particularly during those involving experienced affinity groups), politically effective tactics are the direct result of strategic planning, thorough organization and strict adherence to nonviolent discipline. Spontaneous action is unlikely to be strategically focused or effective. When ruthless repression is a possibility, further preparation and organization is required; this will be considered in a separate section below.

An important strategic consideration concerns the number and experience of the people that should be involved in a particular action. When the intention is to display the strength of the resistance, actions such as street demonstrations (which usually, but not always, provide low-risk opportunities for involvement) might be chosen, as these have the potential to involve large numbers of people. In other cases, small numbers of highly disciplined and experienced activists will be more appropriate. According to Gandhi, "It is possible to fight a non-violent battle even with one satyagrahi. But it . . . cannot be fought with a million non-satyagrahis."[80] This is because effective satyagraha ultimately depends on moral and spiritual resources, not the number of people involved in a particular action. In fact, Gandhi believed, numbers are a source of weakness when discipline is indifferent.[81] For these reasons, Gandhi was much more concerned with quality than with quantity.[82] In some cases, as in the Individual Satyagraha movement, he imposed strict limits on the numbers involved in a campaign.[83] In other cases, as in the Salt March, he limited participation to those with proven commitment, discipline, or experience.[84]

Two related considerations are the location and timing of the action. These were major strengths of Gandhi's campaigns. In relation to timing, Jawaharlal Nehru observed that Gandhi had "a knack of acting at the psychological moment."[85] For example, in order to start the 1930 independence campaign, Gandhi planned to deliberately break the salt laws, and, after much investigation by a team of volunteers and careful deliberation by several co-workers, an obscure and distant beach was chosen as the place for doing so. This meant that Gandhi and his fellow salt marchers had to walk for twenty-five days, a timeframe that reflected Gandhi's preference for building tension gradually. Moreover, he timed his arrival, and the start of civil disobedience, to coincide with the beginning of National Week.[86] In contrast, the cost of failing to make strategic decisions about the location and timing of their tactics was graphically demonstrated by the Chinese pro-democracy activists in 1989. While there is a great deal of contradictory evidence, and therefore considerable uncertainty, regarding the details of the planning and preparation undertaken by activists in Tiananmen

Square for the confrontation with the People's Liberation Army (PLA)[87] during the early hours of 4 June 1989,[88] the accounts that are considered to be the most authoritative, including those of Hou Dejian and Chai Ling, make some details absolutely clear. For example, while the Chinese activists were certainly not lacking in courage, they did lack an adequate strategic goal, as well as the necessary leadership structure, organization, cohesion, and discipline to justify, in a strategic sense, any attempt to maintain their occupation of the square. From the accounts of events leading up to 4 June, it seems clear that they should have decided to conclude their occupation of the square, in favor of other tactics, at the vote taken on 28 May 1989.

Finally, once selected and organized, a tactic should be applied in a manner that is consistent with the conceptions of conflict and Gandhian nonviolence that underpin the strategic theory developed in this study. For instance, as discussed in chapter 7, it should involve a deep respect for the shared humanity of all opponents, it should include a clear willingness to experience self-suffering (with no intention to punish the opponent or to extract revenge), and it should be limited to coercing the opponent elite's participation in a problem-solving process (and must not entail direct coercion of their will).

A strategically focused nonviolent defense should concentrate on the achievement of its strategic aims. For that reason, strategic considerations, including those discussed above, should guide the selection, organization, and application of nonviolent tactics.

Secrecy and Sabotage

There is an ongoing debate in the literature on nonviolent action regarding the utility of secrecy and sabotage. Should tactics involving secrecy or sabotage be employed as part of a nonviolent defense? In the previous chapter, the question of secrecy in relation to the leadership structure of a nonviolent defense was discussed. In this section, the role of secrecy and sabotage in relation to tactics is considered.

In the past, "secret" tactics have been used by many resistance movements. These tactics have been used for a variety of reasons, and they have taken many forms. For example, under the conditions of extreme repression characteristic of Eastern Europe between

1945 and 1989, many forms of indirect resistance, including what Arne Naess calls "microresistance"—resistance by individuals and small temporary groups—were common.[89] But as Václav Havel has noted, even within the context of the "post-totalitarian" system of Eastern Europe during that period, ultimately—if one was to "live within the truth" in order to destroy that system—*one had to act openly*. Such action did not need to be overtly "political"; for example, it may have been cultural in form. Depending on the context, a poem or a rock concert may have the same depth of political meaning as a demonstration or a strike.[90] Similarly, according to the strategic theory developed in this study, a strategy of nonviolent defense has certain requirements for success, and these cannot be met when the tactics employed are applied secretly. Thus, while secret tactics may have played a role in the past and might again in the future, the very limited nature of their contribution *in a strategic sense* must be recognized.

Consequently, as noted earlier, while the period of advance preparation (or even the first stage of the strategy) might require activities or workshops to help people to deal with their fear of acting openly, secret tactics have no part in a strategy of nonviolent defense as it is conceived in this study; as the following explanation illustrates, it is seriously inconsistent with the strategic theory described in chapter 8. First, for the reasons outlined in chapter 7, the use of secrecy precludes the possibility of resolving conflict in terms of human needs. Second, the use of secrecy is contrary to the Gandhian conception of nonviolence. Given the importance he attached to such principles as adherence to truth and respect for the opponent, secrecy had no part to play in Gandhi's scheme of nonviolence: "I detest secrecy as a sin."[91]

Third, the many reasons why nonviolent tactics should not be shrouded in secrecy have been well documented in the literature. For example, secrecy is rooted in fear and contributes to it, whereas nonviolent struggle is essentially about learning to overcome fear. According to Sharp, being truthful and frank with the opponent and third parties is a corollary of the requirements of fearlessness and nonviolent discipline.[92] Moreover, Rajendra Prasad argues, because nonviolent activists, in the Gandhian sense, are always prepared to suffer the consequences of their actions, secrecy is unnecessary. As he notes, the use of secrecy implies a desire to escape those consequences and to shift the responsibility onto others.[93] In addition, secrecy will usually mean that there are fewer active participants. For example, the sense that leaders fear punishment will discourage potential activists.[94]

Fourth, and most importantly, the use of secrecy will not undermine the opponent elite's center of gravity; that is, their sources of power. This is because secrecy interferes with the subtle political and psychological mechanisms at work during nonviolent action. An essential aspect of the power of nonviolence is the way in which personal and group qualities such as honesty, commitment, conviction, courage, and integrity cause shifts of loyalty and thus undermine the power of the opponent. Secrecy subverts this process.

It is an important strategic task to design tactics that do not rely on secrecy for their success. In one sense, this may not be difficult. For example, as noted above, many struggles have been sustained over long periods of time by the use of cultural practices in ways that helped to reinforce the will and power of the people to resist.[95] Nevertheless, in some circumstances the design of nonsecretive tactics will require a certain degree of strategic wisdom and considerable creativity. It might also require audacity and courage. For instance, in Bolivia during the Christmas season of 1977–78, four women commenced a hunger strike in the offices of the Archbishop of La Paz. The hunger strike inspired widespread support (including another 1,380 hunger strikers) and compelled the repressive military dictatorship to "grant the substance of all their demands" in less than a month.[96] And, to elaborate an example cited earlier, in Uruguay in 1983, in order to conclude their fifteen-day fast, two priests and a pastor had called for "an hour of national reflection" so that people could "reflect on their personal responsibility in the face of the violence and repression" inflicted by the military dictatorship. They had also asked that people turn off their lights at 8 P.M. in silent protest. Despite total censorship of the media, at 8 P.M. on the set day the entire city went dark; at 8:15 P.M., people began to bang pots and pans. In this darkened city of one and a half million people busily banging in their homes, "there was nothing" the military could do.[97] Tactics to be employed as part of a strategy of nonviolent defense should be explicitly and publicly declared. Of course, under conditions of extreme repression, as in the examples just cited, additional precautions will need to be taken; these will be identified and discussed in a later section.

Many authors argue that tactics involving sabotage (which, for the purposes of this study, refers to the destruction of property, equipment, or natural phenomena) should be considered, and may be used, as part of a civilian-based defense.[98] However, sabotage, like secrecy, is seriously inconsistent with the strategic theory described in chapter 8. First, as indicated in chapter 7, the use of sabotage precludes the possibility of resolving conflict in terms of human needs. Second, the use of sabotage is contrary to the Gandhian conception of nonviolence. Given the importance he attached to such principles as the unity of means and end, the unity of all life, and the role of self-suffering, sabotage had no part to play in Gandhi's scheme of nonviolence. In fact, according to Gandhi, "Sabotage is a form of violence."[99]

Third, the use of sabotage is widely regarded as contrary to *any* conception of nonviolence, and the arguments against it are comprehensive. According to Sharp, sabotage has never been deliberately applied by a disciplined movement that has consciously chosen to struggle by nonviolent means. In terms of its principles and dynamics, "sabotage is more closely related to violent than to nonviolent action." Sharp gives nine reasons why sabotage will seriously undermine a nonviolent struggle. These include the risk of unintentional injury to opponents or third parties, the need for secrecy in planning and execution, the likelihood that fewer (rather than more) activists will be engaged in the action, its failure to understand the essentially human context of nonviolent struggle and the way in which the support of the opponent and third parties is won, and the possibility of provoking unnecessarily high levels of repression against the activists *as well as* the wider population. Historically, the use of sabotage has often precipitated an unplanned chain of events culminating in violence.[100] Moreover, as George Lakey notes, even when sabotage is used to destroy something that "has no right to exist," such as a military weapon, it still sends a confusing message to the opponent and third parties, given the association of sabotage with violence in the minds of many people.[101]

Fourth, and most importantly, the use of sabotage will not undermine the opponent elite's sources of power. In fact, it may do the opposite. This was graphically illustrated by the failure of the sabotage campaign in South Africa. Following the modest gains of twelve years of nonviolent struggle,[102] in June 1961 Nelson Mandela proposed that the African National Congress adopt a new strategy: a campaign of sabotage.[103] This proposal was accepted, and a separate military wing, Umkonto we Siswe (Spear of the Nation), was created to conduct the sabotage campaign that was launched on 16 December 1961.[104] As outlined by Mandela in his famous speech at the Rivonia trial in 1964, the sabotage campaign was supposed to cause "a heavy drain on the economic life of the country." For example, planned destruction of power plants and communications links was supposed to make it difficult for goods to be transported from industrial areas to the ports; it was also supposed to scare off foreign investors. These attacks, coupled with the sabotage of government buildings and other symbols of apartheid, were supposed to inspire black South Africans, provide an outlet for those advocating violence, and give concrete proof to ANC supporters that a "stronger line" had been adopted in response to government violence. All of this was supposed to compel white voters to reconsider their position, to generate sympathy in other countries, and to put greater pressure on the racist government.[105] In fact, the campaign's impact on the economy was negligible and, rather than being scared off, foreign investors became more deeply involved in the South African economy throughout the next decade. At a political level, however, the damage of the sabotage campaign to the anti-apartheid struggle was devastating. The campaign severely reduced the level of popular participation in the struggle, it reinforced the support of the white electorate for the government's efforts to maintain "law and order," it spurred the government to dramatically increase the level of repression on the grounds that it was dealing with a communist-inspired conspiracy to overthrow the state, and it had no appreciable impact on foreign governments, who remained inactive (apart from issuing token condemnations) in the struggle against apartheid. As a result of government repression, the Umkonto campaign ended with the arrest of its leaders at Rivonia, and other groups involved in sabotage or violent resistance were effectively eliminated by 1964. In terms of the objectives outlined by Mandela during his trial, the sabotage campaign was "a total failure," and the result for the anti-apartheid struggle generally was disastrous. With its leaders in prison and its organizations destroyed, "a silence descended for more than a decade."[106]

For many reasons, then, sabotage has no part in a disciplined nonviolent defense, and as a strategy in itself sabotage is substantially inferior to a strategy based on the principles of nonviolence.

It should be noted that some authors have endorsed the practice of "incapacitation." Incapacitation involves acts such as the removal of key parts from machinery and vehicles, the erasure of sensitive computer data, and the removal or destruction of records; it is intended to be harmless to persons. Some authors suggest that such acts may be carried out against the opponent;[107] others suggest that the practice is useful for disabling defense assets in order to render them useless to the opponent.[108] In addition, some authors even suggest that the careful sabotage of defense assets, such as the destruction of airports or bridges, may be practiced. [109] However, while the removal of sensitive data or the disabling of certain defense equipment may have limited utility (mainly by providing localized opportunities for involvement in the resistance), efforts to disable the opponent's equipment or to sabotage defense assets are strategically irrelevant because they are intended to deny a political objective of the opponent rather than to defend against (what should be) the opponent's strategic aim. Moreover, as the discussion above indicated, sabotage, whatever the target, involves a variety of risks to the defense strategy.

Finally, as Bradford Lyttle noted, secrecy and sabotage generate fear, and this is highly counterproductive. This fear discourages the processes of thought and reflection that lead to self-doubt on the part of the opponent elite's domestic constituency, and it sustains the image, perpetrated by that elite, that the defending society is alien, hostile, and malevolent.[110] As this study has demonstrated, if the strategic aims are to be achieved, fear is one emotional state it is imperative to eliminate. Though the case for employing tactics that involve the use of secrecy or sabotage might be superficially attractive, both the strategic theory developed in this study and the historical evidence (which was only touched upon) indicate that a strategy of nonviolent defense should emphatically reject the use of either.

Peacekeeping

As indicated earlier, to ensure that a nonviolent tactic is effective, it must be strategically focused, thoroughly organized, and disciplined. If it has been decided that a tactic requiring a high level of concentration should be employed, there are additional risks that must be considered. Apart from the risk of ruthless repression, which will be discussed in the next section, disruptions may occur because unchallenged rumors undermine crowd discipline, because hecklers provoke an unintended response, because people are affected by drugs or alcohol, because provocateurs try to incite violence, or because individual soldiers or police behave in an undisciplined manner. To minimize the risk of these disruptions occurring, and to minimize their impact should they occur, the action-planning group should appoint marshals and peacekeepers.

It is the function of marshals to maintain the appropriate mood at the action and to guide the crowd. Marshals should be fully informed about the nature of the action and should assist the action focalizers to make certain that it proceeds as planned. They should be friendly and helpful in dealing with fellow activists, the opponent elite's soldiers and police, and the media. They should be calm, creative, and forthright in encouraging people to follow the guidelines of the planned action and to maintain their nonviolent discipline. For example, during the occupation of Tiananmen Square in 1989, marshals were used for crowd control and for maintaining discipline. One important task was to patrol a three-foot-wide corridor between soldiers and activists in front of Zhongnanhai (the Communist Party compound). This prevented people from touching the soldiers but allowed them to explain the purpose of the movement.[111] Similarly, at an African National Congress rally near Soweto attended by a hundred thousand people on 29 October 1989, concern that provocateurs might initiate violence in order to sabotage the event resulted in more than seven hundred marshals being carefully briefed on how to handle the crowd.[112]

Peacekeeping is a function designed to enhance the discipline and safety of those present at a nonviolent action. Peacekeeping is important, particularly in those circumstances in which provocateurs are likely to be present or in which the opponent elite might respond to the action with violence. Peacekeepers should be chosen because of their commitment to nonviolence as well as their emotional maturity, self-discipline, steadiness under stress, and ability to think quickly and clearly.[113]

The peacekeeping team should be adequately staffed. This should ensure that worst-case contingencies can be handled effectively. It also means that peacekeepers can be rotated, if necessary, to deal with extremely difficult situations. Peacekeepers should be readily identifiable; for example, they might wear clearly labeled and distinctive caps or armbands. They should have radios if possible. Peacekeepers should be educated to anticipate problems so that they can be dealt with promptly. They should work in pairs or small teams, although one might engage a disruptive subject while the partner or partners observe from a short distance.

Peacekeeping begins with the manner in which the action is set up. For example, if the action is a large rally that includes a stage for speakers, access to the stage and sound system should be controlled. If, despite precautions, a disruptive person does gain access, then a masterswitch to cut the power supply or a standby music tape might provide the time necessary to remove the subject with minimum disruption. During the occupation of Tiananmen Square in 1989, increasing attention was devoted to the way in which the occupation was set up. For instance, workers and students were organized into clearly identifiable groups (such as university departments) and positioned systematically around the square. This, coupled with a "pass system" to control access to sensitive areas, was designed to help activists maintain discipline during the occupation.[114]

In response to a disruption, peacekeepers should first attempt to isolate the disruptive individuals from bystanders. Even well-meaning bystanders can make the peacekeeping task more difficult. It is better to rely on peacekeepers who have been educated to perform the role. Individual peacekeepers also should attempt to separate the members of a disruptive group from each other. Because individuals feed off their group's energy, it is easier to respond to them personally once they are separated. In dealing with an individual or, if necessary, a small group, a peacekeeper should adopt a relaxed, nonthreatening body posture with their open hands clearly visible by their sides; they should make only slow and predictable movements. They should stand close enough to occupy the subject's attention, maintain eye contact at all times, and, when speaking, use a calm, steady voice. The most useful skill for reducing tension is reflective listening; often people who are angry or hostile feel that they are not being heard. Reflective listening requires the peacekeeper to listen attentively, to acknowledge feelings, and to accurately restate what has been said by the subject, perhaps several times over; none of which implies that the peacekeeper agrees with what is being said. Once the tension starts to subside, the peacekeeper should ask questions designed to encourage consideration of alternative courses of action. Peacekeepers should keep a log of incidents for subsequent debriefing, evaluation, and learning.

In situations involving several disruptive people or a group of well organized provocateurs, it may be necessary to use an experienced team of peacekeepers to isolate the group or to protect opponent soldiers. One way of doing this is to form a disciplined circle around the group or the soldiers and, perhaps, to sing or hum. For example, just hours before the Beijing massacre, five students wearing headbands locked arms to form a protective ring around a soldier in order to escort him safely through a hostile crowd.[115]

Although the most effective way to avoid disruptions (including the actions of provocateurs) is to design tactics involving dispersion, there are obviously some circumstances in which tactics involving concentration, and therefore the risk of disruption, will be the appropriate strategic choice. In these cases, peacekeeping is an important aspect of organizational efforts to minimize the risk of disruption and to contain its impact should it occur.

Nonviolent Defense Against an Extremely Ruthless Opponent

It is sometimes claimed, usually by those with a limited understanding of its literature and history, that nonviolent resistance to an extremely ruthless or even genocidal opponent, such as the Nazis, would be ineffective.[116] However, this claim cannot be substantiated. To begin with, the argument that nonviolent resistance can be effective against ruthless opponents at the strategic level has been argued persuasively by several authors.[117] More importantly, the effectiveness of nonviolent resistance in these circumstances has been documented in the literature; for example, between 1931 and 1961, no less than ten Central/South American dictators (most with records of ruthless repression) were forced out of office by nonviolent insurrections,[118] and in 1989 a succession of authoritarian communist regimes in Europe (which exercised varying degrees of social control) were forced to relinquish power by nonviolent movements.[119] At the strategic level, then, the effectiveness of nonviolent resistance to ruthless opponents is a matter of historical record; it will not be considered further in this study. Despite these successes—most of which occurred without the benefit of a strategic plan—even advocates of nonviolence have accepted the claim that nonviolent resistance is unlikely to be effective against an extremely ruthless opponent *in a tactical situation*.[120] This claim will be considered below.

In a related claim, it is sometimes argued that nonviolent defense may lead to heavy casualties.[121] In fact, no serious exponent of nonviolent defense discounts this possibility: Resistance usually leads to repression, which might be ruthless. But this is not the point. Assuming that people have decided to reject passive submission to aggression, they must make several choices; central among these choices is the method of struggle. In essence, they can choose violence in one of its various forms or they can choose nonviolent action. If they choose violence, the historical record is clear: Massive casualties should be expected, *and they are highly likely.* For example, during their war of independence against the French, the Algerians suffered nearly one million deaths (out of a population of just ten million).[122] Similarly, and despite the frequent and naive claim that it was the British moral code that made Gandhian nonviolence possible in India,[123] during the Mau Mau uprising in Kenya, the British killed 11,503 Kenyans (out of a resistance movement that numbered little more than 100,000) in a three-year campaign notable for its atrocities in the field and its systematic use of sadistic torture in the fifty-five concentration camps set up to "detain" Mau Mau suspects and prisoners.[124] Alternatively, if people choose nonviolent action, the historical record is equally clear: Substantial casualties should be expected, *but they are not likely.* For instance, during their nonviolent struggle for independence, which lasted for more than thirty years, the Indians, Richard Gregg claims, did not kill one British soldier (although several Indian police were killed) and they suffered only eight thousand deaths (out of a population of 350 million).[125] Similarly, the nonviolent struggle that liberated Zambia from British rule was "virtually bloodless."[126] Algeria, Kenya, India, and Zambia are only four of the examples that could be cited, but they are representative of the historical record.

Violence is grossly dysfunctional. For example, as discussed earlier in this study, it cannot resolve conflict or satisfy human needs. And whenever it has been used in the service of major political goals, it has led to suffering and death, often on a massive scale. Critics of nonviolence often overlook these points—a reflection, in part, of the pervasiveness of an ideological perspective shaped by elites who benefit from the use of violence. In contrast, nonviolence not only has the potential to substantially lower the toll of suffering and death, it has built into it all of the advantages discussed in chapter 7: It facilitates conflict resolution and the satisfaction of human needs and, in so doing, leads to greater human unity. In any case, though massacres of several hundred nonviolent activists have sometimes taken place, there are only two documented cases in which a nonviolent action was so brutally repressed that the number of people killed *may* have exceeded a thousand: in Tehran on 8 September 1978[127] and along Changan Avenue (as the PLA fought its way through makeshift barricades toward Tiananmen Square) during the night of 3–4 June 1989.[128] Moreover, any analysis of these nonviolent actions reveals that neither of them was well organized and that, in both cases, the killing was made worse by a breakdown in nonviolent discipline; these shortcomings seriously undermined the capacity of these actions to minimize the violence that occurred. Of course, these observations do not alter the fact that these massacres were great tragedies, as were those nonviolent actions in which "only" hundreds or even dozens were killed. However, when this historical record is compared with the frightening record of massacres and genocides suffered by groups that have passively submitted to violence, been taken by surprise, or relied on violence to defend themselves,[129] often in the context of the wider use of violence such as during a war, it is starkly evident that the effectiveness of nonviolent action in reducing the number of casualties is a historical fact of considerable significance. Moreover, this is so for specific and identifiable reasons. And there is at least one case in which nonviolent action has been successful in halting a massacre: Gandhi's fast in Calcutta to stop the communal violence following the partition of India at independence.[130] Consequently, while it is important to prepare for the possibility that a nonviolent defense may involve deaths on a large scale, this should be done in the knowledge that well organized nonviolent action has often been extremely effective in minimizing the number of casualties. Given its effectiveness against ruthless opponents at the strategic level and its effectiveness in minimizing casualties, the remaining question is this: Can a strategy of nonviolent defense be effective against a ruthless opponent *at the tactical level?*

As this study has sought to demonstrate, nonviolent action can be very effective in limiting the use of violence, for several interrelated reasons; these include its capacity to directly alter the political milieu, the physical circumstances, and the human psychological conditions (both innate and learned) that make the use of violence possible in the first place. More specifically, nonviolent action can be effective in limiting the use of violence because of its capacity to create a favorable political climate (because of the way in which activist honesty builds trust, for example); its capacity to create a nonthreatening physical environment (because of the nonviolent discipline of the activists); its capacity to reduce or eliminate the opponent's negative emotional states of fear, anger, and depression by satisfying their needs for security, meaning, and self-esteem; and its capacity to humanize the activist in the eyes of the opponent. Nevertheless, a simple commitment to "nonviolence" cannot guarantee the nature of the outcome, as the following two examples grimly illustrate. Despite the nonviolent nature of a crowd of several thousand at a protest meeting in Amritsar on 13 April 1919, 379 Indians were killed, and hundreds wounded, in an unprovoked ten-minute massacre. The massacre was conducted by troops under the command of a British general.[131] Similarly, despite the peaceful and "happy" mood of those attending a Pan-African Congress rally against the pass laws at Sharpeville on 21 March 1960, without provocation or warning the police opened fire into the crowd of about five thousand. The shooting lasted for "forty seconds or more." In total, 69 black South Africans were killed and 180 wounded; three-quarters of these were shot from the back.[132] If a simple commitment to "nonviolence" is inadequate when the opponent is ruthless, can nonviolent resistance be made more effective?

According to several authors, it certainly can. In principle extreme repression can always be applied; in practice the ruthlessness of the opponent can be influenced by the strategy and tactics of the resistance.[133] Thus, in addition to considering the many points discussed previously, the planning process should consider ways in which the strategy can be made less vulnerable to ruthless repression.

First, the strategy can employ tactics that emphasize dispersion rather than concentration. The capacity for tactics involving dispersion to minimize repression has been illustrated in several campaigns. For example, during the 1930–31 independence campaign in India, the main type of repression (imprisonment) used against people throughout India who manufactured salt was relatively mild compared with the repression (beatings) dealt out to the satyagrahis who intended to occupy the Dharasana and other salt works. Even more notably, the widespread boycott of English cotton goods reduced English exports of such products to India by 84 percent at the height of the campaign, without offering a tangible target for repression.[134] During the 1961 "stay-at-home" strike in South Africa, while police went from house to house "beating up Africans and driving them to work,"[135] this method still offered less opportunity for direct repression than did public gatherings, as the 1960 Sharpeville massacre grimly highlighted. Even more effectively, the 1959 potato boycott in South Africa—to protest the use of pass offenders as "slave" labor on potato farms—could not be broken by the government, farmers, and merchants combined and made repression effectively impossible.[136] In a variation on this theme, Rigoberta Menchú describes how her village in Guatemala developed a system of lookouts and signals to warn when the army was approaching. To reduce the risk of their village being massacred like others before it, once the signal was given the whole community left the village and gathered at a previously built camp in the mountains.[137] A similar system has been used in South Africa to defend against vigilante attacks.[138]

Second, the strategy can employ tactics that involve concentration but organize them in a novel way or invest a traditional practice with new meaning. For example, if demonstrations are banned, the action can take the form of a funeral procession or, as is frequently the case in Tibet, a religious ceremony. In Tibet, a group of monks or nuns will sometimes march around the main temple in a city—itself a long-standing religious tradition—carrying a picture of the Dalai Lama in order to indicate their objection to the Chinese occupation. These actions are still repressed, but they have usually been subjected to less extreme violence than other forms of Tibetan protest.[139]

Third, the strategy can emphasize the importance of advance personal contact with the opponent elite's troops. This contact should be designed to reduce troop fears and to counter any ideological conditioning intended to dehumanize the defending populace in the eyes of these troops. If personal contact is to be utilized to minimize the risk of extreme violence, the strategy must plan opportunities for informal contact between activists and troops *prior to and throughout the resistance*. The effectiveness of this form of contact was illustrated by the Chinese pro-democracy activists, whose dialogue with soldiers was instrumental in thwarting the Chinese government's first attempt to clear Tiananmen Square on 20 May 1989.[140] It was also illustrated by those activists in the "Living

Ring"—the name given to those people who surrounded the Russian White House following the 1991 Soviet coup—whose dialogue with Soviet troops led to their refusal to attack the Russian White House and to kill Soviet civilians.[141]

Fourth, the strategy can include a contingency plan for each tactic that might be subjected to extreme violence. The relevant plan should be known by all participants in advance of the action, it may be described in an "action leaflet" distributed as people arrive for the action, it should be explained by the action focalizers at the beginning of the action, and it should be capable of implementation in a matter of seconds. The plan should emphasize the importance of maintaining lookouts during every action in order to eliminate the possibility that activists will be caught by surprise in the way the activists were at Amritsar; activists should always be in a position to choose how they confront their opponents. The plan should include the preparation of simple actions designed to counter the prospect of violence, and it should include simple actions for responding to violence should it start to occur. For example, at Ixopo in South Africa in 1959, a group of protesting women was ordered to disperse. But before police could be ordered to conduct the baton charge, the highly organized women sank quietly to their knees and began to pray. In response, the police "hung around helplessly."[142]

Fifth, the strategy can demand higher levels of courage and discipline. Whatever their commitment, there is little doubt that by running away the activists at Amritsar and Sharpeville helped to create the chaotic scene that made an early halt to the shooting unlikely. Commenting on the first incident, Gandhi asserted that it was "no part of the duty of the Jallianwala Bagh people to run away or even to turn their backs when they were fired upon." In his view, if the Amritsar activists had absorbed the message of nonviolence, they would have stood their ground and faced the troops.[143] While a high level of discipline would not have been possible at the unfocused and poorly organized rally at Sharpeville,[144] it has been possible elsewhere. For example, in response to a tax resistance protest held in the town of Beit Sahour in Palestine during June 1988, Israeli troops besieged the town and ordered the tax resisters to disperse. However, in an act of defiance designed to eliminate any excuse for the troops to fire, the activists sat down in the street and quietly held hands.[145] Similarly, despite considerable provocation by troops at an "illegal gathering" of several thousand people in

Rangoon in 1989—including an order to disperse and the aiming of automatic weapons into the crowd—the Burmese democracy leader Aung San Suu Kyi used some carefully chosen words to maintain the discipline of the crowd; as a result, the government soldiers were compelled to withdraw.[146]

The evidence suggests that, even if threatened or fired upon, individuals in a crowd should not run away or make unnecessary noise, even though this requires tremendous courage and discipline. A disciplined crowd that remains motionless (preferably in a pose of cultural significance, such as one of prayer or meditation) and that remains silent or perhaps hums or sings (possibly a religious hymn or a national anthem) is less likely to be shot at, and, if it is shot at, is less likely to be fired upon for any length of time. The danger of creating circumstances that even appeared to be chaotic was recognized by Hou Dejian, the activist who was instrumental in negotiating the last-minute withdrawal of activists from Tiananmen Square. His realization that a disorderly evacuation of the square (by those who wanted to leave) might create the chaotic conditions in which the soldiers would have a reason to kill indiscriminately was the principal factor in his decision to negotiate the manner of the withdrawal.[147] In the tactical sense, disciplined action of this nature should minimize the number of casualties; in the strategic sense, it should generate the highest level of support for the nonviolent defense.

Sixth, in addition to courage and discipline, the strategy might require activists to withstand a greater degree of suffering. For example, activists protesting against the use of torture in Chile were often sprayed by water cannons loaded with dirty sewer water or water mixed with dangerous chemicals.[148] The women at Greenham Common were subjected to sound, light, or electromagnetic zapping technologies.[149] And, of course, the satyagrahis at Dharasana in India on 21 May 1930 were beaten over the head with steel-tipped clubs, resulting in 320 injuries, including many fractured skulls and two deaths.[150] In each of these cases, the activists withstood the repression.

Seventh, if circumstances allow it, the strategy can utilize the media to expose the possibility of violent repression of nonviolent activists. The use of violent resistance makes violent repression more acceptable culturally and, therefore, more feasible politically;[151] violent repression of nonviolent activists violates major cultural and political norms, as the widespread outrage over the

Beijing massacre in 1989, the Dili massacre in 1991, and the Bangkok massacre in 1992 illustrated. For this reason perpetrators of violent repression, including genocide, usually try to conduct their repression in secret.[152]

Nonviolent resistance to an extremely ruthless opponent offers no certainty about the outcome, whether the action takes place in a major city or, in what is arguably the worst-case scenario, in a remote village confronted by a genocidal opponent. In either case, of course, there is no defense, including access to modern weapons, that can guarantee a successful outcome. Given the increasing sophistication of repression technologies designed to counter it,[153] nonviolent action is becoming more demanding of its practitioners. Nevertheless, whether applied in a strategic or tactical sense, nonviolent action has often been effective in resisting an extremely ruthless opponent. Whatever the circumstances, success is more likely if there is a clear-cut plan for responding to the repression and if it is implemented in an organized and disciplined manner.

13

The Strategic Counteroffensive

This chapter discusses the strategic counteroffensive of a strategy of nonviolent defense based on the strategic theory and strategic framework outlined in chapter 8. Many of the issues dealt with in chapter 12 are relevant here. The discussion identifies important strategic goals and the factors that should be considered when planning the individual campaigns of the strategic counteroffensive. It does not give detailed consideration to the components of the campaigns themselves.

The Opponent Elite's Will

According to the strategic theory outlined in chapter 8, emotions came into existence in response to evolutionary forces because they enhanced the chances of survival. As a direct result of being driven by these emotions, humans have a corresponding set of needs for conditions of life that reduce the negative emotional states of fear, anger, and depression and that thereby permit the positive emotional state of satisfaction. Consequently, the needs for security, meaning, and self-esteem, among others, are innate and universal, and they *must* be satisfied if conflict is to be resolved. For this reason, one aspect of the strategic aim of the counteroffensive is to alter the will of the opponent elite to conduct the aggression by offering a bracket of specific satisfiers that will meet those needs. This requirement is quite specific and should not be confused with the list of political demands that might be issued to mobilize the defense. Moreover, it should not be confused with the type of initiative known as a "peace plan," which tends to identify points to be discussed (the Five-Point Peace Plan that the Dalai Lama of Tibet presented to China in 1987 was of this type).[1]

To formulate a bracket of specific need-satisfiers to offer the opponent elite, it is necessary to identify the needs they are attempting to satisfy through the act of aggression. For example, it is evident from an analysis of Israeli history, the pronouncements of successive Israeli governments, and the statements of ordinary Israeli citizens that the Israeli people experience considerable fear and anger as a result of Palestinian violence, which is widely perceived to threaten the identity and security of Israel.[2] For that reason, if the Palestinians wish to alter the will of the Israeli government to maintain the occupation, they must address the Israeli needs for identity and security. In an attempt to do just this, the Palestine National Council acknowledged Israel's right to exist within secure borders and renounced the use of violence in the Occupied Territories in November 1988.[3] Despite this action, the will of the Israeli government has not yet been fully altered. There are several possible explanations for this. Members of the Israeli government might have other unmet needs, which the Palestinians have not yet identified and offered to satisfy. The sincerity and credibility of the offer is doubted; given the continuing use of violence by some parties of the Palestinian resistance, this reaction is understandable. There are other factors (such as role defense, propaganda, religion, ideology, and culture) that are distorting the Israeli perception of their needs. And finally, Israeli government behavior might be influenced by still other factors: As discussed in chapter 5, these might include nonrational emotions (such as "exaggerated fear" and "macho pride") as well as perceptions, which can be distorted by both unconscious motives (such as a "diabolical enemy-image") and cognitive factors (including the tendency to fit incoming information into preexisting beliefs).

This example illustrates the variety of factors that can complicate any effort to alter the will of the opponent elite; it does not alter the fact that this effort requires the creation of conditions of life that satisfy the opponent's needs. In the above example, this means that the Palestinians must help to create those conditions that satisfy the Israeli needs for identity and security. This requires, among other things, that the Palestinians *completely* forego the use of violence, in order to alleviate the negative emotional states of fear and anger experienced by the Israelis because of it. If the Palestinians are serious about altering the will of the Israeli government, then their offer to satisfy Israeli needs must be reflected in both their attitude and their behavior. Otherwise the offer is meaningless. Once the Israeli government feels less threatened, it will be more likely to participate in a problem-solving process that considers the needs of the Palestinians.

Nevertheless, in attempting to alter the will of the opponent elite by offering to satisfy their needs, it is essential to remember that their perception of their needs is probably distorted, as noted above, by such factors as role defense, propaganda, religion, ideology, and culture. For this reason, efforts to alter the will of the opponent elite should take these factors into account. Consider a situation in which the opponent is an Arab elite. Arab ethics, Raphael Patai explains, revolve around a single focal point, that of self-esteem or self-respect. In turn, self-respect depends on hospitality, generosity, courage, and honor. The outward expression of honor is "face"; and "saving face" is an "overriding imperative" worth almost any price. So strong is the imperative to avoid "loss of face" that prevarication in order to save face is considered justified and lying in order to save face for someone else "becomes a duty."[4] In such circumstances, no Arab with any self-respect could ever submit to a threat. In contrast, given this insight into Arab culture, an appeal to honor would be virtually impossible to ignore because this appeal, in itself, directly satisfies the Arab need for self-esteem.

Despite sincere and concerted effort to alter the will of the opponent elite, this effort will not always be successful. For example, it is evident that distortion caused by such factors as role defense and ideology makes it unlikely that an offer to satisfy the needs of the Chinese government will induce it to withdraw from Tibet. For this reason, the other aspect of the strategic aim of the counteroffensive is to nonviolently coerce the opponent elite to participate in a problem-solving process by subjecting them to a series of strategically focused campaigns of nonviolent action. This will undermine their power to conduct the aggression. This will be achieved by undermining the support of key social groups, in three separate domains, for the opponent elite's act of aggression: the troops who conduct the attack and any repression that goes with it, the social groups within the domestic constituency of the opponent elite that support the elite's aggression, and the social groups that support the allied elites on which the opponent elite depends.[5] To systematically undermine the power of the opponent elite to conduct the aggression, the strategic plan should precisely identify these key social groups and then formulate an appropriate set of strategic goals, each of which should be to alter the will of one (or more) of these groups to support the aggression. Of course, each strategic goal will require its own campaign as part of the overall counteroffensive.

The relative importance of each of these three domains, and the social groups within them, should be determined during the formulation of the strategic plan. Thus, in some circumstances the will of the troops responsible for conducting the aggression might be judged to be decisive in determining the outcome. For example, the refusal by troops to follow orders was a decisive factor in the defeat of the 1991 Soviet coup. In other circumstances it might be judged that the will of the troops is not so important and that the response of other social groups is decisive. For instance, if an attack leads to the occupation of an isolated location,[6] such as an uninhabited island territory, those responsible for strategic planning might decide that it is not useful to confront the opponent elite's troops at the location itself. If they decide that it is strategically useful to do so, nonviolent resistance might be organized at the site, but in most cases of this type it will be strategically more effective to concentrate the counteroffensive in the other two domains identified above. This is because the strategic counteroffensive should be directed against the center of gravity, not simply at the troops where the aggression occurred. This fact should be remembered in those situations in which it is extremely difficult to offer nonviolent resistance at the site, particularly during the act of aggression itself. This would have been the case, for example, when the United States Navy mined Nicaraguan harbors. In these circumstances, greater reliance must be placed on nonviolent campaigns conducted in the other two domains.

The remainder of this chapter will discuss the three domains of the strategic counteroffensive. Of course, like the campaigns of the defense, any campaigns of the counteroffensive must be applied in accordance with the strategic theory outlined in chapter 8. Before discussing the potential of these campaigns, the well known tactic of economic sanctions will be considered.

Economic Sanctions

Within the campaigns of the strategic counteroffensive, there are many tactics that can be used, including economic ones. However, given the traditional use of economic sanctions, this tactic often falls outside the conceptions of conflict and Gandhian nonviolence that underpin the strategic theory developed in this study. Can economic sanctions be used in a manner that is consistent with this theory? And are they an effective tactic within a wider campaign?

Economic sanctions take three primary forms: limits on exports, controls on imports, and restrictions on finance, including aid. Most cases involve a combination of trade and financial sanctions. According to Hufbauer, Schott, and Elliott, while domestic political motives sometimes overshadow concerns about changing foreign behavior, sanctions are usually imposed for one or more of three reasons: to deter, to punish, or to rehabilitate.[7] For reasons explained in chapters 4 and 5, measures that seek to deter or to punish are ineffective when human needs are at stake; consequently, they are inappropriate tools for altering human behavior. Thus, the use of sanctions for these reasons is inconsistent with the strategic theory developed in this study. However, sanctions that are applied in order to genuinely "rehabilitate" an opponent may be a useful tactic in a strategy of nonviolent defense. Rehabilitation, in this sense, may be interpreted to mean the coercion of the opponent elite to participate in a problem-solving process designed to satisfy the needs of all parties. Nevertheless, even if economic sanctions are designed to rehabilitate, there are several other factors that must be considered in order to determine the utility of this tactic.

According to Johan Galtung, the effectiveness of economic sanctions depends on the degree of concentration in the economy, measured in three different ways. In theory, for example, an economy that depended on one product, exported one product, and traded with only one country would be highly vulnerable to economic sanctions. In practice, of course, the economies of imperial states are usually rather diverse and, consequently, much less vulnerable to sanctions of this nature.[8] For this and other reasons, economic sanctions have not been used by small states against large ones.[9] In any case, even if sanctions are applied "effectively," there are four primary counterstrategies that have been used in the past to nullify their impact: States have adapted to any necessary sacrifice (if support for the elite has been widespread), they have reorganized trade patterns and engaged in sanctions-busting, they have restructured their domestic economy in order to achieve a greater degree of self-reliance, and they have relied on a larger state to provide key imports and to accept exports in defiance of any sanctions (as Cuba did when it enlisted the support of the Soviet Union to subvert U.S. sanctions).[10] Are economic sanctions of the traditional kind likely to achieve their goal, then?

In the eighteen cases studied by Peter Wallensteen, it was uncommon for economic sanctions to force compliance with the demands of the sanctioning party.[11] Moreover, his study revealed, there has been a high degree of success in countering sanctions: Total trade has usually returned to normal levels within two years.[12] But these conclusions are contradicted by more recent and elaborate studies. In the 115 cases of economic sanctions studied by Hufbauer, Schott, and Elliott, 34 percent were considered successful, although the success rate varied with the importance of the change sought.[13] And in a specific study of the case of Rhodesia, Hanlon and Omond demonstrate that after an initial downturn and a subsequent recovery spread over several years, which is consistent with the pattern noted by Wallensteen, the Rhodesian economy systematically contracted. Though there were several reasons for this, the long-term impact of sanctions (including the direct cost of sanctions-busting and the lack of foreign exchange) was profound.[14] It seems that the factors that significantly determine the effectiveness of sanctions are many—including the initial health of the target economy, the nature of prior relations between the relevant parties, the goal of the sanctions (including the degree of policy change required), the nature and combination of the sanctions, the cost of imposing them, the speed with which they are applied, the length of time they are imposed, and the level of international support for their application.[15]

An important factor that explains the effectiveness of counterstrategies is that economic sanctions, at least in the beginning, have a tendency to facilitate political integration and to consolidate support for the national elite.[16] Moreover, such sanctions tend to undermine the influence of opposition groups or, in some cases, to eliminate them entirely.[17] In the context of a nonviolent defense, these outcomes would be likely in circumstances in which (1) the sanctions are interpreted to be directed at the society as a whole (rather than just the opponent elite)—the collective nature of many economic sanctions "makes them hit the innocent along with the guilty"; (2) there is a weak or even negative identification with the people of the defending society (which may indicate the need to utilize "the great chain of nonviolence"); and (3) there is a belief in the goals of the opponent elite among the elite's domestic constituency.[18]

The economic sanctions applied against the South African regime illustrate the strengths and weaknesses of this tactic as well as the need to be clear about the role of sanctions. By the late 1950s, economic sanctions against apartheid were being urged by black political organizations despite the knowledge that they would cause additional suffering among the African population.[19] But it was not until after the massacre of students at Soweto in 1976 that sanctions were treated more seriously; for example, the mandatory weapons embargo was imposed by the United Nations in 1977 and, following the fall of the Shah of Iran, the oil embargo began to exact an increasing financial cost (although oil was still readily available).[20] Initially, elite countermeasures within South Africa against these sanctions—including import substitution and sanctions-busting—were quite effective. But the South African economy's vulnerability to sanctions, largely because of the oil embargo, which caused South Africa to accumulate a massive foreign debt, was starkly illustrated in 1985. After years of struggle by the grassroots anti-apartheid network (which had been applying pressure on Western corporations and their allies, such as the U.S. Congress), the major U.S. banks temporarily refused to renew their loans to South African borrowers; this provoked "a major economic crisis"[21] during which foreign investors "deserted South Africa in droves." These financial sanctions, in turn, split the white community in South Africa and led sections of the business community to respond in two ways: to pressure the South African government for meaningful reform and to talk directly with the African National Congress for the first time.[22] Moreover, to save foreign exchange during the crisis, the South African government cut its oil imports and ran down its reserves. Then, when the financial crisis had been averted, it made massive oil purchases to replenish its stocks. It was clear that South Africa would have been in serious trouble had it needed to survive *comprehensive* financial and oil sanctions, combined.[23] This illustrates the strategic importance of selecting, and then working to impose and enforce, an appropriate combination of sanctions, rather than dissipating effort on the more difficult task of trying to impose a total ban.[24] In addition, for various reasons, including the use of censorship by the government to prevent certain information from reaching the white public, the case of South Africa illustrates the importance of combining economic with other sanctions, such as sporting and cultural ones. Whatever impact the economic sanctions had on South Africa (and most of this was probably borne by the blacks themselves), there is little doubt that it was South Africa's sporting and cultural isolation that made the average white South African realize that apartheid was unacceptable to most of the world.[25]

According to Hufbauer, Schott, and Elliott, the historical evidence is consistent with the case of South Africa: Economic sanctions alone are of limited utility in coercing an imperial elite to change its policies in a major way.[26] If this is true, how can economic sanctions be made more effective? First, they should not be used as a form of punishment; in this form, they have many of the same disadvantages as military aggression, including their tendency to consolidate support for the opponent elite. Sanctions should be used only as a means of coercing participation in a problem-solving process designed to satisfy the needs of all parties. The attitude and behavior of sanctioning parties toward the opponent elite and their domestic constituency should reflect this positive goal. Second, the case studies indicate that specific economic sanctions, combined with other tactics and clearly directed, are more likely to influence the opponent elite and its key support groups than is a complete break in trade.[27] For example, trade sanctions might include bans designed to deny the opponent elite key imports such as oil, weapons, and high technology (including that used for purposes of repression). Moreover, because the cost of trade sanctions is usually diffused among the wider population, particular attention might be given to financial sanctions (including trade finance and loans), which have a more direct impact on national elites.[28] And third, because economic sanctions are a means of expressing moral disapproval, they may be more effective, Galtung argues, if they are of a symbolic nature and value deprivation for the opponent is kept low. Further, he maintains, this purpose is better served if self-deprivation as a result of the sanctions is equal to or outweighs the deprivation imposed on the opponent.[29] However, as the case of South Africa illustrates, while the chosen sanctions may require a certain amount of self-sacrifice on the part of the defending population (in this case the blacks), this might not always be politically functional (given the social distance between blacks and whites). Moreover, given the level of suffering that some defending populations are experiencing already, it might be important that any additional burden should not weigh too heavily on that population when solidarity groups can publicly share the burden with them (for example, by buying a boycotted product's more expensive alternative). In any case, and whether or not value deprivation for the opponent elite is kept low, provided that the suffering of the defending population and its solidarity allies is clearly greater, economic sanctions that are applied in accordance with these three points are more effective; they are also consistent with the strategic theory outlined in chapter 8.

Nevertheless, though sanctions of various types can be effective, for reasons discussed in earlier chapters it is evident that national elites will invariably act in concert with elite allies and not in solidarity with ordinary people; as a result, they will resist pressure to apply sanctions or they will apply them ineffectively. For this reason, an examination of the 115 cases cited in Hufbauer, Schott, and Elliott[30] reveals, virtually all of the economic sanctions applied during the period 1914–90 were applied in support of elite goals. A notable exception to this pattern was the sanctions campaign against South Africa. Despite rhetoric to the contrary, it was never a priority of Western elites to end apartheid; too many governments and corporations benefited from black exploitation in South Africa and from the terrorism of the apartheid regime.[31] So how did the sanctions campaign against the apartheid government come about? It was the result of twenty-five years' work, during which grassroots networks built the support necessary to put a reasonably effective (but far from comprehensive) sanctions regime into place.[32] The nature of elite interests also explains why there have been no sanctions measures directed against allied elites in China and Indonesia, despite the ongoing brutalities of the Chinese army in Tibet and the Indonesian military in East Timor. It is also why there have been no sanctions measures directed against the brutal regimes of Burma and Zaire, to name two at random, despite the ongoing military repression these regimes conduct against their own people. And it is one of the reasons why no sanctions packages have been directed against the United States government, despite its deplorable record of interventions in Central/South America and elsewhere. Moreover, while refusal to apply sanctions in solidarity with grassroots struggles is the typical response of governments, in those situations when grassroots pressure has been difficult to resist, governments have simply applied sanctions ineffectively. For example, as Hufbauer, Schott, and Elliott noted, the sanctions imposed on China by the U.S. administration following the Beijing massacre were intended to relieve domestic political pressure in the

U.S.; they were not intended to have any instrumental impact on the Chinese government itself.[33]

Given the vested interests that shape the attitudes of national elites, it is imperative that international solidarity action be taken by grassroots organizations, trade unions, and other groups in order to induce or coerce action by their own elites (and especially governments and corporations) or, more importantly, to impose sanctions directly. As more people and grassroots organizations realize their power to cause change, sanctions such as consumer boycotts (like those against Barclays Bank and Shell),[34] shareholder campaigns, and union bans will prove increasingly effective. For example, as Brian Martin has noted, a well-organized tourist boycott of Fiji following the military coups in 1987 would have had a substantial impact, given that tourism is Fiji's second largest source of export income.[35]

In summary, whatever the value of economic sanctions within the context of a nonviolent defense, they are only one potential tactic in any strategic counteroffensive. If they are to be used effectively, serious thought must be given to the strategic goal, composition, and target of the sanctions package as well as the attitude and behavior toward the sanctioned party; there must also be a clear willingness to experience self-deprivation. Nevertheless, in many cases in which they might be worthwhile, the use of sanctions will be vigorously resisted by national elites. Consequently, even if a defending population decides that it wants to use this tactic, it will take a great deal of solidarity work by grassroots networks to get effective economic sanctions put into place. In most situations, more easily applied tactics are available.

The First Domain: The Opponent Elite's Troops

In virtually all cases (usually including those involving an invasion, occupation, coup, or internal military repression), an important strategic goal of the counteroffensive should be to alter the will of the opponent elite's troops to conduct the attack and any repression that goes with it. This, of course, will seriously undermine the power of the opponent elite to conduct the aggression. This section discusses how to achieve this strategic goal when the defending population and the opponent elite's troops interact.

The historical record demonstrates that dialogue and nonviolent action designed to convince troops to disobey their orders have frequently been successful. For example, it was a vital element of the Czechoslovakian resistance to the Warsaw Pact invasion during 1968,[36] it was the defining feature of the nonviolent revolution in the Philippines in 1986,[37] it was the crucial factor in thwarting the Chinese government's first attempt to clear Tiananmen Square on 20 May 1989,[38] and it was fundamental to the defeat of the Soviet coup in 1991.[39] In each of these cases, the outcome was a direct result of an intuitively understood or clearly defined strategic goal.

Despite these successes, in some cases of nonviolent resistance to military aggression, altering the will of the opponent elite's troops has not been a strategic goal of the resistance. For different reasons, this was the case during the Iranian revolution in 1978–79,[40] during the anti-apartheid struggle in South Africa, and during the Palestinian Intifada; it has also been the case in the Tibetan resistance to Chinese occupation. In other cases, despite some initial successes, it has been incompletely or poorly executed. This has been the case in the resistance to the Burmese junta since 1988.[41]

Of course, in some circumstances this strategic goal may be extremely difficult to achieve. This may be the case when there is considerable social distance between the troops of the opponent elite and the defending population. But it is more complex than this. As a structure of power, the military has many sanctions at its disposal for maintaining the "loyalty" of its troops. On the positive side, the military offers prestige, security, and financial reward to those within its ranks. More negatively, military training, indoctrination, and discipline are designed to foster unquestioning obedience as well as fear of superiors. These factors complicate efforts to alter troop behavior and were, for instance, significant in the failure of most troops to spontaneously join the democracy struggle in Burma during 1988.[42] Nevertheless, irrespective of how difficult it may be to alter the will of the opponent elite's troops, this does not invalidate the utility of this strategic goal in most cases and the importance of working systematically to achieve it.

This strategic goal may be achieved as a result of dialogue with the troops themselves or, if necessary, dialogue combined with carefully selected nonviolent tactics. Communication for this purpose should be undertaken in accordance with the principles described in the previous chapter. During the Soviet coup in 1991, dialogue was the critical factor in altering the will of the troops to carry out orders.[43] Moreover, the defeat of this coup illustrated an important point made by Adam Roberts. In his view, one of the reasons why military coups are so vulnerable to nonviolent resistance (and the dialogue it allows) is that military forces are susceptible to numerous pressures—especially "moral influences"—from a civilian population.[44] If nonviolent action is necessary, it should also be conducted in accordance with principles outlined previously. In the Philippines in 1986[45] and in China on 20 May 1989,[46] the decisive factors were dialogue coupled with massive numbers of people blockading access to a defended location.

Nevertheless, in some circumstances there might be little point in identifying a strategic goal of this nature, or it may be of minor strategic significance. For example, when the opponent elite commands an overwhelming number of troops compared to the number of defenders available to confront them (as the Chinese army does in Tibet) or when the troops are deployed at an isolated location in order to defend a limited political objective of the opponent (such as the Chinese government's use of Chinese labor to exploit Tibet's natural resources), there may be little strategic value in a campaign to alter the will of these troops to perform their duty. Moreover, these circumstances will determine the relevance of particular nonviolent tactics. For instance, in the case just cited, there would be little strategic value in, or opportunity for, tactics of non-cooperation at a mining site. However, in those cases in which action is possible and it has been decided that it is strategically useful to do so, forms of nonviolent persuasion or nonviolent intervention might be attempted.[47]

In most circumstances, altering the will of the opponent elite's troops to conduct the aggression is an important strategic goal of the counteroffensive. Whether it is important or not, however, strategic goals should be identified in the other two domains.

The Second Domain: The Opponent Elite's Domestic Constituency

The strategic counteroffensive of any nonviolent defense should identify an appropriate set of strategic goals in relation to the opponent elite's domestic constituency. Each goal should be specific: to alter the will of a particular social group whose support is necessary for the opponent elite to conduct the aggression. This, of course, will undermine the power of the opponent elite to conduct the aggression. A strategic goal may be achieved as a result of initiatives taken by the defense itself or as a result of a solidarity campaign initiated by, or undertaken on behalf of, the defense. Any solidarity campaign should be based on a modified version of the strategic framework outlined in chapter 8. Apart from economic sanctions, which were considered separately above, this section discusses that domain of the strategic counteroffensive concerned with the society of the opponent elite.

Given the potential of solidarity groups to conduct campaigns on behalf of the nonviolent defense, in those cases in which it is feasible to do so, early attention should be devoted to identifying and contacting such groups (if this has not been done already). Support for the defense might arise from groups within a variety of networks, many of which work within the dominant power structures and spend their time lobbying elites, but it is important to concentrate attention on groups committed to grassroots nonviolent action.[48] Once these solidarity groups have been contacted and, preferably, consulted, the key strategic goals in this domain should be identified. As a result, clearly focused campaigns designed to alter the will of particular social groups within the society of the opponent elite may be formulated quickly and then implemented when appropriate given the prevailing political circumstances.

As noted in the previous section, in most cases it should be an important strategic goal to alter the will of the opponent elite's troops to conduct the aggression. However, action to achieve this goal does not have to be undertaken by the defending population at the site of the aggression. It may also be undertaken by solidarity activists or military personnel within the society of the opponent elite. Often obscured by official secrecy and media censorship, the long and widespread history of resistance by fighting troops to the military aggression of their governments is now being more fully documented.[49] For example, following World War I, resistance by military personnel thwarted the intention of the British government to invade the Soviet Union and overthrow the Bolsheviks. In Britain in January 1919, nonviolent action (mainly in the form of demonstrations, strikes, and refusal to obey orders) by British soldiers forced the government to abandon its plans.[50] This was acknowledged by the secretary of state for war, Winston Churchill, who, despite his enthusiasm for British intervention, was obliged to observe that "we have not the power—our orders would not be obeyed."[51] Resistance to intervention was evident within the military forces of Britain's European allies as well. In the case of France, sailors on five cruisers dispatched to the Baltic "spiked the guns of the French navy" by going on strike.[52]

More recently, the massive opposition within its armed forces was a vital factor in bringing the military intervention by the United States government in Vietnam and Cambodia to an end.[53] In a report prepared for army officers, for instance, statistics reveal that 47 percent of low-ranking soldiers were engaged in some form of resistance at the height of the GI movement during 1970–71 and that, contrary to popular impression, opposition "was far more concentrated among volunteers than among draftees."[54] According to David Cortright, while the major concerns of military personnel included the repressive and undemocratic nature of service life, military racism, and the military justice system, there was a strong element of conscientious objection to the war itself, a consistent anti-imperialist focus, and even a serious questioning of the purpose of the armed forces. This opposition gathered so much momentum, Cortright argues, that by 1969 the plague of disaffection and defiance within the ranks in Vietnam had "crippled the infantry." In response to the increasing unreliability of its ground troops, the U.S. government stepped up naval and then air bombardment. However, this simply led to a large jump in resistance within the Navy and the Air Force. This resistance took a variety of forms. In addition to killing officers and acts of mass rebellion and sabotage (the most serious of which disabled aircraft carriers and partially destroyed bases), military personnel used a wide variety of nonviolent tactics to express their dissent. These included protests of many types at U.S. bases all around the world, the circulation of nearly three hundred underground newspapers, open refusal to carry out combat missions, desertion, and mutiny. Importantly, Cortright observes, links with the civilian resistance were critical, and initiatives such as the "GI coffeehouse movement" were pivotal in sustaining these links and in providing guidance for ongoing and effective resistance within the military. In response to the GI revolt and to prevent further disintegration of its military forces, the U.S. government accelerated troop withdrawals from Vietnam.[55]

As these examples illustrate, and Churchill himself acknowledged, if the will to fight of the opponent elite's military forces can be substantially diminished, then the power of that elite to conduct aggression is completely undermined.

Apart from campaigns to alter the will of military personnel, separate campaigns should be organized to achieve the other strategic goals of the counteroffensive. These campaigns should reflect an astute assessment of the appropriate strategic timeframe, especially in those circumstances in which the defense must begin at the stage of raising awareness of the struggle. For example, following their service with Witness for Peace—an organization that arranged for four thousand activists from the United States to live in communities throughout Nicaragua in order to discourage U.S.-organized Contra attacks—activists were encouraged to engage in a wide range of educational activities designed to raise community awareness of the U.S. government's "war in Central America." Using this increased awareness, activists were then able to mobilize wider opposition to U.S. intervention by, for instance, asking people to sign the Pledge of Resistance.[56] Similarly, the Tibetans need to alert key sectors of the Chinese population to the Tibetan struggle, and they should initiate campaigns for doing so. However, action to achieve this goal does not have to be undertaken by the Tibetans; it can be undertaken by solidarity activists, such as those involved in the pro-democracy movement, in China itself.[57] Of course, as the level of awareness rises and people are mobilized, more specific strategic goals must be given prominence so that precisely focused campaigns can be planned and implemented. This would normally include goals and campaigns to alter the will of key groups of workers.

There is some evidence to suggest that nonviolence works most effectively when the social distance between oppressor and victim is short. But what if the social distance between these two parties is great? According to "the great chain of nonviolence" developed by Galtung, the answer is to identify a third-party that can intervene on behalf of the oppressed group, just as middle-class whites intervened during the civil rights struggle in the United States.[58] Galtung posits a particular social group or groups in each of the examples he cites, but there is some historical evidence to suggest that the "group" most likely to act in solidarity with the oppressed, and most able to close the gap in social distance, is women. While the preponderance of patriarchal analyses of political struggles makes it difficult to document the evidence to justify this claim, two important cases are nevertheless instructive: the role of white women in the anti-apartheid struggle in South Africa and the role of Israeli women during the Palestinian Intifada.

Much of the effective white opposition to apartheid in South Africa was expressed through women's organizations such as the South African Federation of Women and, most notably, the Black Sash. This organization was formed by six white women at a meeting in Johannesburg on 19 May 1955.[59] After an early attempt to form a parallel group composed of white men failed, the Black Sash expanded its own membership to include nonwhites and developed a more sophisticated and radical program.[60] Without discounting the role played by other groups with a substantial white membership—such as the National Union of South African Students and the South African Council of Churches—within several years of its formation the Black Sash was playing a significant part in the nonviolent struggle against apartheid. This was acknowledged by Nelson Mandela on his release from prison.[61] Given its membership in the liberal establishment, the Black Sash aimed at moral influence rather than political power and always operated within the law. Despite this, its nonviolent protests took many forms—petitions, street marches, pickets, silent vigils by members draped with the black sash—and, in testimony to their impact, were often disrupted by hostile crowds. In addition, it established an impressive network of support services, including advice offices, for black South Africans.[62] Though the nonviolent tactics used by the Black Sash were never part of a coherent long-term strategy to compel radical social change,[63] the Black Sash played an important role within the antiapartheid struggle overall and was a vital element in efforts to close the social gap between black and white South Africans.

Similarly, according to Deena Hurwitz, most people would agree that the Israeli women's movement has been the most effective component of the Israeli opposition to the occupation of the West Bank and Gaza. By relating as women first and Israelis or Palestinians second, women have created important bridges across the "Green Line" that separates Israel from Palestine. Solidarity activity has been organized by groups such as the Women and Peace Coalition, Shani, the Women's Organization for Political Prisoners, and, undoubtedly the best known network, Women in Black.[64] According to Yvonne Deutsch: "Women in Black has been the most significant Israeli protest movement since the beginning of the Intifada." In January 1988, a month after the Intifada began, Women in Black began conducting a vigil every Friday in West Jerusalem. By June 1990, vigils were being conducted at thirty locations throughout Israel. By 1993, solidarity vigils were being held in over twenty cities around the world. The women remain silent, dress in black to mourn the killings in the Occupied Territories, and carry placards inscribed with slogans urging an end to the occupation. More importantly, Deutsch argues, by connecting the violence of the occupation to the violence of daily life in Israel, they are creating a feminist political culture that is intended to influence both the grassroots of Israeli society and the political system as a whole.[65] The strategic goal of this powerful witness is to encourage ordinary Israelis and Jewish people everywhere to consider the moral and political implications of the occupation and to decide not to support it.[66] In this way, the power of the Israeli government to maintain the occupation, measured particularly in terms of political and overseas financial support, is undermined. Like the part played by the Black Sash in South Africa, Women in Black (and other women's groups) in Israel have played a vital role in the resistance to the occupation and been instrumental in closing the social gap between Israelis and Palestinians.

From a feminist perspective, it is clear that men collectively derive benefit from the existence of structures of exploitation and the acts of violence conducted by their national elites. Moreover, from this perspective it is clear that men must accept greater responsibility for resisting this exploitation as well as acts of aggression. Nevertheless, until more men have demonstrated their willingness to accept this responsibility, the above two examples strongly suggest that a strategy of nonviolent defense should specifically identify women's groups that are willing to act in solidarity with the defense and which, by doing so, help to close the social gap between the opponent elite and the defending population.

Apart from solidarity *campaigns* initiated by, or undertaken on behalf of, the nonviolent defense, a strategic goal of the counteroffensive may be achieved as a result of initiatives taken in the society of the opponent elite by the defense itself. For example, dialogue with people who represent networks of women, workers, and activists can secure the support of groups whose change of allegiance will functionally undermine (perhaps only minutely, in some cases) the power of the opponent elite to conduct the aggression. In effect, this is the strategic goal of Palestinian women who cross the "Green Line" with the intention of persuading Jewish feminists to support the Palestinian cause.[67]

Although it has been noted previously that planning for each campaign of the strategic counteroffensive should identify a careful selection of tactics that will achieve the strategic goal, there is one form of potential action that requires special mention. In those circumstances in which it is feasible to do so, it may be useful to transport defending (and solidarity) activists onto the territory of the opponent elite in order to carry out a specific nonviolent tactic.[68]

This is what twenty-nine East Timorese activists did on 12 November 1994 when they climbed into the U.S. embassy compound in Jakarta to protest against the Indonesian occupation of East Timor. They timed their action to coincide with a highly publicized meeting of Asia-Pacific government leaders attending a regional economic summit.[69]

In some circumstances solidarity action may involve considerable risk, including the risk of death. Any fully committed nonviolent activist understands and accepts this: It is an inevitable corollary of a belief in the unity of all life. In the words of Brian Willson just before he lost both legs while nonviolently blockading a United States train carrying weapons destined to kill Central Americans: "One truth seems clear: If the munitions train moves past our blockade other human beings will be killed and maimed. We are not worth more. They are not worth less."[70] Nevertheless, relatively few activists are ready to take this degree of risk (or, for that matter, anything like it), and it is for this reason that campaigns staged to gradually build awareness, commitment, discipline, solidarity, and courage are so important.[71]

In most circumstances, strategic goals in relation to the opponent elite's domestic constituency are vitally important to the nonviolent defense. Therefore, campaigns intended to alter the will of key social groups that support the opponent elite's aggression will have a vital bearing on the outcome of the strategic counteroffensive. However, given the ongoing efforts by elites to exacerbate the cleavages between grassroots communities of all types, much work needs to be done to improve communication among grassroots networks and develop their capacity to function fully and effectively as part of any strategy of nonviolent defense.

The Third Domain: The Domestic Constituencies of Allied Elites

The strategic counteroffensive of any nonviolent defense should also identify an appropriate set of strategic goals in relation to the societies of the opponent elite's allies. Again, each goal should be specific: to alter the will of a particular social group (within one of these societies) whose support or "neutrality" is necessary for the opponent elite to conduct the aggression. This will undermine the power of the allied elite to support the aggression or it may undermine the power of the opponent elite directly. A strategic goal can be achieved as a result of initiatives taken by the defense itself or as a result of a solidarity campaign initiated by, or undertaken on behalf of, the defense. Any solidarity campaign should be based on a modified version of the strategic framework outlined in chapter 8. This section discusses that domain of the strategic counteroffensive concerned with the societies of allied elites.

The importance of allied elite support for an opponent intent on countering a strategy of nonviolent resistance has been demonstrated repeatedly. For example, the support of the Soviet government for the Polish government seriously damaged the efficiency of the struggle by Solidarity during the 1980s.[72] And the support of Western elites for the Chinese and Israeli governments has seriously interfered with the resistance strategies developed by the Tibetans and Palestinians, respectively. Given the potential of solidarity groups (or exile communities)[73] within third-party societies to conduct campaigns on behalf of the nonviolent defense, early attention should be devoted, when feasible, to identifying and contacting such groups. Perhaps the key strategic goals in this domain should be identified in consultation with them. As a result, clearly focused campaigns designed to alter the will of particular social groups within these societies can be planned and then implemented when appropriate.

The struggle to achieve the strategic goals of the counteroffensive in third-party societies might need to begin with the modest goal of raising community awareness, so it is important that defense planners make a realistic assessment of the appropriate strategic timeframe and plan their campaigns accordingly. It is politically naive and strategically unwise to assume that certain campaigns, such as those directed at undermining domestic support for the U.S. government's active complicity in the Chinese occupation of Tibet or the use of military violence by its allied elites in Africa, Asia, and Central/South America, will succeed in the short term. In individual cases, strategic goals might be achieved sooner rather than later; but in many cases there is a long struggle ahead. This has been recognized by experienced activists involved in organizing campaigns to undermine public support for U.S. intervention in Central America. For instance, a network of local groups organized blockades of trains carrying weapons (destined to kill people in other parts of the world) from the Concord Naval Weapons Station in California. While their ultimate strategic goals were (presumably) to alter the will of particular social groups that support U.S. intervention in Central America and elsewhere, most of their early work (including their educational efforts and their choice of nonviolent tactics) was directed at the more modest strategic goal of raising community awareness of the U.S. government's role and encouraging U.S. citizens to "listen to their own hearts about what they are called to do to stop this war."[74] Of course, as the level of awareness rises and people are drawn into the struggle, more specific strategic goals must be given prominence so that precisely focused campaigns can be planned and implemented.

Unfortunately, the importance of identifying strategic goals of this nature and of undertaking campaigns to achieve them is not widely recognized. This is usually the result of two primary factors: the inadequacy of the political and strategic assessment that guides the resistance, and the inadequacy of the strategic conception on which the strategy is based. The Palestinian Intifada suffered from both of these shortcomings. As noted by Shmuel Amir, the financial, military, and diplomatic support of the United States government makes the Israeli occupation of Palestine possible. Despite the rhetoric attached to its endorsement of UN resolution 242 (which calls for Israeli withdrawal) and its loudly voiced "objections" to some actions of the Israeli government, U.S. administrations have consistently acted to thwart the establishment of a Palestinian state. In essence, Amir argues, this is for two reasons: It reflects the long-standing U.S. policy of suppressing indigenous national movements, Arab or otherwise, that resist imperial domination and exploitation; and it reflects the U.S. policy of maintaining a strong and dependable military ally in an unstable region of vital strategic and economic importance. Thus, Amir contends, while many observers attribute U.S. government support for Israel to the influence of powerful Jewish organizations in the United States, in fact the interests of the Israeli and U.S. governments coincide and the appearance that U.S. policy is a response to "broad democratic pressure" from within the United States is simply a convenient cloak used to mask the forces that really drive U.S. foreign policy in the region.[75] If the Palestinians are to eliminate the pillar of U.S. government support for the Israeli occupation, they must identify an appropriate set of strategic goals (to alter the will of key social groups, including the main Jewish organizations, that support U.S. government policy in relation to the occupation) and encourage solidarity networks in the United States to conduct the necessary campaigns to achieve those goals. The shortcomings in the widely accepted political analysis (which has resulted in too much attention being concentrated on lobbying elites in Washington) and the absence of clearly identified strategic goals (together with campaigns to achieve them) were fundamental weaknesses of the Intifada. According to Amir, given Israel's complete dependence on it, the U.S. government can easily force Israel to withdraw from the Occupied Territories just as it forced the Israeli retreats from the Sinai in 1956 and 1978.[76]

In some circumstances it might be possible to organize solidarity action that undermines the power of the opponent elite directly. Most effectively, this might include campaigns of noncooperation or intervention by key groups of workers; for example, dock workers might take action to prevent warships or military supplies from leaving their ports. This happened in 1920 when London dockers refused to load the *Jolly George* with ammunition and other supplies for use by the Polish government in its military aggression against the Soviet Union.[77] It also happened between 1945 and 1949 when thirty-one Australian trade unions refused to repair, load, or service 559 Dutch vessels—including warships, merchant ships, oil tankers, and barges—that were intended to assist Dutch military operations to restore colonial rule in Indonesia after World War II. This action (which immobilized or delayed Dutch ships, soldiers, and munitions in Australian ports) temporarily incapacitated the Dutch war machine and inspired bans of a similar nature in several other countries.[78] Similar action took place in 1971 when the International Longshoremen's Association in the United States banned the loading of military cargo onto Pakistani ships following the West Pakistani regime's genocidal assault on East Pakistan (which subsequently became Bangladesh). This ban followed an approach by activists involved in a nonviolent action campaign to halt U.S. military and economic aid to West Pakistan.[79]

In some circumstances it will not be possible for the nonviolent defense to make easy contact with potential allies in third-party societies. This has been the experience of the Tibetan resistance, for example. For this reason it is important that grassroots networks monitor resistance struggles around the world so that information is available to assist activist groups to decide whether solidarity action on their part is appropriate. Western activists have a heavy responsibility in this regard, given the long record of military intervention and resistance to indigenous struggles perpetrated by their governments.

Apart from solidarity *campaigns* initiated by, or undertaken on behalf of, the nonviolent defense, a strategic goal of the counteroffensive may be achieved as a result of initiatives taken in the international arena by the defense itself. For example, dialogue with people who represent international networks of women, workers, and activists—or representations to international bodies such as the World Council of Indigenous Peoples (WCIP) or other nongovernmental organizations—might secure the support of groups whose change of allegiance will undermine the power of the opponent elite to conduct the aggression. In effect, this is the strategic goal of the Dalai Lama in his worldwide travels to gather support for the nonviolent struggle to liberate Tibet from Chinese occupation. It was also the strategic goal of the South African activists posted overseas as part of the anti-apartheid struggle.

In some circumstances, strategic goals in relation to the societies of the opponent elite's allies are vitally important to the nonviolent defense, and campaigns intended to alter the will of key social groups within these societies will have a major bearing on the outcome of the strategic counteroffensive.

Solidarity Action

There are additional kinds of solidarity action. These include action, undertaken in both the opponent elite and third-party societies, that is designed to directly assist the defending population to resist the immediate aggression of the opponent elite. It also includes action designed to undermine the capacity of elites to use violence in the longer term. This section will briefly outline these types of solidarity action.

In some circumstances, particularly those cases in which the opponent elite is very powerful, as the Chinese are in Tibet or the Burmese junta is in Burma, solidarity action to directly assist the defending population can be a vital component of the nonviolent defense. This action can take many forms: providing facilities and services to local representatives of the defense; providing sanctuary for refugees;[80] providing supplies of food, medical equipment, and other vital resources; sending in personnel with special skills and experience; disseminating resistance information, including ideas for action; dispatching equipment such as radio transmitters and printing machinery; and providing external broadcasting facilities for the nonviolent defense.[81] It may also involve more direct action. For example, following the Beijing massacre in 1989, solidarity activists around the world jammed telephone numbers in Beijing set up by the Chinese government so that people could inform on pro-democracy activists.[82]

In some circumstances, it might be appropriate to transport solidarity activists to the scene of the aggression so that they can reinforce the local resistance.[83] Action of this type took place on 15 August 1955 when over three thousand satyagrahis crossed the border from India into the Portuguese colonial enclaves of Goa, Daman, and Diu in support of the local nationalists. At least thirteen Indian activists were killed by Portuguese police.[84] In principle, this type of intervention is similar to, but an extension of, the type of work undertaken by teams working with Witness for Peace[85] and Peace Brigades International (PBI)—an organization that provides nonviolent escorts (from another country) for threatened human rights activists.[86] The effectiveness of transporting affinity groups of activists to bolster the local resistance would obviously vary from one context to the next but should occur only in response to a considered invitation by local activists (and following careful consultation and planning), given the variety of negative outcomes, including increased repression of local people, it might generate.[87]

Another type of solidarity action is designed to undermine the capacity of elites to use violence in the longer term. Given that elites use military violence to defend their imperial interests and structures of exploitation, ongoing nonviolent resistance to these interests and structures is an indispensable component of the struggle overall. In this sense, activities such as conscientious objection to military service, war tax resistance, and campaigns against the various manifestations of militarism, which undermine the power of the militarized state, must be recognized as vitally important solidarity activities of material assistance to present and future strategies of nonviolent defense; they are also necessary components of the wider struggle to transform the nature of society. Action of this type is important because, as Gandhi noted, while there can be situations that require a level of nonviolent power that is not available at the time, there is no excuse for failing to plan and organize to avoid such situations in the future.[88] Arne Naess explains this point: "In facing the future, there are threats of terror and organized violence from many quarters. These threats must be resisted immediately."[89] For this reason, ongoing campaigns of nonviolent resistance, like the one organized by the women at Greenham Common,[90] are very important.

Solidarity work to undermine the capacity of elites to use violence in the longer term also requires constructive programs that, among other things, facilitate the conversion of military production into peaceful manufacturing.[91] This is important, as Hilary Wainwright argues, because people working in the weapons industry cannot be expected to support campaigns against militarism if grassroots movements do not actively concern themselves with the issue of alternative employment.[92] The best known and most influential attempt to initiate a program of major economic conversion was that organized by the workers at Lucas Aerospace in Britain. In response to a decline in their industry and a determination to make a positive contribution to disarmament, the workers at Lucas Aerospace developed a plan to maintain employment that, among other things, proposed a shift in the focus of company production from military components to "socially useful products."[93]

For many reasons, including those indicated in chapter 10, elites generate fear and foster nationalist feeling in order to maintain a perception that ordinary people in one country are in competition with, or are the "enemies" of, the ordinary people in other countries. In this way, the possibilities of cooperation between members of different peripheries can be controlled and minimized. In fact, ordinary people everywhere are natural allies in the struggle against state and corporate elites intent on using military violence to defend their imperial interests. If the military aggression organized by these elites is to be effectively resisted, then solidarity action of various types is a vitally important aspect of both nonviolent defense and the wider struggle.

Conclusion

After fifty years, the peoples of Lithuania, Latvia, and Estonia finally dislodged the Soviet occupation of their countries.[94] After more than forty years, the Tibetans continue to resist Chinese military occupation. As these cases illustrate, if the will to resist is maintained and the center of gravity is adequately defended, the defense cannot be defeated. Moreover, these cases also illustrate that even in circumstances in which the resistance is sporadic and consists of little more than occasional tactics devoid of strategic guidance, improvised nonviolent resistance can be reasonably effective in sustaining a long-term struggle. But the main point of this chapter is that even in the context of extremely unequal struggles such as these, a carefully planned and systematically implemented strategic counteroffensive would vastly enhance the capacity of a strategy of nonviolent defense to compel an opponent elite to withdraw.

Conclusion

This study has identified and discussed four interrelated components of any social cosmology—its pattern of matter-energy use, its social relations, its philosophy of society, and its strategies for dealing with conflict—and argued that, to be functional in the long term, these components of a cosmology must be oriented to the satisfaction of human needs. Using the needs-based conception of human nature derived from this discussion, the study described a conception of security that is radically different from the one that is typical of the literature on international relations and strategic studies. Most importantly, this study has concentrated its attention on the conflict component of any social cosmology, and in this regard it has developed a new strategic theory and a new strategic framework for dealing with military violence. It has done this by synthesizing selected elements taken from three sources: the strategic theory of Carl von Clausewitz, the conceptions of conflict and nonviolence developed by Mohandas K. Gandhi, and recent research in the fields of human-needs and conflict theory. The study then used this new strategic theory and framework to elaborate the strategy of nonviolent defense. One important question remains: How will a strategy of nonviolent defense be introduced? The following discussion offers a preliminary response to this question.

It was noted in chapter 1 that there are political and policy limits on the choice of a defense strategy; these limits, of course, are an expression of the social cosmology. This means that even a defense strategy that is vastly superior in the strategic sense must be both politically acceptable and consistent with policy before it can be implemented. Whether they are superior or not, it is clear that civilian-based defense and social defense have so far lacked the political acceptability to be implemented. An important task for exponents of nonviolent defense, therefore, is to alter those political conditions that constrain the possibility of its implementation.

In advocating the adoption of civilian-based defense, Gene Sharp emphasizes the need for more research, public education, and policy studies in a process that is clearly oriented to persuading political and military elites.[1] Indeed, Sharp is not alone in this approach; it is characteristic of the literature on civilian-based defense.[2] Although there are some scholars in the field who have criticized this approach,[3] the historical evidence conclusively demonstrates that a strategy for social change that relies on intellectual arguments designed to persuade elites is grossly inadequate. In the words of Gandhi, "experience has shown that mere appeal to the reason produces no effect upon those who have settled convictions."[4] For example, the substantial literature that long ago systematically demonstrated the intellectual, logical, and ethical flaws inherent in deterrence theory has not significantly altered elite commitment to deterrence thinking. That these arguments have not been adequate to shift elite reliance on deterrence strategy suggests that elite commitment rests on factors other than rational analysis. Indeed, the arguments outlined in earlier chapters of this study make it clear that there are many complex factors that influence human behavior, including the willingness to accept and act upon new information. These include, but are not limited to, innate human needs (often expressed in the form of a strong commitment to role defense), nonrational emotions (such as "macho pride") and perceptions, which may be distorted by both unconscious motives (such as a moral self-image), and cognitive factors (including the tendency to fit incoming information into preexisting beliefs).

But there is more to it than this. Throughout this study, it has been argued that the components of a society's social cosmology help to shape, as well as reflect, the cosmology itself. There are many existing and possible social cosmologies, but there is one that is dominant, and this one serves the interests of national elites. Moreover, the socializing power of this dominant cosmology is enormous, as is its capacity to distort the perception of individuals within these elites. Under the influence of the dominant cosmology, elites will continue to argue that the political philosophy (that is, the ideology) of realism, with its emphasis on a conception of human nature as violent and selfish, is the only one that is "valid" as an explanation of human affairs; they will continue to promote the idea that military violence is the only "effective" strategy for dealing with many types of conflict; and they will continue to feel justified in using military violence to defend the existing set of exploitative social relations and to gain access to the diminishing supply of nonrenewable sources of matter-energy. Consequently, it should be understood, work toward the adoption of a nonviolent defense will be systematically resisted, not simply because it questions a dominant strategy for dealing with conflict, but because it also challenges the dominant social cosmology and the deep cultural imperatives, such as patriarchy, that have shaped it. For many reasons, then, as Ralph Summy has argued, it is particularly unwise to believe that elites will initiate any change to nonviolent forms of defense. In his view, trying to convince elites will only result in "prolonged frustration" and will end in co-optation.[5]

It seems clear that advocates of nonviolent defense must take these impediments into account and should devise a comprehensive and multifaceted approach in order to work for its "adoption." In essence, this approach requires work in several areas. First, it requires more widespread participation in local campaigns of nonviolent struggle. As Julio Quan has argued: "We have to work at the grassroots level."[6] Second, it requires the establishment of more nonviolent communities in which people participate in efforts to develop cooperative models of social relationships for their economic and political activities, their cultural practices, and their spiritual life.[7] Third, it requires more activists to take the time to reflect upon, analyze, and record what they have learned so that activists and nonviolence scholars can better integrate the insights derived from experience and research. Fourth, it requires the conduct of programs of nonviolence education that are accessible to many more people. Fifth, it requires greater efforts to link existing networks of women, indigenous peoples, workers' organizations and activist groups to the Global Nonviolence Network (GNN) that is gradually taking shape, so that, among other things, information about nonviolent defense can be readily communicated. And sixth, it requires ongoing changes in personal behavior by activists themselves. While each of these points is self-explanatory or has been discussed in a related context in an earlier chapter, the last point will be explained more fully in order to illustrate the pivotal role of each individual within this multifaceted approach to securing the widespread acceptance of nonviolent defense.

A key insight shared by Gandhian nonviolence and feminism is that personal behavior is a vitally important locus for change. Moreover, as Gandhi stressed repeatedly, only powerful individuals are effective agents of social transformation. In his view, a powerful individual is someone who has power-from-within/power-over-one-self. This is why he stressed ongoing review of personal values and attitudes and continuing modification of personal behavior.[8] In addition, as Brian Martin has noted, a personal focus in one's daily life is important. It provides the positive stimulation that results from the knowledge that one is *involved* and *doing something constructive*, and if it is connected with the ongoing work of radical social movements, it also undermines, in a fundamental way, the structures under challenge.[9]

Given the central importance of personal change, what can individuals do? The following suggestions are derived from the evidence presented in earlier chapters that the real (as distinct from declared) reason why national elites use military violence is to defend structures of exploitation. These structures exploit women; indigenous peoples; the people of Africa, Asia, and Central/South America; nonhuman species; the environment; and working people generally. By adopting first one and then more of these suggestions, and understanding the reasons for doing so, an individual gains strength, *on a daily basis*, for the struggle to create a nonviolent cosmology using nonviolent means. This is a vital aspect of the struggle to gain widespread acceptance of nonviolent defense. First, everyone can learn to speak the truth.[10] Second, everyone can learn to deal creatively with the conflict in their personal lives. Third, everyone can learn to respect others more deeply—that is, to refrain from the use of manipulative, exploitative, coercive, or violent behavior in their personal relationships.[11] Fourth, men can continually examine the ways in which they benefit by living in a patriarchal society and work conscientiously to change their own attitudes, language, and behavior to eliminate their personal oppression and exploitation of women. Fifth, nonindigenous peoples can acknowledge the identity and other needs of indigenous peoples and work to create a new and caring relationship with indigenous peoples and their land. Sixth, people who live in industrial societies can minimize their personal consumption and become vegans or vegetarians; this will reduce their exploitation of the people of Africa, Asia, and Central/South America, as well as nonhuman species and the environment. Seventh, everyone can plant indigenous plants as well as their own vegetable gardens (or participate in a community garden or buy organically grown food from a local food cooperative); this will facilitate the shift to an economy based on self-reliance, cooperation, decentralization, and ecological sustainability.

And finally, everyone can devote a higher proportion of their time to creative political activity *outside* the framework of existing state structures by participating in local nonviolent struggles and local efforts to build nonviolent communities. According to Gandhi, personal action will help to cultivate discipline and fearlessness. And the time to act is now: "it is an idle excuse to say that we shall do a thing when . . . others also do it: . . . we should do what we know to be right, and . . . others will do it when they see the way."[12] Action to secure the widespread acceptance of nonviolent defense requires ongoing efforts in several areas. These efforts will be more effective if they are undertaken by powerful individuals.

Like any social movement that concentrates its efforts for radical social change on grassroots constituencies, the struggle to encourage widespread acceptance of the conception of nonviolent defense described in this study will no doubt be laborious. Nevertheless, provided its advocates persist, it will gradually gain acceptance. According to this view, the "adoption" of nonviolent defense is an ongoing process rather than a single event. In the meantime, it will be most productive to work on those sectors of the population who derive the least benefit from the dominant social cosmology as well as those people who have the least ideological commitment to violence.

It should be noted that there are many circumstances in which a strategy of nonviolent defense could be planned and implemented now. Despite the assumption by some authors that nonviolent defense requires unity[13] or widespread participation, the historical evidence suggests that, while these may be desirable, they are not essential. This is because other factors, and particularly the strategy employed, have more bearing on the outcome. For example, there were less than fifty thousand people surrounding the Russian White House during the vital period in 1991,[14] but they were critical to the defeat of the Soviet coup. Conversely, despite the massive participation in the Palestinian Intifada, its successes were limited. As noted previously, those who design strategies of nonviolent defense must consider unity and widespread participation as goals to be achieved, not preconditions for action. The point is this: Even one committed activist, and certainly a small group, can initiate a strategy of nonviolent defense as it is described in this study.

Elites will continue to act in response to the imperatives of the dominant social cosmology for some time yet, as indicated above. Grassroots activists should concentrate their efforts on rediscovering or developing cosmologies that are oriented to the satisfaction of human needs. This will require a shift to patterns of matter-energy use that are based on renewable resources, the development of cooperative models of social relations, the articulation of social philosophies that more accurately reflect the innate determinants of human behavior, and the implementation of strategies of nonviolent defense that can be used to resist the military violence of national elites. As these efforts gather momentum in the decades ahead, the decline of the dominant social cosmology will accelerate.

The strategic theory developed in this study and the strategy of nonviolent defense based on it may be improved, but they cannot be lightly dismissed. Too often in the past, critics have rejected efforts to construct conceptions of nonviolent forms of defense as unrealistic; this rejection usually conceals their ideological commitment to the use of violence in order to preserve the dominant social cosmology. While criticism is a vital part of the process necessary to improve the strategic theory and strategy of nonviolent defense developed in this study, it is necessary to be aware of the preferred cosmology of any critic. And while the comments of any critic should certainly be considered, the criticisms of those who are committed to creating a nonviolent world will usually provide the most thoughtful suggestions for improvement.

The opening sentence in this study posed a question: Can nonviolent defense be an effective strategy against military violence? As this study has demonstrated, nonviolent defense can be very effective in such circumstances. This can be explained theoretically and is consistent with the empirical evidence provided by the historical use of nonviolence. Moreover, if the criterion for judging the effectiveness of any strategy is the extent to which it addresses the causes of the conflict itself, then a strategy of nonviolent defense is the *most effective* response to an act of military aggression.

Notes

Notes to the Introduction

1. In this study, the term *nonviolent defense* has a precise meaning: Nonviolent defense is a defense strategy conducted in accordance with the strategic theory and the strategic framework described in chapter 8. The strategy of nonviolent defense will be fully explained in chapters 10 through 13.

2. In this study, effectiveness is measured by the degree to which a defense strategy diagnoses and addresses the causes of conflict and thus reduces or eliminates the use of military violence.

3. See, for instance, Marx and Engels, *The German Ideology*, 67.

4. On Earth, there are two sources of energy—the terrestrial stock and the solar flow—both of which are limited. The terrestrial stock is of two types: those resources (such as topsoil) that are renewable on a human time scale and those resources (such as fossil fuels) that are only renewable over geological time. For human purposes, resources in the latter category must be treated as nonrenewable. See Herman E. Daly, *Steady-State Economics*, 21.

5. Despite the numerous and widely accepted misconceptions about nonliterate societies—including, for example, the belief that they are led by "chiefs"—many anthropological studies substantiate the characterization of them that is given here. Many of these studies are cited in Bonta, *Peaceful Peoples*. The best general works on the subject are Montagu, ed., *Learning Non-aggression*; Howell and Willis, eds., *Societies at Peace*.

6. In essence, the law in Western "democracies" protects the property interests of elites and the powers of the states that represent those elites. There is, for instance, no equally comprehensive body of law that protects the rights of women; the identity, culture, and land rights of indigenous peoples; the rights of people who are homeless and in poverty; or the rights of nonhuman species and the environment.

7. King-Hall, *Defence in the Nuclear Age*.

8. Lyttle, *National Defense thru Nonviolent Resistance*.

9. Johan Niezing, "The Study of Social Defence: How to Overcome

Stagnation?" (paper presented at the conference "Social Defence," University of Wollongong, Australia, 16 February 1990), 1.

10. Sharp, *Civilian-Based Defense.*

11. Christopher Kruegler, cited in Mel Beckman, "The Washington D.C. Consultation on Civilian-Based Defense," *Civilian-Based Defense* 7 (January 1991): 7.

12. See, for instance, Boserup and Mack, *War without Weapons.*

13. See, for instance, Schmid, *Social Defence;* Sharp, *Making Europe Unconquerable.*

14. For short discussions regarding some of this terminology and its meanings, see Adam Roberts, "Non-violent Resistance As an Approach to Peace," in *Conflict, Violence, and Peace,* ed. Barkat, 89; Galtung, "On the Strategy of Nonmilitary Defense: Some Proposals and Problems," in *Essays in Peace Research,* 2:466 n. 1.

15. Sharp, *National Security,* 47.

16. Christine Schweitzer, "What Is Social Defence? Against the Differentiation of Social Defence and Nonviolent Uprising," trans. Simon Pratt (paper presented at the conference "Nonviolent Struggle and Social Defence," University of Bradford, England, 3–7 April 1990), 3.

17. Julio Quan, "Low Intensity Conflict: Central America," in *Nonviolent Struggle and Social Defence,* ed. Anderson and Larmore, 70.

18. Drago, "Nonviolent Popular Defence," 884.

19. For a brief explanation of why Sharp and other theorists rejected the label *nonviolent defense,* see Sharp, "Promoting Civilian-Based Defense," 12.

20. This tripartite distinction was first made by Lippmann at a conference and was reported in K. W. Thompson, "Toward a Theory of International Politics," 733–46.

21. That is, the study makes no pretense of being "value-free"; such a claim usually disguises the fact that the values of the dominant social cosmology are accepted.

22. Merton, *Social Theory and Social Structure,* 68.

Notes to Chapter 1

1. Peter Paret, "Clausewitz," in *Makers of Modern Strategy,* ed. Paret, 209.

2. Clausewitz, *On War,* 577–78.

3. Paret, "Clausewitz," 193–94.

4. Clausewitz, *On War,* 177.

5. Ibid., 578.

6. Ibid., 70.

7. Peter Paret, "The Genesis of *On War,*" in Clausewitz, *On War,* 4.

8. Liddell Hart, *Strategy,* 340.

9. Aron, *Clausewitz*, ix.
10. Gat, *The Origins of Military Thought*, ix.
11. Howard, *Clausewitz*, 40.
12. Gat, *The Origins of Military Thought*, 252.
13. Gallie, *Philosophers of Peace and War*, 52.
14. Gat, *The Origins of Military Thought*, 230–36.
15. Michael Howard, "The Influence of Clausewitz," in Clausewitz, *On War*, 41.
16. Paret, "Clausewitz," 211–13.
17. Leonard, ed., *Short Guide to Clausewitz on War*, 34–37.
18. Liddell Hart, *Strategy*, 340, 344.
19. Howard, "The Influence of Clausewitz," 27–44.
20. For a discussion of these points, see Smith, "The Womb of War," 58, 41, 55–56, 46.
21. Clausewitz, *On War*, 69, 78.
22. Ibid., 580, 593.
23. Ibid., 585–86.
24. Gallie, *Philosophers of Peace and War*, 52.
25. It could be argued that this relationship is part of a wider *political* theory (that was not elaborated by Clausewitz) rather than part of strategic theory proper. For the purposes of this study, it will be treated as part of Clausewitz's strategic theory.
26. Clausewitz, *On War*, 605, 609, 87, 606. Emphasis in original.
27. Clausewitz does not mean this in the modern "democratic" sense. He is referring to national interests defined by elites.
28. Clausewitz, *On War*, 606–7.
29. Ibid., 81, 75.
30. Smith, "The Womb of War," 52.
31. Clausewitz, *On War*, 159, 77.
32. Ibid., 75.
33. Boserup and Mack, *War without Weapons*, 152.
34. Clausewitz, *On War*, 83.
35. Ibid., 216–17, 579, 585, 119–21, 84.
36. Ibid., 93, 372–73.
37. Boserup and Mack, *War without Weapons*, 154–55. For this interpretation, Boserup and Mack draw extensively on Glucksmann, *Le discours de la guerre*.
38. Clausewitz, *On War*, 617–19, 595–97.
39. Boserup and Mack, *War without Weapons*, 159–61.
40. This is because, as explained above, the center of gravity is determined by the type of defense chosen.
41. Boserup and Mack, *War without Weapons*, 161.
42. Clausewitz, *On War*, 596.
43. Howard, *Clausewitz*, 40.

44. Boserup and Mack, *War without Weapons*, 156–57.

45. Clausewitz, *On War*, 527–28.

46. Boserup and Mack, *War without Weapons*, 164.

47. Collins, *Grand Strategy*, 4.

48. Boserup and Mack, *War without Weapons*, 157; Cincinnatus, *Self-Destruction*, 53.

49. Boserup and Mack, *War without Weapons*, 150–51, 158.

50. Clausewitz, *On War*, 593–94, 87.

51. Liddell Hart, *Strategy*, 319–20.

52. Howard, *Clausewitz*, 66.

53. Boserup and Mack, *War without Weapons*, 177.

54. Lombardi, "Decisive Battle," 2.

55. Paret, "Clausewitz," 208–9.

56. Clausewitz, *On War*, 75.

57. Gallie, *Philosophers of Peace and War*, 61–62.

58. Gat, *The Origins of Military Thought*, 201.

59. Howard, "The Influence of Clausewitz," 29.

60. For a lengthy discussion of this point, see Gat, *The Origins of Military Thought*.

61. Howard, "The Influence of Clausewitz," 44.

62. Clausewitz, *On War*, 92–94.

63. Ibid., 97, 77, 90.

64. Atkinson, *Social Order*, 4, 64, 15, 18, 27–28, 53, 37–40, 97–98, 86–87, 77. For a lengthy explanation of this point, see pp. 10–119. It should be noted that Atkinson draws attention to the difficulties of invading social order in some circumstances. For different reasons, he cites World War I and the Korean War as examples in which the invasion of social order may have been "largely impossible." But because he is essentially concerned with *guerrilla-based* strategies, he ignores the potential of nonguerrilla and nonmilitary strategies in this regard. See Atkinson, *Social Order*, 15–16.

65. The use of absolutes to illustrate concepts was popular with other writers of this time. See, for instance, Kant, *Critique of Pure Reason*.

66. Gallie, *Philosophers of Peace and War*, 54. Despite his trenchant criticism, Gallie argues that it is possible to reconstruct Clausewitz's conceptual system in order to explain this point—see pp. 49–60.

67. Clausewitz, *On War*, 78–80.

68. Atkinson, *Social Order*, 218, 232. For a discussion of the shortcomings and implications of these assumptions, see pp. 209–56.

69. See, for instance, Clausewitz, *On War*, 87, 605–10.

70. Atkinson, *Social Order*, 210–11.

71. Clausewitz, *On War*, 75, 77.

72. Ibid., 87.

73. Liddell Hart, *Strategy*, 338–52.

74. Ibid., 356–57.

75. Ibid., 338–39, 343.

76. Sun Tzu, *The Art of War*, 77, 79.

77. Clausewitz, *On War*, 164.

78. This last position was argued by Liddell Hart in the second half of the 1930s; for a discussion of his view on this point, see Mearsheimer, *Liddell Hart*, 110–19.

79. See, for instance, Buzan, *An Introduction to Strategic Studies*, 31.

80. Boserup and Mack, *War without Weapons*, 157.

81. Atkinson, *Social Order*, 4.

82. Ibid., 72, 77.

83. Howard, *Clausewitz*, 39–40.

84. Clausewitz, *On War*, 90.

85. Leonard, ed., *Short Guide to Clausewitz on War*, 16.

86. Clausewitz, *On War*, 141.

Notes to Chapter 2

1. Clausewitz, *On War*, 95, 128, 177.

2. Ibid., 87, 605–10.

3. Ibid., 78.

4. Ibid., 97, 230, and references throughout book 4.

5. Ibid., 90. Emphasis in original.

6. Ibid., 95–96, 228.

7. Bernard Brodie, "A Guide to the Reading of *On War*," in Clausewitz, *On War*, 647.

8. Clausewitz, *On War*, 96–97.

9. Sun Tzu, *The Art of War*, 77, 79.

10. Gat, *The Origins of Military Thought*, 210.

11. Paret, *Clausewitz and the State*, 369.

12. Howard, "The Influence of Clausewitz," 41.

13. Gat, *The Origins of Military Thought*, 225–26.

14. Clausewitz, *On War*, 97–99, 596; Sun Tzu, *The Art of War*, 77–78.

15. Howard, *Clausewitz*, 43.

16. Clausewitz, *On War*, 97.

17. Liddell Hart, *Strategy*, 321–22.

18. Ibid., 320–21, 213, 324, 349.

19. Freedman, "Indignation, Influence and Strategic Studies," 210.

20. Bull, "Strategic Studies and Its Critics," 593.

21. Howard, *The Causes of Wars*, 85.

22. Wylie, *Military Strategy*, 13.

23. Edward Mead Earle, "Introduction," in *Makers of Modern Strategy*, ed. Earle, viii.

24. Aron, *Clausewitz*, 233.

25. For the most comprehensive reappraisal of Liddell Hart and his legacy, see Mearsheimer, *Liddell Hart*.

26. Ibid., 37–38, 42, 46.

27. Ibid., 84–88.

28. Liddell Hart, *Strategy*, 212.

29. Liddell Hart, *Paris*, 25, 27. For a lengthy discussion emphasizing the importance of will, see pp. 16–43.

30. Liddell Hart, *Strategy*, 212.

31. Liddell Hart, *Paris*, 33.

32. Mearsheimer, *Liddell Hart*, 89, 91, 93.

33. Liddell Hart, *Paris*, 33–35.

34. Liddell Hart, *Strategy*, 334–37.

35. Ibid., 336, 326.

36. Ibid., 327, 135–36, 323.

37. Brian Bond, *Liddell Hart*, 56–57.

38. Mearsheimer, *Liddell Hart*, 87.

39. See, for instance, the discussions in Liddell Hart, *Paris*, 17, 27; Liddell Hart, *Strategy*, 212.

40. Liddell Hart was aware of the value of nonmilitary (or quasi-military) sanctions and even wrote briefly about civilian-based defense. Nevertheless, his vast literary legacy is preoccupied with the military conception of strategy. For discussions by Liddell Hart on civilian-based defense, see Liddell Hart, *Deterrent or Defence*, 217–23; Liddell Hart, "Lessons from Resistance Movements—Guerrilla and Non-violent," in *Civilian Resistance*, ed. Adam Roberts, 228–46. For earlier discussions that touch briefly upon civilian-based defense, see Liddell Hart, *Europe in Arms*, 1–8; Liddell Hart, *Defence of the West*, 62–67.

41. Napoleon, *The Mind of Napoleon*, 203–38.

42. John Shy, "Jomini," in *Makers of Modern Strategy*, ed. Paret, 143–85.

43. Mao, "Problems of Strategy in China's Revolutionary War," in *Selected Works*, 1:199–200; Mao, "Problems of Strategy in Guerrilla War against Japan," in *Selected Works*, 2:82.

44. Marighela, *For the Liberation of Brazil*, 45–51.

45. Liddell Hart, *Strategy*, 334–37.

46. Collins, *Grand Strategy*, 23.

47. Clausewitz, *On War*, 141.

48. Beaufre, *An Introduction to Strategy*, 34.

49. Brodie, *Strategy in the Missile Age*, 23–24.

50. This theory, and its relevance for guiding approaches to conflict in the international system, will be considered in chapter 5.

51. Mao, "On Protracted War," in *Selected Works*, 2:143.

52. In strategic studies, the term *will* refers to the general psychological disposition; it is not used in the specific sense intended by the determinists and libertarians engaged in the free-will debate.

53. Samuel B. Griffith, "Introduction," in Sun Tzu, *The Art of War*, 54.

54. Clausewitz, *On War*, 127, 185, 119, 188.

55. Napoleon, *The Mind of Napoleon*, 219.

56. Liddell Hart, *Strategy*, 146.

57. Gray, *Strategic Studies*, 138, 152, 139.

58. Howard, "The Forgotten Dimensions of Strategy," 975–77.

59. Creveld, *Supplying War*, 233.

60. Howard, "The Forgotten Dimensions of Strategy," 977–78.

61. Ibid., 978–80.

62. Ibid., 981.

63. Taber, *The War of the Flea*, 63.

64. Catudal, *Soviet Nuclear Strategy*, 127–29.

65. Howard, "The Forgotten Dimensions of Strategy," 981.

66. Mack, "Big Nations," 195, 175–79. See also Andrew Mack, "The Strategy of Non-military Defence," in *Strategy and Defence*, ed. Ball, 149–52. For a case study that illustrates this point in some detail, see MacDonald, "French Colonial War in Algeria," 95–108.

67. Howard, "The Forgotten Dimensions of Strategy," 982.

68. Lider, "Towards a Modern Concept of Strategy," 219.

69. Luttwak, "The Operational Level of War," 62–63.

70. Boserup and Mack, *War without Weapons*, 180.

71. Mack, "Big Nations," 178–79; Mack, "Non-military Defence," 149–52.

72. Mao, "On Protracted War," 143.

73. See, for instance, E. L. Katzenbach, Jr., "Time, Space, and Will: The Politico-Military Views of Mao Tse-tung," in *The Guerrilla*, ed. Greene, 18.

74. Kissinger, "The Viet Nam Negotiations," 212–15.

75. Westmoreland, *A Soldier Reports*, 405, 414, 422. There are, of course, other explanations of the U.S. defeat in Vietnam and Cambodia. For an account that systematically exposes the ethical, doctrinal, organizational, strategic, and tactical shortcomings of the U.S. military during this war, as well as the incompetence of its military leadership (including Westmoreland himself), see Cincinnatus, *Self-Destruction*. For an account that argues that the power of the U.S. government to wage war on Vietnam and Cambodia was progressively undermined by resistance within the military itself, see Cortright, *Soldiers in Revolt*.

76. Howard, "The Forgotten Dimensions of Strategy," 982–84.

77. Atkinson, *Social Order*, 72, 77.

78. For discussions of this phenomenon, see Herman and Chomsky, *Manufacturing Consent*; Chomsky, *Necessary Illusions*.

79. For an early example of the now substantial literature documenting this point, see Laura Fraser, "Not Cleared by U.S. Censors," *San Francisco Bay Guardian*, 23 January 1991. One of the more notable postwar analyses

was undertaken by Galtung in "Reporting on a War," 8–11. Discussions of this point were also undertaken by several authors, including Noam Chomsky and Holly Sklar, in the special Gulf War edition of *Propaganda Review* 7 (1991).

Notes to Chapter 3

1. Dahrendorf, *Class and Class Conflict,* 165.

2. John Locke, "An Essay Concerning the True Original, Extent and End of Civil Government," in Locke, Hume, and Rousseau, *Social Contract: Essays by Locke, Hume and Rousseau,* 80–81. For a discussion highlighting the fact that the social contract as it is traditionally conceived presupposes a patriarchal sexual "contract," see Pateman, *The Sexual Contract.*

3. Jean-Jacques Rousseau, "The Social Contract or Principles of Political Right," in Locke, Hume, and Rousseau, *Social Contract: Essays by Locke, Hume and Rousseau,* 255.

4. Durkheim, *Division of Labour in Society,* 68, 329–32.

5. Dahrendorf, *Class and Class Conflict,* 64, 165.

6. Hobbes, *Leviathan,* 223–35.

7. Marx and Engels, "Manifesto of the Communist Party," in *Selected Works in One Volume,* 36.

8. Karl Marx, *Capital,*1:293, 257–58, 689.

9. Karl Marx, *Critique of Political Economy,* 20–21.

10. Bakunin, *The Political Philosophy of Bakunin,* 138–39.

11. Wolff, *In Defense of Anarchism,* 18.

12. Donna Warnock, "Patriarchy Is a Killer: What People Concerned about Peace and Justice Should Know," in *Reweaving the Web of Life,* ed. McAllister, 23.

13. Mary Daly, *Gyn/Ecology,* 355.

14. Pareto, *The Mind and Society,* 3:1421–32.

15. Mills, *The Power Elite,* 3–4.

16. Beres and Targ, *Constructing Alternative World Futures,* 25.

17. Roszak, *Making of a Counter Culture,* 7, 19, 15.

18. Ellul, *The Technological Society,* 138.

19. Beres and Targ, *Constructing Alternative World Futures,* 37.

20. Johan Galtung, lectures (Peace and Conflict Studies Programme, Department of Government, University of Queensland, Australia, 1 July 1991–17 July 1991), lecture dated 10 July 1991.

21. Cleaver, *Soul on Ice,* 85.

22. See, for instance, hooks, *Ain't I a Woman.*

23. Lisa Albrecht and Rose M. Brewer, "Bridges of Power: Women's Multicultural Alliances for Social Change," in *Bridges of Power,* ed. Albrecht and Brewer, 11–13.

24. Albert et al., *Liberating Theory,* 71–84.

25. Burton, *Deviance, Terrorism and War*, 44–47.

26. Ibid., 53.

27. W. E. Moore, "A Reconsideration of Theories of Social Change," in *Readings in Social Evolution and Development*, ed. Eisenstadt, 131.

28. Burton, *Deviance, Terrorism and War*, 52.

29. Berger, *Invitation to Sociology*, 83–94.

30. Burton, *Deviance, Terrorism and War*, 54, 45.

31. Edward E. Azar, "Protracted International Conflicts: Ten Propositions," in *Conflict*, ed. Burton and Dukes, 150–51.

32. Burton, *Deviance, Terrorism and War*, 54.

Notes to Chapter 4

1. This view is shared by many authors. See, for instance, Roger A. Coate and Jerel A. Rosati, "Human Needs in World Society," in *The Power of Human Needs*, ed. Coate and Rosati, 3–5.

2. Karl Marx, "Theses on Feuerbach," in Marx and Engels, *Selected Works in One Volume*, 29.

3. Marx and Engels, *The German Ideology*, 37.

4. Karl Marx, *Critique of Political Economy*, 20–21; Marx and Engels, *The German Ideology*, 42.

5. Stevenson, *Seven Theories of Human Nature*, 64.

6. Freud, *An Outline of Psycho-Analysis*, 17.

7. Freud, *An Outline of Psycho-Analysis*, 2–3; Freud, *Civilization and Its Discontents*, 73.

8. Freud, *An Outline of Psycho-Analysis*, 5–6; Stevenson, *Seven Theories of Human Nature*, 66–67.

9. Freud, *An Outline of Psycho-Analysis*, 3–4.

10. Machiavelli, *The Prince*, 96, 100.

11. Hobbes, *Leviathan*, 118–61.

12. Freud, *Civilization and Its Discontents*, 48–51.

13. Morgenthau, *Politics among Nations*, 3–4.

14. Waltz, *Man, the State and War*, 39–41.

15. Harry Eckstein, "Theoretical Approaches to Explaining Collective Political Violence," in *Handbook of Political Conflict*, ed. Gurr, 138–39.

16. Keith Webb, "Conflict: Inherent and Contingent Theories," in *World Encyclopedia of Peace*, ed. Pauling, 1:170–71.

17. Burton, *Conflict*, 4, 72–73.

18. Howell and Willis, eds., *Societies at Peace*, 10–11.

19. Burton, *Conflict*, 4.

20. Howell and Willis, eds., *Societies at Peace*, 12.

21. For two of the many non-Western conceptions of human nature, see the Dalai Lama, "Relevance of Compassion and Nonviolence Today," 5–11; Signe Howell, "'To Be Angry Is Not to Be Human, But to Be Fearful Is':

Chewong Concepts of Human Nature," in *Societies at Peace*, ed. Howell and Willis, 45–59.

22. See, for instance, Adams et al., "The Seville Statement on Violence," 271–74; Fromm, *The Anatomy of Human Destructiveness*; Montagu, *The Nature of Human Aggression*; Quincy Wright, *A Study of War*, 317–27.

23. Coate and Rosati, "Human Needs in World Society," 3.

24. Galtung, *Methodology and Development*, 145.

25. Burton, *Global Conflict*, 139.

26. Sites, *Control*, 9, 11.

27. Lederer, ed., *Human Needs*, 17.

28. Maslow, *Motivation and Personality*, 15–26.

29. Sites, *Control*, 1, 3, 7, 43.

30. Galtung, "Cultural Violence," 292.

31. Johan Galtung, "International Development in Human Perspective," in *Conflict*, ed. Burton, 312–13.

32. Galtung, *Methodology and Development*, 146.

33. Dennis J. D. Sandole, "The Biological Basis of Needs in World Society: The Ultimate Micro-Macro Nexus," in *Conflict*, ed. Burton, 60–65.

34. Avruch and Black, "A Generic Theory of Conflict Resolution," 91, 95.

35. Boyd and Richerson, *Culture and the Evolutionary Process*, 1–18.

36. Burton and Sandole, "Expanding the Debate," 97.

37. Galtung, "International Development in Human Perspective," 315.

38. Sandole, "Biological Basis of Needs," 68.

39. Paul Sites, "Needs As Analogues of Emotions," in *Conflict*, ed. Burton, 7.

40. Darwin, *Expression of the Emotions*.

41. For one account, which summarizes and synthesizes the research on emotions that has been conducted in several disciplines, see Plutchik, *Emotion*.

42. For one discussion of this, see K. R. Scherer, "On the Nature and Function of Emotion: A Component Process Approach," in *Approaches to Emotion*, ed. Scherer and Ekman, 294.

43. Robert Plutchik, "Emotions: A General Psychoevolutionary Theory," in *Approaches to Emotion*, ed. Scherer and Ekman, 209, 212.

44. For summaries of the research that points to this conclusion, see Plutchik, "Emotions," 200–5; Plutchik, *Emotion*, 131–34.

45. This list, and a summary of the justifications for it, are given in Plutchik, "Emotions," 203.

46. Kemper, "How Many Emotions Are There?" 263–89.

47. Sites, "Needs As Analogues of Emotions," 7–22.

48. Coate and Rosati, "Human Needs in World Society," 3.

49. Burton, *Deviance, Terrorism and War*, 198.

50. Coate and Rosati, "Human Needs in World Society," 13.

51. Buzan, *People, States and Fear,* 18.

52. Coate and Rosati, "Human Needs in World Society," 7.

53. Burton, *Global Conflict,* 39.

54. Burton, *Deviance, Terrorism and War,* 182, 17, 28.

55. Sites, *Control,* 18.

56. Ibid., 10.

57. Box, *Deviance, Reality and Society,* 9.

58. Burton, *Deviance, Terrorism and War,* 182–83.

59. Galtung, lectures, 1 July 1991; Galtung, "International Development in Human Perspective," 310.

60. Victoria Rader, "Human Needs and the Modernization of Poverty," in *Conflict,* ed. Burton, 228.

61. Bull, *The Anarchical Society,* 16.

62. Burton, *Global Conflict,* 17–18.

63. Burton, *Conflict,* 31–33.

64. Burton, *Resolving Deep-Rooted Conflict,* 18.

65. Burton, *Conflict,* 33–34.

66. Burton, *Global Conflict,* 22–23, ix–x.

67. Galtung, *The True Worlds,* 421.

68. Galtung, *Methodology and Development,* 150, 148.

69. Sites, *Control,* 10.

70. Burton, *Global Conflict,* 20.

71. David J. Carroll, Jerel A. Rosati, and Roger A. Coate, "Human Needs Realism: A Critical Assessment of the Power of Human Needs in World Society," in *The Power of Human Needs,* ed. Coate and Rosati, 269.

72. Azar, "Protracted International Conflicts," 147–49.

73. Christian Bay, "Human Needs As Human Rights," in *The Power of Human Needs,* ed. Coate and Rosati, 94.

74. Azar, "Protracted International Conflicts," 151.

Notes to Chapter 5

1. For a review of these authors and a summary of their arguments, see Fink, "Some Conceptual Difficulties," 413–24.

2. Ibid., 413, 416.

3. Max Weber, *Economy and Society,* 1:38.

4. Coser, *The Functions of Social Conflict,* 8.

5. See, for instance, Boulding, *Conflict and Defense,* 5; Deutsch, *The Resolution of Conflict,* 10.

6. It should be noted that recent conflict research has resulted in the development of vastly improved models of negotiation and mediation as well as the creation of several new models for designing conflict outcomes. See, for instance, Fisher and Ury, *Getting to Yes;* Moore, *The Mediation Process;* de Bono, *Conflicts.*

7. Burton, *Conflict*, 247.

8. Ibid., 36–37.

9. Burton, *Deviance, Terrorism and War*, 58–59.

10. Burton, *Global Conflict*, 145.

11. Burton, *Conflict*, 36–38.

12. Ibid., 1–2.

13. Burton, "Conflict Resolution As a Political Philosophy," 62.

14. Burton, *Conflict*, 1–2.

15. Burton, *Global Conflict*, 143.

16. Burton, *Conflict*, 1.

17. Ibid., 18, 3. See also Burton and Dukes, *Conflict*, 161.

18. Burton, *Conflict*, 23.

19. Burton, *Global Conflict*, 137.

20. Ibid., 138.

21. John W. Burton, "History of Conflict Resolution," in *World Encyclopedia of Peace*, ed. Pauling, 1:178.

22. Galtung, *Solving Conflicts*, 4.

23. Ibid., 2–3.

24. Galtung, "Conflict As a Way of Life," in *Essays in Peace Research*, 3:486; Galtung, "A Structural Theory of Imperialism," in *Essays in Peace Research*, 4:438.

25. Galtung, *Peace and Development*, 41.

26. Galtung, *Solving Conflicts*, 5–6.

27. Galtung, lectures, 16 July 1991.

28. Galtung, *The True Worlds*, 140.

29. Otto Klineberg, "Human Needs: A Social-Psychological Approach," in *Human Needs*, ed. Lederer, 21, 32.

30. Herbert C. Kelman, "An Interactional Approach to Conflict Resolution," in *Psychology*, ed. R. K. White, 172–73.

31. R. K. White, *Fearful Warriors*, 128, 109–34, 131.

32. Peck, "An Integrative Model," 14.

33. Jervis, *Perception and Misperception*, 117–202, 356–81.

34. R. K. White, *Fearful Warriors*, 136, 137–54, 168–85, 154–59.

35. Morton Deutsch, "The Malignant (Spiral) Process of Hostile Interaction," in *Psychology*, ed. R. K. White, 136.

36. R. K. White, "Motivated Misperceptions," in *Psychology*, ed. R. K. White, 291.

37. Pruitt and Rubin, *Social Conflict*, 135–36.

38. Frank, *Sanity and Survival*, 125–26.

39. Janis, *Groupthink*, 7–9, 174–75.

40. R. K. White, *Fearful Warriors*, 160.

41. Jervis, *Perception and Misperception*, 113, 409–24.

42. Kelman, "Conflict Resolution," 172.

43. Morton Deutsch, "A Theoretical Perspective on Conflict and Con-

flict Resolution," in *Conflict Management and Problem Solving*, ed. Sandole and Sandole-Staroste, 48.

44. Pruitt and Rubin, *Social Conflict*, 2–3, 25–27.

45. For a discussion of these and other models, see Murray, "Understanding Competing Theories of Negotiation," 179–86.

46. Peck, "United Nations Dispute Settlement Commission," 74. See also Fisher and Ury, *Getting to Yes*, 3–14.

47. Ury, Brett, and Goldberg, *Getting Disputes Resolved*, 4–5, xv. For a discussion of their "dispute resolution system," see pp. 41–64.

48. Ibid., 16.

49. Morgenthau, *Politics among Nations*, 27–40.

50. Bull, *The Anarchical Society*, 283–84.

51. Burton, *Global Conflict*, xi–xii, 7.

52. Ibid., 6–7, 12–13, 8–9.

53. Galtung, "A Structural Theory of Imperialism," 437.

54. Galtung, *Solving Conflicts*, 22–23, 26–27, 33.

55. Galtung, "Violence, Peace, and Peace Research," in *Essays in Peace Research*, 1:114.

56. Azar, "Protracted International Conflicts," 154–55.

57. Burton, *Deviance, Terrorism and War*, 192.

58. Galtung, *Solving Conflicts*, 31–36.

59. Burton, *Deviance, Terrorism and War*, 10, 26, 18–19.

60. Burton, *Resolving Deep-Rooted Conflict*, 11–12.

61. Burton, "Conflict Resolution As a Political Philosophy," 72.

62. Burton, *Conflict*, 202–4.

63. Burton, *Resolving Deep-Rooted Conflict*, 7.

64. Burton, *Global Conflict*, 134.

65. Ibid., 145–46.

66. Fisher and Brown, *Getting Together*.

67. An important shortcoming of Burton's work is his failure to explain how emotions should be dealt with in any conflict resolution process. In fact, the word *emotion* does not even appear in the index of his four major books on conflict. See Burton, *Conflict*; Burton, *Deviance, Terrorism and War*; Burton, *Global Conflict*; Burton, *Resolving Deep-Rooted Conflict*.

68. Fisher and Ury, *Getting to Yes*, 30–33; Cornelius and Faire, *Everyone Can Win*, 88–103.

69. A. J. R. Groom, "Old Ways, New Insights: Conflict Resolution in International Conflict," in *Non-violence in International Crises*, ed. Czempiel, Kiuzadjan, and Masopust, 20–21.

70. Burton, *Global Conflict*, 148; Burton, *Resolving Deep-Rooted Conflict*, 7, 23–24; Burton, *Conflict*, 205–9, 222–23.

71. Galtung, lectures, 9 July 1991.

72. Burton, *Conflict*, 211.

73. Patai, *The Arab Mind*, 228–38.

74. Burton, *Conflict*, 214.

75. John W. Burton, "Unfinished Business in Conflict Resolution," in *Conflict*, ed. Burton and Dukes, 334.

76. See, for instance, Burton, *Deviance, Terrorism and War*, 34, 192; Burton, *Global Conflict*, 11, 41.

77. Burton, *Conflict*, 266. In addition, see the discussions on pp. 249–50, 262–67.

78. Burton, "Unfinished Business in Conflict Resolution," 333–35.

79. Jervis, *Perception and Misperception*, 138–39, 143, 117.

80. Chomsky, *The Chomsky Reader*, 60, 19, 37–39, 44. For a fuller discussion of the responsibility of intellectuals, see pp. 59–136.

81. See, for instance, Burton, *Conflict*, 248–49.

82. Ury, Brett, and Goldberg, *Getting Disputes Resolved*, 16, 18.

Notes to Chapter 6

1. Max Weber, *Economy and Society*, 1:53.

2. See, for instance, Dahl, "The Concept of Power," 202–3; Morgenthau, *Politics among Nations*, 28.

3. Macy, *Despair and Personal Power*, 30.

4. Galtung, *The True Worlds*, 62–64.

5. See, for instance, Macy, *Despair and Personal Power*, 30–34; Margolis, "Considering Women's Experience," 387–416.

6. Starhawk, *Truth or Dare*, 8–18.

7. La Boétie, *The Politics of Obedience*.

8. Sharp, *The Politics of Nonviolent Action*, 10.

9. David Hume, "Of the Original Contract," in Locke, Hume, and Rousseau, *Social Contract: Essays by Locke, Hume and Rousseau*, 211.

10. Sharp, *The Politics of Nonviolent Action*, 10–12.

11. Ibid., 16–18.

12. Hobbes, *Leviathan*, 161–62.

13. Aristotle, *The Politics*, 83. For discussions of the importance of habit to obedience, see, for instance, La Boétie, *The Politics of Obedience*, 60–65; de Jouvenel, *Power*, 27–33.

14. MacIver, *The Web of Government*, 58.

15. Hume, "Of the Original Contract," 214.

16. See, for instance, Milgram, "Behavioral Study of Obedience," 371–78.

17. Starhawk, *Truth or Dare*, 77–81.

18. These sources of obedience have been discussed extensively elsewhere. See, for instance, de Jouvenel, *Power*, 27–33; MacIver, *The Web of Government*, 56–61; Sharp, *The Politics of Nonviolent Action*, 12–25.

19. La Boétie, *The Politics of Obedience*, 69–75.

20. Ibid., 77–78.

21. Mann, *The Sources of Social Power*, 1:7.

22. Sharp, *The Politics of Nonviolent Action*, 27–28, 47–48.

23. Mosca, *The Ruling Class*, 53.

24. Mao, "Problems of War and Strategy," in *Selected Works*, 2:224.

25. Mao, "On Protracted War," 143–44.

26. Gandhi, *Constructive Programme*, 9.

27. Gandhi, *Young India*, 3 November 1927, in *Non-violent Resistance*, 35.

28. Gandhi, *The Hindu*, 19 August 1920, in *Collected Works*, 18:172.

29. Lipsitz and Kritzer, "Unconventional Approaches to Conflict Resolution," 727.

30. Schmid, *Social Defence*, 396; Steven Duncan Huxley, *Constitutionalist Insurgency in Finland*, 22–23, 33. The criticism, as it is explained by Schmid, is partly misconceived. The argument that people are the source of all power does not mean that all people are supporters of a particular elite; some may be opponents or third parties. The point is that nonhuman resources (such as money or weapons) have no value until they are used by people—whether supporters or opponents. In this sense, then, people are the source of all power because they choose how to apply nonhuman resources; for instance, opponents may choose to use weapons or to put them down. Nevertheless, the main focus of this criticism is the irrelevance of consent when there is no dependency relationship, and this aspect of the criticism is important.

31. Rigby, *Living the Intifada*, 195–96.

32. Galtung, *Nonviolence and Israel/Palestine*, 13–33.

33. Summy, "Nonviolence and the Case of the Extremely Ruthless Opponent," 12–13.

34. Pateman, *The Sexual Contract*.

35. McGuinness, "Gene Sharp's Theory of Power," 103–8.

36. La Boétie, *The Politics of Obedience*, 77–78.

37. Martin, "Gene Sharp's Theory of Power," 216, 221.

38. Koch, "Civilian Defence," 3–4.

39. Martin, "Gene Sharp's Theory of Power," 214–15.

40. Millett, *Sexual Politics*, xi, 58, 25.

41. Ibid., 26–44.

42. Ibid., 32–33, 26–27, 46, 54, 58.

43. Starhawk, *The Spiral Dance*, 6–30.

44. Gramsci, *Selections from the Prison Notebooks*, 12–13.

45. Martin, "Gene Sharp's Theory of Power," 217.

46. Marx and Engels, *The German Ideology*, 67.

47. Reus-Smit, "Realist and Resistance Utopias," 3–4. For another discussion of the connection between structures of power and ideology, see Havel, *Living in Truth*, 45–50.

48. Carroll, Rosati, and Coate, "Human Needs Realism," 268.

49. Matthew 5:5.
50. Dickson, *Alternative Technology*, 10.
51. Martin, "Gene Sharp's Theory of Power," 216–17.
52. For a fuller discussion of this point, see ibid., 217.
53. Galtung, *The True Worlds*, 396–98.

Notes to Chapter 7

1. For excerpts of ancient documents from three of these traditions, see Hunter and Mallick, eds., *Nonviolence*, 3–53.

2. For an exceptional variety of historical examples, see Sharp, *The Politics of Nonviolent Action*. For studies that partially redress the bias against recording the contribution of women to human history in this particular context, see McAllister, ed., *Reweaving the Web of Life*; McAllister, *You Can't Kill the Spirit*; McAllister, *This River of Courage*. For studies that partially redress the bias against recording the contribution of non-Western peoples in this regard, see Crow, Grant, and Ibrahim, eds., *Arab Nonviolent Political Struggle*; McManus and Schlabach, eds., *Relentless Persistence*.

3. For a discussion that argues that use of these terms in a "transhistorical" sense is inappropriate, see Steven Duncan Huxley, *Constitutionalist Insurgency in Finland*, 17–21.

4. Sharp, *The Politics of Nonviolent Action*, 64.

5. For a feminist classification, see Carroll, "'Women Take Action!'" 3–24.

6. Sharp, *The Politics of Nonviolent Action*, 117–82.

7. Ibid., 183–356, 315.

8. Ibid., 357–445.

9. Gene Sharp, "A Study of the Meanings of Nonviolence," in *Gandhi*, ed. Ramachandran and Mahadevan, 21–66. See also Sharp, *Gandhi As a Political Strategist*, 201–34.

10. For others, see, for instance, Douglas G. Bond, "Nature and Meanings of Nonviolent Direct Action," 81–89; Summy, "Typology of Nonviolent Politics," 230–42.

11. Sharp, "Meanings of Nonviolence," 28.

12. For a discussion of Gandhi's distinction in this regard, see Iyer, *Mahatma Gandhi*, 192–99.

13. See, for instance, Boserup and Mack, *War without Weapons*, 11–16; Kruegler, "Liddell Hart," passim; Schmid, *Social Defence*, 14–15. More recently, Kruegler has cast his version of this type of distinction differently. See Kruegler, "To the Editor," 13. For Sharp's version of this type of distinction, see Sharp, "To the Editor," 13–15. For an author who thinks this distinction, although justified in certain respects, "can be highly misleading," see Steven Duncan Huxley, *Constitutionalist Insurgency in Finland*, 18 n. 52.

14. See, for instance, Ackerman and Kruegler, *Strategic Nonviolent Conflict*, 2–3. For more complete descriptions of the pragmatic approach, see Boserup and Mack, *War without Weapons*, 12–14, 21; Schmid, *Social Defence*, 14–15.

15. See, for instance, Karl Marx, "Contribution to the Critique of Hegel's 'Philosophy of Right,'" in Marx and Engels, *The Marx-Engels Reader*, 19; Marx and Engels, *The German Ideology*, 47–48.

16. Gandhi, *Harijan*, 16 December 1939, in *Collected Works*, 71:28.

17. Gandhi, in *The Mind of Mahatma Gandhi*, ed. Prabhu and Rao, 254–55.

18. Ibid., 262.

19. Gandhi, *Young India*, 13 October 1921, in *Collected Works*, 21:291.

20. Gandhi, *Hind Swaraj*, 31–33. See also Gandhi, in *Selections from Gandhi*, ed. Bose, 114–22.

21. Gandhi, *Hind Swaraj*, 54–57.

22. Patel, *The Educational Philosophy of Mahatma Gandhi*; Pillai, *The Educational Aims of Mahatma Gandhi*.

23. Gandhi, in *Selections from Gandhi*, ed. Bose, 93–94.

24. Gandhi, *Harijan*, 27 January 1940, in *Collected Works*, 71:130.

25. Gandhi, *Harijan*, 4 August 1946, in *The Mind of Mahatma Gandhi*, ed. Prabhu and Rao, 246.

26. Gandhi, *Harijan*, 28 July 1946, in *Collected Works*, 85:32–33. See also Madan Handa, "The Elements of a Gandhian Social Theory," in *In Theory and In Practice*, ed. Selbourne, 40–41. For a more detailed exposition of Gandhi's social vision, see Pyarelal, *Towards New Horizons*.

27. Gandhi, *Harijan*, 4 November 1939, in *Collected Works*, 70:296.

28. Galtung, *The Way Is the Goal*, 48–50.

29. Gandhi, *Constructive Programme*, 8–10.

30. Ibid., 20–21.

31. Ibid., 10–11, 28–30.

32. Ibid., 12–16.

33. Ibid., 24–26.

34. Gandhi, *Young India*, 13 November 1924, in *Selections from Gandhi*, ed. Bose, 67.

35. Gandhi, *Young India*, 13 July 1921, in *Collected Works*, 20:366.

36. Gandhi, *Harijan*, 1 February 1942, in *Teachings of Mahatma Gandhi*, 321.

37. Pelton, *The Psychology of Nonviolence*, 163.

38. Gandhi, *Harijan*, 25 August 1940, in *Collected Works*, 72:399.

39. Gandhi, *Harijan*, 6 October 1946, in *Collected Works*, 85:369–70.

40. Pelton, *The Psychology of Nonviolence*, 159.

41. Gandhi, in *Selections from Gandhi*, ed. Bose, 35.

42. Gandhi, *Harijan*, 27 May 1939, in *Collected Works*, 69:258.

43. Ramashray Roy, "Three Visions of Needs and the Future: Liberal-

ism, Marxism, and Gandhism," in *The Power of Human Needs*, ed. Coate and Rosati, 71.

44. Gandhi, *From Yeravda Mandir*, 16.

45. Quoted in Pyarelal, *Mahatma Gandhi*, 2:552.

46. Roy, "Three Visions of Needs," 74.

47. Gandhi, *Harijan*, 27 May 1939, in *Collected Works*, 69:258.

48. Pillai, *The Educational Aims of Mahatma Gandhi*, 23.

49. Gandhi, in *The Mind of Mahatma Gandhi*, ed. Prabhu and Rao, 254–55.

50. Naess, *Gandhi and Group Conflict*, 68.

51. Gandhi, *Young India*, 17 November 1921, in *Collected Works*, 21:457.

52. Gandhi, *Young India*, 4 August 1920, in *Collected Works*, 18:112.

53. Gandhi, *Harijan*, 8 July 1933, in *Collected Works*, 55:255.

54. Naess, *Gandhi and Group Conflict*, 98. This, of course, may lead to conflict, and how Gandhi would respond to this conflict is discussed in the next section.

55. Gandhi, *Harijan*, 30 September 1939, in *Collected Works*, 70:206.

56. Galtung, *The Way Is the Goal*, 68.

57. Naess, *Gandhi and Group Conflict*, 111.

58. Gandhi, *Harijan*, 9 March 1940, in *Collected Works*, 71:224–25. See also Naess, *Gandhi and Group Conflict*, 111–12; Galtung, *The Way Is the Goal*, 72.

59. Rattan, *Gandhi's Concept of Political Obligation*, 25, 51.

60. Gandhi, *Harijan*, 22 August 1936, in *Collected Works*, 63:233.

61. Gandhi, *Hind Swaraj*, 72. For a detailed discussion of this, see Rattan, *Gandhi's Concept of Political Obligation*.

62. Galtung, "Conflict As a Way of Life," 490.

63. Galtung, *The Way Is the Goal*, 57.

64. Gandhi, *An Autobiography*, 230.

65. Galtung, *The Way Is the Goal*, 48–49, 57–58.

66. Ibid., 58.

67. Gandhi, *Young India*, 19 March 1925, in *Collected Works*, 26:273.

68. Pelton, *The Psychology of Nonviolence*, 15.

69. Gandhi, *Young India*, 23 March 1921, in *Collected Works*, 19:466.

70. Naess, *Gandhi and Group Conflict*, 59.

71. Galtung, *The Way Is the Goal*, 48.

72. Bondurant, *Conquest of Violence*, 195.

73. Pelton, *The Psychology of Nonviolence*, 17, 19.

74. Johan Galtung, "A Gandhian Theory of Conflict," in *In Theory and In Practice*, ed. Selbourne, 109.

75. Galtung, *The Way Is the Goal*, 75, 87.

76. Gandhi, *Harijan*, 9 March 1940, in *Collected Works*, 71:283.

77. Galtung, "A Gandhian Theory of Conflict," 109–10; Galtung, *The Way Is the Goal*, 87.

78. Bondurant, *Conquest of Violence*, vii, 195, 197. See also Galtung, *The Way Is the Goal*, 87.

79. Galtung, "A Gandhian Theory of Conflict," 110; Galtung, *The Way Is the Goal*, 87–88.

80. Thomas Weber, *Conflict Resolution and Gandhian Ethics*, 62.

81. Gregg, *The Power of Non-violence*, 126.

82. Thomas Weber, *Conflict Resolution and Gandhian Ethics*, 2.

83. Bharatan Kumarappa, "Editor's Note," in Gandhi, *Non-violent Resistance*, iii.

84. Naess, *Gandhi and Group Conflict*, 115–17. Emphasis in original.

85. Gandhi, *From Yeravda Mandir*, 7.

86. Gandhi, *Hind Swaraj*, 71.

87. Gandhi, *Young India*, 17 July 1924, in *Collected Works*, 24:396.

88. Gandhi, *Harijan*, 11 February 1939, in *Collected Works*, 68:390. See also Gandhi, *From Yeravda Mandir*, 7.

89. Aldous Huxley, *Ends and Means*, 9.

90. Arendt, *On Violence*, 4.

91. Pelton, *The Psychology of Nonviolence*, 56.

92. Aldous Huxley, *Ends and Means*, 32.

93. Gregg, *The Power of Non-violence*, 57.

94. Nakamura, *Ways of Thinking of Eastern Peoples*, 70. For a discussion of this notion, see pp. 67–72.

95. Ibid., 67.

96. Dundas, *The Jains*, 138.

97. Thomas Weber, *Conflict Resolution and Gandhian Ethics*, 50.

98. Gandhi, *Ashram Observances in Action*, 40.

99. Gandhi, *Young India*, 4 December 1924, in *Collected Works*, 25:390.

100. Gandhi, *An Autobiography*, 197.

101. See, for instance, Gandhi, *Young India*, 13 September 1928, in *For Pacifists*, 66–67. For discussions of this point, see Bishop, *A Technique for Loving*, 86–87; Dhawan, *Political Philosophy of Mahatma Gandhi*, 64–65; Thomas Weber, *Conflict Resolution and Gandhian Ethics*, 50.

102. Gandhi, *Young India*, 8 October 1925, in *Collected Works*, 28:305.

103. Gandhi, *Hind Swaraj*, 79; Sharp, *The Politics of Nonviolent Action*, 709.

104. Pelton, *The Psychology of Nonviolence*, 15–16, 160.

105. Gandhi, *Hind Swaraj*, 79.

106. See, for instance, the description of police rage engendered by the suffering of satyagrahis at the Dharasana salt depot in Webb Miller, *I Found No Peace*, 134–37. An excerpt of this account is reprinted in Tendulkar, *Mahatma*, 3:40–41.

107. For a discussion of this evidence, see Pelton, *The Psychology of Nonviolence*, 135–43.

108. Ibid., 135, 140, 136–38.

109. Ibid., 139–41.

110. Eleanora Patterson, "Suffering," in *Reweaving the Web of Life*, ed. McAllister, 165–74.

111. For a refutation of the argument by some feminists that the acceptance of suffering by women is inappropriate because it reinforces existing patterns of self-denial and sacrifice, see Lynne Jones, "Perceptions of 'Peace Women' at Greenham Common 1981–85: A Participant's View," in *Images of Women in Peace and War*, ed. Macdonald, Holden, and Ardener, 201–3.

112. Dhawan, *Political Philosophy of Mahatma Gandhi*, 143.

113. Gandhi, *Young India*, 2 August 1928, in *Collected Works*, 37:113.

114. Gandhi, *Harijan*, 1 July 1939, in *Collected Works*, 69:376.

115. Gandhi, *Young India*, 18 September 1924, in *Collected Works*, 25:164.

116. Sharp, "Gandhi As a National Defence Strategist," 257.

117. The Gandhian injunction against secrecy does not mean that the opponent is entitled to "know everything." In some circumstances, openness may constitute betrayal.

118. Thomas Weber, *Conflict Resolution and Gandhian Ethics*, 50.

119. Douglas G. Bond, "Nature and Meanings of Nonviolent Direct Action," 86.

120. Theodor Ebert, "Final Victory," in *Civilian Defence*, ed. Mahadevan, Roberts, and Sharp, 195–96.

121. Gandhi, *Young India*, 12 September 1929, in *Collected Works*, 41:379.

122. Pelton, *The Psychology of Nonviolence*, 204, 207–10. For a lengthy discussion of this point that cites the relevant psychological evidence, see pp. 204–47.

123. Ibid., 205–7.

124. Ibid., 55.

125. Gandhi, *Young India*, 8 January 1925, in *Collected Works*, 25:563.

126. Gandhi, *Young India*, 24 April 1930, in *Collected Works*, 43:306.

127. Gandhi, *Young India*, 8 December 1920, in *Collected Works*, 19:80.

128. Iyer, *Mahatma Gandhi*, 117.

129. Bondurant, *Conquest of Violence*, 164, 35.

130. Gandhi, *Young India*, 11 August 1920, in *Collected Works*, 18:132.

131. Gandhi, *Young India*, 6 May 1926, in *Collected Works*, 30:413.

132. Gandhi, *Young India*, 11 August 1920, in *Collected Works*, 18:133.

133. Iyer, *Mahatma Gandhi*, 96.

134. Gandhi, *Hind Swaraj*, 37.

135. Iyer, *Mahatma Gandhi*, 94, 147.

136. Galtung, lectures, 2 July 1991; Galtung, *The Way Is the Goal*, 63–67.

137. Iyer, *Mahatma Gandhi*, 73.

138. Bay, *The Structure of Freedom*, 93, 274.

139. Pelton, *The Psychology of Nonviolence*, 57.

140. Case, *Non-violent Coercion*, 403.

141. Bondurant, *Conquest of Violence*, 10.

142. Ibid., 9.

143. Deming, *We Are All Part of One Another*, 176–77.

144. Borman, *Gandhi and Non-violence*, 217, 224.

145. Niebuhr, *Moral Man and Immoral Society*, 242.

146. Sharp, *Civilian-Based Defense*, 60–64.

147. Sharp, *The Politics of Nonviolent Action*, 741.

148. Horsburgh, *Mahatma Gandhi*, 33.

149. Gandhi, *Harijan*, 23 July 1938, in *Collected Works*, 67:195.

150. Gandhi, *Harijan*, 24 November 1933, in *Collected Works*, 56:216.

151. Case, *Non-violent Coercion*, 378–79. For a description of the Rowlatt Satyagraha, see Kumar, ed., *Essays on Gandhian Politics*.

152. Thomas Weber, *Conflict Resolution and Gandhian Ethics*, 58.

153. Borman, *Gandhi and Non-violence*, 217–18, 220–21.

154. Gandhi, *Harijan*, 25 March 1939, in *Collected Works*, 69:69.

155. Gandhi, *Harijan*, 24 March 1946, in *Collected Works*, 83:241.

156. Gandhi, *Harijan*, 9 September 1933, in *Collected Works*, 55:411–12.

157. Borman, *Gandhi and Non-violence*, 218, 226.

158. Shridharani, *War without Violence*, 264.

159. Dhawan, *Political Philosophy of Mahatma Gandhi*, 263–66.

160. Naess, *Gandhi and Group Conflict*, 90–91.

161. Ibid., 91–92.

162. Thomas Weber, *Conflict Resolution and Gandhian Ethics*, 58.

163. Naess, *Gandhi and Group Conflict*, 92.

164. Gandhi, *An Autobiography*, 360.

165. Naess, *Gandhi and Group Conflict*, 93.

166. Pelton, *The Psychology of Nonviolence*, 73, 76, 79.

167. Borman, *Gandhi and Non-violence*, 226.

168. Boserup and Mack, *War without Weapons*, 22.

169. Naess, *Gandhi and Group Conflict*, 145.

170. Farmer, *Freedom—When?* 101, quoted in Sharp, *The Politics of Nonviolent Action*, 741.

171. Thomas Weber, *Conflict Resolution and Gandhian Ethics*, 58–59.

172. Naess, *Gandhi and Group Conflict*, 91.

173. Gandhi, *Harijan*, 9 September 1933, in *Collected Works*, 55:412.

174. Gandhi, *Harijan*, 21 July 1940, in *Selections from Gandhi*, ed. Bose, 154.

175. Gandhi, *Harijan*, 9 March 1940, in *Collected Works*, 71:225.

Notes to Chapter 8

1. As we discussed in chapter 1, however, under certain conditions a society can choose a type of defense in order to shift its center of gravity elsewhere.

2. Of course, as the consent theory of power would suggest, in some circumstances the victims of aggression and the people on whom the elite depends for support are identical populations. However, as the modified consent theory recognizes, in many situations this is not the case.

3. The idea of presenting the strategic framework in the form of a strategy wheel was first suggested by Mark Cerin, Kate Kelly, and Margaret Pestorius. This version was developed in collaboration with Mark Cerin and Alexandra Perry.

Notes to Chapter 9

1. Lippmann, *U.S. Foreign Policy*, 51.
2. See, for instance, Buzan, *People, States and Fear*.
3. See, for instance, Adam Roberts, *Nations in Arms*.
4. See, for instance, Møller, *Common Security and Nonoffensive Defense*.
5. There are, of course, other perspectives—such as those of children—that are not considered below.
6. According to Barbara Roberts, a feminist perspective identifies gender as a category of fundamental historical significance. It is based on the recognition that over half of humanity is female and that "human experience must be considered on the basis of that proportion." It is not enough to include women: "it is necessary to look out through women's eyes." See Barbara Roberts, "The Death of Machothink," 196.
7. Wollstonecraft, *Vindication of the Rights of Woman*, 100, 108–9.
8. de Beauvoir, *The Second Sex*, 18.
9. French, *Beyond Power*, 72.
10. Miles, *Women's History of the World*, 69.
11. Barbara Zanotti, "Patriarchy: A State of War," in *Reweaving the Web of Life*, ed. McAllister, 19.
12. Millett, *Sexual Politics*, xi, 58, 25.
13. Brownmiller, *Against Our Will*.
14. Starhawk, *The Spiral Dance*, 10–11.
15. Millett, *Sexual Politics*, 35–36.
16. Starhawk, *The Spiral Dance*, 25.
17. Burger, *Report from the Frontier*, 5–11.
18. Knudtson and Suzuki, *Wisdom of the Elders*, 3.
19. Black Elk and Lyon, *Sacred Ways of a Lakota*, 4.

20. Knudtson and Suzuki, *Wisdom of the Elders*, 3.

21. World Commission on Environment and Development, *Our Common Future*, 114–15.

22. Knudtson and Suzuki, *Wisdom of the Elders*, 66–67, 76–78.

23. Burger, *Report from the Frontier*, 13–14.

24. Crow Dog and Erdoes, *Lakota Woman*, 10–11.

25. World Council of Indigenous Peoples, "Rights of Indigenous Peoples to the Earth," (paper submitted to the Working Group on Indigenous Populations, Commission on Human Rights, Geneva, 30 July 1985), cited in Burger, *Report from the Frontier*, 14.

26. Marcia Langton, "Aboriginals: The Phantoms of the Northern Militarisation," in *The New Australian Militarism*, ed. Cheeseman and Kettle, 169–74.

27. Hong, *Natives of Sarawak*, 2–5, 143–68.

28. World Commission, *Our Common Future*, 115–16.

29. World Commission, *Our Common Future*. For a critical review of this report, see Trainer, "Rejection of the Brundtland Report," 71–84.

30. George, *A Fate Worse than Debt*, 12.

31. For a summary of the extensive documentation of this experience, see Trainer, *Developed to Death*, 1–56.

32. For a summary of the neo-Marxist position, see Todaro, *Economic Development*, 100–6.

33. See, for instance, Herman E. Daly, ed., *Toward a Steady-State Economy*; Herman E. Daly, *Steady-State Economics*.

34. See, for instance, Sale, *Dwellers in the Land*.

35. Galtung, "A Structural Theory of Imperialism," 437–81.

36. Galtung, *Solving Conflicts*, 23.

37. Trainer, *Developed to Death*, 62–64. Emphasis in original.

38. Barbara Ward, "Foreword," in Haq, *The Poverty Curtain*, xii.

39. Haq, *The Poverty Curtain*, 154–55.

40. Trainer, *Developed to Death*, 65–69.

41. George, *How the Other Half Dies*, 16.

42. Sklar, ed., *Trilateralism*, 2.

43. Herman, *The Real Terror Network*, 3, 15.

44. There is extensive documentation of this practice. See, for instance, Chomsky and Herman, *Political Economy of Human Rights*, vol. 1, *The Washington Connection*; Herman, *The Real Terror Network*; Klare and Arnson, *Supplying Repression*; Steve Wright, "New Technologies," 31–62.

45. For some of the many accounts of covert operations and imperial interventions, see Agee, *Inside the Company*; Chomsky, *Turning the Tide*; Chomsky, *The Culture of Terrorism*; Independent Commission of Inquiry, *The U.S. Invasion of Panama*; Woodward, *Veil*.

46. Chomsky, *Turning the Tide*, 72.

47. Okolo, "Dependency in Africa," 245–46.

48. For a summary of the issues associated with land redistribution, see Lappé and Collins, *Food First*, 300–4.

49. Carson, *Silent Spring*.

50. See, for instance, Meadows et al., *The Limits to Growth*.

51. See, for instance, World Commission, *Our Common Future*, 147–67.

52. Naess, "The Shallow and the Deep," 95.

53. Suzuki, *Inventing the Future*, 12.

54. Leopold, *Sand County Almanac*, 204.

55. Singer, *Animal Liberation*, 3.

56. Despite the apparent concurrence, there is an ongoing debate between deep ecologists, who tend to emphasize *the importance of the biotic community as a whole* (and would, if necessary, sacrifice the individual member of it), and the animal liberationists, who tend to emphasize *the rights of the individual organism*. For a discussion of this debate, see Nash, *The Rights of Nature*, 121–60.

57. Mische, "Ecological Security," 393, 396, 424. Emphasis in original.

58. Lovelock, *Gaia*, 9, 11.

59. Mische, "Ecological Security," 413, 425.

60. Rifkin (with Howard), *Entropy*, 47–49.

61. Herman E. Daly, *Steady-State Economics*, 21.

62. The evidence to support this argument is presented systematically in Rifkin, *Entropy*.

63. Lynn White, Jr., "Historical Roots," 1203–7. For a recent summary of the debate on this point, see Nash, *The Rights of Nature*, 87–120. For an account that argues that Christianity, according to its original biblical texts, is intrinsically "green" and that it is the homocentric interpretation of these texts by the Western churches that is at fault, see Bradley, *God Is Green*.

64. Trainer, *Developed to Death*, 130–34.

65. Economic self-reliance and ecological sustainability have been advocated by some prominent activists and theorists, including Gandhi. See Pyarelal, *Towards New Horizons*, 3–97. For other accounts, see Thoreau, *Walden*, 3–247; Schumacher, *Small Is Beautiful*.

66. Sale, "Bioregionalism," 168–69.

67. Sale, *Dwellers in the Land*, 115–18; Trainer, "Sustainable Society," 31.

68. Sale, "Bioregionalism," 171.

69. Merchant, *The Death of Nature*, 293.

70. Roszak, *Person/Planet*, xix.

71. Leopold, *Sand County Almanac*, 224–25.

72. This definition of security is consistent with, but considerably wider than, the meaning used in the human-needs literature.

73. For an early work, see Kropotkin, *Mutual Aid*.

74. Argyle, *Cooperation*, 3, 22, 231.

75. Galtung, lectures, 8 July 1991. Although the approach to security described in this section draws on the work of Galtung, it does not share his statist orientation.

76. Galtung, lectures, 8 July 1991.

77. Narayan Desai, "Nonviolent People's Struggles in India," in *Non-violent Struggle and Social Defence*, ed. Anderson and Larmore, 45.

78. Galtung, lectures, 8 July 1991.

79. Many authors have presented the case for smaller-scale human communities and/or stateless societies. See, for instance, Kohr, *The Breakdown of Nations*; Sale, *Human Scale*.

80. Good examples of this are the World Council of Indigenous Peoples (WCIP), founded in 1975, and those international nongovernmental organizations (INGOs) that are organized on non-statist lines. An interesting discussion of some elements of this idea can be found in Mazrui, *A World Federation of Cultures*.

81. This would include agencies (consisting of representatives of Earth's bioregions) responsible for monitoring ecosystem restoration and coordinating some interbioregional activities.

Notes to Chapter 10

1. See, for instance, Elihu Burritt, "Passive Resistance," in *Nonviolence in America*, ed. Lynd, 93–97; Scott, *Ask That Mountain*.

2. Russell, "War and Non-resistance," 266–74.

3. For brief discussions of the origins of civilian-based defense, see Kruegler, "Liddell Hart," 161–62; Gene Sharp, "Civilian-Based Defense," in *World Encyclopedia of Peace*, ed. Pauling, 1:132; Sharp, "Promoting Civilian-Based Defense," 11. Despite the claim by Kruegler (elaborated in Kruegler, "Liddell Hart," 121–24) that Clausewitz influenced some of the early civilian-based defense literature, there is little evidence to suggest that Clausewitz has been understood and systematically applied by English-language authors on civilian-based defense. The most obvious exception is Boserup and Mack's *War without Weapons*, in which they attempted to fit civilian-based defense into a Clausewitzian framework. For an account of the German struggle, see Wolfgang Sternstein, "The 'Ruhrkampf' of 1923: Economic Problems of Civilian Defence," in *Civilian Resistance*, ed. Adam Roberts, 128–61. For accounts of the Czechoslovakian resistance, see Littell, ed., *The Czech Black Book*; Windsor and Roberts, *Czechoslovakia 1968*.

4. See, for instance, Gandhi, *Young India*, 22 August 1929, in *Collected Works*, 41:310–11.

5. Sharp, "Civilian-Based Defense," 132; Sharp, "Promoting Civilian-Based Defense," 11.

6. King-Hall, *Defence in the Nuclear Age*.

7. Lyttle, *National Defense thru Nonviolent Resistance*. The first edition was published in 1958.

8. It should be noted that the two conceptions are not consistently labeled. Nevertheless, within the limited domain of their use to describe an alternative to military defense, these terms represent conceptions that are consistent with the descriptions given of them below.

9. Kruegler, "Liddell Hart," 1.

10. Martin, *Social Defence Social Change*, 4. See also Brian Martin, "Social Defence: Arguments and Actions," in *Nonviolent Struggle and Social Defence*, ed. Anderson and Larmore, 84.

11. Kruegler, "Liddell Hart," 1–2, 117, 133, 150.

12. Martin, "Revolutionary Social Defence," 98.

13. Kruegler, "Liddell Hart," 2.

14. Sharp, *Civilian-Based Defense*, 6–7.

15. Martin, "Social Defence: Elite Reform or Grassroots Initiative?" 21.

16. Martin, *Uprooting War*, 28.

17. Bristol, "Civilian Defence," 26.

18. Quan, "Low Intensity Conflict," 70.

19. Sharp, *Social Power and Political Freedom*, 233.

20. Freund, *Nonviolent National Defense*, 43.

21. Martin, *Social Defence Social Change*, 5; Martin, "Social Defence: Arguments and Actions," 84.

22. Marko Hren, "Yugoslavia: The Past and the Future," in *Nonviolent Struggle and Social Defence*, ed. Anderson and Larmore, 22–23.

23. Sharp, *Social Power and Political Freedom*, 233.

24. Martin, "Revolutionary Social Defence," 102.

25. Kruegler, "Liddell Hart," 144.

26. Sharp, *National Security*, 57.

27. Kruegler, "Liddell Hart," 23.

28. Ibid., 112–33, 145–47.

29. Ibid., 124, 147.

30. Sharp's classic work draws systematically on the maxims of the indirect approach. See Sharp, *The Politics of Nonviolent Action*, 452–53, 492–510. In contrast, and despite Kruegler's claim (see Kruegler, "Gandhi, Clausewitz, and the 'New World Order,'" 6) that the third part of this work is framed by Clausewitzian concepts, Sharp's references to Clausewitz are incidental and unrelated to the principal tenets of Clausewitzian theory. See Sharp, *The Politics of Nonviolent Action*, 495, 496, 506, 759, 762. Moreover, in more recent works, Sharp's explicitly anti-Clausewitzian conception of strategy is quite stark: It utilizes the strategically flawed "scenario approach," it advocates denial of the opponent's political and other objectives rather than defense against its strategic aim, and it advocates concentrating the counteroffensive against the opponent's weak points rather than against its center of gravity. See the discussions in Sharp, *Civilian-Based Defense*, 105–8; Sharp, *Making*

Europe Unconquerable, 127–44. For a brief discussion of how Liddell Hart's strategic thinking influenced Sharp, see Kruegler, "Liddell Hart," 146–47. There is not space in this study to offer a detailed critique of this influence on Sharp's work on civilian-based defense, but it is apparent, given the inadequacies of the strategy of the indirect approach that were discussed in chapter 2, that Liddell Hart's work is a poor foundation on which to build any defense strategy, including a nonviolent one.

31. See, for instance, Sharp, *Civilian-Based Defense*, 6; Sharp, *Self-Reliant Defense*, 21.

32. See, for instance, Sharp, *Civilian-Based Defense*, 6, 86–88; Sharp, *Self-Reliant Defense*, 21–23. For a fuller discussion of the relationship between civilian-based defense and deterrence, see Theodore Olson, "Social Defence and Deterrence," 33–40.

33. There is a substantial literature demonstrating this point. Apart from the conflict theory, and particularly the work of John Burton, cited in chapter 5, see, for instance, the chapters by Lebow and Stein in *Psychology and Deterrence*, ed. Jervis, Lebow, and Stein.

34. Bristol, "Civilian Defence," 23, 16.

35. Adam Roberts, "Civil Resistance to Military Coups," 32, 29. For an account of the Generals' Revolt, see pp. 23–30.

36. Kruegler, "To the Editor," 13.

37. Gustaaf Geeraerts, "Two Approaches to Civilian Defence: Observations on the Development of the Civilian Defence Concept," in *Possibilities of Civilian Defence*, ed. Geeraerts, 16.

38. Cited in Geeraerts, "Two Approaches to Civilian Defence," 16. The original is in German.

39. Geeraerts, "Two Approaches to Civilian Defence," 13–16.

40. Jahn, "Civilian Defense and Civilian Offense," 286–87.

41. Russell, "War and Non-resistance," 270.

42. Nirmal Kumar Bose, "Non-violence and Defence," in *Gandhi*, ed. Biswas, 27–28.

43. Gene Sharp, "Deterrence and Liberation by Civilian Defence," in *Civilian Defence*, ed. Mahadevan, Roberts, and Sharp, 119.

44. See, for instance, April Carter, "Political Conditions for Civilian Defence," in *Civilian Resistance*, ed. Adam Roberts, 332; Freund, *Nonviolent National Defense*, 42; Jones, "Non-violent Civilian Defence," 9; Lakey, *Powerful Peacemaking*, 13; Adam Roberts, "Civilian Defence Strategy," in *Civilian Resistance*, ed. Adam Roberts, 250, 262; Wolfgang Sternstein, "Through Non-violent Action in Intra-Societal Conflicts to Civilian Defence: Some Remarks on the Past and Future of Civilian Defence Research," in *Possibilities of Civilian Defence*, ed. Geeraerts, 62.

45. Dellinger, *Revolutionary Nonviolence*, 298–99.

46. Karbach and Göttingen, "The Myths of Alternative Defence," 8.

47. Martin, "Social Defence: Elite Reform or Grassroots Initiative?" 21.

48. Jahn, "Civilian Defense and Civilian Offense," 293 n. 1.

49. Ibid., 292.

50. Of course, these advocates usually have personal views about what is needed in order to facilitate wider social change. In Sharp's case, for instance, see Sharp, *Social Power and Political Freedom.*

51. Sharp, "Promoting Civilian-Based Defense," 13.

52. Sharp, *Gandhi As a Political Strategist*, 193–94; Sharp, "Relevance of Civilian-Based Defense," 3–4.

53. Jahn, "Civilian Defense and Civilian Offense," 286.

54. For studies that advocate the consideration or adoption of this type of defense, see, for instance, Alternative Defence Commission, *Defence without the Bomb*, 243–44; Bergfeldt, "Civilian Defence As a Complement," 279–96; Boserup and Mack, *War without Weapons*, 140–47; Galtung, *There Are Alternatives!* 180–84; Salmon, "Can Non-violence Be Combined," 69–80; Sharp, "Relevance of Civilian-Based Defense," 2–6; Sproat, "The Strategy of Social Defence," 25–29; Summy, "An Australian Alternative Defence Strategy," 26–34.

55. Shridharani, *War without Violence*, 263.

56. Randle, "Defence without the Bomb," 27.

57. In particular circumstances, of course, some ordinary people may find themselves in a position to benefit from war. For instance, they may be able to settle on land "won" in an imperial war.

58. Several authors have criticized the civilian-based defense literature for its concentration on two scenarios: invasions and coups. See, for instance, Bergfeldt, "Civilian Defence As a Complement," 283.

59. Lintner, *Outrage.*

60. Yi and Thompson, *Crisis at Tiananmen.*

61. Avedon, *In Exile*; Gyatso, *Freedom in Exile*; Neterowicz, *The Tragedy of Tibet.*

62. Palumbo, *Imperial Israel.* For an account that exposes the complicity of the United States government in this repression, see Chomsky, *The Fateful Triangle.*

63. Budiardjo and Liem Soei Liong, *The War against East Timor*; Ramos-Horta, *Funu*; J. G. Taylor, *Indonesia's Forgotten War.*

64. Dixon, ed., *On Trial*; Sklar, *Washington's War on Nicaragua.*

65. For an account that debunks the official justification for the U.S. intervention in Panama, see the Independent Commission of Inquiry, *The U.S. Invasion of Panama.*

66. Quan, "Low Intensity Conflict," 69–70.

67. Carter, "Civilian Defence," 318.

68. Theodor Ebert, "Final Victory," in *Civilian Defence*, ed. Mahadevan, Roberts, and Sharp, 209.

69. This point is also discussed in Martin, "Revolutionary Social Defence," 98–99.

70. Clausewitz, *On War*, 177. According to Clausewitz, the military aim is always the same: "to disarm the enemy." See p. 77.

71. Jessie Wallace Hughan, "Pacifism and Invasion," in *The Quiet Battle*, ed. Sibley, 327.

72. King-Hall, *Defence in the Nuclear Age*, 191, 204.

73. Sharp, "Civilian-Based Defense," 133; Sharp, *Civilian-Based Defense*, 95.

74. See, for instance, Alternative Defence Commission, *Defence without the Bomb*, 217.

75. Richard Gregg noted this point as well. See Gregg, *The Power of Non-violence*, 59.

76. Boserup and Mack, *War without Weapons*, 163. See also Mack, "Non-military Defence," 156.

77. Adam Roberts, "A Case for Civilian Defence," in *Civilian Defence*, ed. Mahadevan, Roberts, and Sharp, 74.

78. Keyes, "Strategic Non-violent Defense," 133.

79. For another example of a discussion that misconceives this concept, see Ackerman and Kruegler, *Strategic Nonviolent Conflict*, 48–49.

80. Clausewitz, *On War*, 595–96.

81. Sharp, *Social Power and Political Freedom*, 27.

82. Boserup and Mack, *War without Weapons*, 164.

83. This is acknowledged by Sharp. See, for instance, Sharp, *Making Europe Unconquerable*, 122; Sharp, *Civilian-Based Defense*, 96.

84. See, for instance, Sharp, *Civilian-Based Defense*, 83–116.

85. See, for instance, Mack, "Non-military Defence," 167–68; Awad, "The Intifada," 7; Dajani, "Formulation of a Strategy," 41; Rigby, *Living the Intifada*, 114.

86. For an attempt in the peripheral literature, see Šveics, *Small Nation Survival*, 66–69.

87. See, for instance, Sharp, "Civilian-Based Defense," 133; Sharp, *Civilian-Based Defense*, 95.

88. See, for instance, Sharp, *Making Europe Unconquerable*, 140.

89. See, for instance, Alternative Defence Commission, *Defence without the Bomb*, 217.

90. For a discussion of this strategy, see Adam Roberts, "Alternative Strategies in Civilian Defence," in *Civilian Defence*, ed. Mahadevan, Roberts, and Sharp, 137–40.

91. See, for instance, Hughan, "Pacifism and Invasion," 317–32.

92. See, for instance, Theodor Ebert, "Organization in Civilian Defence," in *Civilian Resistance*, ed. Adam Roberts, 298–303.

93. See, for instance, Sharp, *Civilian-Based Defense*, 105–10.

94. Sharp, *Making Europe Unconquerable*, 130; Sharp, *Civilian-Based Defense*, 106.

95. The "scenario approach" involves imagining a range of credible

attack scenarios and then designing defense countermeasures to meet each one of them.

96. See, for instance, Sharp, *Civilian-Based Defense*, 106, 108; Sharp, *Self-Reliant Defense*, 31–33.

97. See, for instance, Galtung, "Two Concepts of Defense," in *Essays in Peace Research*, 2:334.

98. See, for instance, Boserup and Mack, *War without Weapons*, 78–79.

99. See, for instance, Mao, "Problems of Strategy in Guerrilla War against Japan," 84–85.

100. See, for instance, Alternative Defence Commission, *Defence without the Bomb*, 215–17; DeRoose, "Need Military Aggressors Kill People?" 27–37; Galtung, "Nonmilitary Defense," 402; Mack, "Non-military Defence," 158; Sharp, *Making Europe Unconquerable*, 127–44; Sharp, *Civilian-Based Defense*, 92–93, 106; Sharp, *Self-Reliant Defense*, 25, 42.

101. Galtung, "Nonmilitary Defense," 402.

102. Sharp, *Making Europe Unconquerable*, 131–34.

103. This Clausewitzian distinction was clearly understood by Gandhi, as the discussion in chapter 12 will illustrate. It was also understood by Mao: "Make wiping out the enemy's effective strength our main objective; do not make holding or seizing a city or place our main objective. Holding or seizing a city or place is the outcome of wiping out the enemy's effective strength." See Mao, "The Present Situation and Our Tasks," in *Selected Works*, 4:161. See also Mao, "Problems of Strategy in Guerrilla War against Japan," 81.

104. Paradoxically, in one of his more recent articles Sharp argues that defense against coups does not require "defense of points of geography or even governmental buildings." See Sharp, "An Anti-Coup Defense," 3. However, there is no indication that Sharp realizes the profound implications of this insight for his long-standing advocacy of a conception of civilian-based defense that is based on defense against the opponent's political and other objectives.

105. It may be noted, for the sake of completeness, that in those circumstances in which it is judged that resistance to specific instructions, objectives, or acts of aggression by the opponent will consolidate the power and will of the defense (or undermine the power of the opponent), then it *might* be appropriate to offer resistance at those particular points. In most cases, however, tactics that are selected and designed to enable the defense to retain the initiative will serve the strategic aims more effectively.

Notes to Chapter 11

1. Clausewitz, *On War*, 177.

2. For discussions of these campaigns, with some reference to their strategic shortcomings, see, respectively, Kuper, *Passive Resistance in South*

Africa, 122–45; Windsor and Roberts, *Czechoslovakia 1968*, 111–43; Sharp and Jenkins, "Nonviolent Struggle in China," 1–7.

3. For a discussion illustrating the existence of this type of tension during the Solidarity struggle in Poland, see the "underground debate" between Kuron, Bujak, and Kulerski: Kuron, "Theses on Solving an Insoluble Problem," 150–54; Bujak, "Positional Warfare," 155–57; Kulerski, "The Third Possibility," 158–59. This tension is also raised in Zielonka, "Strengths and Weaknesses," 101–2.

4. See, for instance, the words used in the first communiqué, reprinted in part in Schiff and Ya'ari's *Intifada*, 193.

5. Palestinian Center for the Study of Non-Violence, "Intifada," 2.

6. Rigby, *Living the Intifada*, 1, 191, 197–98, 16.

7. Ibid., 198, 196.

8. The shortcomings of the pragmatic conception of nonviolence were discussed in chapter 7.

9. Rigby, *Living the Intifada*, 1. Emphasis in original.

10. The tax resistance by the residents of Beit Sahour is a classic example. See Sharples, "Palestinian Tax Resistance," 4–7.

11. Andrew Rigby and Nafez Assaily, "The Intifada," in *Nonviolent Struggle and Social Defence*, ed. Anderson and Larmore, 31–35.

12. Lakey, *Powerful Peacemaking*, 58.

13. Michael N. Nagler, "Nonviolence As New Science," in *Perspectives on Nonviolence*, ed. Kool, 138.

14. Frank, *Sanity and Survival*, 265.

15. Horsburgh, *Non-violence and Aggression*, 176–77.

16. Frank, *Sanity and Survival*, 264.

17. Gandhi, *Young India*, 7 July 1920, in *Collected Works*, 18:14.

18. Gandhi, *Harijan*, 3 June 1939, in *Non-violent Resistance*, 365. See also Gandhi, *Young India*, 20 October 1921, in *Collected Works*, 21:313–14.

19. Gandhi, *Young India*, 19 March 1925, in *Collected Works*, 26:272.

20. Sharp, *The Politics of Nonviolent Action*, 621.

21. Gandhi, *From Yeravda Mandir*, 30.

22. Sharp, *The Politics of Nonviolent Action*, 616.

23. For excellent discussions of the vital importance of discipline, and the ways to achieve and maintain it, see Gregg, *A Discipline for Non-violence*; Sharp, *The Politics of Nonviolent Action*, 615–33.

24. Tendulkar, *Mahatma*, 3:39–41; Thomas Weber, "'The Marchers,'" 267–89. For a discussion of the importance and effectiveness of nonviolent discipline in the Czechoslovakian resistance to Soviet occupation in 1968, see Šveics, *Small Nation Survival*, 206–11.

25. Gandhi, "Some Rules of Satyagraha," in *Young India*, 27 February 1930, in *Collected Works*, 42:491–93.

26. Barbé, *Grace and Power*, 150; Domingos Barbé, "The Spiritual Basis of Nonviolence," in *Relentless Persistence*, ed. McManus and Schlabach, 280.

27. For an example from the nonviolent revolution in East Germany in 1989, see Randle, *People Power*, 65–66. For an example from one of the campaigns conducted in South Africa during 1989, see Smuts and Westcott, eds., *The Purple Shall Govern*, 40. For an example of a set of "respected policies" designed to guide women's participation in the Seneca Women's Peace Camp in the United States in 1983, see Rhoda Linton, "Seneca Women's Peace Camp: Shapes of Things to Come," in *Rocking the Ship of State*, ed. Harris and King, 244–45.

28. Action focalizers are the people appointed by the group to coordinate the action. Their role is discussed in the next chapter.

29. This injunction against secrecy does not mean that the opponent is entitled to "know everything." In some circumstances, openness may constitute betrayal.

30. See, for instance, the many examples discussed in McManus and Schlabach, eds., *Relentless Persistence*.

31. Gandhi, *Young India*, 28 July 1920, in *Collected Works*, 18:93.

32. For a discussion of the organizational and other shortcomings of the Western Areas and Bantu Education campaigns, see Feit, *African Opposition in South Africa*.

33. See, for instance, Freund, *Nonviolent National Defense*, 43; Salmon, "Can Non-violence Be Combined," 74.

34. Ratna, "Sarvodaya Democracy," 38.

35. Chadwick Alger, "The Limits of the Nation-State," in *In Theory and In Practice*, ed. Selbourne, 89–90.

36. Burnheim, *Is Democracy Possible?* 5.

37. Ebert, "Organization in Civilian Defence," 309.

38. Dolgoff, ed., *The Anarchist Collectives*; Leval, *Collectives in the Spanish Revolution*.

39. Barbé, *Grace and Power*, 88–106.

40. Sharp, *Civilian-Based Defense*, 148. It should be noted that several experts on the coup d'état have argued that societies with strong and independent political institutions are much less vulnerable to military seizures of power. See, for instance, Finer, *The Man on Horseback*, 77–98; Luttwak, *Coup d'Etat*, 28–56.

41. Carter, "Civilian Defence," 324.

42. Wehr, "Nonviolent Resistance to Nazism," 77–95.

43. Gene Sharp, "Tyranny Could Not Quell Them," in *The Quiet Battle*, ed. Sibley, 170–86.

44. Ebert, "Organization in Civilian Defence," 311.

45. Although group size has been a research focus in the social sciences for a long time, there is no consensus on the exact size "small groups" should be. This is because the optimum size depends on many factors, including, notably, the task of the group. According to the research cited by Mancur Olson, for instance, "action-taking" groups usually have between five and

eight members. See Mancur Olson, *The Logic of Collective Action*, 54. For a discussion of some of the factors that help to determine optimum group size in different circumstances, see Hare, *Handbook of Small Group Research*, 214–31.

46. Carter, "Civilian Defence," 325.

47. Mansbridge, *Beyond Adversary Democracy*, 8–9.

48. Ibid., 283, 24–27.

49. In this context, the term *collective* is used in its "modern" social movement sense; not, as in the case cited above, in the sense used by anarchists during the Spanish Revolution.

50. Janice L. Ristock, "Canadian Feminist Social Service Collectives: Caring and Contradictions," in *Bridges of Power*, ed. Albrecht and Brewer, 172–79.

51. Gloria Anzaldua, "Bridge, Drawbridge, Sandbar or Island: Lesbians-of-Color Hacienda Alianzas," in *Bridges of Power*, ed. Albrecht and Brewer, 225.

52. Starhawk, *The Spiral Dance*, 48–68.

53. Lakey, *Powerful Peacemaking*, 78–79.

54. Roxanna Carillo, "Feminist Alliances: A View from Peru," in *Bridges of Power*, ed. Albrecht and Brewer, 205.

55. See, for instance, Lyons' description of the "Grassroots" network in West Germany, in *The "Grassroots" Network*, 4–6.

56. For a sobering discussion of the problems that can arise within groups attempting to use these processes, see Landry et al., *What a Way to Run a Railroad*.

57. For a discussion of this point, see Mansbridge, *Beyond Adversary Democracy*, 279–80.

58. West and Blumberg, eds. *Women and Social Protest*, 39.

59. Boserup and Mack, *War without Weapons*, 61–67. Despite this last claim, underground organizations have often been destroyed. For a discussion of the usual methods for doing so, see Theodor Ebert, "Initiating Popular Resistance to Totalitarian Invasion," in *Civilian Defence*, ed. Mahadevan, Roberts, and Sharp, 171–72.

60. Paul Wehr, "Nonviolent Resistance to Occupation: Norway and Czechoslovakia," in *Nonviolent Action and Social Change*, ed. Bruyn and Rayman, 220–22.

61. Jutikkala (with Pirinen), *A History of Finland*, 199. For accounts of this struggle, see pp. 194–206; Steven Duncan Huxley, *Constitutionalist Insurgency in Finland*, 143–252.

62. G. T. Marx, *Undercover*.

63. Ebert, "Organization in Civilian Defence," 305.

64. Nehru, *An Autobiography*, 69.

65. Quoted in Dhawan, *Political Philosophy of Mahatma Gandhi*, 223.

66. See, for instance, Rigby, *Living the Intifada*, 33; Schiff and Ya'ari, *Intifada*, 189.

67. Schiff and Ya'ari, *Intifada*, 190, 210, 215–16.

68. For different interpretations of this relationship, see Rigby, *Living the Intifada*, 27–30; Schiff and Ya'ari, *Intifada*, 188–92.

69. Ebert, "Organization in Civilian Defence," 307.

70. Arne Naess, "Nonmilitary Defense," in *Preventing World War III*, ed. Wright, Evan, and Deutsch, 130.

71. Ebert, "Organization in Civilian Defence," 303.

72. Nehru, *An Autobiography*, 85.

73. Gopal, *The Viceroyalty of Lord Irwin*, 77–78.

74. Keyes, "Strategic Non-violent Defense," 144.

75. For an account of this, see Windsor and Roberts, *Czechoslovakia 1968*, 131–40.

76. For an account of this, see Feit, *South Africa*, 6–10.

77. Adam Roberts, "Civil Resistance to Military Coups," 23–30.

78. McAllister, *You Can't Kill the Spirit*, 20–24; Fisher, *Mothers of the Disappeared*; Philip McManus, "Argentina's Mothers of Courage," in *Relentless Persistence*, ed. McManus and Schlabach, 79–99.

79. Kulerski, "The Third Possibility," 159.

80. Martin, "Democracy without Elections," 16. Perhaps the most sophisticated historical examples of federal organization are those of the various Native American confederacies prior to the European invasion. For brief descriptions of several of these, together with a bibliography on traditional forms of Native American governance, see Rebecca L. Robbins, "Self-Determination and Subordination: The Past, Present, and Future of American Indian Governance," in *The State of Native America*, ed. Jaimes, 87–89.

81. Lyons, *The "Grassroots" Network*, 4; for a discussion of the organizational experience of the "Grassroots" nonviolence network in West Germany during the period 1972–85, see pp. 16–37.

82. An example of a network facilitator is Peace Movement Aotearoa. See Hager, "Peace Movement Aotearoa," 15.

83. For a fuller explanation of demarchy, see Burnheim, *Is Democracy Possible?* 106–24.

84. For a fuller explanation of policy juries and variations on it, including "citizens panels" and "planning cells," see Crosby, "The Peace Movement," 33–37; Crosby, Kelly, and Schaefer, "Citizens Panels," 170–78; Peter C. Dienel, "Contributing to Social Decision Methodology: Citizen Reports on Technological Projects," in *Social Decision Methodology*, ed. Vlek and Cvetkovich, 133–51.

85. Rigby, *Living the Intifada*, 19–20, 24–25, 33, 40–42.

86. Starhawk, *Truth or Dare*, 268–87.

87. This criticism is not intended to underrate the immense difficulties associated with trying to implement a strategy of nonviolent defense in the circumstances presented by the Israeli occupation. These include the ongoing debate between the advocates of violence—including the ascen-

dant Islamic Resistance Movement (Hamas)—and nonviolence, the ongoing debate between Islamic and secular organizations regarding the role of religion in the struggle, the competition between the different factions of the PLO, and the practical difficulties presented by the arrest of experienced activists who provide the street leadership necessary to control the activities of more volatile Palestinians. See Rigby, *Living the Intifada*, 35–47. For a discussion of how nonviolent defenders should treat collaborators, see Theodor Ebert, "The Crisis," in *Civilian Defence*, ed. Mahadevan, Roberts, and Sharp, 181–83.

88. For a brief discussion of the circumstances in which this vote was taken, see Yi and Thompson, *Crisis at Tiananmen*, 71.

89. Gandhi, *Harijan*, 28 July 1940, in *Collected Works*, 72:217.

90. Walzer, *Just and Unjust Wars*, 332.

91. Schmid, *Social Defence*, 28.

92. Kuper, *Passive Resistance*, 131.

93. Mandela, *No Easy Walk to Freedom*, 96–98.

94. Given available surveillance technologies, even these communication systems can be detected and disrupted. See Wehr, "Nonviolent Resistance to Nazism," 93.

95. Wehr, "Nonviolent Resistance to Occupation," 219–22.

96. Adam Roberts, "Civil Resistance to Military Coups," 26–27.

97. Martin, *Social Defence Social Change*, 20.

98. Martin, "Lessons in Nonviolence," 332.

99. Pronozin, "Social Defence," 7.

100. For a description of a community research project that investigated how telecommunications could be used to facilitate nonviolent defense, see Martin, *Social Defence Social Change*, 111–19.

101. Barnett, "Tibet," 8.

102. The evidence to support this claim has been presented by several authors. See, for instance, Chomsky, *Deterring Democracy*, 27–28, 32–33; Trainer, *Developed to Death*, 162–71. For a historical survey of the U.S. government's efforts to systematically destroy the sovereignty and right to self-determination of Native Americans, see Robbins, "Self-Determination and Subordination," 87–121.

103. Role-plays to teach nonviolent action date from the civil rights struggle in the United States. See King, *Stride Toward Freedom*, 163.

104. For a detailed account of one highly informative exercise in "nonviolent defense," see Olson and Christiansen, *The Grindstone Experiment*.

105. Ebert, "Preparations for Civilian Defence," 284–85.

106. Quan, "Low Intensity Conflict," 72.

107. Desai, "Nonviolent People's Struggles in India," 45.

108. For discussions of media complicity in "manufacturing consent," see Herman and Chomsky, *Manufacturing Consent*; Chomsky, *Necessary Illusions*.

109. Some authors have noted the possibility of stockpiling food and fuel as well. See, for instance, Hughan, "Pacifism and Invasion," 324; Mack, "Non-military Defence," 160; Adam Roberts, "Alternative Strategies in Civilian Defence," 141; Sharp, "Deterrence and Liberation," 123.

110. Gandhi made strategic and tactical recommendations for three defense situations: how to liberate India from British occupation, how to defend India against a possible Japanese invasion during World War II, and how to defend an independent India. For a discussion of these, see Sharp, "Gandhi As a National Defence Strategist," 254–73. For a statement by Gandhi on nonviolent defense, see Gandhi, "Can India Be Defended?" in Pyarelal, *Mahatma Gandhi*, 1:813–15.

111. Gandhi, *Hind Swaraj*, 101–4.

112. The constructive program outlined below describes only the important principles of such a program because how these principles are applied in practice will vary from one defense context to another. In practice, any constructive program should be just as "concrete" as that implemented by Gandhi in India.

113. Galtung, *The Way Is the Goal*, 66.

114. Havel, *Living in Truth*, 117–18.

115. Gandhi, *From Yeravda Mandir*, 15.

116. Galtung, *The Way Is the Goal*, 66.

117. Gandhi, *From Yeravda Mandir*, 17–19.

118. Despite their very limited vision in this regard, the Solidarity leaders in Poland during 1989 recognized that their premature election to government would create serious problems because "basic structures remained unchanged." See Ash, *We the People*, 36–39.

119. Havel, *Living in Truth*, 100–4, 117–20.

120. For a brief description of the alternative structures created by the Palestinians during the Intifada, see Rigby, *Living the Intifada*, 21–24. For a case study of the serious problems they faced in conducting alternative education, see pp. 98–113.

121. Zielonka, "Strengths and Weaknesses," 105–6.

Notes to Chapter 12

1. This diagram was developed in collaboration with Anita McKone and Mark Cerin.

2. Gandhi, *Constructive Programme*, 34.

3. These demands are cited in Tendulkar, *Mahatma*, 3:10.

4. Gopal, *The Viceroyalty of Lord Irwin*, 56.

5. The Freedom Charter is reprinted in Mermelstein, ed., *The Anti-Apartheid Reader*, 208–11. For a discussion of the divisiveness generated by the content of the Freedom Charter, particularly given its emphasis on racial equality and its socialist orientation, see Feit, *South Africa*, 14–18, 29–34.

6. For a fuller discussion of this point, see Feit, *South Africa*, 65–67, 70–73. For a discussion that reveals that the United Democratic Front (UDF) recognized the importance of basing its campaigns during the 1980s on the concrete demands of ordinary Africans, see Lekota, "Anti-Apartheid Struggle," 13.

7. Desai, "Nonviolent People's Struggles in India," 45.

8. Rigby, *Living the Intifada*, 26–27, 10–11.

9. There are a variety of tools widely used in nonviolence education programs that can be modified to assist in the identification of strategic goals. These include the "social speedometer" (described in Jones, ed., *Keeping the Peace*, 135–36); the "web chart" (described in Coover et al., *Resource Manual*, 250–53); and the "force field analysis" (described in Coover et al., *Resource Manual*, 256–57).

10. Rigby, *Living the Intifada*, 195–96.

11. Ibid., 196.

12. Although Rigby notes that there was an increasing awareness among Palestinians of the need to influence Israeli public opinion, he concluded that "the determining impetus necessary to make Israel withdraw . . . must come from within Israel itself." Similarly, while he notes Palestinian efforts to elicit the sympathy of Washington, he concluded that the Palestinians "lack the resources to vitally affect the self-interest of the United States." See Rigby, *Living the Intifada*, 189, 193, 199–200. However, according to the strategic theory developed in this study, shifts in public opinion in Israel or elsewhere should, whenever possible, be the direct result of strategic initiatives by the Palestinians. Moreover, efforts to alter U.S. support for the occupation should focus on undermining the support of key social groups within that country; they should not rely on appeals to the sympathy of the U.S. elite. Initiatives of this nature will be considered further in the next chapter.

13. Given the deep cultural imperatives that have shaped the collective unconscious of Israeli society and the vulnerability of this collective unconscious to elite manipulation, this aspect of the strategic aim would have been no easy task. However, it is evident that Palestinian violence makes the task more difficult by inflaming the feelings of fear and insecurity historically entrenched within Israeli society. See Amos Gvirtz, "Peace: A Necessary Condition," in *Walking the Red Line*, ed. Hurwitz, 163. For a discussion that identifies Israeli intransigence in the face of violence, see Philip Grant, "Nonviolent Political Struggle in the Occupied Territories," in *Arab Nonviolent Political Struggle*, ed. Crow, Grant, and Ibrahim, 71.

14. Ishai Menuchin, "Occupation, Protest, and Selective Refusal," in *Walking the Red Line*, ed. Hurwitz, 78–83. For a discussion of the stresses created within the Israeli army by the Intifada as it was, see Schiff and Ya'ari, *Intifada*, 132–69.

15. Rigby, *Living the Intifada*, 1, 191, 197.

16. See, for instance, Gandhi, *Young India*, 20 March 1930, in *Collected Works*, 43:108; Gandhi, *Hindi Navajivan*, 20 March 1930, in *Collected Works*, 43:112–13; Gandhi, *Young India*, 24 April 1930, in *Collected Works*, 43:306.

17. See, for instance, Gandhi, "Letter to Lord Irwin," 2 March 1930, in *Collected Works*, 43:6; Gandhi, *Navajivan*, 23 March 1930, in *Collected Works*, 43:106.

18. Adam Roberts, "Civil Resistance to Military Coups," 32.

19. Schmid, *Social Defence*, 28–29.

20. Pronozin, "Social Defence," 6.

21. Schmid, *Social Defence*, 28.

22. Carter, "Civilian Defence," 319.

23. Rigby, *Living the Intifada*, 35–38.

24. For a discussion of this point, see Feit, *South Africa*, 11–18.

25. For accounts of this lack of a unified strategy, see Luthuli, *Let My People Go*, 221–22; William Robert Miller, *Nonviolence*, 277–86.

26. Frank, *Sanity and Survival*, 264. For an account of the Danish nonviolent resistance to the Nazi occupation, see Jeremy Bennett, "The Resistance against the German Occupation of Denmark 1940–1945," in *Civilian Resistance*, ed. Adam Roberts, 182–203. For an account of the Norwegian nonviolent resistance, see Magne Skodvin, "Norwegian Non-violent Resistance during the German Occupation," in *Civilian Resistance*, ed. Adam Roberts, 162–81.

27. See, for instance, Gandhi, "How to Work Non-co-operation," in *Young India*, 5 May 1920, in *Collected Works*, 17:389–92. Mao also appreciated the importance of working to a realistic strategic timeframe. See Mao, "On Protracted War," 144.

28. For a discussion of this, see Maria Serena I Diokno, "People Power: The Philippines," in *Nonviolent Struggle and Social Defence*, ed. Anderson and Larmore, 24–29.

29. For an account of the North American struggle in the ten years prior to the war of independence, see Conser et al., eds., *Resistance, Politics, and the American Struggle*. There is a summary of the stages on pp. 6–9.

30. For an account of the Chinese pro-democracy movement, in which this shortcoming is starkly evident, see Yi and Thompson, *Crisis at Tiananmen*.

31. Gandhi, *Young India*, 7 July 1920, in *Collected Works*, 18:13.

32. Lekota, "Anti-Apartheid Struggle," 12.

33. This point has also been noted elsewhere. See, for instance, Lars Porsholt, "On the Conduct of Civilian Defence," in *Civilian Defence*, ed. Mahadevan, Roberts, and Sharp, 146.

34. Ebert, "Initiating Popular Resistance," 174–75.

35. Barnett, "Tibet," 9.

36. Eglitis, *Nonviolent Action*, 5–6.

37. Wehr, "Nonviolent Resistance to Nazism," 86–88.

38. For a description of one of Gandhi's campaigns—the 1940–41 Individual Satyagraha movement—that illustrates his attention to these factors, see Tendulkar, *Mahatma*, 6:1–16. See also Gandhi, "Statement by Non-co-operation Committee," in *Young India*, 7 July 1920, in *Collected Works*, 18:13–14.

39. See, for instance, Gyatso, *Freedom in Exile*, 285–86.

40. Adam Roberts, "Non-violent Resistance," 105.

41. See, for instance, Nanda, *Mahatma Gandhi*, 171–74.

42. Gandhi, "Speech on Provisional Settlement," Karachi Congress, 30 March 1931, in *Collected Works*, 45:364–65.

43. Prasad, *At the Feet of Mahatma Gandhi*, 206.

44. Douglass, *The Non-violent Cross*, 265.

45. Adam Roberts, "Non-violent Resistance," 105.

46. Windsor and Roberts, *Czechoslovakia 1968*, 127.

47. Adam Roberts, "Non-violent Resistance," 97.

48. Ebert, "Final Victory," 204.

49. Pronozin, "Social Defence," 7.

50. Schmid, *Social Defence*, 29.

51. Clausewitz, *On War*, 582–83.

52. Mao, "Problems of Strategy in Guerrilla War against Japan," 84–85.

53. For one discussion that illustrates the importance of cultural factors—including philosophical, religious, artistic, and literary traditions—in shaping the style and manner of nonviolent struggle in each particular context, see True, "Nonviolence in Cultural Contexts," 72–77.

54. These have been discussed elsewhere and will not be considered further in this study. See Sharp, *The Politics of Nonviolent Action*.

55. For discussions that explain Gandhi's reservations about some forms of "blockading"—because they entail a form of moral blackmail and might humiliate the opponent—see Dhawan, *Political Philosophy of Mahatma Gandhi*, 231; Horsburgh, *Non-violence and Aggression*, 147–48.

56. Rigby, *Living the Intifada*, 114–38.

57. Sharp, "Gandhi As a National Defence Strategist," 264.

58. Gandhi, *Young India*, 20 March 1930, in *Collected Works*, 43:41–42.

59. Sharp, "Gandhi As a National Defence Strategist," 264.

60. Gandhi, *Young India*, 4 August 1921, in *Collected Works*, 20:466.

61. Sharp, "Gandhi As a National Defence Strategist," 264.

62. Gandhi, "Evidence before Disorders Inquiry Committee," Ahmedabad, 9 January 1920, in *Collected Works*, 16:386–87. For a description of another occasion of this type, see Tendulkar, *Mahatma*, 3:9–10.

63. Theodor Ebert, "Non-violent Resistance against Communist Regimes?" in *Civilian Resistance*, ed. Adam Roberts, 226–27; Christopher

Kruegler, "Why Nonviolent Sanctions Fail: Typical Strategic Blunders and their Antidotes," (photocopy, 24 September 1986), 15–19; Sharp, *The Politics of Nonviolent Action*, 550.

64. Zielonka, "Strengths and Weaknesses," 103–6.

65. Gandhi, "Letter to Viceroy," 4 May 1930, in *Collected Works*, 43:391–92.

66. Even in this case, it should be noted, the satyagrahis organized their approach to the salt works in groups separated by intervals of several minutes. In this way, they compelled the troops to pause for reflection. See Ebert, "The Crisis," 192. For an analysis of the political and psychological factors at work during and after the salt raids at Dharasana, see Thomas Weber, "'The Marchers,'" 267–89.

67. Gandhi, *Harijan*, 27 May 1939, in *Selections from Gandhi*, ed. Bose, 235.

68. Luthuli, *Let My People Go*, 127–28.

69. Bondurant, *Conquest of Violence*, 38.

70. See, for instance, Alternative Defence Commission, *Defence without the Bomb*, 215–17; Galtung, "Nonmilitary Defense," 402; Mack, "Nonmilitary Defence," 158; Sharp, *Making Europe Unconquerable*, 127–44; Sharp, *Civilian-Based Defense*, 92–93, 106.

71. Katherine Roberts, "Nonviolent Resistance and the Pedagogy of Human Rights," in *Relentless Persistence*, ed. McManus and Schlabach, 102, 110.

72. Šveics, *Small Nation Survival*, 208–10.

73. Wehr, "Nonviolent Resistance to Occupation," 226.

74. For a discussion of the important role of symbols in society, see Duncan, *Symbols in Society*.

75. For an account of the two weeks in Tiananmen Square leading up to 4 June 1989, see Yi and Thompson, *Crisis at Tiananmen*, 69–91. For another illustration of the danger of concentrating too intently on a symbol and thus losing the flexibility to shift the focus of the resistance, the role of the bell in the Grindstone experiment is particularly instructive. See Olson and Christiansen, *The Grindstone Experiment*, 15–20, 40.

76. Sharp has also noted the danger of confusing "mere physical occupation" of a building with actual control of political processes. See Sharp, "An Anti-Coup Defense," 3.

77. It should be noted that this argument also applies to a leadership group. Leaders, in this sense, are merely highly vulnerable symbols: They represent a particular type of political system that can be managed by others. Unless the leaders have particular skills that the defense might require, their loss should be understood to be strategically insignificant. The failure to recognize this fact severely interfered with the Czechoslovakian resistance to Soviet occupation in 1968.

78. There is a detailed account of the Salt March in Thomas Weber, "On the Salt March."

79. Amy S. Hubbard, "'Killing the Messenger': Public Perceptions of Nonviolent Protest," in *Perspectives on Nonviolence*, ed. Kool, 125–26.

80. Gandhi, *Young India*, 7 May 1931, in *Collected Works*, 46:107.

81. Dhawan, *Political Philosophy of Mahatma Gandhi*, 224–25.

82. Gandhi, *Young India*, 30 April 1925, in *Collected Works*, 26:564.

83. Tendulkar, *Mahatma*, 6:1–7.

84. Thomas Weber, "On the Salt March," 128–33.

85. Nehru, *An Autobiography*, 253.

86. Thomas Weber, "On the Salt March," 115–19.

87. Despite reports that it was the 27th Army that "cleared" Tiananmen Square, there were actually several army groups—including elements from the 14th, 24th, 39th, and 54th armies—involved in the confrontation. For an account of the role played by the PLA, see Michael T. Byrnes, "The Death of a People's Army," in *The Broken Mirror*, ed. Hicks, 137–41.

88. For four separate eyewitness accounts of the events in Tiananmen Square during this period, see Yi and Thompson, *Crisis at Tiananmen*, 239–69.

89. Naess, "Nonmilitary Defense," 133, 135 n. 6.

90. Havel, *Living in Truth*, 55–60. It was one of the strengths of Solidarity in Poland that the authorities were unable to curtail the movement's educational and cultural activities, which were highly political in nature. See Zielonka, "Strengths and Weaknesses," 106.

91. Gandhi, *Young India*, 11 August 1920, in *Collected Works*, 18:134.

92. Sharp, *The Politics of Nonviolent Action*, 485.

93. Prasad, *At the Feet of Mahatma Gandhi*, 293.

94. Sharp, *The Politics of Nonviolent Action*, 486. For a fuller discussion of the arguments against secrecy, see pp. 481–92.

95. This was the case in Latvia during the Soviet occupation, for instance. See Eglitis, *Nonviolent Action*, 5–6.

96. W. T. Boots, "Miracle in Bolivia: Four Women Confront a Nation," in *Relentless Persistence*, ed. McManus and Schlabach, 48–62.

97. Katherine Roberts, "Nonviolent Resistance and the Pedagogy of Human Rights," 100–16.

98. See, for instance, Kruegler, "Liddell Hart," 2.

99. Gandhi, *Harijan*, 10 February 1946, in *Non-violent Resistance*, 379. See also Diwakar, *Saga of Satyagraha*, viii.

100. For a fuller discussion of the arguments against sabotage, see Sharp, *The Politics of Nonviolent Action*, 608–11.

101. Lakey, *Powerful Peacemaking*, 108–9. The quoted words cited by Lakey are those of Daniel Berrigan.

102. It is clear that during the years from 1949 to 1961 the African National Congress was deeply committed to nonviolence and that escalating levels of government repression made organization increasingly difficult; it should nevertheless be noted that the nonviolent struggle conducted

in South Africa during this period was based on an inadequate understanding of the dynamics of nonviolent action and that it lacked a coherent strategic orientation—it was, therefore, seriously flawed. The lack of understanding is evident, for instance, in the explanation given by Mandela to justify the sabotage campaign. This explanation is outlined below. For an account that documents some of the strategic shortcomings of the ANC, see Feit, *South Africa.*

103. Meredith, *In the Name of Apartheid,* 98.

104. The founding statement of Umkonto we Siswe is reprinted in Mermelstein, *The Anti-Apartheid Reader,* 218–20.

105. Mandela, *No Easy Walk to Freedom,* 171. For a description of Mandela's analysis of the political situation in South Africa at the time, and a fuller explanation of the ANC's decision to resort to sabotage, see pp. 162–89.

106. Meredith, *In the Name of Apartheid,* 105–7.

107. See, for instance, Keyes, "Strategic Nonviolent Defense," 8–12.

108. See, for instance, Martin, "Science for Non-violent Struggle," 57.

109. See, for instance, Galtung, "Nonmilitary Defense," 390–91.

110. Cited in American Friends Service Committee, *In Place of War,* 54.

111. Sharp and Jenkins, "Nonviolent Struggle in China," 4.

112. Chris Erasmus, "ANC Rally Attracts Massive Support," *Age* (Melbourne), 30 October 1989.

113. Some of the ideas in the next few paragraphs are taken from Yeshua Moser, "Domestic Peace Brigades," (photocopy, n.d.); Yeshua Moser, "Peacekeeping: Reclaim the Test Site II," (photocopy, 1989).

114. Sharp and Jenkins, "Nonviolent Struggle in China," 4.

115. Ibid.

116. See, for instance, Aron, *Peace and War,* 629–35; Orwell, *Collected Essays, Journalism and Letters,* 4:468–69; Walzer, *Just and Unjust Wars,* 329–35; Stratford, "Can Nonviolent National Defence Be Effective," 49–57. The Stratford article generated a dialogue. The first response was that of Martin, "The Nazis and Nonviolence," 47–49.

117. See, for instance, Semelin, *Unarmed against Hitler;* Sharp, *The Politics of Nonviolent Action,* 521–655; Stoltzfus, "Dissent in Nazi Germany," 87–94; Summy, "Nonviolence and the Case of the Extremely Ruthless Opponent."

118. Parkman, *Insurrectionary Civic Strikes.*

119. Randle, *People Power;* Adam Roberts, *Civil Resistance.* For other accounts describing the nonviolent removal of ruthless dictators or authoritarian regimes, see Hoveyda, *The Fall of the Shah;* Parkman, *Nonviolent Insurrection in El Salvador.*

120. See, for instance, Kruegler and Parkman, "Identifying Alternatives," 110; Summy, "Nonviolence and the Case of the Extremely Ruthless Opponent," 3–4.

121. Keyes, "Heavy Casualties and Nonviolent Defense," 75–88.

122. Sharp, *The Politics of Nonviolent Action*, 552. For an account of the Algerian War, see Talbott, *The War without a Name*.

123. See, for instance, Dawidowicz, *The War against the Jews*, 334; Kaunda, *Kaunda on Violence*, 25, 27; Seifert, *Conquest by Suffering*, 157. For one rebuttal of this claim about British morality, see Galtung, *Nonviolence and Israel/Palestine*, 21–22. For a brief discussion that exposes the brutality of the British in India and cites more detailed references, see Chomsky, *Year 501*, 6–14.

124. The actual number of Kenyans killed during the Mau Mau uprising is unknown. The figure cited is the official British one; it is widely regarded to be a substantial and intentional underestimate. For a sixty-page summary of British atrocities in Kenya during the Mau Mau uprising, including the systematic use of starvation, rape, castration, electric shock, and the roasting of live prisoners, see Edgerton, *Mau Mau*, 143–203. The official death toll is cited on p. 107.

125. Gregg, *The Power of Nonviolence*, 100. As Gregg offers no indication of how he arrived at the figures of zero and eight thousand, they should be treated with some circumspection. Nevertheless, there is no evidence to suggest that these figures are serious underestimates.

126. Kaunda, *Kaunda on Violence*, 35.

127. Fischer, *Iran*, 199; Halliday, *Iran*, 292. Estimates of the number of people killed in the Tehran massacre range from several hundred to as many as three thousand; the exact figure is unknown.

128. The evidence indicates that relatively few activists were killed in Tiananmen Square; the massacre (of an unknown number) took place along Changan Avenue. See Yi and Thompson, *Crisis at Tiananmen*, 81–83, 91; Simmie and Nixon, *Tiananmen Square*, 175–96.

129. For a discussion of massacres and genocides of groups in these categories, see Kuper, *Genocide*.

130. Kuper, *Genocide*, 68. For a more detailed account of this fast and its effects, see Tendulkar, *Mahatma*, 8:101–11.

131. For a description of the Amritsar massacre, see Tendulkar, *Mahatma*, 1:257–58.

132. For a full description of the Sharpeville massacre and some compelling photographic evidence and firsthand accounts, see Reeves, *Shooting at Sharpeville*, 51–160.

133. Alternative Defence Commission, *Defence without the Bomb*, 224; Boserup and Mack, *War without Weapons*, 168–69.

134. For discussions of the cloth boycott figures, see Brown, *Gandhi and Civil Disobedience*, 127–30; Shridharani, *War without Violence*, 30–31.

135. Mandela, *No Easy Walk to Freedom*, 120.

136. Luthuli, *Let My People Go*, 217–19.

137. Menchú, *I, Rigoberta Menchú*, 122–49.

138. Jacqui Boulle, Lawrence Sibisi, and Rob Goldman, "Low Intensity Conflict: South Africa," in *Nonviolent Struggle and Social Defence*, ed. Anderson and Larmore, 74–75.

139. Barnett, "Tibet," 8–9.

140. Yi and Thompson, *Crisis at Tiananmen*, 67–68.

141. Hartsough, "Faces of Courage and Hope," 6–7.

142. Luthuli, *Let My People Go*, 196.

143. Gandhi, *Young India*, 20 October 1921, in *Collected Works*, 21:313.

144. Reeves, *Shooting at Sharpeville*, 56–57.

145. For an account of this action, see Sharples, "Palestinian Tax Resistance," 5.

146. For an account of this incident, see Benjamin, "Under the Boot," 25.

147. Hou Dejian, "Blame Me if You Want!" in Yi and Thompson, *Crisis at Tiananmen*, 241–42.

148. McManus and Schlabach, eds., *Relentless Persistence*, 120.

149. Gwyn Kirk, "Our Greenham Common: Feminism and Nonviolence," in *Rocking the Ship of State*, ed. Harris and King, 126.

150. Tendulkar, *Mahatma*, 3:40–41; Thomas Weber, "'The Marchers,'" 275–77.

151. Boserup and Mack, *War without Weapons*, 169.

152. Kuper, *Genocide*, 137, 139.

153. Steve Wright, "Undermining Nonviolence," 157–65.

Notes to Chapter 13

1. Gyatso, *Freedom in Exile*, 273.

2. The *government* pronouncements in this regard also reflect the long-standing elite practice of demonizing the Palestinians as part of the strategy to maintain elite power within Israeli society.

3. Rigby, *Living the Intifada*, 10–11.

4. Patai, *The Arab Mind*, 84–96, 101–6.

5. These three domains are a revised version of classifications offered by earlier theorists. See, for instance, King-Hall, *Defence in the Nuclear Age*, 147; Adam Roberts, "Civilian Defence Strategy," 250–51; Boserup and Mack, *War without Weapons*, 169.

6. Several studies have expressed concern that civilian-based defense and social defense cannot adequately defend remote regions. See, for instance, Alternative Defence Commission, *Defence without the Bomb*, 233, 243–44; Atkeson, "Relevance of Civilian-Based Defense," part 2, 50–54; Boserup and Mack, *War without Weapons*, 75; Kritzer, "Nonviolent National Defense," 13; Mack, "Non-military Defence," 158; Theodore Olson, "Social Defence and Deterrence," 35; Adam Roberts, "Civilian Defence Twenty

Years On," 295; Sharp, *Making Europe Unconquerable*, 132–34; Summy, "One Person's Search," 39. This concern, it should be noted, is one legacy of using the "scenario approach": an approach that involves imagining a range of credible attack scenarios and then designing defense countermeasures to meet each one of them. As the discussion in chapter 1 illustrated, this approach is strategically flawed.

7. Hufbauer, Schott, and Elliott, *Economic Sanctions Reconsidered*, 36, 41, 10–11. For a general bibliography of the extensive literature on economic sanctions, see pp. 117–19.

8. Galtung, "Economic Sanctions," 385–86.

9. Hufbauer, Schott, and Elliott, *Economic Sanctions Reconsidered*, 10–11, 16–32; Wallensteen, "Characteristics of Economic Sanctions," 259.

10. Doxey, *International Sanctions in Contemporary Perspective*, 110–18; Galtung, "Economic Sanctions," 387–98; Hanlon and Omond, *The Sanctions Handbook*, 212–15; Hufbauer, Schott, and Elliott, *Economic Sanctions Reconsidered*, 12.

11. In his study, only two cases out of eighteen resulted in "some kind" of compliance. It should be noted, however, that the demands were usually perceived as onerous by the sanctioned party. See Wallensteen, "Characteristics of Economic Sanctions," 249.

12. Ibid., 258.

13. Hufbauer, Schott, and Elliott, *Economic Sanctions Reconsidered*, 93.

14. For a fuller discussion of the impact of sanctions on Rhodesia, see Hanlon and Omond, *The Sanctions Handbook*, 204–9.

15. For a list of nine propositions that Hufbauer, Schott, and Elliott believe should be used to guide the application of traditional economic sanctions, see Hufbauer, Schott, and Elliott, *Economic Sanctions Reconsidered*, 91–105.

16. Galtung, "Economic Sanctions," 389, 398; Hufbauer, Schott, and Elliott, *Economic Sanctions Reconsidered*, 12; Wallensteen, "Characteristics of Economic Sanctions," 258.

17. Wallensteen, "Characteristics of Economic Sanctions," 257–58.

18. Galtung, "Economic Sanctions," 389–90.

19. See, for instance, Luthuli, *Let My People Go*, 208–10; Mandela, *No Easy Walk to Freedom*, 111.

20. Hanlon and Omond, *The Sanctions Handbook*, 191, 305–8, 209–11.

21. Ibid., 210, 200.

22. Meredith, *In the Name of Apartheid*, 202–6.

23. Hanlon and Omond, *The Sanctions Handbook*, 209–11.

24. Recognition of this point led the Commonwealth Committee of Foreign Ministers on Southern Africa to appoint an Expert Study Group to devise an appropriate package of sanctions to be applied against South Africa. See Expert Study Group, *South Africa*, 167–77.

25. Hanlon and Omond, *The Sanctions Handbook*, 225–26; Expert Study Group, *South Africa*, 60.

26. Hufbauer, Schott, and Elliott, *Economic Sanctions Reconsidered*, 92–93.

27. Wallensteen, "Characteristics of Economic Sanctions," 264–65.

28. Hufbauer, Schott, and Elliott, *Economic Sanctions Reconsidered*, 70–71.

29. Galtung, "Economic Sanctions," 412.

30. Hufbauer, Schott, and Elliott, *Economic Sanctions Reconsidered*, 16–32.

31. For one discussion of this point, see Herman, *The Real Terror Network*, 73–76.

32. Expert Study Group, *South Africa*, 68–71.

33. Hufbauer, Schott, and Elliott, *Economic Sanctions Reconsidered*, 93.

34. For a description of these boycott campaigns, see Hanlon and Omond, *The Sanctions Handbook*, 201–2.

35. Martin, "Lessons in Nonviolence," 332.

36. Windsor and Roberts, *Czechoslovakia 1968*, 127.

37. Diokno, "People Power," 26.

38. Yi and Thompson, *Crisis at Tiananmen*, 67–68.

39. Pronozin, "Social Defence," 6–7.

40. For one discussion that clearly indicates that no concerted attempt was made to influence the Shah's troops and that efforts were concentrated on other strategic goals, see Hoveyda, *The Fall of the Shah*, 119–51.

41. The early successes of the Burmese activists in undermining troop loyalty have been largely obscured, but they occurred nevertheless. For instance, in August 1988 the Burmese army and police abandoned the town of Kowsong because they would not shoot democracy activists. In an official Thai report of this incident a Burmese soldier is quoted as saying: "We are patriots. We absolutely cannot shoot civilians." See "Burmese Rebels 'Capture Town,'" *Age* (Melbourne), 12 August 1988. There are brief discussions of this point, together with further examples, in Lintner, *Outrage*, 126–27; Helvey, "Nonviolent Pro-Democracy Movement in Burma," 9.

42. In fact, among other initiatives, the Burmese junta paid its troops for six months in advance during the early stages of the uprising. See Lintner, *Outrage*, 120, 139.

43. Pronozin, "Social Defence," 6–7.

44. Adam Roberts, "Civil Resistance to Military Coups," 31.

45. Diokno, "People Power," 26.

46. Yi and Thompson, *Crisis at Tiananmen*, 67–68.

47. Adam Roberts, "Non-violent Resistance," 104.

48. A good example of an organization of this type, until it closed down in 1993, was the Pledge of Resistance network, which was established to organize civil disobedience and other forms of nonviolent resistance to

any escalation of U.S. intervention in Central America. See Butigan, Mess-man-Rucker, and Pastrick, eds., *¡Basta!*

49. For one recent and comprehensive overview, see Cortright and Watts, *Left Face.*

50. For a discussion of this resistance and its impact, as well as references to the relevant documentary evidence, see Rothstein, *The Soldiers' Strikes of 1919.*

51. Cited in Gilbert, *Winston S. Churchill,* 4:236.

52. Allen, *The Fight for Peace,* 2:633.

53. The evidence to support this claim is presented systematically in Cortright, *Soldiers in Revolt.* See also Cincinnatus, *Self-Destruction.*

54. The report and its figures are discussed in Cortright and Watts, *Left Face,* 19–22.

55. Cortright, *Soldiers in Revolt,* 76, 145, 153, 47–49, 110, 126, 123–25, 130–37, 50–55, 28.

56. Richard K. Taylor, "Witness for Peace," 16; Griffin-Nolan, *Witness for Peace,* 87–105.

57. Links between the Tibetan struggle and the Chinese pro-democracy movement have existed since 1989. See Moser, "Political Struggle for the Land of Snows," 11.

58. Galtung, *Nonviolence and Israel/Palestine,* 19–27.

59. The Black Sash was originally known as the Women's Defence of the Constitution League. For a description of its first year, see Rogers, *The Black Sash.*

60. Michelman, *Black Sash of South Africa,* 47–49, 84–89.

61. Guida West and Rhoda L. Blumberg, "Reconstructing Social Protest from a Feminist Perspective," in *Women and Social Protest,* ed. West and Blumberg, 17.

62. Michelman, *Black Sash of South Africa,* 9, 153, 132, 111–29.

63. Ibid., 153–57.

64. Deena Hurwitz, "Introduction," in *Walking the Red Line,* ed. Hurwitz, 4–5.

65. Yvonne Deutsch, "Israeli Women: From Protest to a Culture of Peace," in *Walking the Red Line,* ed. Hurwitz, 51.

66. Jill Sanguinetti, "Black for Grief and Hope," *Age* (Melbourne), 7 June 1989.

67. Abdo, "Women of the *Intifada,*" 25–26.

68. Alternative Defence Commission, *Defence without the Bomb,* 240; Freund, *Nonviolent National Defense,* 48, 51–52.

69. Lindsay Murdoch, "Escort Whisks Clinton Past Protest Group," *Age* (Melbourne), 15 November 1994. Although it did not involve an attempt to transport activists directly onto the territory of the opponent elite (which, in this example, would have been Britain), a more elaborate initiative of this general nature occurred in 1962 when the World Peace Brigade

planned to organize an international "freedom march" to cross from Tanganyika into Northern Rhodesia (Zambia) as part of the latter's struggle for independence from Britain. According to Charles Walker, the planned march was one of the factors in the British decision to grant independence. See Charles C. Walker, "Nonviolence in Eastern Africa 1962–4: The World Peace Brigade and Zambian Independence," in *Liberation without Violence,* ed. Hare and Blumberg, 157–77.

70. Cited in Philip McManus, "Introduction: In Search of the Shalom Society," in *Relentless Persistence,* ed. McManus and Schlabach, 10.

71. For a thoughtful explanation by one activist not yet ready to go to jail for what she believes, see Daphna Golan, "Letter to Deena," in *Walking the Red Line,* ed. Hurwitz, 101–5.

72. Zielonka, "Strengths and Weaknesses," 108.

73. Exile communities scattered around the world played a prominent role in the Latvian resistance to Soviet occupation. See Eglitis, *Nonviolent Action,* 7.

74. Hartsough, "Keeping the Vigil in California," 20–22.

75. Shmuel Amir, "After the Gulf War," in *Walking the Red Line,* ed. Hurwitz, 173–76.

76. Ibid., 174, 180. See also Stanley Cohen, "Resuming the Struggle," in *Walking the Red Line,* ed. Hurwitz, 192–94.

77. Graubard, *British Labour,* 92.

78. Lockwood, *Black Armada.*

79. Richard K. Taylor, *Blockade.*

80. For instance, there is an elaborate sanctuary movement in North America to provide shelter to victims of aggression conducted or sponsored by the U.S. government in Central/South America. For one account of this, see McAllister, *This River of Courage,* 137–42.

81. Alternative Defence Commission, *Defence without the Bomb,* 240; Adam Roberts, "Civilian Defence Strategy," 260.

82. "Protest Calls Ring Up a Win," *Sun* (Melbourne), 13 June 1989.

83. Alternative Defence Commission, *Defence without the Bomb,* 240; Bell, *Alternative to War,* 51.

84. *Keesing's Contemporary Archives,* 3–10 September 1955, 14401–2.

85. Griffin-Nolan, *Witness for Peace.*

86. For a good introduction to the work of PBI, see Dijkstra, "Peace Brigades International," 391–406. For a discussion of the historically related idea of placing nonviolent teams between opposing military forces, see Thomas Weber, "From Maude Royden's Peace Army," 45–64.

87. Although the group's intervention was not intended to resist military aggression, the experience of the SOS Sarawak Action Group in 1991 illustrates the risks of foreign intervention of this type. This group of eight activists from various countries was arrested after they occupied timber cranes and barges at the port of Kuala Baram in Sarawak in order to focus

attention on the destructive impact of the rainforest timber trade. One of several negative outcomes of this action was the increased level of police repression directed at local activists long after the foreign activists had departed. For a sobering account of this action and its lessons, see Lockhead, "The Sarawak Campaign," 4–7.

88. Pyarelal, *Mahatma Gandhi*, 2:505; Gandhi, *Satyagraha in South Africa*, 105–6; Thomas Weber, *Conflict Resolution and Gandhian Ethics*, 60–61, 142.

89. Naess, *Gandhi and Group Conflict*, 145–46.

90. Cook and Kirk, *Greenham Women Everywhere*. For a feminist critique of Greenham, see *Breaking the Peace*.

91. For two of the many discussions of conversion, see Martin, *Uprooting War*, 51–62; Melman, *The Demilitarized Society*.

92. Hilary Wainwright, "The Women Who Wire Up the Weapons: Workers in Armaments Factories," in *Over Our Dead Bodies*, ed. Dorothy Thompson, 143.

93. Albrecht, "New Concepts for Conversion Strategies," 348–58. For an evaluation of this initiative, see Wainwright and Elliott, *The Lucas Plan*. The plan was actively resisted by the company and opposed by the government and trade union hierarchies.

94. While the resistance to Soviet occupation of the Baltic states included guerrilla warfare and other forms of violence during the years immediately following World War II, most of the resistance offered throughout the occupation period was nonviolent in nature. For a case study of the Lithuanian resistance, see Schmid, *Social Defence*, 213–54. For a case study of the Latvian resistance, see Eglitis, *Nonviolent Action*.

Notes to the Conclusion

1. Gene Sharp, "Transitions to Civilian-Based Defence," in *Nonviolent Struggle and Social Defence*, ed. Anderson and Larmore, 18; Sharp, *National Security*, 41–46.

2. See, for instance, Alternative Defence Commission, *Defence without the Bomb*, 243; Adam Roberts, "Transarmament to Civilian Defence," in *Civilian Resistance*, ed. Adam Roberts, 338.

3. See, for instance, Sternstein, "Through Non-violent Action," 63–64.

4. Gandhi, *Young India*, 19 March 1925, in *Collected Works*, 26:327.

5. Summy, "One Person's Search," 44, 38.

6. Quan, "Low Intensity Conflict," 72.

7. For one description of a nonviolent community, see Desai, *Handbook for Satyagrahis*, 8–19.

8. For one easily accessible reference in which Gandhi explained the importance he attached to personal behavior and his suggestions in this regard, see Gandhi, *From Yeravda Mandir*.

9. Martin, "Mobilising against Nuclear War," 9–10. See also Thomas Weber, *Conflict Resolution and Gandhian Ethics*, 113–14.

10. For a fuller explanation of what truth meant to Gandhi, see Gandhi, *From Yeravda Mandir*, 3–5. See also Thomas Weber, *Conflict Resolution and Gandhian Ethics*, 43–47.

11. Gandhi, *From Yeravda Mandir*, 5–7; Bok and Moyers, "Role of Nonviolence," 11.

12. Gandhi, *Hind Swaraj*, 103.

13. See, for instance, Boserup and Mack, *War without Weapons*, 163.

14. Hartsough, "Faces of Courage and Hope," 6–7.

Bibliography

Abdo, Nahla. "Women of the *Intifada*: Gender, Class and National Liberation." *Race and Class* 32 (April–June 1991).

Ackerman, Peter, and Christopher Kruegler. *Strategic Nonviolent Conflict: The Dynamics of People Power in the Twentieth Century.* Westport, Conn.: Praeger, 1994.

Adams, David, and others. "The Seville Statement on Violence," *Alternatives* 12 (1987).

Agee, Philip. *Inside the Company: CIA Diary.* Harmondsworth, England: Penguin, 1975.

Albert, Michael, Leslie Cagan, Noam Chomsky, Robin Hahnel, Mel King, Lydia Sargent, and Holly Sklar. *Liberating Theory.* Boston: South End Press, 1986.

Albrecht, Lisa, and Rose M. Brewer, eds. *Bridges of Power: Women's Multicultural Alliances.* Philadelphia: New Society, 1990.

Albrecht, Ulrich. "New Concepts for Conversion Strategies in Western Europe: Analysing the Lucas Experience." *Bulletin of Peace Proposals* 9, no. 4 (1978).

Allen, Devere. *The Fight for Peace.* 2 vols. New York: Garland, 1971.

Alternative Defence Commission. *Defence without the Bomb.* New York: Taylor & Francis, 1983.

American Friends Service Committee. *In Place of War: An Inquiry into Nonviolent National Defense.* New York: Grossman, 1967.

Anderson, Shelley, and Janet Larmore, eds. *Nonviolent Struggle and Social Defence.* London: War Resisters' International, 1991.

Arendt, Hannah. *On Violence.* London: Allen Lane; Penguin Press, 1970.

Argyle, Michael. *Cooperation: The Basis of Sociability.* London: Routledge, 1991.

Aristotle. *The Politics.* Trans. T. A. Sinclair. Reprint, Harmondsworth, England: Penguin, 1962.

Aron, Raymond. *Clausewitz: Philosopher of War.* Trans. Christine Booker and Norman Stone. Englewood Cliffs, N.J.: Prentice-Hall, 1985.

———. *Peace and War: A Theory of International Relations.* Trans. Richard Howard and A. B. Fox. London: Weidenfeld & Nicolson, 1966.

Ash, Timothy Garton. *We the People: The Revolution of '89 Witnessed in Warsaw, Budapest, Berlin and Prague.* Cambridge: Granta Books, 1990.

Atkeson, Edward B. "The Relevance of Civilian-Based Defense to U.S. Security Interests." Parts 1 and 2. *Military Review* (May/June 1976).

Atkinson, Alexander. *Social Order and the General Theory of Strategy.* London: Routledge & Kegan Paul, 1981.

Avedon, J. F. *In Exile from the Land of Snows.* London: Michael Joseph, 1984.

Avruch, Kevin, and Peter W. Black. "A Generic Theory of Conflict Resolution: A Critique." *Negotiation Journal* 3 (January 1987).

Awad, Mubarak. "The Intifada: Nonviolent Struggle in the Middle East." *Nonviolent Sanctions* 1/2 (Spring/Summer 1990).

Bakunin, Mikhail. *The Political Philosophy of Bakunin: Scientific Anarchism.* Ed. G. P. Maximoff. New York: Free Press, 1953.

Ball, Desmond, ed. *Strategy and Defence: Australian Essays.* Sydney, Australia: George Allen & Unwin, 1982.

Barbé, Dominique. *Grace and Power: Base Communities and Nonviolence in Brazil.* Trans. John Pairman Brown. Maryknoll, N.Y.: Orbis, 1987.

Barkat, Anwar M., ed. *Conflict, Violence, and Peace.* Geneva: World Council of Churches, 1970.

Barnett, Robbie. "Tibet: Resistance and Survival." *Peace News* 2352 (March 1992).

Bay, Christian. *The Structure of Freedom.* Stanford University Press, 1970.

Beaufre, André. *An Introduction to Strategy.* Trans. R. H. Barry. London: Faber & Faber, 1965.

de Beauvoir, Simone. *The Second Sex.* Ed. and Trans. H. M. Parshley. Harmondsworth, England: Penguin, 1972.

Bell, R. G. *Alternative to War.* London: James Clarke, 1959.

Benjamin, Daniel. "Under the Boot." *Time,* 14 August 1989.

Beres, Louis René, and Harry R. Targ. *Constructing Alternative World Futures: Reordering the Planet.* Cambridge, Mass.: Schenkman, 1977.

Berger, Peter L. *Invitation to Sociology: A Humanistic Perspective.* Harmondsworth, England: Penguin, 1966.

Bergfeldt, Lennart. "Civilian Defence As a Complement." *Cooperation and Conflict* 20 (1985).

Bishop, Peter D. *A Technique for Loving: Non-violence in Indian and Christian Traditions.* London: SCM Press, 1981.

Biswas, S. C., ed. *Gandhi: Theory and Practice—Social Impact and Contemporary Relevance.* Simla, India: Indian Institute of Advanced Study, 1969.

Black Elk, Wallace H., and William S. Lyon. *The Sacred Ways of a Lakota.* San Francisco: HarperCollins, 1990.

Bok, Sissela, and Bill Moyers. "Role of Non-violence: An Interview." *Sansthakul* 21 (July 1991).

Bond, Brian. *Liddell Hart: A Study of His Military Thought.* London: Cassell, 1977.

Bond, Douglas G. "The Nature and Meanings of Nonviolent Direct Action: An Exploratory Study." *Journal of Peace Research* 25, no. 1 (1988).

Bondurant, Joan V. *Conquest of Violence: The Gandhian Philosophy of Conflict.* Rev. ed. Berkeley: University of California Press, 1965.

de Bono, Edward. *Conflicts: A Better Way to Resolve Them.* London: Harrap, 1985.

Bonta, Bruce D. *Peaceful Peoples: An Annotated Bibliography.* Metuchen, N.J.: Scarecrow Press, 1993.

Borman, William. *Gandhi and Non-violence.* Albany: State University of New York Press, 1986.

Bose, Nirmal Kumar. *Selections from Gandhi.* 2d ed. Ahmedabad, India: Navajivan, 1957.

Boserup, Anders, and Andrew Mack. *War without Weapons: Non-violence in National Defense.* New York: Schocken, 1975.

Boulding, Kenneth E. *Conflict and Defense: A General Theory.* New York: Harper, 1962.

Box, Steven. *Deviance, Reality and Society.* 2d ed. London: Holt, Rinehart & Winston, 1981.

Boyd, Robert, and P. J. Richerson. *Culture and the Evolutionary Process.* Chicago: University of Chicago Press, 1985.

Bradley, Ian. *God Is Green: Christianity and the Environment.* London: Darton, Longman & Todd, 1990.

Breaking the Peace. London: Onlywomen Press, 1983.

Bristol, James E. "The Nature and Limitations of Civilian Defence." *Gandhi Marg* 9 (January 1965).

Brodie, Bernard. *Strategy in the Missile Age.* Princeton: Princeton University Press, 1970.

Brown, Judith M. *Gandhi and Civil Disobedience: The Mahatma in Indian Politics 1928–34.* Cambridge: Cambridge University Press, 1977.

Brownmiller, Susan. *Against Our Will: Men, Women and Rape.* London: Secker & Warburg, 1975.

Bruyn, Severyn T., and Paula M. Rayman, eds. *Nonviolent Action and Social Change.* New York: Irvington, 1981.

Budiardjo, Carmel, and Liem Soei Liong. *The War against East Timor.* London: Zed Books, 1984.

Bujak, Zbigniew. "Positional Warfare." *Survey: A Journal of East and West Studies* 26 (Summer 1982).

Bull, Hedley. *The Anarchical Society: A Study of Order in World Politics.* London: Macmillan, 1977.

———. "Strategic Studies and Its Critics." *World Politics* 20 (1968).

Burger, Julian. *Report from the Frontier: The State of the World's Indigenous Peoples.* London: Zed Books, 1987.

Burnheim, John. *Is Democracy Possible? The Alternative to Electoral Politics.* Cambridge: Polity Press, 1989.

Burton, John W. *Conflict: Resolution and Provention.* London: Macmillan, 1990.
———. "Conflict Resolution As a Political Philosophy." *Interdisciplinary Peace Research* 3 (May/June 1991).
———. *Deviance, Terrorism and War: The Process of Solving Unsolved Social and Political Problems.* Canberra: Australian National University Press, 1979.
———. *Global Conflict: The Domestic Sources of International Crisis.* Brighton, England: Wheatsheaf Books, 1984.
———. *Resolving Deep-Rooted Conflict: A Handbook.* New York: University Press of America, 1987.
———, ed. *Conflict: Human Needs Theory.* London: Macmillan, 1990.
Burton, John W., and Frank Dukes. *Conflict: Practices in Management, Settlement and Resolution.* London: Macmillan, 1990.
———, eds. *Conflict: Readings in Management and Resolution.* London: Macmillan, 1990.
Burton, John W., and Dennis J. D. Sandole. "Expanding the Debate on Generic Theory of Conflict Resolution: A Response to a Critique." *Negotiation Journal* 3 (January 1987).
Butigan, Ken, Terry Messman-Rucker, and Marie Pastrick, eds. *¡Basta! No Mandate for War: A Pledge of Resistance Handbook.* Philadelphia: New Society, 1986.
Buzan, Barry. *An Introduction to Strategic Studies: Military Technology and International Relations.* London: Macmillan, 1987.
———. *People, States and Fear: An Agenda for International Security Studies in the Post–Cold War Era.* 2d ed. New York: Harvester Wheatsheaf, 1991.
Carroll, Berenice A. "'Women Take Action!' Women's Direct Action and Social Change." *Women's Studies International Forum* 12, no. 1 (1989).
Carson, Rachel L. *Silent Spring.* New York: Fawcett Crest, 1962.
Case, Clarence Marsh. *Non-violent Coercion: A Study in Methods of Social Pressure.* 1923. Reprint, Jerome S. Ozer, 1972.
Catudal, Honoré M. *Soviet Nuclear Strategy from Stalin to Gorbachev: A Revolution in Soviet Military and Political Thinking.* London: Mansell, 1988.
Cheeseman, Graeme, and St John Kettle, eds. *The New Australian Militarism: Undermining Our Future Security.* Sydney, Australia: Pluto Press, 1990.
Chomsky, Noam. *The Chomsky Reader.* Ed. James Peck. New York: Pantheon, 1987.
———. *The Culture of Terrorism.* Montreal: Black Rose Books, 1988.
———. *Deterring Democracy.* London: Vintage, 1992.
———. *The Fateful Triangle: The United States, Israel and the Palestinians.* London: Pluto Press, 1983.
———. *Necessary Illusions: Thought Control in Democratic Societies.* London: Pluto Press, 1989.
———. *Turning the Tide: U.S. Intervention in Central America and the Struggle for Peace.* Boston: Pluto Press, 1985.

―――. *Year 501: The Conquest Continues.* London: Verso, 1993.

Chomsky, Noam, and Edward S. Herman. *The Political Economy of Human Rights.* Vol. 1, *The Washington Connection and Third World Fascism.* Boston: South End Press, 1979.

Cincinnatus. *Self-Destruction: The Disintegration and Decay of the United States Army during the Vietnam Era.* New York: W. W. Norton, 1981.

Clausewitz, Carl von. *On War.* Ed. and Trans. Michael Howard and Peter Paret. 1832. Reprint, Princeton: Princeton University Press, 1976.

Cleaver, Eldridge. *Soul on Ice.* London: Panther, 1970.

Coate, Roger A., and Jerel A. Rosati, eds. *The Power of Human Needs in World Society.* Boulder: Lynne Rienner, 1988.

Collins, John M. *Grand Strategy: Principles and Practices.* Annapolis: Naval Institute Press, 1973.

Conser, Walter H., Jr, Ronald M. McCarthy, David J. Toscano, and Gene Sharp, eds. *Resistance, Politics, and the American Struggle for Independence, 1765–1775.* Boulder: Lynne Rienner, 1986.

Cook, Alice, and Gwyn Kirk. *Greenham Women Everywhere: Dreams, Ideas and Actions from the Women's Peace Movement.* London: Pluto Press, 1983.

Coover, Virginia, Ellen Deacon, Charles Esser, and Christopher Moore. *Resource Manual for a Living Revolution.* Philadelphia: New Society, 1981.

Cornelius, Helena, and Shoshana Faire. *Everyone Can Win: How to Resolve Conflict.* Sydney, Australia: Simon & Schuster, 1991.

Cortright, David. *Soldiers in Revolt: The American Military Today.* Garden City, N.Y.: Anchor Press/Doubleday, 1975.

Cortright, David, and Max Watts. *Left Face: Soldier Unions and Resistance Movements in Modern Armies.* New York: Greenwood Press, 1991.

Coser, Lewis A. *The Functions of Social Conflict.* London: Routledge & Kegan Paul, 1972.

Creveld, Martin van. *Supplying War: Logistics from Wallenstein to Patton.* Cambridge: Cambridge University Press, 1977.

Crosby, Ned. "The Peace Movement and New Democratic Processes." *Social Alternatives* 8 (January 1990).

Crosby, Ned, Janet M. Kelly, and Paul Schaefer. "Citizens Panels: A New Approach to Citizen Participation." *Public Administration Review* 46 (March/April 1986).

Crow, Ralph E., Philip Grant, and Saad E. Ibrahim, eds. *Arab Nonviolent Political Struggle in the Middle East.* Boulder: Lynne Rienner, 1990.

Crow Dog, Mary, and Richard Erdoes. *Lakota Woman.* New York: HarperCollins, 1991.

Czempiel, Ernst-Otto, Liparit Kiuzadjan, and Zdenek Masopust, eds. *Nonviolence in International Crises.* International Social Science Council, 1990.

Dahl, Robert A. "The Concept of Power." *Behavioural Science* 2 (July 1957).

Dahrendorf, Ralf. *Class and Class Conflict in Industrial Society.* London: Routledge & Kegan Paul, 1969.

Dajani, Souad. "Towards the Formulation of a Strategy of Nonviolent Civilian Resistance: The Occupied Palestinian Territories As a Case Study." *International Journal of Nonviolence* 1 (September 1993).

Dalai Lama. "Relevance of Compassion and Nonviolence Today." *Gandhi Marg* 13 (April–June 1991).

Daly, Herman E. *Steady-State Economics.* 2d ed. Washington D.C.: Island Press, 1991.

———, ed. *Toward a Steady-State Economy.* San Francisco: W. H. Freeman, 1973.

Daly, Mary. *Gyn/Ecology: The Metaethics of Radical Feminism.* London: Women's Press, 1979.

Darwin, Charles. *The Expression of the Emotions in Man and Animals.* 1872. Reprint, Chicago: University of Chicago Press, 1965.

Dawidowicz, Lucy S. *The War against the Jews 1933–45.* Harmondsworth, England: Penguin, 1987.

Dellinger, Dave. *Revolutionary Nonviolence.* Indianapolis: Bobbs-Merrill, 1970.

Deming, Barbara. *We Are All Part of One Another: A Barbara Deming Reader.* Ed. Jane Meyerding. Philadelphia: New Society, 1984.

DeRoose, Frank. "Need Military Aggressors Kill People?" *Interdisciplinary Peace Research* 2 (May–June 1990).

Desai, Narayan. *Handbook for Satyagrahis: A Manual for Volunteers of Total Revolution.* New Delhi: Gandhi Peace Foundation, 1980.

Deutsch, Morton. *The Resolution of Conflict: Constructive and Destructive Processes.* New Haven: Yale University Press, 1978.

Dhawan, Gopinath. *The Political Philosophy of Mahatma Gandhi.* 4th ed. New Delhi: Gandhi Peace Foundation, 1990.

Dickson, David. *Alternative Technology and the Politics of Technical Change.* Glasgow, Scotland: Fontana, 1974.

Dijkstra, Piet. "Peace Brigades International." *Gandhi Marg* 8 (October 1986).

Diwakar, R. R. *Saga of Satyagraha.* New Delhi: Gandhi Peace Foundation, 1969.

Dixon, Marlene, ed. *On Trial: Reagan's War against Nicaragua: Testimony of the Permanent Peoples' Tribunal.* London: Zed Books, 1985.

Dolgoff, Sam, ed. *The Anarchist Collectives: Workers' Self-Management in the Spanish Revolution 1936–1939.* Montreal: Black Rose Books, 1974.

Douglass, James W. *The Non-violent Cross: A Theology of Revolution and Peace.* London: Geoffrey Chapman, 1968.

Doxey, M. P. *International Sanctions in Contemporary Perspective.* London: Macmillan, 1987.

Drago, Antonino. "Towards a Political Programme for a Nonviolent Popular Defence." *Gandhi Marg* 4 (February 1983).

Duncan, H. D. *Symbols in Society.* London: Oxford University Press, 1972.

Dundas, Paul. *The Jains.* London: Routledge, 1992.

Durkheim, Emile. *The Division of Labour in Society.* Trans. W. D. Halls. 1893. Reprint, London: Macmillan, 1984.

Earle, Edward Mead, ed. *Makers of Modern Strategy: Military Thought from Machiavelli to Hitler.* Princeton: Princeton University Press, 1944.

Ebert, Theodor. "Preparations for Civilian Defence." *Gandhi Marg* 9 (October 1965).

Edgerton, Robert B. *Mau Mau: An African Crucible.* New York: Ballantine, 1989.

Eglitis, Olgerts. *Nonviolent Action in the Liberation of Latvia.* Cambridge, Mass.: Albert Einstein Institution, 1993.

Eisenstadt, S. N., ed. *Readings in Social Evolution and Development.* Oxford: Pergamon Press, 1970.

Ellul, Jacques. *The Technological Society.* Trans. John Wilkinson. New York: Vintage, 1964.

Expert Study Group. *South Africa: The Sanctions Report.* London: Penguin, 1989.

Farmer, James. *Freedom—When?* New York: Random House, 1965.

Feit, Edward. *African Opposition in South Africa: The Failure of Passive Resistance.* Stanford: Hoover Institution on War, Revolution and Peace, 1967.

————. *South Africa: The Dynamics of the African National Congress.* London: Oxford University Press, 1962.

Finer, S. E. *The Man on Horseback: The Role of the Military in Politics.* 2d ed. Harmondsworth, England: Penguin, 1976.

Fink, Clinton F. "Some Conceptual Difficulties in the Theory of Social Conflict." *Journal of Conflict Resolution* 12, no. 4 (1968).

Fischer, Michael M. J. *Iran: From Religious Dispute to Revolution.* Cambridge: Harvard University Press, 1980.

Fisher, Jo. *Mothers of the Disappeared.* London: Zed Books, 1989.

Fisher, Roger, and Scott Brown. *Getting Together: Building a Relationship That Gets to Yes.* London: Business Books, 1989.

Fisher, Roger, and William Ury. *Getting to Yes: Negotiating Agreement without Giving In.* London: Hutchinson Business, 1982.

Frank, Jerome D. *Sanity and Survival: Psychological Aspects of War and Peace.* New York: Vintage, 1967.

Freedman, Lawrence. "Indignation, Influence and Strategic Studies." *International Affairs* 60 (Spring 1984).

French, Marilyn. *Beyond Power: On Women, Men, and Morals.* New York: Summit Books, 1985.

Freud, Sigmund. *Civilization and Its Discontents.* Ed. James Strachey. Trans. Joan Riviere. London: Hogarth Press, 1963.

————. *An Outline of Psycho-Analysis.* Trans. James Strachey. London: Hogarth Press, 1969.

Freund, Norman C. *Nonviolent National Defense: A Philosophical Inquiry into Applied Nonviolence.* New York: University Press of America, 1987.

Fromm, Erich. *The Anatomy of Human Destructiveness.* New York: Fawcett Crest, 1973.

Gallie, W. B. *Philosophers of Peace and War: Kant, Clausewitz, Marx, Engels and Tolstoy.* Cambridge: Cambridge University Press, 1979.

Galtung, Johan. "Cultural Violence." *Journal of Peace Research* 27, no. 3 (1990).

———. *Essays in Peace Research.* 6 vols. Copenhagen: Christian Ejlers, 1975–88.

———. *Methodology and Development: Essays in Methodology.* Vol. 3. Copenhagen: Christian Ejlers, 1988.

———. *Nonviolence and Israel/Palestine.* Honolulu: University of Hawaii Institute for Peace, 1989.

———. "On the Effects of International Economic Sanctions with Examples from the Case of Rhodesia." *World Politics* 19 (April 1967).

———. *Peace and Development in the Pacific Hemisphere.* Honolulu: University of Hawaii Institute for Peace, 1989.

———. "Reporting on a War: The Gulf War." *Social Alternatives* 11 (April 1992).

———. *Solving Conflicts: A Peace Research Perspective.* Honolulu: University of Hawaii Institute for Peace, 1989.

———. *There Are Alternatives! Four Roads to Peace and Security.* Nottingham, England: Spokesman, 1984.

———. *The True Worlds: A Transnational Perspective.* New York: Free Press, 1980.

———. *The Way Is the Goal: Gandhi Today.* Ahmedabad, India: Gujarat Vidyapith Peace Research Centre, 1992.

Gandhi, M. K. *Ashram Observances in Action.* Trans. Valji Govindji Desai. Ahmedabad, India: Navajivan, 1955.

———. *An Autobiography or The Story of My Experiments with Truth.* Trans. Mahadev Desai. Ahmedabad, India: Navajivan, 1927.

———. *The Collected Works of Mahatma Gandhi.* 90 vols. New Delhi: Government of India, Publications Division, 1958–84.

———. *Constructive Programme: Its Meaning and Place.* 2d ed. Ahmedabad, India: Navajivan, 1945.

———. *For Pacifists.* Ed. Bharatan Kumarappa. Ahmedabad, India: Navajivan, 1949.

———. *From Yeravda Mandir: Ashram Observances.* Trans. Valji Govindji Desai. Ahmedabad, India: Navajivan, 1932.

———. *Hind Swaraj or Indian Home Rule.* Rev. ed. Ahmedabad, India: Navajivan, 1939.

———. *Non-violent Resistance (Satyagraha).* Ed. Bharatan Kumarappa. New York: Schocken, 1961.

————. *Satyagraha in South Africa*. 2d ed. Trans. Valji Govindji Desai. Ahmedabad, India: Navajivan, 1950.

————. *Teachings of Mahatma Gandhi*. Ed. Jag Parvesh Chander. Lahore, India: Indian Printing Works, n.d.

Gat, Azar. *The Origins of Military Thought: From the Enlightenment to Clausewitz*. Oxford: Clarendon Press, 1989.

Geeraerts, Gustaaf, ed. *Possibilities of Civilian Defence in Western Europe*. Amsterdam: Swets & Zeitlinger, 1977.

George, Susan. *A Fate Worse than Debt*. London: Penguin, 1988.

————. *How the Other Half Dies: The Real Reasons for World Hunger*. Harmondsworth, England: Penguin, 1977.

Gilbert, Martin. *Winston S. Churchill*. Vol. 4. London: Heinemann, 1975.

Glucksmann, André. *Le discours de la guerre*. Paris: L'Herne, 1967.

Gopal, S. *The Viceroyalty of Lord Irwin 1926–1931*. Oxford: Clarendon Press, 1957.

Gramsci, Antonio. *Selections from the Prison Notebooks*. Ed. and Trans. Quintin Hoare and Geoffrey Nowell Smith. London: Lawrence & Wishart, 1971.

Graubard, Stephen Richards. *British Labour and the Russian Revolution 1917–1924*. Cambridge: Harvard University Press, 1956.

Gray, Colin S. *Strategic Studies: A Critical Assessment*. Westport, Conn.: Greenwood Press, 1982.

Greene, T. N., ed. *The Guerrilla—and How to Fight Him: Selections from the Marine Corps Gazette*. New York: Frederick A. Praeger, 1964.

Gregg, Richard B. *A Discipline for Non-violence*. Ahmedabad, India: Navajivan, 1959.

————. *The Power of Non-violence*. Ahmedabad, India: Navajivan, 1949.

————. *The Power of Nonviolence*. 2d ed. London: James Clarke, 1960.

Griffin-Nolan, Ed. *Witness for Peace: A Story of Resistance*. Louisville: Westminster/John Knox Press, 1991.

Gurr, Ted Robert, ed. *Handbook of Political Conflict: Theory and Research*. New York: Free Press, 1980.

Gyatso, Tenzin. *Freedom in Exile: The Autobiography of His Holiness the Dalai Lama of Tibet*. London: Abacus, 1992.

Hager, Nicky. "Peace Movement Aotearoa." *Nonviolence Today* 20 (April/May 1991).

Halliday, Fred. *Iran: Dictatorship and Development*. 2d ed. Harmondsworth, England: Penguin, 1979.

Hanlon, Joseph, and Roger Omond. *The Sanctions Handbook*. Harmondsworth, England: Penguin, 1987.

Haq, Mahbub ul. *The Poverty Curtain: Choices for the Third World*. New York: Columbia University Press, 1976.

Hare, A. Paul. *Handbook of Small Group Research*. 2d ed. New York: Free Press, 1976.

Hare, A. Paul, and Herbert H. Blumberg, eds. *Liberation without Violence: A Third-Party Approach.* London: Rex Collings, 1977.

Harris, Adrienne, and Ynestra King, eds. *Rocking the Ship of State: Toward a Feminist Peace Politics.* Boulder: Westview Press, 1989.

Hartsough, David. "Faces of Courage and Hope." *Civilian-Based Defense* 7 (December 1991).

———. "Keeping the Vigil in California." *Nonviolence Today* 12 (December 1989/January 1990).

Havel, Václav. *Living in Truth.* Ed. Jan Vladislav. London: Faber & Faber, 1987.

Helvey, Robert. "The Nonviolent Pro-Democracy Movement in Burma." *Nonviolent Sanctions* 1/2 (Spring/Summer 1990).

Herman, Edward S. *The Real Terror Network: Terrorism in Fact and Propaganda.* Boston: South End Press, 1982.

Herman, Edward S., and Noam Chomsky. *Manufacturing Consent: The Political Economy of the Mass Media.* New York: Pantheon, 1988.

Hicks, George, ed. *The Broken Mirror: China after Tiananmen.* Harlow, Essex, England: Longman, 1990.

Hobbes, Thomas. *Leviathan.* Ed. C. B. Macpherson. 1651. Reprint, Harmondsworth, England: Penguin, 1968.

Hong, Evelyne. *Natives of Sarawak: Survival in Borneo's Vanishing Forest.* 2d ed. Penang, Malaysia: Institut Masyarakat, 1987.

hooks, bell. *Ain't I a Woman: Black Women and Feminism.* Boston: South End Press, 1991.

Horsburgh, H. J. N. *Mahatma Gandhi.* London: Lutterworth Press, 1972.

———. *Non-violence and Aggression: A Study of Gandhi's Moral Equivalent of War.* London: Oxford University Press, 1968.

Hoveyda, Fereydoun. *The Fall of the Shah.* Trans. Roger Liddell. London: Weidenfeld & Nicolson, 1980.

Howard, Michael. *The Causes of Wars and Other Essays.* London: Temple Smith, 1983.

———. *Clausewitz.* Oxford: Oxford University Press, 1983.

———. "The Forgotten Dimensions of Strategy." *Foreign Affairs* 57 (Summer 1979).

Howell, Signe, and Roy Willis, eds. *Societies at Peace: Anthropological Perspectives.* London: Routledge, 1989.

Hufbauer, Gary Clyde, Jeffrey J. Schott, and Kimberly Ann Elliott. *Economic Sanctions Reconsidered: History and Current Policy.* 2d ed. Washington D.C.: Institute for International Economics, 1990.

Hunter, Doris A., and Krishna Mallick, eds. *Nonviolence: A Reader in the Ethics of Action.* 2d ed. New York: University Press of America, 1990.

Hurwitz, Deena, ed. *Walking the Red Line: Israelis in Search of Justice for Palestine.* Philadelphia: New Society, 1992.

Huxley, Aldous. *Ends and Means: An Enquiry into the Nature of Ideals and into the Methods Employed for their Realization.* London: Chatto & Windus, 1946.

Huxley, Steven Duncan. *Constitutionalist Insurgency in Finland: Finnish "Passive Resistance" against Russification As a Case of Nonmilitary Struggle in the European Resistance Tradition.* Helsinki: Finnish Historical Society, 1990.

Independent Commission of Inquiry on the U.S. Invasion of Panama. *The U.S. Invasion of Panama: The Truth behind Operation "Just Cause."* Boston: South End Press, 1991.

Iyer, Raghavan N. *The Moral and Political Thought of Mahatma Gandhi.* Oxford: Oxford University Press, 1973.

Jahn, Egbert. "Civilian Defense and Civilian Offense." *Journal of Peace Research* 10, no. 3 (1973).

Jaimes, M. Annette, ed. *The State of Native America: Genocide, Colonization, and Resistance.* Boston: South End Press, 1992.

Janis, Irving L. *Groupthink: Psychological Studies of Policy Decisions and Fiascoes.* 2d ed. Boston: Houghton Mifflin, 1983.

Jervis, Robert. *Perception and Misperception in International Politics.* Princeton: Princeton University Press, 1976.

Jervis, Robert, R. N. Lebow, and Janice G. Stein. *Psychology and Deterrence.* Baltimore: Johns Hopkins University Press, 1985.

Jones, Lawrence. "Non-violent Civilian Defence: An Alternative to Collective Security." *Social Alternatives* (Spring 1977).

Jones, Lynne, ed. *Keeping the Peace: A Women's Peace Handbook 1.* London: Women's Press, 1983.

de Jouvenel, Bertrand. *Power: The Natural History of Its Growth.* Trans. J. F. Huntington. London: Hutchinson, 1948.

Jutikkala, Eino (with Kauko Pirinen). *A History of Finland.* 3d ed. Trans. Paul Sjoblom. London: Heinemann, 1974.

Kant, Immanuel. *Critique of Pure Reason.* Trans. J. M. D. Meiklejohn. 1787. Reprint, London: J. M. Dent and Sons, 1934.

Karbach, Hajo, and G. A. Göttingen. "The Myths of Alternative Defence." *Graswurzelrevolution* (Summer 1981).

Kaunda, Kenneth David. *Kaunda on Violence.* Ed. Colin M. Morris. London: Collins, 1980.

Kemper, Theodore D. "How Many Emotions Are There? Wedding the Social and the Autonomic Components." *American Journal of Sociology* 93 (September 1987).

Keyes, Gene. "Heavy Casualties and Nonviolent Defense." *Philosophy and Social Action* 17 (July–December 1991).

———. "Strategic Non-violent Defense: The Construct of an Option." *Journal of Strategic Studies* 4 (June 1981).

———. "Strategic Nonviolent Defense: Five Policies." Paper presented at the annual meeting of the Canadian Political Science Association, Vancouver, 1983.

King, Martin Luther., Jr. *Stride toward Freedom: The Montgomery Story.* San Francisco: Harper & Row, 1958.

King-Hall, Stephen. *Defence in the Nuclear Age.* London: Victor Gollancz, 1958.

Kissinger, Henry A. "The Viet Nam Negotiations." *Foreign Affairs* 47 (January 1969).

Klare, M. T., and Cynthia Arnson. *Supplying Repression: U.S. Support for Authoritarian Regimes Abroad.* Washington D.C.: Institute for Policy Studies, 1981.

Knudtson, Peter, and David Suzuki. *Wisdom of the Elders.* Sydney, Australia: Allen & Unwin, 1992.

Koch, Koen. "Civilian Defence: An Alternative to Military Defence?" *The Netherlands' Journal of Sociology* 20–1 (1984).

Kohr, Leopold. *The Breakdown of Nations.* London: Routledge & Kegan Paul, 1986.

Kool, V. K., ed. *Perspectives on Nonviolence.* New York: Springer-Verlag, 1990.

Kritzer, Herbert M. "Nonviolent National Defense: Concepts and Implications." *Peace Research Reviews* 5 (1974).

Kropotkin, Petr. *Mutual Aid: A Factor of Evolution.* Boston: Extending Horizons Books, n.d.

Kruegler, Christopher. "Gandhi, Clausewitz, and the 'New World Order.'" *Nonviolent Sanctions* 3/4 (Spring/Summer 1992).

———. "Liddell Hart and the Concept of Civilian-Based Defense." Ph.D. diss., Syracuse University, 1984.

———. "To the Editor." *Civilian-Based Defense* 8 (October 1992).

Kruegler, Christopher, and Patricia Parkman. "Identifying Alternatives to Political Violence: An Educational Imperative." *Harvard Educational Review* 55 (February 1985).

Kulerski, Wiktor. "The Third Possibility." *Survey: A Journal of East and West Studies* 26 (Summer 1982).

Kumar, R., ed. *Essays on Gandhian Politics: The Rowlatt Satyagraha of 1919.* Oxford: Clarendon Press, 1971.

Kuper, Leo. *Genocide: Its Political Use in the Twentieth Century.* New Haven: Yale University Press, 1982.

———. *Passive Resistance in South Africa.* New Haven: Yale University Press, 1960.

Kuron, Jacek. "Theses on Solving an Insoluble Problem." *Survey: A Journal of East and West Studies* 26 (Summer 1982).

La Boétie, Étienne de. *The Politics of Obedience: The Discourse of Voluntary Servitude.* Trans. Harry Kurz. 1576. Reprint, Montreal: Black Rose Books, 1975.

Lakey, George. *Powerful Peacemaking: A Strategy for a Living Revolution.* Philadelphia: New Society, 1987.

Landry, Charles, Dave Morley, Russell Southwood, and Patrick Wright.

What a Way to Run a Railroad: An Analysis of Radical Failure. London: Comedia, 1985.

Lappé, Frances Moore, and Joseph Collins. *Food First.* London: Abacus, 1982.

Lederer, Katrin, ed. *Human Needs: A Contribution to the Current Debate.* Cambridge, Mass.: Oelgeschlager, Gunn & Hain, 1980.

Lekota, Patrick. "The Anti-Apartheid Struggle in South Africa." *Nonviolent Sanctions* 1/2 (Spring/Summer 1990).

Leonard, Roger Ashley, ed. *A Short Guide to Clausewitz on War.* London: Weidenfeld & Nicolson, 1967.

Leopold, Aldo. *A Sand County Almanac and Sketches Here and There.* New York: Oxford University Press, 1989.

Leval, Gaston. *Collectives in the Spanish Revolution.* Trans. Vernon Richards. London: Freedom Press, 1975.

Liddell Hart, B. H. *Defence of the West.* New York: William Morrow, 1950.

———. *Deterrent or Defence: A Fresh Look at the West's Military Position.* London: Stevens, 1960.

———. *Europe in Arms.* London: Faber & Faber, 1937.

———. *Paris or the Future of War.* London: Kegan Paul, Trench, Trubner, 1925.

———. *Strategy.* 2d ed. New York: Praeger, 1967.

Lider, Julian. "Towards a Modern Concept of Strategy." *Cooperation and Conflict* 16 (1981).

Lintner, Bertil. *Outrage: Burma's Struggle for Democracy.* 2d ed. London: White Lotus, 1990.

Lippmann, Walter. *U.S. Foreign Policy: Shield of the Republic.* Boston: Little, Brown, 1943.

Lipsitz, Lewis, and Herbert M. Kritzer. "Unconventional Approaches to Conflict Resolution: Erikson and Sharp on Nonviolence." *Journal of Conflict Resolution* 19 (December 1975).

Littell, Robert, ed. *The Czech Black Book.* London: Pall Mall Press, 1969.

Locke, John, David Hume, and Jean-Jacques Rousseau. *Social Contract: Essays by Locke, Hume and Rousseau.* Reprint, London: Oxford University Press, 1947.

Lockhead, James. "The Sarawak Campaign: Perspectives for Discussion." *World Rainforest Report* 22 (June 1992).

Lockwood, Rupert. *Black Armada: Australia and the Struggle for Indonesian Independence 1942–49.* Sydney, Australia: Hale & Iremonger, 1982.

Lombardi, Ben. "The Idea of the Decisive Battle and Its Role in War." Occasional Paper 16, Programme in Strategic Studies, University of Manitoba (August 1992).

Lovelock, J. E. *Gaia: A New Look at Life on Earth.* Oxford: Oxford University Press, 1987.

Luthuli, Albert. *Let My People Go: An Autobiography.* London: Collins, 1962.

Luttwak, Edward. *Coup d'Etat: A Practical Handbook.* Harmondsworth, England: Penguin, 1969.

———. "The Operational Level of War." *International Security* 5 (Winter 1980/1981).

Lynd, Staughton, ed. *Nonviolence in America: A Documentary History.* Indianapolis: Bobbs-Merrill, 1966.

Lyons, Matthew Nemiroff. *The "Grassroots" Network: Radical Nonviolence in the Federal Republic of Germany 1972–1985.* Ithaca, N.Y.: Cornell University, Center for International Studies, 1988.

Lyttle, Bradford. *National Defense thru Nonviolent Resistance.* 2d ed. Chicago: Shahn-ti Sena, 1959.

MacDonald, Brian. "The French Colonial War in Algeria: Asymmetric Conflict and the Military Bias." *Australian Journal of Defence Studies* 1 (October 1977).

Macdonald, Sharon, Pat Holden, and Shirley Ardener, eds. *Images of Women in Peace and War: Cross-Cultural and Historical Perspectives.* Basingstoke, Hampshire, England: Macmillan, 1987.

Machiavelli, Niccolò. *The Prince.* Trans. George Bull. c 1514. Reprint, Harmondsworth, England: Penguin, 1961.

MacIver, Robert M. *The Web of Government.* Rev. ed. New York: Free Press, 1965.

Mack, Andrew. "Why Big Nations Lose Small Wars: The Politics of Asymmetric Conflict." *World Politics* 27 (January 1975).

Macy, Joanna Rogers. *Despair and Personal Power in the Nuclear Age.* Philadelphia: New Society, 1983.

Mahadevan, T. K., Adam Roberts, and Gene Sharp, eds. *Civilian Defence: An Introduction.* New Delhi: Gandhi Peace Foundation, 1967.

Mandela, Nelson. *No Easy Walk to Freedom.* London: Heinemann, 1965.

Mann, Michael. *The Sources of Social Power.* Vol. 1, *A History of Power from the Beginning to A.D. 1760.* Cambridge: Cambridge University Press, 1986.

Mansbridge, Jane J. *Beyond Adversary Democracy.* Chicago: University of Chicago Press, 1983.

Mao Tse-tung. *Selected Works of Mao Tse-tung.* 4 vols. Beijing: Foreign Languages Press, 1961–65.

Margolis, Diane Rothbard. "Considering Women's Experience: A Reformulation of Power Theory." *Theory and Society* 18 (1989).

Marighela, Carlos. *For the Liberation of Brazil.* Trans. John Butt and Rosemary Sheed. Harmondsworth, England: Penguin, 1971.

Martin, Brian. "Democracy without Elections." *Social Alternatives* 8 (January 1990).

———. "Gene Sharp's Theory of Power." *Journal of Peace Research* 26, no. 2 (1989).

———. "Lessons in Nonviolence from the Fiji Coups." *Gandhi Marg* 10 (September 1988).

————. "Mobilising against Nuclear War: The Insufficiency of Knowledge and Logic." *Social Alternatives* 1, no. 6/7 (1980).

————. "The Nazis and Nonviolence." *Social Alternatives* 6 (August 1987).

————. "Revolutionary Social Defence." *Bulletin of Peace Proposals* 22, no. 1 (1991).

————. "Science for Non-violent Struggle." *Science and Public Policy* 19 (February 1992).

————. "Social Defence: Elite Reform or Grassroots Initiative?" *Social Alternatives* 6 (April 1987).

————. *Social Defence Social Change.* London: Freedom Press, 1993.

————. *Uprooting War.* London: Freedom Press, 1984.

Marx, G. T. *Undercover: Police Surveillance in America.* Berkeley: University of California Press, 1988.

Marx, Karl. *Capital.* 3 vols. Ed. Frederick Engels. 1887–94. Reprint, Moscow: Progress, 1956–71.

————. *A Contribution to the Critique of Political Economy.* Ed. Maurice Dobb. Trans. S. W. Ryazanskaya. 1859. Reprint, Moscow: Progress, 1970.

Marx, Karl, and Frederick Engels. *The German Ideology.* 3d ed. Reprint, Moscow: Progress, 1976.

————. *The Marx-Engels Reader.* Ed. Robert C. Tucker. New York: W. W. Norton, 1972.

————. *Selected Works in One Volume.* New York: International, 1968.

Maslow, Abraham H. *Motivation and Personality.* 3d ed. New York: Harper & Row, 1987.

Mazrui, Ali A. *A World Federation of Cultures: An African Perspective.* New York: Free Press, 1976.

McAllister, Pam. *This River of Courage: Generations of Women's Resistance and Action.* Philadelphia: New Society, 1991.

————. *You Can't Kill the Spirit.* Philadelphia: New Society, 1988.

————, ed. *Reweaving the Web of Life: Feminism and Nonviolence.* Philadelphia: New Society, 1982.

McGuinness, Kate. "Gene Sharp's Theory of Power: A Feminist Critique of Consent." *Journal of Peace Research* 30 (February 1993).

McManus, Philip, and Gerald Schlabach, eds. *Relentless Persistence: Nonviolent Action in Latin America.* Philadelphia: New Society, 1991.

Meadows, Donella H., Dennis L. Meadows, Jørgen Randers, and William W. Behrens III. *The Limits to Growth: A Report for the Club of Rome's Project on the Predicament of Mankind.* London: Pan, 1974.

Mearsheimer, John J. *Liddell Hart and the Weight of History.* Ithaca, N.Y.: Cornell University Press, 1988.

Melman, Seymour. *The Demilitarized Society: Disarmament and Conversion.* Nottingham, England: Spokesman, 1988.

Menchú, Rigoberta. *I, Rigoberta Menchú: An Indian Woman in Guatemala.* Ed. Elisabeth Burgos-Debray. Trans. Ann Wright. London: Verso, 1991.

Merchant, Carolyn. *The Death of Nature: Women, Ecology, and the Scientific Revolution.* San Francisco: HarperCollins, 1990.

Meredith, Martin. *In the Name of Apartheid: South Africa in the Postwar Period.* London: Hamish Hamilton, 1988.

Mermelstein, David, ed. *The Anti-Apartheid Reader: The Struggle against White Racist Rule in South Africa.* New York: Grove Press, 1987.

Merton, Robert K. *Social Theory and Social Structure.* Enlarged ed. New York: Free Press, 1968.

Michelman, Cherry. *The Black Sash of South Africa: A Case Study in Liberalism.* London: Oxford University Press, 1975.

Miles, Rosalind. *The Women's History of the World.* London: Paladin Grafton, 1989.

Milgram. Stanley. "Behavioral Study of Obedience." *Journal of Abnormal and Social Psychology* 67, no. 4 (1963).

Miller, Webb. *I Found No Peace: The Journal of a Foreign Correspondent.* Harmondsworth, England: Penguin, 1940.

Miller, William Robert. *Nonviolence: A Christian Interpretation.* New York: Schocken, 1964.

Millett, Kate. *Sexual Politics.* London: Virago, 1977.

Mills, C. Wright. *The Power Elite.* London: Oxford University Press, 1956.

Mische, Patricia M., "Ecological Security and the Need to Reconceptualize Sovereignty." *Alternatives* 14 (October 1989).

Møller, Bjørn. *Common Security and Nonoffensive Defense: A Neorealist Perspective.* Boulder: Lynne Rienner, 1992.

Montagu, Ashley. *The Nature of Human Aggression.* Oxford: Oxford University Press, 1976.

———, ed. *Learning Non-aggression: The Experience of Non-literate Societies.* Oxford: Oxford University Press, 1978.

Moore, Christopher W. *The Mediation Process: Practical Strategies for Resolving Conflict.* San Francisco: Jossey-Bass, 1987.

Morgenthau, Hans J. *Politics among Nations: The Struggle for Power and Peace.* 5th ed. New York: Knopf, 1973.

Mosca, Gaetano. *The Ruling Class.* Ed. Arthur Livingston. Trans. Hannah D. Kahn. New York: McGraw-Hill, 1939.

Moser, Yeshua. "Political Struggle for the Land of Snows." *Nonviolence Today* 32 (May/June 1993).

Murray, John S. "Understanding Competing Theories of Negotiation." *Negotiation Journal* (April 1986).

Naess, Arne. *Gandhi and Group Conflict: An Exploration of Satyagraha—Theoretical Background.* Oslo: Universitetsforlaget, 1974.

———. "The Shallow and the Deep, Long-Range Ecology Movement. A Summary," *Inquiry* 16 (1973).

Nakamura, Hajime. *Ways of Thinking of Eastern Peoples: India, China, Tibet, Japan.* Ed. P. P. Wiener. Honolulu: East-West Center Press, 1964.

Nanda, B. R. *Mahatma Gandhi: A Biography*. Abridged ed. London: Unwin, 1965.

Napoleon. *The Mind of Napoleon: A Selection from His Written and Spoken Words*. Ed. and Trans. J. Christopher Herold. New York: Columbia University Press, 1955.

Nash, R. F. *The Rights of Nature: A History of Environmental Ethics*. Sydney, Australia: Primavera Press, 1990.

Nehru, Jawaharlal. *An Autobiography*. London: John Lane The Bodley Head, 1942.

Neterowicz, E. M. *The Tragedy of Tibet*. Washington D.C.: Council for Social and Economic Studies, 1989.

Niebuhr, Reinhold. *Moral Man and Immoral Society: A Study in Ethics and Politics*. New York: Charles Scribner's Sons, 1932.

Okolo, Amechi. "Dependency in Africa: Stages of African Political Economy." *Alternatives* 9 (Fall 1983).

Olson, Mancur. *The Logic of Collective Action: Public Goods and the Theory of Groups*. Cambridge: Harvard University Press, 1971.

Olson, Theodore. "Social Defence and Deterrence: Their Interrelationship." *Bulletin of Peace Proposals* 16, no. 1 (1985).

Olson, Theodore, and Gordon Christiansen. *The Grindstone Experiment: Thirty-One Hours*. Toronto: Canadian Friends Service Committee, 1966.

Orwell, George. *The Collected Essays, Journalism and Letters of George Orwell*. Vol. 4. Ed. Sonia Orwell and Ian Angus. London: Secker & Warburg, 1968.

Palestinian Center for the Study of Non-Violence. "Intifada: Palestinian Nonviolent Protest—an Affirmation of Human Dignity and Freedom." (May 1988).

Palumbo, Michael. *Imperial Israel: The History of the Occupation of the West Bank and Gaza*. London: Bloomsbury, 1990.

Paret, Peter. *Clausewitz and the State*. New York: Oxford University Press, 1976.

———, ed. *Makers of Modern Strategy: From Machiavelli to the Nuclear Age*. Princeton: Princeton University Press, 1986.

Pareto, Vilfredo. *The Mind and Society: A Treatise on General Sociology*. 4 vols. Trans. Andrew Bongiorno and Arthur Livingston. 1935. Reprint, New York: Dover, 1963.

Parkman, Patricia. *Insurrectionary Civic Strikes in Latin America 1931–1961*. Cambridge, Mass.: Albert Einstein Institution, 1990.

———. *Nonviolent Insurrection in El Salvador: The Fall of Maximiliano Hernandez Martinez*. Tucson: University of Arizona Press, 1988.

Patai, Raphael. *The Arab Mind*. New York: Charles Scribner's Sons, 1973.

Patel, M. S. *The Educational Philosophy of Mahatma Gandhi*. Ahmedabad, India: Navajivan, 1953.

Pateman, Carole. *The Sexual Contract.* Cambridge: Polity Press, 1988.

Pauling, Linus, ed. *World Encyclopedia of Peace.* Vol. 1. Oxford: Pergamon, 1986.

Peck, Connie. "The Case for a United Nations Dispute Settlement Commission." *Interdisciplinary Peace Research* 3 (May/June 1991).

————. "An Integrative Model for Understanding and Managing Conflict." *Interdisciplinary Peace Research* 1 (May 1989).

Pelton, Leroy H. *The Psychology of Nonviolence.* New York: Pergamon, 1974.

Pillai, N. P. *The Educational Aims of Mahatma Gandhi.* Trivandrum, India: Kalyanmandir, 1959.

Plutchik, Robert. *Emotion: A Psychoevolutionary Synthesis.* New York: Harper & Row, 1980.

Prabhu, R. K., and U. R. Rao, eds. *The Mind of Mahatma Gandhi.* Rev. ed. Ahmedabad, India: Navajivan, 1967.

Prasad, Rajendra. *At the Feet of Mahatma Gandhi.* Westport, Conn.: Greenwood Press, 1961.

Pronozin, Alexander. "Social Defence, the Coup, and a Sort of Revolution: Three Days That Counted for More than Six Years of Perestroika." *Peace News* 2346 (September 1991).

Pruitt, Dean G., and Jeffrey Z. Rubin. *Social Conflict: Escalation, Stalemate, and Settlement.* New York: Random House, 1986.

Pyarelal. *Mahatma Gandhi: The Last Phase.* 2 vols. Ahmedabad, India: Navajivan, 1956, 1958.

————. *Towards New Horizons.* Ahmedabad, India: Navajivan, 1959.

Ramachandran, G., and T. K. Mahadevan, eds. *Gandhi: His Relevance for Our Times.* 2d ed. New Delhi: Gandhi Peace Foundation, 1967.

Ramos-Horta, Jose. *Funu: The Unfinished Saga of East Timor.* Trenton, N.J.: Red Sea Press, 1987.

Randle, Michael. "Defence without the Bomb." *Reconciliation Quarterly* (June 1982).

————. *People Power: The Building of a New European Home.* Stroud, England: Hawthorn Press, 1991.

Ratna, Anurag. "Sarvodaya Democracy." *Social Alternatives* 8 (January 1990).

Rattan, Ram. *Gandhi's Concept of Political Obligation.* Calcutta, India: Minerva Associates, 1972.

Reeves, Ambrose. *Shooting at Sharpeville: The Agony of South Africa.* London: Victor Gollancz, 1960.

Reus-Smit, Christian. "Realist and Resistance Utopias: Community, Security and Political Action in the New Europe." *Millennium* 21, no. 1 (1992).

Rifkin, Jeremy (with Ted Howard). *Entropy: Into the Greenhouse World.* Rev. ed. New York: Bantam, 1989.

Rigby, Andrew. *Living the Intifada.* London: Zed Books, 1991.

Roberts, Adam. "Civilian Defence Twenty Years On." *Bulletin of Peace Proposals* 9, no. 4 (1978).

———. *Civil Resistance in the East European and Soviet Revolutions*. Cambridge, Mass.: Albert Einstein Institution, 1991.

———. "Civil Resistance to Military Coups." *Journal of Peace Research* 12, no. 1 (1975).

———. *Nations in Arms: The Theory and Practice of Territorial Defence*. 2d ed. London: Macmillan, 1986.

———, ed. *Civilian Resistance As a National Defence: Non-violent Action against Aggression*. Harmondsworth, England: Penguin, 1969.

Roberts, Barbara. "The Death of Machothink: Feminist Research and the Transformation of Peace Studies." *Women's Studies International Forum* 7, no. 4 (1984).

Rogers, Mirabel. *The Black Sash: The Story of the South African Women's Defence of the Constitution League*. Johannesburg, South Africa: Rotonews, 1956.

Roszak, Theodore. *The Making of a Counter Culture: Reflections on the Technocratic Society and Its Youthful Opposition*. London: Faber & Faber, 1970.

———. *Person/Planet: The Creative Disintegration of Industrial Society*. Garden City, N.Y.: Anchor, 1979.

Rothstein, Andrew. *The Soldiers' Strikes of 1919*. London: Macmillan, 1980.

Russell, Bertrand. "War and Non-resistance." *Atlantic Monthly* (August 1915).

Sale, Kirkpatrick. "Bioregionalism: A New Way to Treat the Land." *Ecologist* 14, no. 4 (1984).

———. *Dwellers in the Land: The Bioregional Vision*. Philadelphia: New Society, 1991.

———. *Human Scale*. London: Secker & Warburg, 1980.

Salmon, Jack D. "Can Non-violence Be Combined with Military Means for National Defense?" *Journal of Peace Research* 25, no. 1 (1988).

Sandole, Dennis J. D., and Ingrid Sandole-Staroste, eds. *Conflict Management and Problem Solving: Interpersonal to International Applications*. London: Frances Pinter, 1987.

Scherer, K. R., and Paul Ekman, eds. *Approaches to Emotion*. Hillsdale, N.J.: Erlbaum, 1984.

Schiff, Ze'ev, and Ehud Ya'ari. *Intifada: The Palestinian Uprising—Israel's Third Front*. Ed. and Trans. Ina Friedman. New York: Simon & Schuster, 1990.

Schmid, Alex P. (in collaboration with E. Berends and L. Zonneveld). *Social Defence and Soviet Military Power: An Inquiry into the Relevance of an Alternative Defence Concept*. Leiden, Netherlands: State University of Leiden, Centre for the Study of Social Conflict, 1985.

Schumacher, E. F. *Small Is Beautiful: A Study of Economics as if People Mattered*. London: Abacus, 1974.

Scott, Dick. *Ask That Mountain: The Story of Parihaka*. Auckland, New Zealand: Reed/Southern Cross, 1981.

Seifert, Harvey. *Conquest by Suffering: The Process and Prospects of Nonviolent Resistance*. Philadelphia: Westminster, 1965.

Selbourne, David, ed. *In Theory and In Practice: Essays on the Politics of Jayaprakash Narayan*. Delhi: Oxford University Press, 1985.

Semelin, Jacques. *Unarmed against Hitler: Civilian Resistance in Europe, 1939–1943*. Trans. Suzan Husserl-Kapit. Westport, Conn.: Praeger, 1993.

Sharp, Gene. "An Anti-Coup Defense: Prerequisite for a Lasting Democracy." *Civilian-Based Defense* 8 (December 1992).

———. *Civilian-Based Defense: A Post-military Weapons System*. Princeton: Princeton University Press, 1990.

———. "Gandhi As a National Defence Strategist." *Gandhi Marg* 14 (July 1970).

———. *Gandhi As a Political Strategist*. Boston: Porter Sargent, 1979.

———. *Making Europe Unconquerable: The Potential of Civilian-Based Deterrence and Defence*. Cambridge, Mass.: Ballinger, 1985.

———. *National Security through Civilian-Based Defense*. Omaha: Association for Transarmament Studies, 1985.

———. *The Politics of Nonviolent Action*. Boston: Porter Sargent, 1973.

———. "Promoting Civilian-Based Defense: Lessons from the History of Development of the Policy." *Civilian-Based Defense* 7 (August 1992).

———. "The Relevance of Civilian-Based Defense for the 1990s." *Civilian-Based Defense* 8 (October 1992).

———. *Self-Reliant Defense without Bankruptcy or War: Considerations for the Baltics, East Central Europe, and Members of the Commonwealth of Independent States*. Cambridge, Mass.: Albert Einstein Institution, 1992.

———. *Social Power and Political Freedom*. Boston: Porter Sargent, 1980.

———. "To the Editor." *Civilian-Based Defense* 8 (October 1992).

Sharp, Gene, and Bruce Jenkins. "Nonviolent Struggle in China: An Eyewitness Account." *Nonviolent Sanctions* 1 (Fall 1989).

Sharples, Vivien. "Palestinian Tax Resistance." *Conscience and Military Tax Campaign Newsletter* 46 (Autumn 1992).

Shridharani, Krishnalal. *War without Violence*. 1939. Reprint, Bombay, India: Bharatiya Vidya Bhavan, 1962.

Sibley, Mulford Q., ed. *The Quiet Battle: Writings on the Theory and Practice of Non-violent Resistance*. New York: Anchor, 1963.

Simmie, Scott, and Bob Nixon. *Tiananmen Square*. Seattle: University of Washington Press, 1989.

Singer, Peter. *Animal Liberation*. New York: Avon Books, 1975.

Sites, Paul. *Control: The Basis of Social Order*. New York: Dunellen, 1973.

Sklar, Holly. *Washington's War on Nicaragua*. Boston: South End Press, 1988.

———, ed. *Trilateralism: The Trilateral Commission and Elite Planning for World Management*. Montreal: Black Rose Books, 1980.

Smith, Hugh. "The Womb of War: Clausewitz and International Politics." *Review of International Studies* 16 (1990).

Smuts, Dene, and Shauna Westcott, eds. *The Purple Shall Govern: A South African A to Z of Nonviolent Action*. Cape Town, South Africa: Oxford University Press, 1991.

Sproat, Peter. "The Strategy of Social Defence: An Introduction and Evaluation." Occasional Paper 7, Department of Politics, University of Reading (March 1991).

Starhawk. *The Spiral Dance: A Rebirth of the Ancient Religion of the Great Goddess*. Rev. ed. San Francisco: HarperCollins, 1989.

———. *Truth or Dare: Encounters with Power, Authority, and Mystery*. San Francisco: HarperCollins, 1987.

Stevenson, Leslie. *Seven Theories of Human Nature*. New York: Oxford University Press, 1974.

Stoltzfus, Nathan. "Dissent in Nazi Germany." *Atlantic Monthly* (September 1992).

Stratford, Michael C. "Can Nonviolent National Defence Be Effective if the Opponent Is Ruthless? The Nazi Case." *Social Alternatives* 6 (April 1987).

Summy, Ralph. "An Australian Alternative Defence Strategy: From Swords and Spears to Shields and Snares." *Social Alternatives* 6 (April 1987).

———. "Nonviolence and the Case of the Extremely Ruthless Opponent." *Pacifica Review* 6 (May/June 1994).

———. "One Person's Search for a Functional Alternative to Violence." *Gandhi Marg* 5 (April 1983).

———. "Typology of Nonviolent Politics." *Australian Journal of Politics and History* 31, no. 2 (1985).

Sun Tzu. *The Art of War*. Trans. Samuel B. Griffith. Reprint, London: Oxford University Press, 1963.

Suzuki, David. *Inventing the Future*. Sydney, Australia: Allen & Unwin, 1990.

Šveics, V. V. *Small Nation Survival: Political Defense in Unequal Conflicts*. New York: Exposition Press, 1970.

Taber, Robert. *The War of the Flea: A Study of Guerrilla Warfare, Theory and Practice*. London: Paladin, 1970.

Talbott, John. *The War without a Name: France in Algeria, 1954–1962*. London: Faber & Faber, 1981.

Taylor, J. G. *Indonesia's Forgotten War: The Hidden History of East Timor*. London: Zed Books, 1991.

Taylor, Richard K. *Blockade: A Guide to Non-violent Intervention*. New York: Orbis Books, 1977.

———. "Witness for Peace and the Pledge of Resistance." *Nonviolent Sanctions* 1/2 (Spring/Summer 1990).

Tendulkar, D. G. *Mahatma: Life of Mohandas Karamchand Gandhi*. Rev. ed. 8 vols. New Delhi: Government of India, Publications Division, 1960.

Thompson, Dorothy, ed. *Over Our Dead Bodies: Women against the Bomb.* London: Virago, 1983.

Thompson, K. W. "Toward a Theory of International Politics." *American Political Science Review* 49 (September 1955).

Thoreau, Henry David. *Walden or Life in the Woods and On the Duty of Civil Disobedience.* Reprint, New York: Harper & Row, 1965.

Todaro, M. P. *Economic Development in the Third World.* 4th ed. New York: Longman, 1990.

Trainer, Ted. *Developed to Death: Rethinking Third World Development.* London: Green Print, 1989.

———. "A Rejection of the Brundtland Report." *IFDA Dossier* 77 (May/June 1990).

———. "Sustainable Society: A Radical View." *Chain Reaction* 66 (April 1992).

True, Michael. "Nonviolence in Cultural Contexts: China." *Interdisciplinary Peace Research* 4 (October/November 1992).

Ury, William L., Jeanne M. Brett, and Stephen B. Goldberg. *Getting Disputes Resolved: Designing Systems to Cut the Cost of Conflict.* San Francisco: Jossey-Bass, 1989.

Vlek, Charles, and George Cvetkovich, eds. *Social Decision Methodology for Technological Projects.* Dordrecht, Holland: Kluwer Academic, 1989.

Wainwright, Hilary, and Dave Elliott. *The Lucas Plan: A New Trade Unionism in the Making?* London: Allison & Busby, 1982.

Wallensteen, Peter. "Characteristics of Economic Sanctions." *Journal of Peace Research* 5, no. 3 (1968).

Waltz, Kenneth N. *Man, the State and War: A Theoretical Analysis.* New York: Columbia University Press, 1959.

Walzer, Michael. *Just and Unjust Wars: A Moral Argument with Historical Illustrations.* New York: Basic Books, 1977.

Weber, Max. *Economy and Society: An Outline of Interpretive Sociology.* 2 vols. Ed. Guenther Roth and Claus Wittich. Berkeley: University of California Press, 1968.

Weber, Thomas. *Conflict Resolution and Gandhian Ethics.* New Delhi: Gandhi Peace Foundation, 1991.

———. "From Maude Royden's Peace Army to the Gulf Peace Team: An Assessment of Unarmed Interpositionary Peace Forces." *Journal of Peace Research* 30 (February 1993).

———. "'The Marchers Simply Walked Forward until Struck Down': Nonviolent Suffering and Conversion." *Peace and Change* 18 (July 1993).

———. "On the Salt March: Gandhi's Epic March to Dandi Remembered." Manuscript, 1992.

Wehr, Paul. "Nonviolent Resistance to Nazism: Norway, 1940–45." *Peace and Change* 10 (Fall/Winter 1984).

West, Guida, and Rhoda L. Blumberg, eds. *Women and Social Protest.* New York: Oxford University Press, 1990.

Westmoreland, William C. *A Soldier Reports*. New York: Da Capo Press, 1989.

White, Lynn., Jr. "The Historical Roots of Our Ecologic Crisis." *Science* 155 (10 March 1967).

White, R. K. *Fearful Warriors: A Psychological Profile of U.S.–Soviet Relations*. New York: Free Press, 1984.

————, ed. *Psychology and the Prevention of Nuclear War: A Book of Readings*. New York: New York University Press, 1986.

Windsor, Philip, and Adam Roberts. *Czechoslovakia 1968: Reform, Repression and Resistance*. London: Chatto & Windus, 1969.

Wolff, Robert Paul. *In Defense of Anarchism*. New York: Harper & Row, 1970.

Wollstonecraft, Mary. *A Vindication of the Rights of Woman*. Ed. Miriam Brody. 1792. Reprint, London: Penguin, 1992.

Woodward, Bob. *Veil: The Secret Wars of the CIA 1981–1987*. London: Simon & Schuster, 1987.

World Commission on Environment and Development. *Our Common Future*. Oxford: Oxford University Press, 1989.

Wright, Quincy. *A Study of War*. Abridged ed. Chicago: University of Chicago Press, 1964.

Wright, Quincy, William M. Evan, and Morton Deutsch, eds. *Preventing World War III: Some Proposals*. New York: Simon & Schuster, 1962.

Wright, Steve. "The New Technologies of Political Repression: A New Case for Arms Control?" *Philosophy and Social Action* 17 (July–December 1991).

————. "Undermining Nonviolence: The Coming Role of New Police Technologies." *Gandhi Marg* 14 (April–June 1992).

Wylie, J. C. *Military Strategy: A General Theory of Power Control*. New Brunswick, N.J.: Rutgers University Press, 1967.

Yi Mu, and Mark V. Thompson. *Crisis at Tiananmen: Reform and Reality in Modern China*. San Francisco: China Books and Periodicals, 1990.

Zielonka, Jan. "Strengths and Weaknesses of Nonviolent Action: The Polish Case." *Orbis* 30 (Spring 1986).

Index